O9-BUC-269

WORLD FOOD AND YOU
Nan Unklesbay, PhD

SOME ADVANCE REVIEWS

"An easy-to-read book that provides an excellent overview of the world food situation. It has numerous citations of specific countries and their situations and combines a global perspective on essential topics such as nutrition, processing and marketing along with other topics of contemporary interest. Unklesbay has attempted to address the complex interdependent issues affecting the global food supply. I recommend the book as an excellent resource manual for food scientists, marketing professionals, and others interested in the world food supply. Should be required reading for food science and technology academic programs."

Mario de Figueiredo, PhD
Vice President, Research & Development
Golden Dipt Company, St. Louis, Missouri

"Covers a broad array of international food issues of interest and concern. Provides readers with the background knowledge necessary to become an informed member of society ready to tackle complex global food issues such as biotechnology, foreign aid, global warming and its impact on agriculture, chemicals in the food supply, food waste and packaging, and others. This book provides coverage of content that is urgently needed. To my knowledge, no book exists on the topic. . . ."

Lucy M. McProud, RD
Chairperson, Department of Nutrition and Food Science
San Jose State University

"Current, complete, comprehensive, and fills a void of resources of this type. It combines essential principles of nutrition with vital topics relating to food technology, hunger, and world food issues."

Dennis Ponton, PhD
Chairman, Nutrition and Food Science Department
Buffalo State College

"Unklesbay has brought together a wide variety of resources, and in a readable format has produced a reference for use in undergraduate courses that provides a global perspective to the science of food. She deals with many aspects of world food and brings in specific examples from around the globe. Throughout the text she consistently interrelates these aspects and by doing so, reinforces the interdependency of the many factors underlying the science of food and feeding all people inhabiting this planet."

Yvonne K. Bushland, MS
Senior Lecturer, Department of Food Science
University of Wisconsin-Madison

NOTES FOR PROFESSIONAL LIBRARIANS AND LIBRARY USERS

This is an original book title published by Food Products Press, an imprint of The Haworth Press, Inc. Unless otherwise noted in specific chapters with attribution, materials in this book have not been previously published elsewhere in any format or language.

CONSERVATION AND PRESERVATION NOTES

The paper used in this publication meets the minimum requirements of American National Standard for Information Sciences — Permanence of Paper for Printed Material, ANSI Z39.48-1984.

World Food and You

FOOD PRODUCTS PRESS
An Imprint of The Haworth Press, Inc.
Robert E. Gough, Senior Editor

New, Recent, and Forthcoming Titles:

Vintage Wine Book: A Practical Guide to the History of Wine, Winemaking, Classification, and Selection, Second Edition by Sommelier Executive Council

Winemaking Basics by C. S. Ough

Statistical Methods for Food and Agriculture by Filmore E. Bender, Larry W. Douglass, and Amihud Kramer

World Food and You by Nan Unklesbay

Understanding the Japanese Food and Agrimarket: A Multifaceted Opportunity edited by A. Desmond O'Rourke

Highbush Blueberry Management by Robert E. Gough

Nutrition Care of People with Diabetes Mellitus: A Nutrition Reference for Health Professionals by Penelope S. Easton et al.

Operations Manual for a Dietetic Service in Long-Term Care Facilities by Karen Kolasa

Managing the Potato Production System by Bill Dean

Marketing Livestock and Meat by William H. Lesser

Economics of Aquaculture by Curtis M. Jolly and Howard A. Clonts

Culture of Freshwater Crayfish edited by Jay V. Huner

World Food and You

Nan Unklesbay, PhD

Food Products Press
An Imprint of The Haworth Press, Inc.
New York • London • Norwood (Australia)

Published by

Food Products Press, an imprint of The Haworth Press, Inc., 10 Alice Street, Binghamton, NY 13904-1580

Library of Congress Cataloging-in-Publication Data

Unklesbay, Nan.
    World food and you/ Nan Unklesbay.
      p. cm.
    Includes bibliographical references (p.) and index.
    ISBN 1-56022-010-4 (acid-free paper). — ISBN 1-56022-011-2 (pbk.)
     1. Food industry and trade. 2. Food supply. I. Title.
TP370.U53 1991
363.8 — dc20

                                                       91-8347
                                                          CIP

In memory of my mentor,
Betty Rigby

ABOUT THE AUTHOR

Nan Unklesbay, PhD, is Professor in the Department of Food Science and Human Nutrition at the University of Missouri-Columbia, and Research Professor at the Environmental Trace Substance Research Center, also at the University of Missouri. Before entering the teaching profession, she worked for three years with the Inuit and Newfoundlanders in Canada while serving as dietary consultant for the Department of Health in St. John's, Newfoundland. This experience made her aware of how aboriginal societies can be greatly affected by changes in their food supplies. She is particularly interested in teaching nonagricultural students about the global food situation, because she firmly believes that every college-educated person should have an appreciation of how food and nutrition affect their lives. Her interests have an international focus as a result of extensive travel and her readings in the area of foreign affairs. Dr. Unklesbay is the author or co-author of 70 papers in the discipline of food science and nutrition, many of which have had an educational focus.

CONTENTS

Preface

Everyone is an expert on food in one way or another. However, the subject is so multifaceted that most people are somewhat limited both in experience and understanding. This text was written especially for you to both satisfy your intellectual needs and to cook up possible career opportunities for you. The finished product is the first comprehensive treatise that provides you with essential principles of nutrition, as well as other important topics that relate to food science and international food issues.

World Food and You can serve you in many ways, depending on your background and interests. The text can be used as a basis for development of an international food course to understand scientific principles and dynamic interactions involved in food production, processing, nutrition, shelf life, and marketing. Special attention has been given to career options over a wide range of food-related disciplines. The book contains a vast array of information dealing with world food problems and other issues to furnish a valuable resource for those trained in physical and social sciences.

For your convenience, the text is divided into four parts that are subdivided into chapters. Each chapter contains an introduction that spells out precisely what is in it for you in order to catalyze interpretation from your perspective. By addressing the reader as "you," the author's intention was to help the reader identify with the material.

Part One, "Global Food Production and You," deals with important international issues including populations relative to food supply, food production, food marketing, food problems, and foreign aid. The changing world population is addressed, as well as spotlighting major areas around the world for crop growth compared to food stores, as well as other relevant topics. Part Two, "Agricultural Production, Processing, and Consumption and You," includes chapters that embrace production of plant crops, livestock, fish, and shellfish. Food processing operations describe the scientific impact to engineer the conversion of raw materials to safe, packaged products for your consumption. The importance of maximizing utilization and minimizing wastes and other costs relative to global consumers is described.

Part Three, "Nutrition and You," addresses the two contrasting nutritional conditions found in the world—overnutrition in developed countries and undernutrition in developing countries. The author details the effects of various types of malnutrition including various vitamin and mineral diseases. Information assists understanding your personal need for specific nutrients. In Part Four, "Current Food Issues and You," the author exposes you to ideas for solving some of the problems you have become familiar with through extensive media coverage. Selected examples presented are: the role of biotechnology in improving agricultural production and processing; safe use, potential physiological effects, and regulation of chemicals in the food supply; global warming's potential impact on global agriculture; and interaction of physical and social scientists in multidisciplinary research programs to improve nutritional status of a targeted population.

Of special interest to you is the inclusion of an appendix on "Career Opportunities in International Agriculture." The author describes a wide range of opportunities along with academic and personal qualities needed for those of you with career interests in international agriculture. Further information may be obtained from ten citations listed.

George N. Bookwalter, Research Food Technologist
Food Quality and Safety Research
National Center for Agricultural
Utilization Research, ARS-USDA
Peoria, IL

Acknowledgements

Many colleagues and friends have made this book possible. I wish to especially thank R. L. Mitchell and W. C. Stringer for their encouragement, interest, and support. Given its global nature, many have contributed information to the following pages. I wish to especially thank: M. Abu Shaar, K. Biedrzycki, A. L. Clausen Vangen, J. Davidson, B. Ely, N. Ibrahim, B. Keller, S. Pare, and E. Sandeman. As friends residing in, and traveling to, different countries, they have all readily shared specific information about our global food supply.

It is my hope that the following pages will help many, from a variety of disciplines, begin to understand how their professional and personal actions can influence our global food situation. If any of them are motivated to further study and actions, my personal objectives will have been realized.

The preparation of this manuscript could not have been possible without the technical support of J. Lewis and the love and understanding of my husband, Kenneth.

PART ONE:
GLOBAL FOOD PRODUCTION AND YOU

As you picked up this book, you no doubt observed that you were referred to in the title. Perhaps you wondered how you are involved with all of the issues that you have come to associate with global agriculture and trade. Your personal frame of reference may be one of detachment or involvement. In a passive sense, you may frequently observe television pictures of starving children with extended stomachs, or by contrast, you may be involved in one of the vital phases of agriculture, from food production to consumption. In any case, what you have in common with all other human beings throughout the world is that you need to derive sustenance for growth and maintenance from food. The actual manner in which that sustenance is received around the globe and throughout societies varies greatly.

Your food consumption may be influenced by religious beliefs. On some occasions you use food in a social setting, where the focus is far from your need to reduce your personal sense of hunger. Food customs in your location, region, and nation affect how and where you consume food. Your daily life-style influences your food consumption trends. Food policies established by your government affect how your nation trades, and thus what foods are available for you to enjoy. In many nations, an abundant supply of foods has enabled you to develop particular food preferences which directly affect your food selection patterns. In many nations, and in areas within nations, the luxury of food selection is not so obvious.

If you are in a position of having an adequate nutritional daily

1

diet, served within the bounds of sanitation and appropriate social settings, and within your financial ability to pay for it, you may still be wondering why you have chosen to study the wide range of topics presented throughout this book. There are several obvious reasons. Informed citizens can make a difference. Given the political nature of agriculture and its interdependent role with other nations and other issues such as the environment, your knowledge can affect your political preferences and thus have an impact upon your nation's future.

Depending on your personal interests, you may decide to pursue further study or even a career in one or more of the diverse food and agricultural disciplines. For example, as you read about the U.S. Food for Peace Program, you may think about the food scientist responsible for developing food products that are shipped around the world each day to eliminate hunger and improve the quality of life. You may relate to the personal sense of satisfaction now possessed by that scientist. The food technologies that have been developed have made a difference around the world. In any case, as an educated person, you can share your knowledge with others who, in turn, may wish to expand their level of expertise.

The diverse, interrelated areas of agriculture offer unique opportunities to people with aptitudes for many disciplines. If you have an interest in the social sciences, you may choose to study issues surrounding the food aid issues. If you have a strong interest in the physical sciences, you may choose a career in biotechnology where you acquire the needed skills to manipulate genes and influence our global food supply. Information presented in this book will at least expose you to many opportunities and give suggestions for further study.

Throughout this book, you will notice that many viewpoints are presented, from extremely optimistic to extremely pessimistic. Due to the reliance upon future global projections for population and food, this is inevitable. Once you understand the scientific facts of an issue, you will be in a position to attain your personal viewpoint along the continuum from pessimism to optimism. Ideally, your opinions should be based on informed, scientific knowledge. The one fact that you will acquire is that, through research activities, the scientific community has made a difference around the world. Further, this trend will accelerate. Throughout the world, cooperation among all social and physical scientists and politicians will be crucial. Will you be one of those individuals?

Personal travel to other countries can accelerate your understanding of the role of food and agriculture. If you have travelled to any of the countries mentioned in this book, your understanding of the issues should be enhanced. If your travel has been limited, locating these countries on a world map will help you focus on the issues. Subsequent travel made at any level, whether on a first-class tour package or with a friend and a backpack, will give you unlimited opportunities to observe the role of food and agriculture in diverse societies. Understanding issues presented to you by people in different societies will assist you with understanding domestic food issues and policies. Many former Peace Corps volunteers can attest to this fact; many will tell you that their lives have been enriched by their experiences.

When the phrase "world food" is used, people's perceptions of it range from visualizing a variety of ethnic food delights served in international settings, to absolute poverty in many nations. World food encompasses both of those extremes, plus a great deal more. As the environmental issue becomes the global issue of the 1990s, material presented in this book will assist you with your personal understanding of how food and agriculture and the environment are related. As food and feed trade policies unfold in the 1990s, you will be in a more knowledgeable position to assess their impact. Given all of these reasons to continue your study, enjoy finding your role in our world food situation.

Chapter One

World Population and Food

INTRODUCTION

After studying information in this chapter, you will be in an informed position to discuss:

- the changing world population, including future projections and reasons for rapidly evolving alterations;
- the major areas around the world for the growth of crops for human food and animal feed, and for the production of animals for human food and agricultural work.

In addition, you will be initially exposed to many of the issues which are causing common disparities between human hunger and food supplies. These issues will be briefly introduced to enable you to understand why the world food situation is such a dynamic one. They will be expanded upon for you in future chapters.

Since scientific research in agriculture has been responsible for much of our progress, the role of scientists and some of the challenges and unknowns they still face will be delineated for you. Finally, the topic of establishing world food and trade policies will be introduced, enabling you to gain perspective on the challenging, changing, and vital issues surrounding our global food and agriculture situations.

THE GLOBAL FOOD SITUATION

Food is a complex, multifaceted phenomenon with different properties and meanings, affecting everyone in several important ways. Food contains nutrients essential to the survival and well-being of all species. Food is an economic phenomenon, the end result of agriculture and food systems, with varied divisions of resources and labor. Food has religious, cultural, and social functions, being part of rituals, beliefs, and patterns of social interaction. Food has become a worldwide object of dispute, and therefore has important political dimensions.

Few issues are more vital to the well-being of the world population than the food we eat. Food is one of the largest industries in most countries. Food is the largest item in a typical household budget, except in the developed countries.

During the last two centuries, all the populations in the world have experienced dramatic changes in their dietary patterns. In industrialized countries, these changes have been associated with improved levels of nutrition and public health, and some increase in the recognition of nutrition-related diseases. Food varieties, production methods, and consumption patterns have been disseminated throughout the world in an increasing and intensifying network of socioeconomic and political interdependency.

An increasing portion of the daily diet in the U.S. comes from distant places, usually through commercial channels. This fact was recognized as early as 1916 in an article in the *National Geographic* magazine. An example of a simple menu and the location of the foods served is given in Exhibit 1.1. With all the food additives and preservatives used in processed foods today, the geographic food sources for this historical exhibit would be greatly expanded upon.

In developed countries, changes in dietary patterns have become associated with increases in the diversity of available foods and the quantity of food imports, as well as in improved diets. In developing countries, these changes have tended to produce opposite effects on the quality of daily diets, except for the elite members of some populations. As some of these countries have become engaged in full commercial participation with developed countries, economic and political forces have encouraged them to concentrate on one or two main cash crops, with an accompanying deterioration of their indigenous food diversity. Thus, worldwide food distribution and food-use transformations have often occurred at the expense of economically marginal populations. About 25 percent of

Exhibit 1.1.   A U.S. Meal Served in 1916; Made Possible by
               Agriculturalists and Businessmen From
               Around the World.

Menu	Origin
Olives and salted nuts	Olives (Spain), almonds (California, U.S.), pecans (Texas, U.S.), salt (New York, U.S.)
Celery	Michigan (U.S.)
Chesapeake Bay Clam Chowder	Pepper (Africa)
Salmon	Alaska (U.S.)
Prime Ribs of Beef	Kansas City (Packing Town), (Missouri, U.S.)
Potatoes	Maine (U.S.)
Boiled Rice	China
String Beans	Florida (U.S.)
Tomatoes	Maryland (U.S.)
Salad and salad dressing	Mexican peppers, Hawaiian pineapple, Sicilian cherries, Pennsylvania lettuce, Iowa eggs, Spanish olive oil, Ohio vinegar, California mustard, and Guiana red pepper.
Ice Cream	Virginia cream, Cuban sugar, Ecuadorean vanilla, Mexican chocolate.
Cake	Butter (Illinois, U.S.), flour (Minnesota, U.S.), wheat (North Dakota, U.S.), baking powder (Pennsylvania, U.S.).
Coffee	Turkish Arabia and Dutch Java

"Food Servants" in 1916[1]	Distribution "Modes" in 1916[1]
African Savage	Autos
Alaskan Inuit Fisherman	Backs of Donkeys
American Stock Grower	Camels
California Truck Farmer	Carts drawn by Water Buffalo
Chesapeake Bay Fisherman	Delivery cars
Chinese Coolie	Heads of Indians

Dakota Wheat Farmer	Railroads
Hawaiian Sugar Grower	Steamships
Javanese Coffee Picker	Trucks
Mexican Peon	Wheelbarrows
New York Orchardist	
Puerto Rican Planter	
South American Indian	
Spanish Olive Packer	
Turbaned Arabian	
Virginia Dairyman	

---

[1] Language as used in 1916.

A quote from 1916:

"Truly the man who dines well ought to be a deep student of
geography, for all races, all nationalities, all types of
people, all points of the compass, all latitudes -- continent,
island, river, and sea -- all must come to him as he looks
over the bill of fare and tries to find those things that
delight his palate."

Source: Showalter, William Joseph. 1916. How the world is fed. The
National Geographic Magazine. 29(1):1-110.

the population in the developed world consumes 80 percent of the world's resources.

The concern for agricultural productivity often obscures the need for improved marketing effectiveness. A large part of the price of food items pays for the processing, packaging, advertising, and shipment of foods, as well as the profits of various entrepreneurs in the food chain. Poor people cannot afford to pay these added costs, and hence they are reduced to a narrower selection of cheaper foods.

There have been massive changes in local food systems over the last 250 years as the world community has become knit into a tightly interconnected network of economic, social, and political relations. Worldwide food production capabilities have increased greatly. Serious problems of maldistribution of food resources remain, and many problems are becoming worse.

Income distribution is the primary factor in controlling which populations, or groups within populations, will be well-nourished. Today, the wealthy consume the finer cuts of beef and imported liquors and pâtés. Access to foods, beyond the staples necessary for nutrition and satisfaction of hunger, is an integral aspect of the struggle for improved standards of living.

This desire influences many political decisions around the world today, for example, many of the issues prevalent within Latin American politics. The working classes in most of Latin America today, while reasonably secure from famine and extreme hunger, do not have the luxury that their North American and European counterparts enjoy, of choosing between steak three nights per week and a new automobile.

Our global food problem can be defined as: "the inability to reconcile the increasing commercialization of domestic and international agricultural trade with divergent national agricultural policies, any food surpluses, and shifting and expanding populations."

DEFINITION OF AGRICULTURE

Agriculture includes every aspect of the system that puts food on the table: the manufacture of farm machinery and chemicals; the transport of food by rail, truck, barge, air, car, and animal; food processing and packaging industries; supermarkets, hyperr arkets, and commercial and nonprofit foodservice operations or restaurants; the production of food preparation, holding, and storage equipment, e.g., stoves and refrigerators; chemicals for sanitary functions; and so on. Defined in this manner, agriculture is much more than simply growing or raising food; agriculture is the largest industry in the U.S. and accounts for one-sixth of the Gross National Product (GNP).

WORLD POPULATION

Our world population is expanding, shifting, and influencing agricultural production in an integral manner. About 90 million people are added to the world's population each year. The total population of the world in 1988, along with the agricultural population, is given in Exhibit 1.2. Country classifications for "developed" and "developing" are given in Appendix A.

As recently as July 11, 1987, the world's population passed the

Exhibit 1.2. Total Population and Agricultural Population - 1988.

Region/Country	Population (in thousands)		% in Agriculture
	Total	Agricultural*	
North and Central America	417276	56279	13
Europe	496812	46132	9
Oceania	25757	4526	18
South America	285024	70053	25
Africa	609922	375261	62
Asia	2994005	1755110	59
USSR	285993	40615	14
All Developed Countries	1235303	109996	9
All Developing Countries	3879485	2237980	58
World	5114788	2347976	46

*Defined as all persons depending for their livelihood on agriculture, comprising all persons actively engaged in agriculture and their non-working dependents.

Source: FAO Production Yearbook. Vol. 42. 1988. Food and Agriculture Organization of the United Nations: Rome.

5 billion mark. One year later, by July 11, 1988, a net growth of another 83 million had occurred, an increase greater than the population of Mexico. Given that the amount of arable land on our planet decreased during that time, in one sense our planet actually became smaller as that astronomical rate of net human growth occurred. In those same 366 days, arable land diminished by 8,700 square miles, an area greater than twice the size of Jamaica. The world's farmers

are trying to feed almost 90 million more people a year with 24 billion fewer tons of topsoil, an amount equal to the soil on all of Australia's wheatland.

Putting this growth into perspective, from prehistory until about the year 1000 B.C., the world's population increased extremely slowly. In those early times, life was so precarious, and food supplies so unreliable, that a rough balance could be maintained between births and deaths, notwithstanding an undoubtedly high fertility rate. The slow development and introduction of agricultural practices enabled a greater certainty of food supplies.

However, for a long time these increases were largely offset by recurring crises of plagues, wars, infestations, and so on. World population growth throughout the civilized world was modest for many centuries, ranging from about 300 million at the time of Christ to 800 million in the middle of the seventeenth century. At the beginning of this period, doubling the world's population took about 1,600 years. Further, the rate of growth was approximately the same in all populated regions of the world.

From about the year 1850 A.D., the rate of population growth accelerated immensely. Human rates of mortality decreased as progress in science, technology, and medicine increased. The next doubling period of the world's population was reduced by 90 percent; the world required only 150 years to grow from 800 million to 1.7 billion in 1900. That acceleration continues today. By 1950 the world population had reached 2.5 billion (Exhibit 1.3), by 1987, 5 billion. Doubling the world's population, which had once taken 1,500 years, was accomplished in 37 years during this century.

The World Bank's best estimate for the year 2000 is an increase of 1.2 billion, for a total world population of 6.2 billion, as we celebrate the beginning of a new century. These figures are difficult to put into perspective. We now have an annual increase of close to 100 million people. The population of Bangladesh is about 100 million. Every year, from now until the year 2000, the world's population will grow by the equivalent of one new Bangladesh.

The earth's population, now approximately 5.2 billion, rose in 1989 by an estimated 87.5 million, maintaining a growth rate that could double the number of human beings by the year 2,025. An-

Exhibit 1.3. World Population Growth by Decade, 1950-90, With
Projection to 2000.

Year	Population	Increase by Decade	Average Annual Increase
	(billion)	(million)	
1950	2,515	---	---
1960	3,019	504	50
1970	3,698	679	68
1980	4,450	752	75
1990	5,292	842	84
2000	6,251	959	96

Source: Reprinted from STATE OF THE WORLD 1990, A Worldwatch Institute
on Progress Toward a Sustainable Society, Project Director:
Lester R. Brown. By permission of W. W. Norton & Company, Inc.
Copyright (c) 1990 by Worldwatch Institute.

other billion people will be added to the world in 11 years. Population growth is not expected to level off until early in the twenty-second century. According to the United Nations (UN), by then it could be as high as 14 billion.

Every 10 seconds, the world's population grows by 25 people; every 14 seconds, the planet's stock of arable land falls by one hectare. Clearly, this process cannot continue. Although some progress was made in reducing rates of population growth during the 1970s, the decline has been so gradual that the annual increment (Exhibit 1.3) grows larger each year. During the last decade, the average population increase was 84 million each year. As the excess of births over deaths widens in the 1990s, the average annual increase will approach at least 96 million.

Getting birth control information and devices to the 2.5 billion people beyond the present reach of family planning programs will require U.S. $8 billion annually, a $5 billion rise from current levels. In 1989, the U.S. contributed $245 million to such programs, less in real terms than in 1979. Will America reverse its present policy? Does it send a message to the world that mass starvation is preferable to the prevention of some pregnancies?

Population Facts of Selected Countries

Many factors interplay with these astounding population figures. Citizens of New York City complain of "traffic" jams; those in Beijing, of "people" jams. Both groups have developed schemes for coping and remaining mobile. To help you comprehend the population figures given in billions in Exhibit 1.3, a few statistics from individual countries and cities follow.

United States

The American population expands by roughly 1.9 million people each year. By 2000, there will be more than 100,000 Americans over 100 years old.

China

China's population is 1.096 billion and growing at a rate of more than 20 million per year. In 1980, China indicated it wanted to limit its population to 1.2 billion by the year 2000. According to some experts, population growth is now running out of control, making it increasingly difficult for the country to feed its people and threatening its decade-long modernization program. China, with 1.1 billion people in early 1990, will have nearly 200 million more mouths to feed in the year 2000 and must substantially improve its stagnating agricultural output if it is to remain self-sufficient.

Hong Kong

In Hong Kong, 5.7 million people are crowded into 270 square kilometers of habitable land.

India

At an annual population growth rate of 2 percent, India will reach 1.6 billion by 2075, rivalling China, now the world's most populous country.

Japan

The population in Japan is aging even more rapidly than the population in the U.S. During 1990, about one-fifth of the 1985 working population retired on pensions paying 80 percent of their final salaries. Today, Tokyo is a monster. The city proper—23 city wards with 8.2 million people crammed into 580 square kilometers—has mutated into a megalopolis of 30 million, engulfing Yokohama, Kawasaki, Chiba, and more than 100 other smaller cities and towns, once serenely surrounded by rice paddies.

Kenya

Kenya has one of the world's highest growth rates—4.2 percent—and will double its population of 23 million people by 2005.

Uganda

In Africa, Acquired Immunodeficiency Syndrome (AIDS) is so widespread that it will nearly destroy some entire nations. By the year 2000, one-third of the population of Uganda may die from AIDS.

Future Population Projections

Accepted projections distribute the population for the year 2000 as 4.9 billion for the developing countries and 1.3 billion for the industrialized countries. In an attempt to counter this disequilibrium, increasing numbers of people from developing countries are seeking entry into the industrialized countries, searching for refuge and opportunities. Changing demographic compositions are accelerating this movement.

In May 1989, the UN Population Fund estimated that the world population would settle at 14 billion. The world is now projected to add 959 million people during the 1990s (Exhibit 1.3), the largest increment ever for a decade.

The most optimistic projections show the world's population levelling off at 10 billion people, almost double the number who live on our planet today. Ninety percent of this population growth will occur in the poorest countries, three-quarters in areas of the world that are already grossly overcrowded.

Gross National Product (GNP) Values

Another way of classifying populations is to distinguish them from one another by the Gross National Product (GNP) of their respective countries. In order to classify countries according to their GNP per person, they have been identified as belonging to the First, Second, Third, or Communist or Socialist World. About 840 million people live in the First World (North America, Western Europe, Japan, South Africa, Israel, Australia, and New Zealand). Their GNP averages U.S. $10,000 per person and annual grocery store expenditures average about $1,000 per person or 10 percent of their income. Three hundred and sixty million people live in the Second World (Mexico, Brazil, Argentina, and the Pacific Basin, excluding Japan). Their GNP ranges from U.S. $1,500 to 3,000 per person. Also, 2.2 billion people live in the Third World (Africa, excluding South Africa; India; Pakistan; and Indonesia). Their GNP is several hundred dollars per person. Finally, 1.6 billion people live in the Communist or Socialist World (Eastern Europe, Russia, China, and Southwest Asia). This latter classification will change as Eastern Europe develops market economies. Their GNP per person cannot be estimated.

The concept of GNP per person can be deceiving. For example, in some Latin American countries, the top 20 percent of the population earn as much as 30 times the income of the bottom 20 percent of the population. These vast inequalities have played a large role in the onset of the debt crisis and greatly influence countries' food situations.

In the 41 Least Developed Countries (LDCs), the world's poorest people have an average per capita GNP of slightly over U.S. $200 (1985 data). The wealthiest LDC was Botswana, with a per capita GNP of U.S. $1,030; the poorest was Ethiopia, with U.S. $120. The inhabitants of the LDCs comprise about 8 percent of the world's population, or about 370 million people. Most of these countries are in Africa; only one, Haiti, is in the western hemisphere.

Contrasting Global Populations

There are sharp contrasts between communities of hunter-gatherers, which have remained small in number, are illiterate, and apply stone-age technologies, and sophisticated societies. As a result of a long process of interrelated demographic and technological development, the latter have large populations and have reached high levels of development with advanced industrial technology, general literacy, and a sizable, scientifically trained, elite population. Sharp contrasts exist among the foods that are consumed and how they are acquired.

In industrialized countries, most people are only cognizant of the food and agriculture system at the supermarket checkout and at the restaurant as they pay their bills. The bulk of the U.S. population is far removed from food production and processing. In developed countries, eating habits are largely determined by habit and custom. Prolonged hunger seldom occurs. Although meal patterns are shifting as populations adopt more time flexibilities, breakfast, midday, and evening meals have traditionally been consumed around a fixed time.

In the Triad markets of Western Europe, North America, and the Pacific Rim, with about 300 million people each, consumers have different cultures, but similar food values: quality, convenience, nutrition, availability, variety, safety, and value. Consumers begin to exhibit similar characteristics around the world, but only in the context of the particular country's culture, heritage, trade practices, and competition.

People in developed countries will spend more money on food as incomes rise because they will be eating more meals away from home and buying more services, such as convenience, with their food.

A billion or more of the world's population already spend 70 percent of their income on food. In the U.S., a $1 loaf of bread contains about 5 cents worth of wheat. If the price of wheat is doubled, the price of the loaf increases to $1.05. However, in developing countries, if wheat is purchased and ground into flour at home, a doubling of retail grain prices doubles bread prices. A food price increase that is merely annoying to the world's affluent population can drive consumption below the survival level for the poor.

As an international trade and cultural phenomenon, the interdependence of food among countries is only partial. The large rural hinterlands, in which the masses of poor people live, are not fully integrated into the system of world trade. Small farmers growing food for their own consumption, and rural workers relying largely on local markets, are only partially integrated into national markets, and even less integrated into international markets.

Since the poor and the rich do not spend their money on the same kind of food, policies that encourage greater production of poor people's food, such as cassava, corn, sorghum, and millet, can help reduce malnutrition. Food marketing and storage programs can help reduce regional, seasonal, and annual variations in supplies and prices.

In nearly all developed countries, food exports have helped finance their industrialization. The potential benefits of trade have also not been realized because the vast majority of the world's people do not have adequate incomes to meet nutritional needs or satisfy their food preferences.

Contrasts and extremes in food production, distribution, and consumption are found throughout Latin America. Indians sacrifice maize to increase harvests, while scientists work in biotechnology laboratories to produce new strains of wheat and corn. Ambulatory vendors of tamales compete with McDonald's for fast-food trade. Argentines consume 100 g of protein and 3,235 calories per capita a day; Haitians survive on 39 g of protein and 1,750 calories.

A radical change in foreign policy in favor of investments in food production, replacing food imports whenever possible, could reduce the risk of famine in developing countries.

Urban vs. Rural Populations

The physical location of the world's population, whether "urban" or "rural," influences the food they demand as well as its availability. As with the total world population, these classifications are also shifting.

The term, urban, has different meanings for much of the world's population. By the year 2000, 51.2 percent of the world's population will be located in urban areas, ranging from exclusive high-rise condominiums and secluded dachas, to shanty towns beside abandoned highways. Forty-five of the 60 largest cities in the world will be in the southern hemisphere, 18 of them larger than 10 million people.

While populations are aging in the northern hemisphere, the reverse is true in the South where residents of cities will be overwhelmingly young. In the developing countries by the year 2000, 35 percent of the total population will be under 14 years old. Increasingly, these youths roam the streets: abandoned, uneducated, unemployed, frequently undernourished, and alienated from traditional societal norms.

Cities that will triple in population by 2000 include: Dhaka, Bangladesh; Dar-es-Salaam, Tanzania; Lusaka, Zambia; and Nairobi, Kenya. Cities that will be inhabited by populations greater than 10 million will include: Bangkok, Bombay, Cairo, Calcutta, Delhi, Jakarta, Karachi, and Seoul. The Mexican capital, with a population estimated at 20 million or more, up from the last official census figure of 14 million in 1980 and 10 million in 1970, is expected to contain more than 26 million people by the turn of the century.

The pressure of 50 million Egyptians living on 4 percent of the land in Egypt has created one of the highest population densities in the world: 1,300 people per square kilometer. Cairo and Alexandria, with 14 million and 5 million respectively, are the biggest cities in the Arab world.

By the year 2000, 39 percent of Africans will live in urban areas. Also, by this future landmark date, 76.8 percent of Latin Americans and 35 percent of Asians will live in cities and be classified as "urban dwellers." Overall, in developed regions of the world, 74.4 percent of all citizens will reside in cities by 2000, while 39.3 percent will reside in less-developed regions.

As people move from the countryside to cities, there are fewer food producers, more consumers, and more pressure to urbanize productive land. About 42 percent of the current world's population is in urban areas, up from 34 percent in 1960.

In Africa, the population is growing at about 3 percent per annum, whereas food production growth is barely half of that rate. Rapid population growth has contributed directly to high rates of urbanization, which in turn has accentuated Africa's deteriorating food situation.

Rural populations degrade the environment during their quest for forage, firewood, and food. According to the Brandt Commission, planetary forest cover was reduced by 25 percent of the earth's surface to 20 percent in two recent decades. The Brundtland Commission estimates that for every tree planted in tropical regions, ten are destroyed; in sub-Saharan Africa, this ratio is estimated to be 1:29.

In Central America, about 80 percent of farm families are unable to feed themselves from their holdings. Since the 1960s, the number of landless peasants in the region has tripled, forcing the rural poor to exist on increasingly marginal ground, where the effects of cultivation wreak the worst environmental devastation. Easily depleted mountain soils are laid bare through deforestation.

Population, properly supported, is an immense natural resource and an incomparable source of accomplishment. Poor people, without basic necessities or the hope of attaining them, turn upon themselves and upon their landscape with distressing results. Population pressures are inconsistent with a wholesome environment and demeaning to human dignity, making social contact impossible, and contributing to political and economic insecurity. According to the World Bank, one of every five persons lives in "absolute poverty," defined as: "the state of those persons suffering from malnutrition to the point of being unable to work."

Influence of Refugees

In the twentieth century, the refugee problem has become persistently contentious and destabilizing. The shifting populations greatly impact upon available food supplies. Refugees can be defined as: "People who are forced to flee or are expelled from their homelands due to war, civil conflict, pestilence, natural disaster or persecution based on ethnicity, race, tribal affiliation, religion or political beliefs." Internal refugees include millions of persons around the world who are displaced from their homes for the same reasons. However, they either cannot or choose not to leave their country. They frequently are not the recipients of international relief efforts. In 1989, they included: 700,000 to 1.5 million Ethiopians, 2 million Mozambiquans, 3.6 million South African blacks resettled in tribal homelands, and 150,000 to 500,000 Salvadorans uprooted by civil war.

Significant parts of our globe continue to be marred by strife, privation, and bigotry. These refugees, or displaced men, women, and children, are indicators of the state of human relations. The quest for freedom from repression and intolerance is typically expressed through the ebb and flow of population movements. Exhibit 1.4 shows all of the countries (printed in black) from which refugees had fled by 1988.

Around the globe, population flows can exacerbate interstate and regional tensions, drain the economies of host nations, overextend humanitarian support mechanisms including food aid, and put a strain on the world's compassion threshold. In the fall of 1989 as the West Germans welcomed 200,000 East Germans who initially escaped via Hungary, the doors closed on thousands of Vietnamese boat people in Hong Kong. The former situation was quickly resolved as the Berlin Wall crumbled and, with respect to food, an undue burden was not placed on the citizens of West Germany. About 400,000 Indochinese have languished for years in camps in Thailand. Hundreds of thousands of ethnic Turks have been expelled from Bulgaria. Millions of refugees have been dispersed in Africa and Latin America. One million refugees have fled from Haiti in the past decade, less because of its political repression than because of its exhausted soil.

People in camps or designated settlement areas have no resources to enable them to engage in productive work. They are usually not allowed to integrate into the economic life of the local population. When they are recognized as international problems, the international community attends to their welfare. Emergencies of this kind are largely unpredictable.

Influence of World Travel

Travellers for pleasure and business have different influences on the local food industry than refugees have. The former are catered to, and they increase the GNP of the countries visited. The influx of American tourists to Europe has lead to the establishment of the American hamburger with accompanying marketing techniques. Americans, having travelled to Europe to enjoy a new culture and

Exhibit 1.4. Influence of Refugees on World Population and Food Supplies.

REFUGEES 1988: WHERE THEY'RE FROM, WHERE THEY'VE GONE

Refugees have fled from these countries.

Vietnam
Philippines
Indonesia
Cambodia
Laos
China
Burma
Sri Lanka
Bangladesh
Soviet Union
Afghanistan
South Yemen
Iran
Iraq
Mozambique
Poland
Romania
Somalia
Zimbabwe
Uganda
Rwanda
Burundi
Czechoslovakia
Hungary
Yugoslavia
Ethiopia
Chad Sudan
Zaire
South Africa
Western Sahara
Guinea-Bissau
Angola
Namibia
Chile
Cuba
Haiti
Nicaragua
El Salvador
Guatemala

Source: *The Wall Street Journal*, September 28, 1989.

their food habits, are bombarded by highway signs "American Hamburger," perhaps obscuring the vista of a Norwegian fjord and mountain landscape. In Germany, McDonald's hamburgers are served to Americans with beer, adapting the local food and beverage customs. The food regulations of Germany classify beer as a food; the U.S. classifies it as a beverage.

Travelling consumers influence what foods are available for them, and how it is marketed to them. World travel also has profound impacts upon the domestic food industry and consumer demands for foods. In the U.S., there has been a recent proliferation of Oriental restaurants, widening the taste spectrum beyond the entrenched Americanized Chinese establishments. Japanese, Korean, and Southeast Asian restaurants originally catered to the recent influx of Oriental immigrants and executives. They now cater to the American public who has transferred this new cuisine to the home. Increased travel by Americans to the Orient will likely stimulate interest in their fermented foods. The rapid upward mobility of Oriental immigrants has accelerated the spread of their culture, especially their ethnic foods. Concern about health and appearance has increased interest in natural, low-calorie, low-cholesterol, high-fiber foods, which translates into more cereal grains and vegetables in the diet. These have been established features of Oriental diets for centuries.

FOOD SECURITY VERSUS FOOD INSECURITY

The magnitude of the world population, the disparities among populations, the shifting nature of populations, the inherent food demands, and world trade all interact to produce nations and regions with either food security or food insecurity.

Food security can be defined as: "the assured physical and economic access to food, at all times, to all citizens and noncitizens." In many countries, such as India, the main causes of food insecurity are domestic ones. "Food insecure" people are defined by the World Bank as: "those people not having enough food for normal health and physical activity." The global total of food insecure people is about 100 million. For example, nearly one-third of the citizens of Ethiopia, about 14.7 million, are undernourished. Nigeria has 13.7 million people classified as food insecure.

The two most useful global indicators of food security are the per capita grain production and the carryover stocks of grain. The first indicator gives a sense of whether overall food availability is improving or deteriorating. Changes in carryover stocks indicate whether production is exceeding consumption or falling short of it.

Countries which have severe levels of food insecurity generally have low levels of, and unequal distribution of, food, plus an unequal distribution of land and other assets to produce food. They will usually also have low levels of investment to increase and stabilize their food production. Small countries, frequently threatened by political food embargos, encounter large changes in the price of foods and grains they need to import.

To summarize, food security and, thus, food insecurity, can be chronic or transitory situations. Either event may or may not be anticipated by the country's government or worldwide watchers and global food policymakers. Furthermore, the food security situation may occur at regular or random intervals, i.e., it can have seasonal and year-to-year implications. Although the world produces a 4-billion-ton cornucopia of food each year, more than enough to give everyone a basic diet if evenly distributed, hunger still affects a large segment of humanity.

The Intrigue of Famines

Experts disagree about who the world's hungry are, where they are located, and the best way to help them. Since World War II, famines and various emergency needs have led to a drive to establish strategic or emergency food reserves. Globally, experts express the principal nutritional problem as inadequate food consumption in terms of quantity, rather than quality. They justify this approach because most diets meet protein requirements as long as people consume them in quantities adequate to satisfy energy needs.

One common bond of undernourished people is poverty. The majority of undernourished people live in rural areas. The undernourished in urban areas also face severe difficulties in meeting their food needs. Their incomes are drastically altered by economic downturns, inflation, fixed wage dependency, and unemployment. Their health, due at least partially to crowded living conditions, may be worse than that of the rural poor of equivalent, or even lower, incomes.

These chronic situations are not frequently stressed or encountered in the media in developed countries. Instead, the tragedy of famines has been emphasized. There was more famine in 1985 than in 1975. At no time in history has the fate of hundreds of millions of starving and malnourished people — particularly in Africa, and especially in Ethiopia — been more vividly portrayed to the western world via the media. Benefits have been received from this needed attention.

Why have there been famines? Famines are traditionally seen as the result of unforeseeable and uncontrollable vagaries of nature, but modern scholarship suggests that the cause is much more often social and political.

Famines have frequently been local, especially in Europe, and have often occurred when food was plentiful and not too far away. The costs of transportation can be prohibitively high because of poor roads. Poverty-stricken people cannot afford to pay the high prices for the food, which is often available locally.

For food relief efforts, several target groups have been identified as hard to reach. These include children under 5 years of age, large families, and landless households. In some areas of the world, they are even harder to reach during wet seasons when access is difficult. Geographic location is a prime factor in obtaining food. Thus refugee camps "spring" up in more food-accessible areas.

Food-increasing mechanisms are often not initiated immediately when scarcities become apparent. For example, the world is still adjusting to the Organization of Petroleum Exporting Countries (OPEC) crises of the 1970s when the costs of energy-intensive agricultural production, and thus food, skyrocketed. To increase the food supplies, changes in farming practices involving effort and risk are often required. Neither of these are inherently attractive, and progress is slow.

In developing countries, where 80 percent of the population is needed for agriculture, many people still suffer from malnutrition. Insufficient intakes of food energy plus debilitating illnesses are the cause. Medical treatment includes immunization and anti-parasitic treatments, in addition to dietary regimes. Hunger is our oldest enemy. There are more hungry people in the world today than when the 1980s began.

WORLD AGRICULTURAL PRODUCTION

The objectives of world agriculture confront the aspirations of the developing nations and their formidable problems. Agriculture is an account of human control over nature. Defined in the manner previously given, agriculture has both on- and off-farm sectors. The on-farm sector of agriculture involves growing and harvesting raw crops and animal products. One of its unique qualities is the intimate relationship shared with the global environment. The off-farm sector is responsible for everything that happens to raw commodities after they leave the farm, from transportation through processing, packaging, storage, and consumption. Within this sector, food is an industrial product that is managed as a scarce resource, with consideration for its physical properties to maintain its nutritional and economic values.

World Crop Production

Data about the total world agricultural production in 1988 are given in Exhibit 1.5. Throughout the world, there are four categories of crops. The first category is subsistence crops which are either consumed by those who produce them, or sold by them in local markets. They include such crops as: sorghum, millet, cassava, pulses, yams, teff, and root crops. The second category is grains which are sold and bought in national and international markets, and include: wheat, rice, maize, and barley. The third category is nongrain food cash crops which are grown for local consumption and for export. These include: sugar, vegetable oils, nuts, and fruits and vegetables. The final category is nonfood cash crops which are grown mainly for the export market. These include: coffee, tea, cocoa, tobacco, pyrethrum, and agricultural fibers such as cotton, sisal, jute, kenaf, and rubber.

Developing nations are dependent on a narrow base of crops and

Exhibit 1.5. Selected Commodities of World Agricultural Production - 1988.

Product	Amount (1000 MT)		
	World	Developed Countries	Developing Countries
Total Cereals	1742985	773887	969098
Wheat	509952	293018	216934
Rice	483466	25531	457935
Coarse Grains	749567	455337	294230
Maize	405460	220080	185380
Barley	168423	140514	27909
Root Crops	571182	195639	375543
Potatoes	269702	192891	76811
Total Pulses	54652	19137	35515
Vegetables and Melons	426187	153420	272767
Fruits	329506	126463	203043
Grapes	59776	44429	15347
Citrus Fruit	67398	25893	41505
Bananas	41913	922	40991
Apples	40860	27812	13048
Nuts, total	4098	1883	2215
Sugar, raw	102779	42801	59978
Cocoa Beans	2230	0	2230
Coffee, Green	5515	1	5514
Tea	2499	266	2233
Eggs, Hen	34880	19405	15475
Wool, Greasy	3124	2192	932

Source: <u>FAO Production Yearbook</u>. Vol. 42. 1988. Food and Agriculture Organization of the United Nations: Rome.

need external supplies of feed and grains, with accompanying volatile commodity prices.

Cash versus Food Crops

In sub-Saharan Africa, inadequate emphasis has been given to the production of traditional crops identified as millet, sorghum, cassava, yams, pulses, bananas, and plantains. These indigenous crops hold considerable promise for sub-Saharan Africa and other regions where subsistence households have traditionally cultivated them. In addition to supplying calories, they are important for effective land use, labor absorption, family and community food security, national food self-sufficiency, and the involvement of women. They are more drought-resistant and easier to store than imported cereals.

Imported cereals have imposed burdens on foreign exchange resources, as well as on the storage and transport capacities of developing countries. In spite of the advantages of subsistence crops, they are considered "poor man's crops" and their production has suffered because improved agricultural technologies have not been developed for them. Research is needed to improve varieties, develop better pest and disease control methods, and develop processing methods to increase their preservation.

World Grain Trade

In 1950, most of the international grain trade flowed from North America to Western Europe. In the 1980s, Western Europe ended two centuries of dependence on imported grain. This was achieved by implementing advanced agricultural technologies, establishing farm support prices above the world market level, and achieving a population growth rate approaching zero.

In 1950, except for Western Europe, the rest of the world was essentially self-sufficient in grains. Since then, annual North American grain trade has increased from 23 to 119 million tons, and customers and recipients of grains have been drastically altered. From 1950 to 1984, per capita world grain production increased from 246 to 345 kilograms, a 40 percent increase, leading to improved diets and increased livestock production. Between 1950 and

1984, per capita production in Western Europe was climbing. Grain production in Africa peaked in 1967 and has declined by 27 percent since then. Since 1981, the grain output in Latin America has fallen by 10 percent.

In 1988, Latin America imported 11 million tons of grains. Although rapidly developing their domestic production, Brazil regularly imports both wheat and feed grains.

In 1988, China imported 5 percent of its grain, about 15 million tons. If China were to import 15 percent of its needs by 1995, the amount would total 45 million tons. This would represent more than the 28 and 24 million tons bought by Japan and the Soviet Union, respectively, in 1988. These two countries were the leading grain importers in 1988.

Even with continental imports of about 28 million tons of grains in 1988, millions of people in sub-Saharan Africa were hungry and malnourished. Asia is the largest food importing region because of shrinking cropland area per person and rising prosperity in many countries.

As recently as 1985, the U.S., Canada, and the European Community (EC) had a cereal stock of about 125 million tons, compared to the total world stock of about 290 million tons. Most of the 125 million tons of cereal stocks in developing countries were concentrated in China, India, and several Far Eastern countries.

The U.S. and Canada control a larger share of grain exports than the Middle East does of oil. During the 1980s, North American grain exports averaged about 110 million tons per year. This rate has been achieved because nearly 40 percent of harvested acres in the U.S. are devoted to export production. With respect to world trade, the U.S. provides more than 75 percent of all the corn and soybeans, over 40 percent of the wheat, and 25 percent of the rice to other markets.

International interdependence has become a slogan with significant ramifications. World grain trade is so tightly integrated that a crop failure anywhere in the world may adversely affect extremely remote villages. The lives of the 800 million persons living in absolute poverty are put at risk every time there is a drought in the central U.S., or floods in India, or a late frost in the Ukraine. Interdependence has clearly increased. During the 1980 Soviet grain embargo, Soviet grain imports reached record levels during the 15 months of the embargo and Soviet livestock herds continued to expand. This was true in spite of the fact that the U.S. then supplied more than 40 percent of the wheat, and nearly two-thirds of the coarse grains traded on the international market.

WORLD ANIMAL PRODUCTION

About 35 percent of the calories of the average U.S. diet consists of animal products. Almost 60 percent of these animal foods is derived from unimproved pasture or rangelands. Approximately 90 percent of the U.S. corn crop is fed to domestic animals. U.S. grazing and pasturelands are inadequate to meet the demand for animal products. Most of the circa 650 million acres used to graze livestock are being degraded through overuse. Almost 70 percent of this land is in below-normal condition, because of overgrazing. Almost 11,000 kilocalories (kcal) of crops are required to produce the 700 kcal of crop-fed animal products in the average U.S. daily diet, a ratio of more than 15:1.

For range and small-scale farms, animals and livestock are a vital and often necessary part of crop production systems. Worldwide, 40 to 80 percent of livestock are associated with mixed crop and livestock farming systems. In warm climate regions, animals provide 150 million horsepower per year, predominately being used for cropping. Needs for animal power will increase in the future. Small landholders rarely grow forage crops because it reduces the area needed for producing food crops. Residues from their food crops, such as rice, wheat, and barley straw, peanut hay, soybean hulls, and sweet potato leaves, are their main livestock feeds.

Agricultural production data, such as those given in Exhibit 1.5, only give gross figures and do not take into account the quantities normally put aside for seed stock for reserves, buffer stocks for price stabilization, etc., some of which may have to be compensated for out of food aid.

AGRICULTURE AND WATER RESOURCES

Water is projected to be the most critically limiting natural resource for agriculture. When there is less water, more thirsty people fight for it. When there is less arable land, more desperate people search for it. Water use doubled between 1940 and 1980, and is expected to double again by the year 2000. Eighty countries already suffer severe water shortages. In Ethiopia and Mozambique, only about 15 percent of the population has access to safe drinking water.

FUTURE AGRICULTURAL PRODUCTION PROSPECTS

At the beginning of the 1987 harvest, world grain stocks reached the record level of 459 million tons, enough to feed the world for 101 days. Grain reserves account for one-half of all human caloric intake when consumed directly, and part of the remainder, in the form of meat, milk, cheese, butter, and eggs. At the beginning of the 1989 harvest, stocks were expected to drop to 54 days of consumption, lower than the 57 days at the beginning of 1973 when grain prices doubled.

Grain stocks have dropped as food demands have continued to respond to the population-driven rise. Grain production has recently fallen at a record rate. In recent years, conditions in a number of countries have contributed to the worldwide decline in grain stocks. In 1987, a monsoon failure in India reduced grain production by 85 million tons. In 1988, drought-induced harvests in the U.S., Canada, and China reduced world output by 76 million tons. North America maintained exports during the 1988/89 trade year by selling carryover stocks.

The growth of world food production is losing momentum. Between 1950 and 1984, world grain output climbed from 624 million tons to 1,645 million tons, a 2.6-fold increase that raised per capita grain production by 40 percent. During the mid-1980s, grain production plateaued in some of the world's most populous countries: India, Indonesia, Mexico, and China. In response to the Green Revolution, the wheat harvest in India more than tripled between 1965 and 1983. Since then, grain production has not risen. Between 1970 and 1984, the rice harvest in Indonesia doubled, but production has since leveled off. Between 1950 and 1984, Mexico's grain harvest increased four times, and has since declined. Between 1976 and 1984, grain production in China increased by about 50 percent, largely by applying previously underutilized agricultural technologies. Since 1984, China's output has fallen slightly. Since 1984, global output per person has declined by 14 percent each year. In part, this decline measures the unsustainable use of soil and water. Because of world grain reserves, the drop in consumption per capita was limited to 3 percent. As a result of the production losses of 1987 and 1988, prices increased by almost 50 percent.

For approximately one-sixth of mankind, human progress has now become a retreat and, in many nations, development is being reversed. Meeting adequate food needs during the 1990s and beyond will require increased attention of, and informed action from, all political leaders, particularly those in the Third World. National governments must be prepared to wage wars against hunger on extremely broad fronts. A massive international effort is needed to protect soil, conserve water, and restore productivity of degraded lands. A worldwide scarcity of cropland and irrigation water, combined with a diminished response to the use of additional chemical fertilizers, is slowing the growth in world food output. If fertilizer use were abruptly discontinued, world food output would decrease by about 40 percent.

The Food and Agricultural Organization (FAO) projections for the year 2000 indicate that the volume of agricultural produce processed through the primary stage will double between 1980 and 2000. The most rapidly growing processing operations will be for fruits and vegetables. For produce, accelerating domestic demands and export opportunities are expected to support an annual expansion rate of 6 percent.

Experts have stated that one of our agricultural goals should be to double crop production by 2035. For several reasons, this cannot be achieved without increasing agricultural research. First, international competition in commodity markets is increasing, coupled with increasing competition for limited energy, water, and land resources. Second, labor costs are rising around the world, responding to the needs of all people to have food-purchasing powers. Of equal importance is the human demand for improved diets which increases the amount and variety of crops and animals desired. The complexity of the latter issue is also compounded by rates of population growth.

FOOD MARKETING SYSTEMS

Food marketing systems in industrialized countries have changed drastically during the last three decades. New technology in food packaging, processing, transport, storage, and information processing have enabled the development of supermarket chains that are closely integrated, both horizontally and vertically. Concentration of wholesale purchasing through these food marketing chains has important repercussions for the organization of food supply at the farm, assembly, and processing levels. The demand for large quantities of well-packed and standardized food products has permitted mass marketing. The productivity of labor in food marketing has increased, reducing costs and opening up new and expanded markets for farmers' produce.

Food problems on a global scale cannot be solved without establishing protocols for efficient and effective food storage and improved utilization. Densely populated countries encounter enormous pre- and post-harvest wastes and losses in nutritional values of foods that are locally produced, as well as imported. These losses occur because of the poor keeping-quality of some foods and food products, inadequate storage facilities, and inadequate food packaging and distribution systems. They also occur when any food surpluses are either not stored effectively or processed to preserve them for later use.

THE FOOD PROCESSING INDUSTRY

The food industry is a complex set of many integral parts with many different products and processes and large numbers of people working in food manufacturing, processing, and distribution enterprises. In recent years, there have been changes in the kinds and qualities of food produced and marketed, the technologies used, numbers and size of enterprises, channels of distribution used, efficiency in production and distribution, industry orientation and organizational structures, procurement and merchandising methods used, and the nature of competition. These changes and developments are occurring at an accelerated pace. The rate varies among countries. However, in every country, the food industry is dynamic. Generally, food expenditures constitute a large percentage of an average family's budget. Developments in food marketing and distribution are an integral part of economic development of all countries.

The discipline of food science is represented in the U.S. by the Institute of Food Technologists (IFT) which has 23,000 professional members in 60 countries. Graduate and undergraduate education in food science is offered in 60 programs in North America. The disciplines of microbiology, engineering, chemistry, physics, and molecular biology have made diverse contributions to the education of food scientists.

Non-Nutritional Food Factors

Some adverse effects of food supply on human populations are not limited to nutritional deficiencies. Food contaminants and adulterants have significant historical roles. Chronic lead poisoning is suspected to have played a role in the fall of the Roman Empire. The use of lead vessels in wine making and lead-lined cooking pots could have resulted in mental impairment of the aristocracy. The heavy bacteriological contamination of the milk fed to young infants in nineteenth century Europe is linked with their high rates of infant mortality. Today, high infant mortality in many developing countries is caused by contaminated weaning foods.

NUTRITIONAL SURVEILLANCE

Management procedures known as nutritional surveillance are offering considerable prospects for reducing the malnourished population. For example, nutritional surveillance can assist by indicating whether malnutrition occurs as shifts are made from subsistence to cash crops. Observing vulnerable groups in different areas, regions, or countries may indicate whether certain crops, cultures, or conditions are associated with especially high risks of malnutrition. Recommendations which include the need for, and identification of, remedial activities should result from effective nutritional surveillance programs.

WORLD FOOD POLICIES AND STRATEGIES

Nutritional status of children is now regarded as a central indicator for monitoring progress towards health for all people at program, national, and global levels. This is considered to be a huge advance, made in a very few years. Nutritional policies are impacting food policies and food policies in turn arc affecting agricultural policies.

Policymakers in developing countries want high prices for food to encourage agricultural production. They want low food prices so the poor can afford to purchase food. Agricultural producers have been discriminated against in many low-income countries. This has countered productivity, and inequity and unemployment have resulted. Clearly, poverty has not been alleviated. An adequate supply of food is not enough to eliminate malnutrition, hunger, and starvation. Poor people need access or exchange entitlements to food, i.e., in the form of adequate incomes and low food prices.

Future international political stability and global economic security may depend on controlling population growth more than any other single factor. The world's consumers do not have access to food at competitive prices from countries which produce it most competitively. Governments intervene in domestic food and agricultural markets. Further, they adopt trade policies to facilitate these interventions. Such trade policies often shift the burden of domestic policies onto buyers in other countries and deny domestic consumers free access to world trade. The cost of these barriers is $60 billion to the Organization for Economic Cooperation and Development (OECD) countries each year (U.S., Canada, Japan, Australia, New Zealand, and Western Europe). In the European Community (EC), consumers' food bills would be reduced by U.S.

$40-50 billion if they were allowed to buy their food at competitive world prices annually.

In the current Food Aid Convention, which represents a multi-annual legal minimum commitment of donor countries, the UN target of 10 million tons of cereals has been satisfied to the degree of 76 percent. The food aid requirements now estimated by the FAO and World Food Program (WFP) are 18 and 20 million tons, respectively.

Either the total or partial removal of hunger and malnutrition calls for sound global food strategies. Disregarding distribution problems, the world production of grain in 1987 could have provided everyone with more than 3,000 calories and 65 g of protein per day. Further, 2 percent of the world's grain output would be sufficient to eliminate malnutrition among the world's 400 to 600 million undernourished. However, 40 percent of the world's grain is fed to livestock. An additional problem occurs because of inadequate distribution systems. Food is ineffectively transported among countries and regions. Once located within an area, unequal distribution to different income groups can occur. Further, in some societies, food is unequally distributed between the two sexes.

Finally, within households, food consumption practices can be based on traditional roles rather than human needs. For example, after women have walked all day for water, they may not be given enough to eat to offset their caloric expenditure. Women's health can be improved by reducing the need for long walks to collect firewood or water, as well as other forms of hard work. Further, reducing unwanted pregnancies decreases caloric requirements of women. In some cases, some family members consume more because of their extra physical efforts, and the rest of the family receives less. Calorie deficiencies vary by geographical area, season, and year, increasing the drastic effects from the distribution of food based on cultural practices or traditions.

Receiving more food is not necessarily a guarantee that basic needs of poor people may be met. If they have parasites in their stomachs, the nutrients will not be absorbed for the benefit of their bodies. Food needs can be met by reducing unnecessary requirements raised by infections and illness. Health authorities say as many as 30,000 children die each year of respiratory disease and diarrhea caused by contaminated air and water.

Effective food policies encompass all components of the complex agriculture and food industry. For example, in the U.S., federal policies affect almost every aspect of food production and consumption. These policies are implemented by more than 350 food, nutrition, and agriculture programs that perform several key functions: food industry regulation, nutrition surveys, food assistance, research, agriculture support, nutrition education, and foreign food aid. In 1984, these programs cost $36 billion. They are distributed among 28 government departments and regulate the food and agriculture industry with additional assistance from agencies responsible for the regulation of alcohol, seafood, weights and measures, radioactive contamination, and food containers.

The developing nations that are self-sufficient in food at low per capita income levels have a propensity to spend any increased income on more or different foods. This additional expenditure usually outruns their agricultural output capacity.

The average share of agriculture in central government public expenditures in developing countries has varied between 5 and 10 percent. This sector accounts for a very large share of their gross development product, employment, and export. Within agriculture, the food sector has traditionally lagged in public support in favor of the cash crop sector which earns needed foreign exchange. The food sector cannot be improved if the export sector fails to grow. The export sector is the source of foreign exchange necessary to import inputs and equipment for the food sector.

We have a constantly changing world. The industrial life-style of the past 300 years is unravelling conditions on earth that took a billion years to develop. Political decisions have undue influence upon agricultural production. For example, around 1960 in China, Chairman Mao Tse-tung declared war on the country's sparrow population, believing the birds were consuming tons of badly needed grain in the fields. The result was carnage for the country's bird population. Millions of Chinese trapped and killed not only sparrows but millions of other small birds, including insect-eating varieties beneficial to farmers.

Role of Global Scientists

We are in a global economy. Research, fundamental and applied, has become an international competitive resource of decisive value. The number of scientists, engineers, and technicians engaged in Research and Development (R&D) in the developing countries is less than 1.5 per 10,000 inhabitants, compared with 16.6 in the market economies of the industrialized countries. In an age where technological advances are occurring with breathtaking speed, the gap in capacity between North and South is rapidly widening. Although there are exceptions, the term "North" is often used to refer to industrialized countries; the term "South," to developing countries.

Throughout our recent history, technology has been the most effective change agent. Knowledge now available in agricultural production and primary health care is not simply transferable around the globe. It needs to be understood, appropriately revised and updated, and absorbed by developing countries to be used in a geographically and culturally sensitive fashion. Developing countries must acquire the means to pursue the newer biological and physical science technologies and adapt them to their own needs.

Rigorous scientific activity must be encouraged within the developing countries to permit them to identify their own problems and gain the competence to resolve them. In their own institutions, Third World scientists should engage in research on their priority problems. In addition to dedication and a willingness to share, worldwide dissemination of public knowledge requires the use of new computer and satellite technologies. Worldwide communication advances include road, rail, and air links; telephone, telex, and satellite systems; and the extensive use of computerized data.

Relevant technology depends on a long-term commitment to agricultural research concomitant with relevant research in the social and nutritional sciences. Technologies to increase product yields in all the diverse environments where the poor and the undernourished live are still in their early stages of development. The harsh, resource-poor areas, such as arid regions, require considerable research in dry-farming technologies. The application of new technologies can cause significant shifts in local traditions, economic relationships, and labor market conditions.

At the international level, tens of thousands of foreign alumni of U.S. land grant and other universities are now abroad. They consist of agricultural leaders throughout the world with a loyalty to their home institutions and former thesis advisors. These alumni provide a great opportunity to act as a link for encouraging scientific exchanges and cooperative research efforts.

AGRICULTURE AND YOU

Agriculture is one of the oldest and most essential human pursuits. It is also one of the most complex and confounding. A basic question is: What can be done to bring the world's food supply and population into balance? Because of emergent biotechnologies, including genetic engineering, we will have greater control and we will experience record-breaking product yields. In the year 2000, the productivity and imagination of agriculturists will be taxed as never before. What will your social, political, or professional role be?

REFERENCES

Abbott, J. C. 1986. *Marketing improvement in the developing world: what happens and what we have learned*. FAO Economic and Social Development Series No. 37. Rome: Food and Agriculture Organization of the United Nations.

Alsudery, Abdelmuhsin. 1985. The world food problems: assessment and solutions. In *Crop productivity – research imperatives revisited*, eds. M. Gibbs and C. Carlson, 71-80. An international conference held at Boyne Highlands Inn, October 13-18, 1985 and Airlie House, December 11-13, 1985.

Boserup, Ester. The impact of scarcity and plenty on development. In *Hunger and history*, eds. R. I. Rotberg and T. K. Rabb, 185-209. Cambridge: Cambridge University Press.

Brown, Lester R. 1989. Feeding six billion. *World-Watch* 2(5):32-40.

Brown, Lester R. 1989. Reexamining the World Food Prospect. In *State of the world 1989*, ed. L. R. Brown, 41-58. New York: W. W. Norton & Company.

Cetron, Marvin and Owen Davies. 1989. *American renaissance – our life at the turn of the 21st century*. New York: St. Martin's Press.

Evans, D. and W. Sharp. 1986. Potential applications of plant cell culture. In *Biotechnology in food processing*, eds. S. K. Harlander and T. P. Labuza, 133-43. New Jersey: Noyes Publications.

Falcon, W. P., C. T. Kurien, F. Monckeberg, A. P. Okeyo, S. O. Olayide, F. Rabar, and W. Tims. 1987. The world food and hunger problem: changing perspectives and possibilities, 1974-84. In *Food policy integrating supply, distribution, and consumption*, eds. J. P. Gittinger, J. Leslie and C. Hoisington, 15-38. Baltimore: The Johns Hopkins University Press.

Gever, J., R. Kaufman, D. Skole, and C. Vorosmarty. 1986. *Beyond oil*. Cambridge: Ballinger Publishing Company.

Gibbs, M. and C. Carlson, eds. 1985. *Crop productivity – research imperatives revisited*. An international conference held at Boyne Highlands Inn, October 13-18, 1985 and Airlie House, December 11-13, 1985.

Harwood, R. R., R. J. Battenfield, B. D. Knezek, and J. L. Davidson. 1985. Production systems. In *Crop productivity – research imperatives revisited*, eds. M. Gibbs and C. Carlson, 216-238. An international conference held at Boyne Highlands Inn, October 13-18, 1985 and Airlie House, December 11-13, 1985.

Haswell, Margaret. 1985. *Energy for subsistence*, 2d. ed. London: The Macmillan Press Ltd.

Hood, Lamartine F. 1988. The role of food science and technology in the food and agriculture system. *Food Technology* 42(9):131-34.

Kaynak, Erdener. 1986. *World food marketing systems*. London: Butterworth & Co. (Publishers) Ltd.

Lee, John E. 1988. Trends in world agriculture and trade in high-value food products. *Food Technology* 42(9):119-27.

Lester, R. 1990. The illusion of progress. In *State of the World 1990*, ed. L. Starke, 3-16. New York: W. W. Norton & Company, Inc.

Mason, J. B., J-P. Habicht, H. Tabatabai, and V. Valverde. 1984. *Nutritional surveillance*. Geneva: World Health Organization.

McGovern, R. Gordon. 1988. Worldwide consumer trends and the competitive position of the U.S. food industry. *Food Technology* 42(9):128-9.

Nestle, Marion. 1985. *Nutrition in medical practice*. Greenbrae, California: Jones Medical Publications.

Pelto, G. H. and P. J. Pelto. 1983. Diet and delocalization: dietary changes since 1750. In *Hunger and history*, eds. R. I. Rotberg and T. K. Tabb, 309-330. Cambridge: Cambridge University Press.

Scrimshaw, Nevin S. 1983. The value of contemporary food and nutrition studies for historians. In *Hunger and history*, eds. R. I. Rotberg and T. K. Rabb, 331-336. Cambridge: Cambridge University Press.

Singer, H., J. Wood, and T. Jennings. 1987. *Food aid: the challenge and the opportunity*. New York: Oxford University Press.

Streeten, Paul. 1987. *What price food?* New York: St. Martin's Press.

Wittwer, Sylvan H. 1983. The new agriculture: a view of the twenty-first century.

In *Agriculture in the twenty-first century*, ed. J. W. Rosenblum, 337-67. New York: John Wiley & Sons.

Wittwer, Sylvan H. 1985. Crop productivity—research imperatives: a decade of change. In *Crop productivity—research imperatives revisited*, eds. M. Gibbs and C. Carlson, 1-6. An international conference held at Boyne Highlands Inn, October 13-18, 1985 and Airlie House, December 11-13, 1985.

Chapter Two

Global Food Production

INTRODUCTION

This chapter will give you the facts about where crops and livestock are grown throughout the globe. You will also be introduced to a few of the issues that affect the location and efficiency of food production. You will be introduced to the interrelated dimensions of the world food problem. After studying this material, you should be able to:

- discuss where specific crops and livestock are produced around the world;
- discuss some of the current agricultural issues affecting crop and livestock production;
- understand the complexity of the world food problem, realizing that it is being accentuated by the changing resource base.

Because of the complexity of these issues, they will be discussed in detail throughout later chapters of this book. In this chapter, you will be introduced to agronomic resources as well as changes which are occurring to them, and how they are being used for food and agriculture throughout the world. Having stated the objective of making you aware of where major crops and livestock are grown, it would seem to be optimal if data could be given to you which stated, for example, that XXX tons of grains were grown on XXX acres of land in China, using XXX cu. ft. of water and XXX tons of nitrogen fertilizer. Obviously, the crop yields are affected by more than water, soil, and fertilizer, and thus you would expect them to vary from season to season. However, with erosion of topsoils occurring at rapid rates, the amount of arable lands also changes;

some regions have higher disappearing or erosion rates than others. In addition, fertilizer use is adjusted by plant and soil needs, as well as economic conditions. For these reasons, and others which will become apparent to you, this and other chapters will concentrate upon trends; data in the exhibits are intended to help you understand these trends.

THE CROPLAND BASE

Throughout arable lands around the world, grasslands provide the human population with meat, milk, leather, and wool; croplands provide food, feed, and industrial raw materials such as fiber and vegetable oils. Exhibit 1.5 provided data about the total crop production made possible by agriculture and the effective use of agronomic resources. Data in Exhibits 2.1, 2.2, and 2.3 provide

Exhibit 2.1. Total Production of Wheat, Rice, and Soybeans - 1988.

Region/Country	Wheat		Rice		Soybeans	
	Production (1000 MT)	Yield (Kg/HA)	Production (1000 MT)	Yield (Kg/HA)	Production (1000 MT)	Yield (Kg/HA)
North and Central America	68702	1942	9426	5147	43477	1803
Europe	124599	4586	2232	5135	2360	2303
Oceania	14337	1532	778	6446	65	1414
South America	15941	1727	17183	2336	29761	1869
Africa	13630	1682	9467	1738	472	1088
Asia	188242	2263	441480	3402	15438	1254
USSR	84500	1760	2900	4394	760	950
All Developed Countries	293018	2415	25531	5667	46598	1803
All Developing Countries	216934	2189	457935	3246	45734	1587
World	509952	2314	483466	3320	92333	1690

Source: <u>FAO Production Yearbook</u>. Vol. 42. 1988. Food and Agriculture Organization of the United Nations: Rome.

Exhibit 2.2. Total Production of Vegetables and Melons, Fruit and
            Treenuts - 1988.

Region/Country	Vegetables and Melons (1000 MT)	Fruit (1000 MT)	Treenuts* (1000 MT)
North and Central America	36812	45275	866
Europe	70036	71387	868
Oceania	2169	4260	15
South America	13599	49348	206
Africa	30851	41398	270
Asia	238940	10334	1750
USSR	33781	14503	124
All Developed Countries	153420	126463	1883
All Developing Countries	272767	203043	2215
World	426187	329506	4098

*Nuts include: almonds, pistachios, hazelnuts, cashew nuts, chestnuts, and
walnuts; and others sold mainly for dessert or table nuts such as Brazil nuts,
pili nuts, sapucaia nuts and macadamia nuts.

Source: FAO Production Yearbook. Vol. 42. 1988. Food and Agriculture
        Organization of the United Nations: Rome.

information about the selected crops, namely: wheat, rice, and soybeans; vegetables, fruits, and nuts; and sugarcane and sugar beets,
respectively. The regions or countries referred to in these exhibits
are defined in Appendix A. Data in Exhibits 2.4 and 2.5 provide
information about animal and milk production around the world,
respectively. Together, these commodities supply much of the protein, fat, and carbohydrates consumed by the world's population.
They are grown in different regions in response to agronomic, eco-

Exhibit 2.3. Total Production of Sugar Cane and Sugar Beets - 1988*

Region/Country	Sugar Cane		Sugar Beet	
	Production (1000 MT)	Yield (Kg/HA)	Production (1000 MT)	Yield (Kg/HA)
North and Central America	181656	65106	23219	42425
Europe	226	65318	144822	43372
Oceania	31043	77112	-------	-------
South America	327544	62921	2678	48326
Africa	73185	61120	3902	44825
Asia	374556	55493	32268	29172
USSR	-------	-------	87800	25824
All Developed Countries	78175	80175	259601	35285
All Developing Countries	910034	59194	35089	29796
World	988209	60445	294690	34527

*These data cover all crops except those grown explicitly for feed. In several countries considerable quantities are used for seed, feed, fresh consumption, and the manufacture of alcohol and other uses.

Source: FAO Production Yearbook. Vol. 42. 1988. Food and Agriculture Organization of the United Nations: Rome.

nomic, and political conditions. International trade and foreign aid are the principal vehicles used to distribute them throughout the world. With the fact in mind that the population of the developing world is 214 percent larger than that in developed countries (Exhibit 1.2), calculating per capita consumption data from these tables yields discovery of some of the disparities existing in food supplies today.

Exhibit 2.4. Total Production of Meat, Horse Meat, Beef and Buffalo Meat,
              Sheep and Goats, Pig Meat and Poultry Meat - 1988.

Country/Region	Total Meat (1000 MT)	Horse Meat (1000 MT)	Beef and Buffalo*** (1000 MT)	Sheep and Goat Meat* (1000 MT)	Pig Meat* (1000 MT)	Poultry** Meat (1000 MT)
North and Central America	34817	203	13675	241	9149	11369
Europe	42861	144	11153	1464	21199	8255
Oceania	4239	12	2181	1341	367	470
South America	12188	89	6863	326	1989	3401
Africa	8267	16	3420	1447	483	1983
Asia	41955	92	4537	3329	24868	8256
USSR	19213	---	8359	869	6300	3127
All Developed Countries	101948	286	34627	3996	37593	24029
All Developing Countries	61592	270	15561	5020	26762	12833
World	163540	556	50188	9016	64354	36862

*Data include the meat equivalent of exported live animals and exclude the meat
equivalent of imported live animals.

**Data include meat form all domestic birds and refers to ready-to-cook weight.

***Data include veal meat.

Source: FAO Production Yearbook. Vol. 42. 1988. Food and Agriculture
         Organization of the United Nations: Rome.

Surface land available around the world today is about 13 billion
hectares. Of these lands, 1.5 billion hectares are used to produce
crops. About 25 percent of this area is cultivated for pasture or
rangelands from grass and forage for domestic livestock and wild
herbivores. An additional 31 percent is forest, including the vast
savannahs which are partly treed. The remaining portion, or 33 percent, supports limited biological activity, being either paved to support urban life, or being classified as deserts or other wastelands.
Examination of history of these percentages leads to the conclusion

Exhibit 2.5. Total Production of Animal Milk for Human Consumption - 1988.

| Country/Region | Milk | | | |
	Cow (1000 MT)	Buffalo (1000 MT)	Sheep (1000 MT)	Goat (1000 MT)
North and Central America	85184	-----	-----	345
Europe	172557	94	3716	1663
Oceania	14209	-----	-----	-----
South America	29119	-----	39	153
Africa	12523	1420	1512	1990
Asia	48820	36743	3665	3787
USSR	105950	-----	86	360
All Developed Countries	377913	94	3823	2047
All Developing Countries	90449	38163	5194	6252
World	468362	38257	9017	8299

Source: FAO Production Yearbook. Vol. 42. 1988. Food and Agriculture Organization of the United Nations: Rome.

that cultivated areas and forests are decreasing, and wastelands are increasing.

Since 1950, four-fifths of the increase in world food output has come from expanding cultivated areas. This area was increased by 24 percent from 1950 to 1981. Since then, cultivated areas have fallen by 7 percent. The areas of newly reclaimed land have been offset by degradation and conversion to non-farm uses. Forest lands have been decreasing since 1980. Overgrazing of animals slowly converts grasslands to deserts, which are developing on every continent. As grasslands diminish, pressure is placed on croplands to produce more grain to feed livestock and the competition between human and animal food supplies increases.

Some of the animal production given in Exhibit 2.4 is expected to decline, along with the milk production (Exhibit 2.5). As grasslands deteriorate, soil erosion accelerates and the capacity to sustain livestock diminishes. Currently, 600 million tons of grain are needed each year to feed the world's livestock. The fodder needs of livestock already exceed the sustainable yield of grasslands and other forage sources. By 2000, projections have been made that the demand for fodder will be 700 million tons and the supply will be 540 million tons. Currently, fodder supplies only 50 to 60 percent of the needs in some Indian states, such as Rajasthan and Karnataka, leaving large numbers of emaciated cattle. To help correct this situation, India has established fodder relief camps for cattle that are threatened by starvation.

CHANGES IN THE AGRICULTURE RESOURCE BASE

Human activities and natural events are affecting the biosphere through changes in land cover and biological productivity, soil moisture, groundwater reserves, atmospheric carbon dioxide, and trace compounds including pollutants and toxic substances. These rates of change appear to be exceeding our understanding of their implications and our ability to cope with them.

The agricultural systems of Japan, Taiwan, Western Europe, and China are said to be both biologically-based and scientifically-oriented, resulting in the sparing and effective use of land, energy, and water resources. Their technologies produce higher yields per unit of land area, but are not as productive per farm worker as those in the U.S. and Canada. Scientists in the developed countries are slowly realizing that they will have to alter their demand-driven economy with its perceived unlimited resources. Instead, they will also have to adopt procedures adapted to a resource-limited economy. Many experts state that worldwide agriculture will have to shift in this direction.

These statements or realizations are being made at the same time that experts, such as Lester Brown of the Worldwatch Institute, argue that global annual food production already falls short of human consumption and that environmental degradation reduces yields 1 percent annually at a time when world population is growing by 2 percent. A tremendous challenge lies ahead: making the shift to a resource-limited economy while supplying sufficient foods for the nutritional status and sense of well-being of people throughout the globe.

Changing Lands

Land is the most valuable natural resource of a nation. There have never been so many competitive forces affecting global land resources, essential for future crop productivity, in human recorded history. Problems in soil such as salinity, alkalinity, and aluminum toxicity constitute a significant impediment to crop productivity. As a capital good, man has been investing in land, i.e., improving its capacity for productivity, for decades. In the humid tropics, development of technologies of soil and crop management, i.e., conservation tillage and alley cropping, is needed so that continuous cropping can be a viable alternative to the slash and burn, shifting cultivation systems now used. There is increasing public support for the improvement and conservation of natural resources.

Erosion

Globally, 8 million hectares are being lost to soil erosion, and 2 million each from desertification and toxification. Twenty-six billion tons of topsoil are lost annually and 26 million hectares are reduced to zero productivity as a result of desertification. Conditions differ among countries and regions.

Several examples of soil erosion illustrate how cultivated areas are being reduced. About 6 billion tons of soil per year are eroded from one-third of India's cultivated land. In 1975, India was losing 5 billion tons of topsoil each year, compared to 3 billion tons in the U.S., which had equivalent cultivated areas. However, by the late 1970s, erosion surpassed soil formation on one-third of U.S. cropland, much of it in the Midwest. Fifteen years later, the U.S. still loses about three billion tons of topsoil per year. Soil degradation affects one-fifth of Canadian farmland, costing farmers about $1 billion per year. Canada lags behind the U.S. and some other countries in effective programs to protect and maintain or enhance land productivity.

The U.S. Agency for International Development (AID) estimates that 680 million tons of U.S. topsoil per year, 130 tons per hectare coming from prime farmland, are being washed into the sea, down the country's three chains of steep mountain slopes leading to its oceans. Due to the complex nature of detecting erosion rates around the globe, estimates of true erosion are conflicting.

China's topsoil is vanishing at the rate of 5 billion tons per year. More than 50 million hectares of grassland are being lost each year, and the country's deserts are expanding by 1,500 square kilometers. In 1978, 1 billion tons of topsoil were washing down from Ethiopia's highlands each year. Since that time, Ethiopia has been subjected to droughts.

At the end of the 1980s, soil erosion was slowly reducing the inherent productivity of up to one-third of the world's cropland. However, increased use of chemical fertilizers was temporarily masking this deterioration. An estimated 25 billion tons of topsoil is now being lost each year from cropland around the globe. This is roughly the amount of topsoil that covers all of Australia's wheatlands.

More than 80 percent of the Canadian prairie grasslands, which supported herds of bison before they were slaughtered in the 1800s, has been converted to agricultural and other uses. Most of the land receives regular applications of chemicals. Fertilizer and pesticide sales in Canada have more than tripled since 1972. The soil is degrading, however. The organic content of prairie soils has declined to 36 from 49 percent, and worse, the loss is closer to 50 percent in the provinces of Ontario and Quebec. Because of acceptable economic climates, the developed world can better withstand environmental degradations than the undeveloped world. Today, soil erosion may cost Canada about $1 billion in reduced yields per year, but people do not starve there because of the consequences of this erosion. Can this continue with positive results?

Desertification

Soil erosion and encroaching desert areas claim about 6 million hectares per year of cultivated cropland around the world. This is an area twice the size of Belgium. Further, this area is lost beyond any practical hope of reclamation, according to the UN Environment Program. By 2000, desertification is expected to erode more than

75,000 square kilometers in China, more than twice the area of Taiwan.

Further, the UN Environment Program estimates that 35 percent of the earth's land surface, on which food for one-fifth of the world's population is grown, is threatened by desertification. Ethiopia, India, and Mauritania are severely affected by desertification, and human survival itself is questionable.

In the Sahel region of Africa, where the desert is advancing about 50 miles per year, desert nomads and rural small farmers are erecting plastic and palm fiber fences to protect their oases and threatened agricultural lands. This simple, easily maintained, and low-cost technology has successfully halted the immediate advancement of the desert in some areas.

Deforestation

The world's native forests are being cleared at an accelerating pace. Much of this land is infertile and is being settled by subsistence farmers. In the past, there was a tendency for large international lending agencies to support land-clearing schemes without providing guidelines for improving impoverished soils. Such neglect lead to erosion, exposure of soils to acids, and more impoverished subsoils.

As a result of logging, the world's forests are being shaved at the rate of 11 million hectares per year. More than one-third of the world's rain forests have already been destroyed. The chronic demand for fuel has left woodland slopes naked in Haiti and Nepal. Once the trees are removed, erosion, landslides, and floods increase. The familiar Dover cliffs of England were once forested before the trees were needed for fuel as civilizations advanced. By 2020, there may be little old growth cover of trees anywhere in the world.

Crop Diversity

By the 1950s, 70 percent of all cultivated land was planted with improved varieties that had not existed in the 1930s. In the U.S. in 1955, 80 percent of the wheat planted, 86 percent of the corn, 92 percent of the oats, 95 percent of the cotton, and 98 percent of the soybeans were new genetic varieties.

The term "Green Revolution" was coined by the U.S. AID in 1968 to refer to certain breakthroughs in wheat and rice farming which had the potential to double or triple the supplies of these grains for developing countries. The father of the Green Revolution, Norman Borlaug, received the Nobel Peace Prize in 1970 for his breeding of new high-yielding varieties of wheat.

Green Revolution technologies focused on biological and yield-increasing technologies. They emerged in order to increase output per land unit when land is scarce or labor is cheap. Green Revolution research sought to improve the production of high-yielding cereal grains. The production of these grains was emphasized, frequently at the expense of nutritious staples such as peas, lentils, and beans, consumed by the poor indigenous population.

Continued high rates of population growth coupled with the difficulty of developing "miracle" strains in genetically complex food crops, such as vegetables, are partly responsible for restricting the success of the Green Revolution. Recent discussions of the Green Revolution have centered on the second wave of techniques in which high-yielding varieties, bred for disease and insect resistance, will fix their own nitrogen.

Today, countries in coastal West Africa, the Caribbean, and similar climatic zones in Asia do not depend on one major cereal for their basic food supplies. Yams, cassava, and other tubers can be grown to harvest in different seasons. Cassava can be stored by leaving it in the ground. However, as more of the population shifts and becomes urbanized, preference for grains, as opposed to tubers, becomes stronger. Many successes are being made through genetic engineering. For example, drought-resistant wheat can now be grown in desert areas of Australia and North America.

PHOTOSYNTHESIS

Unlike other agronomic resources, the life-sustaining process of photosynthesis is stable and is not increasing or decreasing the amount of food available to the world's population. Undisturbed natural ecosystems demonstrate little net productivity. That is, the amount of plant and animal material usually does not increase very much from year to year. Most of the solar energy captured by the *biota*, or plant and animal life in the region, is used to support daily metabolic needs; little remains for new growth. When some of the *biota* is removed by humans, regrowth occurs slowly. Peter Raven, Director of the Missouri Botanical Garden, points out that humanity consumes or wastes 40 percent of the total amount of energy stored by photosynthesis in terrestrial vegetation. How much more can people devour before they begin to exhaust resources and crowd out vital ecosystems?

WATER RESOURCES

Water will likely become the most limited and one of the most expensive of all resources for future global food production. Although water covers about three-fourths of the earth's surface, only 3 percent of the world's water is fresh, and 75 percent of that is contained in glaciers and the polar ice caps. In the early 1980s, an Arab country tried unsuccessfully to alter these statistics by towing icebergs from the polar regions to their country.

Water resources are limited in each of the five most populous countries on earth: China, India, the former U.S.S.R., U.S., and Indonesia. Water is the most critical natural resource for future agricultural development in the Middle East, Southern Europe, Egypt, the Sudan, sub-Saharan Africa, Taiwan, Pakistan, Australia, Argentina, Brazil, Canada, and most countries in Central and South America.

Throughout the Arabian peninsula, water threatens to replace oil as the precious commodity of the future. Agricultural projects are rapidly polluting and depleting ground water supplies. Countries have been driven to the use of expensive desalination programs or to importing water. The transportation of icebergs from the poles to the Middle East has been discussed and eliminated as a source of water. Saudi Arabia is self-sufficient in grain, but production costs are six times higher than world market rates. Irrigation is using 90 percent of Saudi Arabia's nonrenewable fossil water supplies, causing the water table to drop at an alarming rate.

Canada has 20 percent of the world's fresh water supply. However, regional water shortages are now a common occurrence. Nominal charges to consumers and industry encourage both overuse and waste. Further, consumer fears about contamination of drinking water has increased sales of bottled water by at least fourteenfold since 1980.

Pollution and Water Resources

The effects of polluted ground water on plants needs further investigation. Chemical dumps, septic tanks, and leakage from contaminated areas may lower the quality of ground water. Sewage releases from chemical industries and surface runoff may adversely affect the quality of surface waters. Irrigation water from such contaminated sources may adversely affect crop production.

Irrigation

In 1900, 1950, and 1980, there were 40, 94, and 249 million hectares, respectively, of irrigated cropland around the world. Since 1980, irrigated land area has increased by 8 million hectares. Not all of the irrigation expansion during the preceding three decades is sustainable. For example, irrigation in the U.S. southern Great Plains is based on the use of fossil water, which will eventually be depleted.

Agriculture is the world's largest water user, consuming, mostly through crop irrigation, 80 to 85 percent of the fresh water resources in the U.S. What is the actual impact of irrigation systems? One-third of the world's food is now grown on the 18 percent of the cropland that is irrigated. Different situations related to irrigation are prevalent throughout the world. A few examples from different countries and regions will be presented.

From Turkey to Egypt, only three river systems water the arid deserts. Political discussions are evolving around alternative uses for them. Turkey's plan to tap the headwaters of the Tigris-Euphrates is straining relations with Syria and Iraq; Iraqi villages are already importing water by truck. Palestinians and Israelis are feuding over the Jordan River and the underground reserves in the West Bank and Gaza. Underground water in both Jordan and Syria is expected to be exhausted early in the next century. In the late 1980s, the turbines of the Aswan dam on the Nile River were within inches of grinding to a halt until rains in the Ethiopian highlands brought a temporary reprieve. Before 2000, the struggle over limited and threatened water resources could destroy the fragile ties among these nations, leading to unprecedented upheaval within the area.

Important decisions about water use for agriculture versus industrial and urban needs add to the frustrating political climate in this region. Economic and technological influences are affecting environmental trends and resource constraints such as the waterlogging and salting of irrigation systems, the falling water tables, the diversion of irrigation water to nonfarm uses, and the possible adverse effects of climatic changes.

In the U.S.S.R., the excessive use of water for irrigation diminishes the flow of two central Asian rivers, the Syr-Darya and Amu-Darya. Irrigation diversions from these rivers have greatly reduced the flow into the landlocked Aral Sea, reducing the water level by at least 12 meters. Since 1960, the area covered by this sea has shrunk more than 40 percent, leading to sandstorms which affect the surrounding crops.

In Gambia, farmers can take advantage of coastal sea breezes for irrigation systems. At wind speeds of 10-12 m.p.h, a wind pump can draw water at a rate of 1200 gallons per hour from a 50-ft. well into a 10-ft. high storage tank. Although time and human energy savings would be enormous with this pump compared to the traditional "rope and hand" methods with irrigation buckets, concerns have been raised that this system is still more expensive.

Although irrigated areas in the U.S. have been reduced by 7 percent since 1978, water tables are still falling by 6 inches to 4 feet per year beneath one-fourth of U.S. irrigated cropland. In the U.S. corn and wheat belts, spring moisture is a determinant factor for agriculture productivity. In these relatively low population areas, agriculture consumes 83 percent of the water supplies. Currently, 63 percent of orchard land and 52 percent of vegetable crop areas in the U.S. are not irrigated.

The Ogallala Aquifer is a vast reservoir from which Nebraska, Kansas, and parts of Colorado, New Mexico, Oklahoma, and Texas draw most of their water supplies. Since 1945, irrigation systems pumping water up from the Ogallala have turned the Dust Bowl of the 1930s into a farming center that grows most of the corn, wheat, sorghum, and cotton in the U.S. These crops are worth more than

$20 billion per year. Thirty years ago, the Ogallala contained about as much water as one of the Great Lakes, namely, Lake Huron. The supply is now drying up because far more water is drained from the aquifer every year than is restored by rain. In parts of Texas, New Mexico, and Kansas, the water table has dropped more than 100 feet since the mid-1950s.

In these regions, farmers are attempting to reduce their water consumption. Because they require less water for production, some farmers have substituted cotton, wheat, or sorghum for corn. Some farmers are using water-conserving irrigation methods and have graded their fields billiard-table flat, so that desperately needed water does not run off. However, these techniques can only slow the depletion of the Ogallala.

By 2000, projections are being made that many farmers will have returned to dry-land farming, working harder to produce less crops. By 2020, the six states that depend on the Ogallala will have lost more than 5 million acres of irrigated farmland, an area the size of the state of Massachusetts.

A proposed alternative is to import vast quantities of water up to 1,100 miles uphill from Arkansas, Missouri, and South Dakota. If agreement among the states could be reached, the estimated costs would exceed $25 billion. At the turn of the century, that alternative may seem more acceptable than allowing the Great Plains to return to the near-barrenness of the 1930s.

By 2000, California's fertile San Joaquin Valley will face a catastrophe of another kind. Today the valley is one of the world's most productive farming areas. The valley receives too little rain to support most crops, so farming is heavily dependent on irrigation. As California's population grows, people are beginning to compete for the irrigation water. What use is more important? In addition, the same water that sustains the otherwise arid valley also deposits mineral salts in the ground. Slowly, the soil is becoming too salty to support the growth of crop plants. A decade from now, San Joaquin harvests will be dropping rapidly. Ten years after that, it will be nearly impossible to survive as a farmer in the valley, unless salt-tolerant plants are available.

There is a theoretical way to repair this environmental problem. Flooding the affected lands with water could wash the salt from the soil and into the rivers and out to sea. However, this would require far more water than is available. Scientists are being challenged to develop genetically engineered crops capable of living in toxic soil. For another alternative, perhaps physicists could develop technologies for cheaply desalinating ocean water to flood the San Joaquin fields. Unless one or more solutions are quickly found, this valley could remain nearly barren for decades.

The efficiency of conventionally applied irrigation water varies between 20 and 40 percent in the U.S., and 80 to 85 percent in Israel. Drip or trickle irrigation will be increasingly important for future agricultural food production. Drip systems use water and fertilizer more efficiently and reduce labor costs. Their use will expand to include both high-value crops and the main food crops around the world.

THE CHANGING ATMOSPHERE AND CROPS

Ozone, by itself and combined with sulfur and nitrogen oxides, accounts for about 90 percent of all crop losses in the U.S. caused by air pollutants. These annual crop losses range from 2 to 4 percent. Legumes are particularly susceptible. No major agricultural areas throughout the world are free from the adverse effects of air pollution. Atmospheric gases indirectly affect soil fertility and the water status of the soil. The aerial environment, plants, and soil microorganisms are a highly interactive ecosystem.

Acid Rain

The principal components of acidic deposition are sulfur dioxide and nitrogen oxides, found principally as nitrogen dioxide and nitrogen oxide. These are precursors for the principal components of acid precipitation. They are the primary chemicals concerning crop production, reaching the plant as gasses in "acid rain" or directly as "dry deposition."

In parts of Europe, these gases are the principal atmospheric chemicals affecting crop production. They are emitted in large quantities from power stations, smelter operations, and other industrial sources. The automobile is a primary source of nitrogen oxides.

Heavy metals and other atmospheric chemicals are principally local problems associated with specific sources. When dissolved in water or on leaf surfaces, heavy metals and soluble components of particulate matter may enter the plant through the leaf or the root systems.

In the industrialized world, acid rain has killed 31 million hectares of trees, an area about the size of the Canadian province of Saskatchewan. The first international treaty to reduce acid rain, approved by twenty-seven nations, became effective in 1990. This was the first step toward environmental cooperation on a worldwide scale. Ecosystems can begin to recover almost as soon as the acid rain stops falling. However, the full restoration of the original environment will take hundreds of years.

LAND PRODUCTIVITY POTENTIAL

Ancient civilizations calculated yield as the ratio of grain harvested to that sown. Grain was their scarce commodity. Today, land is our scarce commodity. The global food prospect in the 1990s is directly linked to the potential for raising land productivity. Between 1950 and 1980, world grain yield per hectare increased from 1.1 tons to 2.3 tons.

Concurrently, from 1950 to 1980, the use of fertilizer increased from 14 million to 125 million tons, a gain of more than 11 percent per year. From 1984 to 1988, fertilizer usage increased from 125 to 134 million tons, an annual increase of less than 2 percent. If land is to remain fertile, nutrients must be replaced with commercial fertilizers, manure obtained elsewhere, or nonfood cover crops. All of these alternatives require the management of energy resources.

Monoculture farming, such as rice in Asia, has led to oversupply, depressed prices, and depleted land resources. Improperly chosen crops drastically reduce soil nutrients and undermine future prospects for productivity.

Since 1970, Japan has increased its rice yield per acre by 0.9 percent per year. If every farm in every country throughout the world could duplicate the Japanese increase, global grain output would increase by 158 million tons, for an overall increase of 9 percent. Can the world do this? Other nations recognize that Japan has farmers that are skilled, literate, and scientifically oriented. Can other nations duplicate these human factors?

ENERGY AND AGRICULTURE

Farmers invest energy in plowing, seeding, weeding, and all the other aspects of sedentary agriculture. The amount of food produced is vastly increased by mechanization, but at decreasing energy efficiency levels and increasing energy costs. For every kilocalorie of energy invested in a slash-and-burn or other nonsedentary farming system, between 13 and 67 kcal of food are produced. In an unmechanized sedentary system, when most farm work is done by people and domestic animals, a kilocalorie invested yields between 2 and 12 kcal of food. Compared to a modern, mechanized farming system, a kilocalorie invested increases food production by 0.67 to 3.1 kcal of food.

Using renewable energy resources is the most desired alternative for reducing energy costs for agricultural production. Today, thirteen countries that have the greatest potential for economic commercial wind energy development are: Jordan, India, Pakistan, China, Mauritania, Morocco, Chile, Sri Lanka, Jamaica, Syria, Yemen P.D.R., Romania, and Tanzania. Experimental wind farms are underway in several countries, including the developed nation of Denmark.

Human Energy

Many experts note that too little effort has been focused upon the critical need to reduce the massive waste of human resources for agricultural production. The negative energy balance among adult female farmers during planting, cultivating, and harvesting supports the belief that there will soon be insufficient human labor both to continue traditional processing of cereals and to cultivate additional quantities. Clearly, a malnourished population cannot be a productive one. Many examples abound about how human energies can be conserved. For example, substituting a simple dry mechanical dehuller for traditional wet-milling processing saves human energy expended for fetching water, hand pounding, and winnowing.

MANAGING AGRICULTURAL PRODUCTION

Given the agronomic resources needed for crop and livestock production and the demand for food by the world's population, most nations have an established farming community. Ideally, it is organized to halt the depletion of agronomic resources as much as possible. The U.S. farming system will be used as an example of how agricultural production is managed.

In the U.S., farming is one of the most publicized instances of the trend to bimodal distribution. Generally, huge commercial farms are prospering; most of the small, part-time farms are at least surviving; and the mid-sized farms are in transition. Part-time farms (i.e., less than $100,000 per year in gross sales, profits under $20,000, and owners with second jobs) survive because of off-farm income. Ninety-three percent of small farms have at least one person with an outside job; more than 50 percent have two.

In 1986, 2 million small farms produced 35 percent of U.S. crops and earned 15 percent of the farm profit. By 2000, one-fourth of these vest-pocket farms will have disappeared, with 1.5 million remaining. They will then produce 15 percent of the nation's crops but will receive only 5 percent of farm profits because of their relatively high production costs. By 2000, projected income from outside jobs will more than compensate for any loss of farm income. Debts that now threaten them will have been paid off. Further, the most imaginative small farmers will have found new profits in the growing specialty produce market.

Large commercial farms, operations with substantial investments in agribusiness and more than $500,000 in gross farm sales each year, are flourishing throughout the U.S. Such giant farms have advantages over their smaller competitors. They purchase raw materials at prices about 10 percent lower than small farmers and sell produce at prices 5 percent higher. Because of higher profit rates, they can afford to adopt computer systems, biotechnology developments, and similar high technological innovations almost as soon as they become available. In 1986 there were 23,000 U.S. farms in this category, growing 25 percent of the nation's crops and making 50 percent of the farm profits. By the turn of the century, there will be 50,000 large commercial farms. The giant agribusinesses benefit from automation, wholesale mechanization, and the ability to manage their farms with a single, integrated corporate staff. They will grow two-thirds of the crops and, because of their lower cost-per-unit, they will earn three-fourths of the farm profit.

Moderate-size farms do not have the advantages possessed by their competitors. In 1986 there were 250,000 U.S. farms with sales between $100,000 and $250,000 per year. They grew 40 percent of U.S. agricultural products and earned one-third of the farm profits. With effective management, some of these farms are gradually becoming eligible for the $500,000 category. They need more than a single family's hands to bring in the crop, yet are not profitable enough to pay for the high technology tools of the corporate owners. By 2000, there will be only 100,000 moderate-size farms left, accounting for 20 percent of the nation's farm products and profits. Their competitive abilities are hindered by their inability to perform additional off-the-farm work coupled with their lack of clout to win favorable prices from suppliers and buyers. Most of these farms will eventually be absorbed by large commercial agribusinesses.

Industrial Agricultural Products

Although most emphasis is placed on growing plants and animals for food, numerous industrial products are made from agricultural products. For example, coconuts are an important export of Malaysia, being processed into coconut water to drink, coconut oil for cooking, and coconut cakes and sauces from the meat and milk portions. Fermented coconut tree sap, toddy, is a popular beverage. Industrial products are also made from the coconut palm: medicine, soap, fuel, rope, dye, yeast, fertilizer, corks, cups, bowls, musical instruments, decorations, and jewelry. Thatched roofs made from coconut leaves and treated with copper sulphate and cashew nut oil will last 4 years instead of 1 year for untreated coconut leaves. Many countries are promoting this trend toward nonfood uses for agriculture crops. For example, acknowledging the importance of industrial products, India has established a Center for Alternative Technology.

Cash versus Food Crops

Controversies continue to surround the agricultural production of crops for cash versus food crops for the indigenous population. Obviously, the former are needed to meet the debt payments of many nations. In addition, cash can be used to purchase food crops. However, farmers who produce crops for export have more income and are better fed than subsistence farmers who produce only basic food crops for home consumption.

In Africa, Asia, and Latin America, small farmers who shifted into sugarcane, maize, vegetables, and rice for export maintained or slightly improved the nutrition levels of their families while raising their incomes. Farmers produce subsistence crops as insurance against market, employment, and production risks. However, if cash crop production is to be increased, it will be necessary to improve the technology for staple food crop production, particularly sweet potatoes, maize, millet, and sorghum, the principal subsistence crops in these regions.

Sustainable versus Industrial Agriculture

The U.S. can maintain current trends in industrial agriculture through 2025 by achieving technological improvements in on-farm efficiency and avoiding most of the negative effects of land degradation. If this is not achieved, the U.S. will lose its export capabilities. Globally, the loss of U.S. export capacity would be a catastrophe.

Many industrial farming techniques accelerate the decline in the quality of the resource base. Two approaches to this problem have been recently observed. Some farmers, acknowledging the drawbacks of industrial farming, have adopted several techniques such as avoiding chemical fertilizers and pesticides, avoiding or minimizing the use of mechanized equipment, establishing contours and windbreaks to reduce erosion, and planting soil-regenerating cover plants in rotation with food crops.

Other farmers have tried to apply modern techniques as efficiently as possible. They have adopted new fertilizer, irrigation, tillage, and pest control technologies. Their objective is to be almost as effective or productive as conventional or industrial farming techniques enable, but to reduce or eliminate their unpleasant side effects.

Sustainable Agriculture

A key concept for farming operations today is sustainable agriculture. The subsistence farmers buy few agricultural inputs and consume most of their output. They are almost totally self-sufficient. Highly commercialized farmers buy nearly 100 percent of their input and sell nearly 100 percent of their output. The goal of sustainable development is to have economic growth that relies on renewable resources, thereby avoiding permanent damage to the environment. Sustainable development is a concept that means putting the environment above all else. For this concept to work, agricultural policies need to be supportive. A major drawback for the U.S. and Canada is that sustainable agricultural practices require more labor, time, and management skills than conventional approaches. What share of world food output is unsustainable?

MULTIPLE DIMENSIONS
OF THE WORLD FOOD PROBLEM

When analyzing agricultural production and food processing and distribution on a global scale, five dimensions have been considered: seasonal, cyclical, geographical, marketing and purchasing power, and policy and planning. The latter two dimensions will be discussed in Chapter Three. Each interdependent dimension has a significant impact upon agricultural productivity every year, and thus on the data generated in tables such as those in Exhibits 2.1-2.5. Differing from the agronomic resources briefly discussed, they further demonstrate the complexity of the world food and agricultural system.

Seasonal dimensions. Seasonality in both food availability and price affects dietary intakes, food storage, transportation, and marketing as well as employment and income. This regional and local dimension to agriculture will always be prevalent.

Cyclical dimensions. Natural disasters, market swings, wars, and civil disorders have been part of life in the twentieth century. The consequences of the two African droughts of 1972-1974 and 1982-1984 are well known. In the early 1970s, food supply shortages in the international markets seriously eroded the ability of food deficit countries to obtain necessary food imports. During that period, the Ethiopian famine cost 500,000 lives. The famine in Bangladesh claimed close to 1 million lives. Bangladesh was unable to buy food in the international market and emergency food shipments arrived too late.

During 1982-1984, the African countries suffered from drought-related food shortages. Along with other food deficit countries, they found themselves in a disadvantaged situation. Although supplies were then abundant in the international market, they had insufficient cash to import foods. This was largely caused by sharp declines in prices for their commodities and high energy costs for the production of those commodities.

Problems created by war and civil disorders are also very familiar. Populations become dislocated from their agricultural production base. Emergency food supplies often have to be delivered under very hostile political and/or religious conditions. Throughout extended periods of social disorder, productive capacities usually remain very low. Resumption of adequate food production requires both financial and physical assistance, as well as strategic forward planning. Examples of recent populations that have been affected by war and civil disorders include: 10 million Bangladesh refugees who fled to India in 1971 during the Pakistan civil war, the Afghan refugees who fled to Pakistan during the Afghanistan War, the Cambodian population both during and after the Vietnam War, and the Ethiopian population in the continuing civil war-torn areas.

Geographical dimensions. Regions of the world differ in their intrinsic capacity to produce food. Sharp contrasts in all of the agronomic resources prevail throughout the globe. For example, there was a strong recent contrast when the EC suffered from unprecedented food surpluses while thousands died from starvation in sub-

Saharan Africa and over 100 million remained exposed to the threat of starvation.

The Process of Management

Planning for industrial or large-scale agriculture requires competent and local interest groups that can effectively communicate with administrators or government officials. Generally, countries suffer when there is no well-organized, domestic interest group for basic needs or nutrition. Thus, progress towards a healthy diet is slow. This same argument can be applied to a nation's desire to have a viable sustainable agricultural system.

Although effective management is required if we are to meet the world food demands, an argument has been made against this process. Specifically, while the effective management of agricultural production tends to increase the amount of food obtained, it also usually increases the amount of effort required to obtain each unit of food. Further, management can disrupt the normal cycles of nutrients among plants, animals, earth, and air. For example, land clearing can leave the soil vulnerable to erosion which carries nutrients away. Crop harvesting also removes nutrients from the soil. Tillage eventually reduces the soil's organic matter content. Manure and crop residues can be returned, but they often do not contain all the nutrients removed with the *biota*. This argument fails to consider that, when research findings about agronomic resources precede management practices, optimal solutions to the above conditions can be obtained. In all cases, substantial investments in sustained human efforts are mandatory for establishing effective agricultural production.

In addition to technology, appropriate institutions, and infrastructure, technical and entrepreneurial skills must be in place. Production can be controlled by placing constraints on the generation of new technology and the utilization of old technology. Agricultural and food production cannot be automatically expanded by improving technology.

Although not ranked by order of importance, the food production systems of the developing world have been disturbed by five complex interrelated factors:

• *Cash crops:* The introduction of cash crop production on good lands, leaving lands of marginal quality for the production of food crops.
• *Purchasing power:* When increasing proportions of the population must obtain their basic foods through the market, their purchasing power abilities become key elements for their food availability.
• *Land tenure:* Changes in land tenure systems affect all facets of agricultural production.
• *Environmental losses:* Environmental degradation leads to the loss of land productivity.
• *Population:* Populations continue to grow beyond the carrying capacity of the land.

To nullify the effect of these on food production in developing countries, policies related to these interrelated factors will require major improvements in technology, institutions, and education. Substantial increases in funding for agricultural research will be required. Increases in cultivated acreage must occur without causing intolerable erosion, pollution, and food chain contamination.

SUMMARY

The annual world food production of 4 billion tons is still more than enough to feed the globe's 5.2 billion people, yet one-fifth of humanity goes hungry every day because of regional disparities in production and distribution. Explosive population growth means there will be one-half the productive food land per person that there was 35 years ago.

An optimistic viewpoint is still being projected, given these conditions. The sense of this view is that people expand the areas of arable lands by opening up new lands, planting more intensively, and inventing and adopting new food-producing techniques in response to perceived needs and opportunities. Infrastructures such as roads and communication links result from sufficiently high income and dense population settlements. From these and other mechanisms, long-run increases in productivity are possible. These increases overcome short-term scarcities and produce historical trends toward cheaper food with less famine and higher consumption per person in the world. In the developed countries, this increased food for more people is produced by a smaller number of farmers; the same reduction in the total number of farmers may be expected in the developing countries as they achieve more wealth.

REFERENCES

Abbott, J. C. 1986. *Marketing improvement in the developing world: what happens and what we have learned*. FAO Economic and Social Development Series No. 37. Rome: Food and Agriculture Organization of the United Nations.

Agri-Energy Roundtable, Inc. 1985-86. *Agri-enterprise in development: New leadership and technology for food security*. Sixth and Seventh Annual International Forum. Geneva.

Alsudery, Abdelmuhsin. 1985. The world food problems: assessment and solutions. In *Crop productivity – research imperatives revisited*, eds. M. Gibbs and C. Carlson, 71-80. An international conference held at Boyne Highlands Inn, October 13-18, 1985 and Airlie House, December 11-13, 1985.

Brown, Lester R. 1989. Feeding six billion. *World-Watch* 2(5):32-40.

Brown, Lester R. 1989. Reexamining the World Food Prospect. In *State of the world 1989*, ed. L. R. Brown, 41-58. New York: W. W. Norton & Company, Inc.

Brown, Lester R. 1990. The illusion of progress. In *State of the world 1990*, ed. L. Starke, 3-16. New York: W. W. Norton & Company, Inc.

Brown, L. R. and J. E. Young. 1990. Feeding the world in the nineties. In *State of the world 1990*, ed. L. Starke, 59-78. New York: W. W. Norton & Company, Inc.

Cetron, Marvin and Owen Davies. 1989. *American renaissance – our life at the turn of the 21st century*. New York: St. Martin's Press.

Davidson, J. M., A. D. Hanson, and D. R. Nielsen. 1985. Environmental constraints. In *Crop productivity – research imperatives revisited*, eds. M. Gibbs and C. Carlson, 196-215. An international conference held at Boyne Highlands Inn, October 13-18, 1985 and Airlie House, December 11-13, 1985.

deSousa, I. S. F., E. G. Singer, and W. L. Flinn. 1985. Sociopolitical forces and technology: critical reflections on the green revolution. In *Food, politics, and society in Latin America*, eds. J. C. Super and T. C. Wright, 228-245. Lincoln and London: University of Nebraska Press.

French, Hilary F. 1990. Clearing the air. In *State of the world 1990*, ed. L. Starke, 98-118. New York and London: W. W. Norton & Company, Inc.

Gever, J., R. Kaufman, D. Skole, and C. Vorosmarty. 1986. *Beyond oil*. Cambridge: Ballinger Publishing Company.

Gibbs, M. and C. Carlson, eds. 1985. *Crop productivity – research imperatives revisited*. An international conference held at Boyne Highlands Inn, October 13-18, 1985 and Airlie House, December 11-13, 1985.

Hansen, Art and D. E. McMillan, eds. 1986. *Food in sub-Saharan Africa*. Boulder: Lynne Rienner.

Haswell, Margaret. 1985. *Energy for subsistence*, 2d. ed. London: The Macmillan Press Ltd.

Johnson, Glenn L. 1985. Agricultural surpluses—research on agricultural technologies, institutions, people, and capital growth. In *Crop productivity—research imperatives revisited*, eds. M. Gibbs and C. Carlson, 57-70. An international conference held at Boyne Highlands Inn, October 13-18, 1985 and Airlie House, December 11-13, 1985.

Lawrence, Peter, ed. 1986. *World recession and the food crisis in Africa*. Boulder: Westview Press.

Lee, John E. 1988. Trends in world agriculture and trade in high-value food products. *Food Technology* 42(9):119-27.

Lyng, Richard E. 1988. Food and agriculture in a global economy. *Food Technology* 42(9):115-16.

Mason, J. B., J-P. Habicht, H. Tabatabai, and V. Valverde. 1984. *Nutritional surveillance*, 22. Geneva: World Health Organization. Explanation for subsidies for agricultural products.

Mickelsen, Olaf. 1983. Nutritional considerations in planning for food production. In *Sustainable food systems*, ed. D. Knorr, 394-410. Westport, Conn.: AVI Publishing Company, Inc.

Postel, Sandra. 1990. Saving water for agriculture. In *State of the world 1990*, ed. L. Starke, 39-58. New York: W. W. Norton & Company, Inc.

Simon, Julian L. 1983. The effects of population on nutrition and economic wellbeing. In *Hunger and history*, ed. R. I. Rotberg and T. K. Rabb, 215-239. Cambridge: Cambridge University Press.

Wittwer, Sylvan H. 1983. The new agriculture: a view of the twenty-first century. In *Agriculture in the twenty-first century,* ed. J. W. Rosenblum, 337-67. New York: John Wiley & Sons.

Wittwer, Sylvan H. 1985. Crop productivity—research imperatives: a decade of change. In *Crop productivity—research imperatives revisited*, eds. M. Gibbs and C. Carlson, 1-6. An international conference held at Boyne Highlands Inn, October 13-18, 1985 and Airlie House, December 11-13, 1985.

Yermanos, D. M., M. Neushul, and R. D. MacElroy. 1983. Crops from the desert, sea, and space. In *Agriculture in the twenty-first century*, ed. J. W. Rosenblum, 144-65. New York: John Wiley & Sons.

Chapter Three

Global Food Marketing

INTRODUCTION

To distribute food and agricultural products from countries, regions, or areas where they can be grown and processed to populations requiring them, an international food marketing system has been established. Most people, whether they live near a transnational highway system, a river with barge traffic, or a bustling port city, observe the movement of foods in their daily lives. At least, people observe food containers or carriers before they are purchased, or otherwise obtained, from some form of a food marketing outlet. This movement of foods may go unnoticed by you until an unusual event happens such as a highway accident where foods are strewn across the highway, a severe drought, or ice jam which halts river barge traffic. By studying the information in this chapter, you will become familiar with:

- the vast scope of the food marketing system, involving traditional or small scale, modern or large scale, and institutional food marketing systems;
- the importance of effective food policies to ensure a fair and equal distribution of foods, with inherent profits;
- implications of the latest round of discussions on the General Agreements on Tariffs and Trade (GATT) for world food marketing and distribution.

Information about the European Community (EC) will be emphasized in this chapter, demonstrating for you how changes in this market will have dramatic effects around the world for the foreseeable future.

World food marketing commenced with the worldwide dissemination of domesticated plants and animals around the globe. Without the findings of early traders, vegetation throughout the globe would be very different today. European acquisitions were influenced by Columbus's voyages to North America. European settlers, missionaries, and adventurers spread knowledge, seeds, animals, and other materials from both the Old and New World to other parts of the world. Although by 1970, maize, rice, wheat, barley, oats, potatoes, cattle, and other livestock had spread throughout most of the world, international food trade was still required.

For centuries, gold was the measure of currency. All other currencies were measured against it. A fixed standard for currency exchange rates made international trade easy: if you contracted to sell, any changes in the value of local currencies could alter your profits. Successful exporting countries collected large sums of foreign currency and importing countries depleted stocks of their own money. In 1973, the fixed rate of exchange was dropped and currency values now float in response to the markets.

The global distribution of plant seeds and livestock has dramatically affected global food production. For example, the adoption of maize and sweet potatoes in China at the end of the eighteenth century greatly increased their food supply. In Africa, slave traders introduced maize and other crops to West Africa to have provisions for their ships. Before the Europeans arrived, the natives of North and South America ate only wild turkeys, dogs, llamas, chickens, and guinea pigs as sources of meat.

Until sugarcane production was begun in the New World, where favorable growing conditions, large acreages, and the availability of slave labor enabled rapid increases in production, sugar was a luxury item. Using sugarcane by-products for the manufacturing of rum contributed to sugar profits.

These and numerous other examples have contributed greatly to local food supplies, and have increased the complexity of world food marketing requirements.

Although food imports by developing countries constituted a financial burden during the 1970s and early 1980s, they improved the nutritional standards for many countries. The share of imports of food, calculated in total calorie supplies, increased in all regions, for example: from 6 to 13 percent in Africa; 8 to 15 percent in Latin America; 12 to 23 percent in the Near East; and 5 to 7 percent in the Far East. However, developing countries had to curtail their imports in the 1980s. In 1985, low-income developing countries required about $2 billion (U.S.) in food aid and loans to finance their required food imports. The world economic crisis reduced demand for their exports and their capacity to pay for imports.

WORLD FOOD MARKETING SYSTEMS

A diagram of world food marketing systems is given in Exhibit 3.1. Throughout the world, the one feature that all nations have in common is that their food supplies come from two sources: food production and food imports. In the diagram in Exhibit 3.1, food imports include products which are received through food aid programs. After that point, even though the markets are classified as traditional, modern, and institutional, all countries have different systems. For example, EC countries are building hypermarkets; the U.S. and Canada continue to build smaller supermarkets. Self-service stores in Mexico can be interpreted as making food selections, and bartering for them, from open-market tables. For all food marketing outlets, the functions and services shown in Exhibit 3.1 are required.

Technologies for food marketing must be compatible with local conditions, labor costs, marketing organization, and the sociocultural environment. Two problems of food marketing systems predominate in developing countries. First, there is a bias toward providing sophisticated physical facilities, instead of facilities which can be easily maintained and still enable the efficient distribution of foodstuffs. Second, there are pervasive negative attitudes of governments toward private enterprises for food marketing systems. The latter situation is slowly changing throughout the world.

Marketing and International Organizations

As the foods, such as those listed in Exhibits 2.1-2.5, are distributed around the globe, a need has been identified for research funding to ensure that food supplies reach consumers with acceptable

Exhibit 3.1. World Food Marketing Systems.

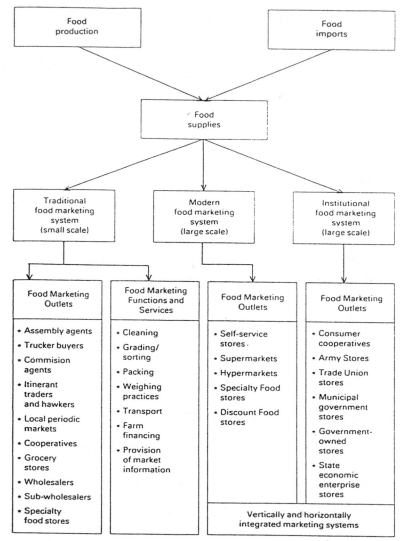

Source: Kaynak, E. 1986. World food marketing systems: integrative
          statement. In World Food Marketing Systems. ed. E. Kaynak,
          London: Butterworth & Co. "by permission of the publishers,
          Butterworth-Heinemann Ltd., ©".

levels of food quality and minimal levels of food waste. The recognition for this need on an international scale has come slowly. The FAO traditionally allocated less than 1 percent for marketing activities from its regular program budget. In 1984/85 their budget for marketing support was 1.9 percent of its technical and economic programs. Fortunately, recent trends toward efforts for alleviating postharvest food losses have increased this amount.

International agencies are gradually increasing funding for the food marketing aspects of agricultural production and rural development projects. A few examples follow. The International Bank for Reconstruction and Development Program (IBRDP) budgets about 2 percent for marketing activities. The International Rice Research Institute (IRRI) has gradually become more involved with postharvest problems of processing and marketing. Within the International Fund for Agricultural Development (IFAD), one-third of their projects have been explicitly involved in improving storage facilities and/or other marketing aspects.

Since 1975, the International Food Policy Research Institute (IFPRI) has emphasized production and consumption projections. Focusing on Chinese and Soviet food grain imports, their projects have determined the impact of food subsidies, food distribution systems, international stockholding and food security, agricultural research investments, and international food grain markets on production and consumption patterns.

In addition to these official organizations, some international firms have consultants that specialize in food marketing in developing countries. They frequently provide expertise in internationally traded commodities that is greater than their expertise in local food marketing. Marketing specialists are frequently used as adjuncts to engineering, storage, and transportation projects. Unfortunately, improving the food marketing system, or integrating it with transportation systems, is frequently not an integral part of development projects. Obviously, a partial analysis of the food marketing systems can be harmful.

In a report by the FAO entitled "Agriculture Toward 2000," authorities projected that from 1980 to 2000, food production that required a system of marketing would increase from 35 to 54 percent of agricultural production. This implies a need for massive

intrastructural investments in marketing as well as the need to improve marketing systems substantially. However, the FAO envisaged an investment increase for storage and marketing from $3 to
$4 billion during this period. Investments in agriculture are pro-
jected to increase from $16 to $24 billion during these two decades.

Agricultural Trade Values

All agricultural products contain a value-added component.
When raw wheat is exported, one-fifth to one-sixth of its value is
derived from trade and transportation services between the farm and
export market. Low-value products include bulk commodities, such
as grains and oilseeds, and raw materials, such as cotton and tobacco. Raw bulk products contain the lowest value-added proportion of all U.S. agricultural exports.

High-value products include unprocessed foods (e.g., eggs, fresh
fruits and nuts, and fresh vegetables); semiprocessed products
(e.g., flour, oilseed products, and meats); and highly processed
products (e.g., prepared and preserved meats, dairy products, bakery products, and prepared foods, including soups).

Both agricultural production and food processing techniques are
responsible for these classifications. For example, meat represents
corn with value added through transformation into livestock and
then into meat and by-products. Fresh fruit and vegetables have
higher levels of value because they are highly perishable and require special distribution to reduce spoilage. By creating jobs at
home for transforming products, high-value exports are desirable.

Data in Exhibit 3.2 are categorized according to processed and
unprocessed foods, the former mainly comprising those which contain a substantial value-added component, i.e., foods, beverages,
feeds, and tobacco products. In 1985, on a worldwide basis, processed foods accounted for about 40 percent of agricultural trade.
About 25 to 30 percent of U.S. agriculturally related exports are
processed. Note that the U.S. share of that trade amounted to 11
percent. The U.S. tends to export more raw agricultural products
than other high-income exporting nations. In U.S. dollars, processed foods amounted to 74 billion dollars, with 8.4 billion being

Exhibit 3.2. U.S. and World Exports of Raw Agricultural and
Processed Food Products, Selected Years, 1961-1965
to 1985

Export Category	1961-1965	1963-1965	1969-1971	1979-1981	1985
			Billion dollars		
Total merchandise:					
World	157	165	315	1,863	1,587
U.S.	24	25	41	215	214
Total food & agriculture, excluding fish:					
World	39	41	50	239	183E
U.S.	6.0	6.0	7.0	42	30
Total processed food, beverage, tobacco:					
World	--	--	21	95	74
U.S.	--	--	2.1	8.6	8.4
			Per cent		
U.S. shares of world trade:					
Total	15	15	13	12	11
Food & Agriculture	16	15	14	18	16
Processed Food	--	17	10	9	11
Unprocessed Food	--	14E	17	23	20
Ag./total World Trade	25	23	19	21	12
Processed Food/ Agriculture World Trade	--	--	42	40	40

Source: Reprinted by permission of the publisher, from Food
Processing: An Industrial Powerhouse In Transition by
John M. Connor. (Lexington, Mass: Lexington Books, D.C.
Heath and Company, copyright 1988, Lexington Books.)

Note: "World" excludes USSR and most Eastern Europe countries.

-- = Not available.

E = Estimated.

exported by the U.S. Effective food policies are required to promote such international food export trade.

Food Distribution

Efficient food distribution is paramount to the success of global food trade whether it is by truck, train, barge, airplane, or some other mode of transportation, given in Exhibit 1.1. In many countries, inefficiencies have led to delays and subsequent food losses. For example, a drawback of the Polish food distribution system is that the food product flow from producer to end-user is excessively long. This increases the social costs of the functioning of the system. With a conversion to a market economy, inefficiencies in this system will likely be reduced.

Other concerns about the Polish system in the past have centered around the uncoordinated activities of the marketing institutions responsible for product supply; adding to the problem was a severe lack of adjustment of agricultural marketing to spatially differentiated conditions of agriculture. For any food distribution system responding to the types of food marketing systems depicted in Exhibit 3.1, the point of view of the end-user is of utmost importance when policy decisions are being formulated.

Energy Consumption and Food Distribution

Energy is needed at every step of the journey of food from field to table. Today, 4 percent of the U.S. energy budget is used to grow food, while 10 to 13 percent is needed for service in homes and restaurants.

Consumer demand for some quality foods has increased energy expenditures by transporting fresh artichokes for example, from California to New Hampshire, or by transporting live lobsters from Maine to Nebraska, and so on. These foods increase the quality of life in the U.S. at the expense of increasing dependence upon foreign countries for energy supplies. As fuel supplies fail to keep pace with population growth, consumer conveniences will become increasingly costly to maintain.

Several ideas have been discussed regarding changes that would reduce energy consumption in the off-farm sectors. Two ideas include: (1) a partial return to regional diets, consisting of food grown locally, to substantially reduce transportation energy, and (2) diets composed of in-season food, reducing fuel needed to refrigerate, freeze, and process food. Home gardens offer additional opportunities to reduce off-farm energy needs.

Such diets would restrict consumers' choice of foods and increase the amount of time spent in food purchasing and preparation. A return to regional, seasonal, home-grown meals would involve trading consumer convenience for lower food prices, but would provide more fuel for other purposes such as jet travel. However, some of these changes have inherent energy costs. For example, if New England grew more of its own food, it might require extensive clearance of forests that now provide firewood. Further, they may require power for a hot-house agriculture system. The Government of Newfoundland and Labrador recently acknowledged that their multi-million dollar investment in growing cucumbers in large greenhouses on the Avalon peninsula, near the capital of St. John's, was a failure after several unsuccessful, and expensive, years of production.

CLIMATIC OPPORTUNITIES FOR FOOD EXPORTS

Opportunities arise from climatic advantage to supply fruit and vegetables to consumers in areas where, and when, they are not available from local sources. This can be a major stimulus for development. Such opportunities enable foreign exchange earnings and substantially augment farm incomes. Countries with this climatic advantage are located in several regions: Mediterranean, Central Africa, Caribbean, and the Indo-Pakistan subcontinent. They market to Europe, North America, West Asia, and the Orient.

When produce is grown in one climatic zone and transported to consumers in another, movements to physical storage facilities may include: a local assembly point, a port, ship transport to another port, rail/truck distribution to a central wholesale market, and retail distribution. Ideal conditions include pre-cooling equipment at the assembly and packing points, and refrigerated ship and transport storage to the terminal markets. This transport requires considerable investment in physical facilities; quality damage and serious losses can occur at any point when coordination of efforts is not perfected.

In the future, considerable exports from developing to more developed countries is anticipated. Governments will respond to good markets and government pressure to earn foreign exchange.

Israel Promotes Food Exports

Establishing world trade of the magnitude presented in Exhibit 3.2 does not automatically occur. In many countries, food marketing research is conducted and efforts are made to establish a demand for a country's food exports.

Israel has one of the world's outstanding examples of fruit and vegetable marketing. Fruit and vegetable production, processing, and marketing are carefully integrated. Produce for export is actively promoted. Produce is promoted into alternative markets so as to avoid depressing prices and avoid attracting competitors. The key factor in these operations is their central control of quality and deliveries through the Citrus Board and Agrexco.

Methods used in the 1960s to promote the sale of Israeli avocados are noteworthy. At that time, consumer demand for avocados in the United Kingdom (U.K.) was limited to a few London specialty shops. To change this trend, the Israeli export company employed people to go to fruit and vegetable shops in prosperous U.K. towns and ask for avocados. As a result, new weekly orders came from all over the country for avocados. Retailers were soon impressed and ordered supplies of avocados. The U.K. market for avocados quickly expanded.

FOOD TRADE AND THE EUROPEAN COMMUNITY (EC)

European food shortages during and after World War II led to increasing governmental intervention in the agriculture sector. This was dictated by the need to have adequate food supplies and to counter balance-of-payments problems. As agricultural production caught up with demand around 1953, there was a change in emphasis. Instead of concentrating upon increased production, efforts were directed towards achieving selective expansion and raising agricultural efficiencies. In 1968, the structures of European agriculture were reshaped with a view to becoming competitive without detriment to the family character of farming operations.

The EC, one of the world's largest trading blocks, is now a substantial exporter and importer of agricultural products. It is an important market for developing countries of both agricultural and industrial products. Its member states have historical, political, and economic ties with countries on every continent, and its trade activities have profound effects on many countries. A move toward increased protectionism would have damaging effects on these countries.

The EC is the largest trading partner in the world, representing about 20 percent of world trade compared with 14 percent for the U.S. Its share in world exports represents about 15 percent of its GNP. Comparable figures for the U.S. and Japan are between 7 and 12 percent, respectively.

The EC has a vital interest in being open to imports and being able to export to the rest of the world. EC exports to the Third World amount to U.S. $121.2 billion. Third World exports to the EC are $113.7 billion. There is no risk that the EC will be closed to the rest of the world when it completes the single market transitions in 1992.

The Common Agricultural Policy (CAP) is based on regulatory mechanisms aimed at supporting farm incomes by means of relatively high guaranteed prices, or direct subsidies for products in unlimited quantities that are not necessarily adapted to market requirements. Refer to the summary of objectives in Exhibit 3.3 and the three main principles in Exhibit 3.4 for an expanded discussion of CAP. Outside the EC, the CAP is perceived by some nations as being highly protectionistic, inefficient, and disruptive of world agricultural markets.

Community preference means that domestic European producers are given priority over all other suppliers. The EC will run a number of 1992 seminars to help inform its partner countries, still in various stages of development, about the technical aspects of the single market. This involves, for example, very technical information about harmonization of standards, industrial norms, and the like. In airport bookstores all over Europe, travèllers can purchase guides to dealing with the EC after 1992.

The EC's new master plan will help developing countries boost their trade with Europe by virtue of an increased growth rate of the new community. EC imports are expected to increase about 7 percent which could mean new trading opportunities for the Third World.

The decision to unify the European market by 1992 has restored a sense of purpose to Western Europe. Human energies, coined "1992 fever" are sweeping the continent, capturing everyone's imagination. The cartoon in Exhibit 3.5 depicts the twelve countries which now comprise the EC. A free trade zone, including food products, will be created by 1992. Each of the countries have different food preferences, as well as growing conditions and food processing capabilities which will influence EC food trade among the twelve countries and the rest of the world.

After 1992, others may apply to join the new confederation: Switzerland, Norway, Denmark, Sweden, Finland, and Yugoslavia. By 2000, Europe will be an enormous market with over 400 million consumers compared to the U.S. and Japanese markets of some 250 and 125 million people, respectively. Responding to this development, as they did in Asia in the 1960s, Japanese companies have been cultivating markets in Latin America and Africa with the objective of having a foot in the door when those economies begin to grow rapidly.

Exhibit 3.3. Objectives of the Common Agricultural Policy (CAP)

---

1. Increase agricultural productivity by promoting technical progress and ensuring the rational development of agricultural production and the optimum use of production factors, including labor.

2. Ensure a fair standard of living for the agricultural community, by increasing the earnings of persons engaged in agriculture.

3. Stabilize markets.

4. Assure the availability of supplies.

5. Ensure that supplies reach consumers at reasonable prices.

Source: McMahan, Joseph A. 1988. European trade policy in agricultural products. Netherlands: Martinus Nijoff Publishers.

Exhibit 3.4. Three main principles of Common Agricultural Policy
(CAP)

---

1. *Unified market.* Free movement of commodities among member States
   without customs duties, taxes, or subsidies prejudicial to competition.
   Common prices, coordination of health and veterinary regulations. Stable
   currency equivalences.

2. *Community preference.* Protects the single market from cheap imports and
   from fluctuations in the world market. When world market prices are
   lower than those in the EC, a variable tax or "levy" raises the prices
   of products purchased from Third World countries to the level of the
   common prices. When the EC prices are below world prices, the system
   operates in reverse to protect European consumers by discouraging
   exports.

3. *Financial solidarity.* The *guarantee* section finances public expenditures
   arising from establishing common agricultural market organizations, including
   regulations, and refunds applicable to exports to third countries which
   facilitate the sale of European agricultural products on the world market.
   The *guidance* section participates in the financing of the common policy of
   improving the structures of agriculture in the member countries.

Source: McMahan, Joseph A. 1988. <u>European trade policy in agricultural
products</u>. Netherlands: Martinus Nijoff Publishers.

Food marketing in Europe after 1992 is still being debated. On
one side, there is evidence of broadening consumer taste preferences. For example, a decade ago few people would have projected
that pasta would be included in "power lunches" across Europe.
Preference for Mexican food in Europe has also been surprising. In
1984, the Mexican food leader in the U.S., IC Industries Inc., introduced their Old El Paso unit in their familiar red and yellow label
to Europe. By 1990, the company estimated the total Mexican food
market would be worth £16 million in the U.K., although Norway
had the biggest per capita consumption.

New foods, such as Mexican, can be introduced throughout Europe without any adaptations. However, taste remains chauvinistic
in many areas. For example, junk food is not universally craved. In
a recent study of European youth, only 17 percent of French respondents said they "really like" junk food, well below the survey average of 49 percent. On the other hand, 61 percent of youths in
Greece "really like" junk food.

Convenience food is more popular in northern Europe than in the

Exhibit 3.5. Cartoon of the Euro Man.

EURO MAN

*As 1992
approaches,
the Old World
takes on
a new look*

● **A German head**
for business and for managing
the EC's inflation policy

● **Danish eyes**
for design, which often set the
EC's high-tech standards

● **A Belgian ear**
for languages, which despite wars
between the country's own French and
Dutch speakers, enables it to be host
to the EC's major institutions

●**A Portuguese nose**
sniffing enviously at richer
partners as it hopes to smell
more of the benefits of 1992 ● **An Irish mouth**

● **An English** using blarney to extract
stiff upper lip money for farmers
to fight off the "socialist"
tendencies on the Continent

● **A Dutch finger**
in the dike against the dreaded
flood of Japanese imports

● **Italian hands**
capable of talking rings around EC rules
without speaking a word.

● **The deep pockets
of Luxembourg,**
the EC's tax haven, which hopes
to keep its privileged status
despite cries for reform

● **A French chest**
deflated by adapting many
French business customs to
more rational German ones

● **A Greek heel,**
the Achilles' heel of the EC, in that Greece
is the least willing to pay the price for
benefits of the Community

● **Spanish feet**
doing a nimble flamenco to
adapt to modern EC standards
while remaining Spanish

Source: *The Wall Street Journal*, September 22, 1989

south. A recent survey found that 43 percent of British respondents own a microwave compared with just 3 percent of the Italians.

Examples of European Food Preferences

Because people's food preferences vary throughout the world, extensive efforts are made to ensure that they always receive the products most desired by them. This is certainly the case in the EC where the twelve nations depicted in Exhibit 3.5 have considerably different preferences for many items. Standardized, legal specifications will be used to order food products throughout the EC, thereby ensuring that uniform products travel in the food trade routes. Agreement among twelve countries with varying food preferences is proving to be a formidable task. Several examples follow.

Food Specifications

Consumers in Holland spread very smooth jam on bread for breakfast. French consumers eat jam right from the jar with a spoon, preferring it lumpy and fruity. As a result, the Dutch want more sugar in their jam specifications; the French want more fruit. These arguments, just one of many now ongoing, are depicted in the cartoon in Exhibit 3.6.

Throughout Europe, low-quality jam has traditionally been called marmalade. Because British consumers take pride in their excellent quality marmalades, use of this term for jams of low quality throughout the EC has been opposed by Britons. After 25 years of negotiations, a specification for the production and marketing of jam throughout the EC was developed. Following this achievement, efforts were directed towards working on a standard for low-calorie jam.

In other examples, Danish consumers prefer creamy mayonnaise over the oily version produced by the Italians. French beer is weaker than German beer. In Holland, national health standards prevent the sale of France's *baguette* bread loaf because it has been judged to be lacking in nutrients.

Exhibit 3.6. Cartoon of the Jam Specification Controversy.

Source: *The Wall Street Journal*, September 22, 1989

Rum Trade and the EC

As the EC regulations are established, many special cases involving food trade will need consideration from the EC Parliament. For example, the accession of the U.K. to the EC necessitated special arrangements for traditional imports of rum from the African, Caribbean, and Pacific (ACP) States. It was desired to have rum imported duty-free into the EC under such conditions as to permit the development of traditional trade flows between the ACP States and the EC and between the member states. The quantities allowed to be imported are fixed each year on the basis of the largest annual quantities imported into the EC from the ACP States in the last 3 years. Allowance is made for an annual growth rate of 37 percent for the U.K. market and 27 percent for all other member state markets. The annual quota is set at 170,000 hectoliters of pure alcohol, but may be increased if this hampers the development of traditional trade flows. Provision has been made for trade promotion measures to encourage the expansion of sales in nontraditional markets. Although this may appear to be an unimportant commodity with respect to nutritional health, the point can be emphasized that the EC is establishing regulations for every commodity that is traded among its members and the rest of the world.

U.S. FOOD PRODUCTS FOR EXPORT

Nearly 40 percent of harvested acres in the U.S. are devoted to export production. The U.S. provides more than three-quarters of the corn and soybeans, over 40 percent of the wheat, and 25 percent of the rice traded in world markets.

During 1988, Japan imported 49 million bushels of food-quality soybeans, the largest single customer for U.S. soybeans. The imported soybeans included 19.8 and 7.1 million bushels for tofu and natto, respectively. About 1.1 million bushels were used for products such as soy sauce and soy protein additives. The demand for soybeans used for direct consumption is increasing about 2, 3, and 5 percent per annum for tofu, miso, and natto, respectively. The U.S. supplies nearly 80 percent of the soybeans for tofu, 25 percent for natto, and 65 percent of total food soybean demand.

The volume and value of international trade are growing faster than the U.S. domestic market. From 1960 to 1980, the value of merchandise trade grew at an average annual rate of 16 percent (Exhibit 3.2). Excluding seafood, the growth rate in the value of food and agricultural exports was about 12 percent per year during that period. Adjusting for inflation, the rate of growth of agriculturally related exports was about 6 percent per year, about double the rate of growth of the U.S. market.

The major factor influencing the value of world trade is effective demand, that is, the GNPs of importing nations. The severe 1980-1983 worldwide recession reduced the volume of all exports.

The U.S. share of world trade in agricultural products has been about 14 to 18 percent for the last three decades. The U.S. share of world trade in processed foods has fallen. The U.S. has a rising share of trade in unprocessed agricultural products. The U.S. share of world trade in processed foods is below that of the EC, appearing to have stabilized at about 10 percent.

The U.S. economy is developing greater links with the world economy. Imports and exports of goods and services now represent a much higher share of U.S. economic activity than 10 to 20 years ago. Since the early 1960s, the U.S. has been a net exporter of foods and agricultural products, with 1981 being a peak year.

Newly industrialized countries of South Korea, Taiwan, Hong Kong, and Singapore must act quickly so as not to be frozen out of the huge European and North American markets. By 2000, East Asia's aggregate GNP will be comparable with the EC or North America, with about 22 percent of the world's total. Growth throughout this region has been tremendous. In 1960, it was only one-half the size of Europe's GNP and only one-third that of North America's.

Food Processing and Food Trade

Only 4 percent of U.S. food processing shipments in the 1980s involved exports. International exports are only one way that food processors sell in foreign markets. The other two principal methods are licensing and foreign direct investment. With licensing, a U.S. food processor exchanges the right to produce and sell a trade-marked product or patented process in a foreign market for a royalty or other form of payment. With foreign direct investment, a food processor markets a product by establishing or buying about 90 percent of a subsidiary manufacturing facility that ships its products to the local foreign market. Most countries retain a 10 percent level of ownership. In 1985, U.S. food processors owned $9.3 billion of equity in, and loans to, foreign subsidiaries. Processing forms the largest component of foreign direct investment abroad in the food marketing industries.

The U.S. exports 4 percent of its domestic production; other countries export far greater proportions. The Netherlands exports 55 percent of its processed food production and imports 40 percent of all the processed foods consumed in the country. Similarly, Belgium's export share and import penetration both exceed 60 percent. Germany exports 21 percent and imports 27 percent of its processed food. These three developed countries have small domestic markets and must export foods to enable them to operate large, efficient food processing plants. Managers of these companies deal with multiple languages, cultures, and regulatory environments.

A large market for value-added food products will develop when economic growth begins in the developing countries. The ability of food scientists to innovate and adapt their products using technologies to improve efficiency and quality will become a decisive factor for market expansion. This economic growth will only be realized once developing countries have solved their debt problems and possess sufficient investment capital.

It is widely accepted that developing countries should use the food technologies most appropriate to their circumstances. In countless instances, developing countries have adopted or retained technologies clearly unsuitable to their circumstances. Why does this situation continue to occur? Foreign consultants or advisers may advocate the technology with which they are most familiar. Local engineers, if educated abroad or as the heirs of a colonial legacy, may have acquired a similar bias in favor of advanced technology, or they may simply presume that what is most modern is best. Special interest groups may favor a particular technical approach. Deep-seated customs and traditions may favor certain solutions and make others unacceptable. Lack of knowledge or reluctance to experiment may limit the available choices.

THE U.S.S.R:
GRAIN PURCHASES AND AN EMBARGO

Trade between the U.S.S.R. and U.S. offers two examples of imbalances that can occur when drastic changes in policies are made. First, the large Soviet Union grain purchase in 1972 was one of the factors precipitating the 1973-1974 world food crisis. This crisis was preceded by a slight shortfall in U.S. production below the established trend, the first time in 25 years that such decreases had occurred.

Second, the day before the U.S. presidential announcement of an embargo of Soviet grain in response to the Soviet invasion of Afghanistan in 1979, the Soviets had placed a last-minute order for an additional 3 million tons of American grain. The U.S.S.R. had already allocated 1 million tons of grain to Vietnam and North Korea, and another million to Afghanistan. The poor Soviet 1979 harvest meant that they would need to import 34 million tons of grain — 25 million tons were on order from the U.S.

In response to the U.S. embargo, Soviet purchasers swarmed out to scour world markets for alternative sources. Their biggest finds were made in Latin America. They closed long-term contracts with 15 countries. They imported coffee and sugar from Colombia, fruit conserves and spices from Mexico, rice from Costa Rica, and bananas from Ecuador. They purchased grain from Canada and Argentina, purchasing 83 percent of Argentina's total grain exports. In addition to these developments, Europeans purchased large quantities of American soybeans for further processing and resale to the Soviets. By October of that year, *Pravda* boasted that President Carter's grain embargo had failed.

The Soviet Union spent more than 2 billion dollars on contracts with new agricultural partners. Their attempts to substitute barter arrangements for cash payments failed. Because most of the grain sellers demanded hard currency, Moscow traders sold millions of dollars worth of oil, diamonds, and precious metals. The next year, when commodity prices drastically declined, they were forced to finance their continuing grain imports with short-term loans, at interest rates of 17 percent.

These actions were taken because bread is the mainstay of the Soviet diet and is seldom scarce. Despite the squeeze of the embargo, Soviet officials assured their population that they could continue to meet the demand for grain. The problem was complicated by their extensive use of feed grains for livestock. Given that herds were consuming American grain, the embargo would have affected people living on their agricultural collectives. If an impending deficit forced the slaughter of their cattle and swine, the situation could have become explosive. Meat shortages in Eastern-bloc countries have been known to cause social upheavals and rioting.

In summary, the Soviets seemed able to cope with the American embargo with relative ease. This fact has been interpreted by many countries as evidence of the futility of international trade sanctions. Throughout the embargo, most American farmers cooperated voluntarily with government regulations. However, the action of President Carter failed to capture the public imagination. Did people understand what guns for the battlefields of Afghanistan had to do with bread for Soviet citizens? The brunt of the embargo was felt by the small American farmer who had nothing to do with the invasion. At that time, the grain embargo failed to provide an adequate response to Moscow's mounting aggression. From the Kremlin's perspective, the cost of the grain embargo was acceptable because it could be reduced to a fiscal situation.

FOOD POLICIES AND EXPORT TRADE

Every developed country has an agricultural policy. An example was given for the EC in Exhibits 3.3 and 3.4. The rationale given for government intervention in this sector of the economy can be characterized by the interactions among social, economic, and political concerns. The goal of socioeconomic interactions is to provide adequate food supplies for the country's population. Politico-economic concerns promote an adequate rate of economic growth. Finally, sociopolitical concerns promote the welfare of the rural population.

Pricing decisions are political. Generally, acceptable possibilities exist for improving the diets of malnourished people. For example, when different regions or socioeconomic groups eat different staples, lowering the price of one staple while raising that of another, consumers can make substitutions. For example, high-cost energy crops such as rice can be swapped for low-cost energy from other staples. By intervening in the marketplace, importing countries take advantage of low food costs to either raise prices to producers or lower them to consumers. The policy followed depends on the political power of producers and consumers.

In 1988 there was a chronic supply imbalance in agricultural products caused largely by the use of government subsidies. Government policies can displace or distort the supply-and-demand forces of the marketplace as the main factor in determining trading practices for agricultural products.

The EC has adopted agricultural policies which have overstimulated its farm sectors. This has resulted in an excess of production which is dumped on the world market at prices well below the cost of production. To make this work, export subsidies, called restitutions, are used.

Developed countries that remain net food importers have adopted various forms of agricultural protection. For example, small farmers are protected in Japan at great expense to their consumers.

Besides subsidies, governments have erected barriers to market entry such as tariffs, nontariff barriers, and other restrictions, including sanitary or health standards. Often these are caused by emotional motivation or excessive caution.

U.S. Food Policies

Although most experts believe that the only effective solution to the world food crisis is to provide everyone with an adequate income, little agreement exists about how this desired result can be accomplished.

Because U.S. surveys identified poor Afro-Americans, young children, adolescents, pregnant women, and the elderly as high-risk groups, federal food assistance programs are targeted toward them. As program costs have risen, they have been increasingly scrutinized. Critics argue that the programs do not reach all of the intended people. Others complain of widespread fraud and of inadequate evaluation systems to prove that they improve nutritional status. The size and diversity of the recipient population impede data collection and design of control groups to evaluate them. However, people who use food stamps have been shown to increase their intake of some key nutrients. Their relatively high costs, combined with uncertain effectiveness and politically weak constituencies, make them vulnerable to elimination or reduction of services.

Farm Subsidies

Large portions of U.S. wheat, flour, rice, vegetable oils, and dairy products exports are subject to various federal government subsidies. U.S. farm price supports amount to about $25 billion per year in federal spending, representing about one-third of farm income.

Strategies to industrialize countries have had mixed economic results. Economic growth rates often accelerate in average terms, especially in market economy countries, but frequently without a great impact on poverty and with deleterious effects on income distribution. Bias towards concentrated and capital-intensive industrialization has resulted in low prices for agriculture products. Low prices translate to little output growth for the rural population. Governments soon realize that a stagnant agricultural sector will ruin chances for their sustained growth. Instead of raising farm prices to world levels, most governments decide to subsidize inputs, providing research findings, technical advice, subsidized fertilizers, machinery, irrigation, and access to low-cost credit. In some countries, these subsidies have frequently aided the larger and more commercially oriented farmers more than the smaller farmers or landless laborers. It appears that the debate about farm subsidies will continue for many years.

Impact of Policy Shifts:
The Colombian Example

Throughout the world, policy shifts affect food prices and, thus, the quality of people's lives. For example, in 1989, the President of Colombia claimed that the failure of the U.S. to support renewal of an international coffee agreement triggered a 50 percent fall in world coffee prices. This was projected to cost Colombia U.S. $400 million per year, an amount six times greater than the $65 million in emergency aid that was already being sent to Colombia for its drug war. Officials warned that the price cut made it harder to prevent farmers from diverting to coca whose dried leaves are made into cocaine. Could Colombia be helped through increased access for Colombian products, especially coffee, to the U.S.?

GENERAL AGREEMENT ON TRADE
AND TARIFFS (GATT)

The trading nations of the world are now inextricably linked to one another, receiving an average of one-quarter of their GNPs from exports. About one-half of export profits come from the operations of large multinational organizations.

In 1986, for the eighth time since the GATT organization was established in 1947, representatives of the 94 member nations met at the seaside resort of Punta del Este, Uruguay. The members have come to realize the disastrous results of current trade policies. In September 1986, the Uruguay Round of their negotiations was agreed to with the decision to establish new trading rules for agriculture. The three major thrusts in the discussions of the Uruguay Round of GATT were: (1) remove distortions of government interference in agricultural trade; (2) reduce the waste of scarce resources that are in vital demand; and (3) stop the misallocation of time, energy, and effort.

Failure of the talks which terminated in December 1990, could lead to a new wave of protectionism. There is a danger that a cycle of retaliations could sabotage future GATT talks and protectionist fever could spread worldwide. In that event, nations would become further entrenched in regional trading blocs. For the U.S., a breakdown in the mechanism of trade would make it overwhelmingly difficult to reduce the country's trade deficit.

Members considered an American proposal to do away with costly, unproductive agricultural subsidies. In July 1987, the U.S. tabled the proposal to phase out all direct and indirect subsidies affecting agricultural trade and all tariff and nontariff trade barriers over 10 years. The U.S. negotiators desired a harmonization of health and sanitary regulations on a worldwide basis, guided by safety and science, and established by the Codex Alimentarius Commission. The Commission, composed of 25 committees, develops and promotes coordinated standards to facilitate world trade. Its network also assists with the introduction of new food products to international markets.

The EC and Japan have great opposition to the U.S. proposal. Two other areas of contention are trade in services and intellectual property rights. Countries in the developing world are seeking preferential access to patents, copyrights, and computer software from industrialized countries.

Although it is hard to dispute the logic of free trade (e.g., the Free Trade Agreement recently initiated between the U.S. and Canada), interest groups in countries throughout the world are attempting to sabotage efforts toward global economic integration. For example, the EC banned the importation of American beef which had been treated artificially with hormones. The U.S. retaliated by imposing duties on EC agricultural products roughly equal to the beef sales American producers would forfeit under the ban, approximately $100 million per year.

Trade liberalization, if successfully negotiated in future GATT talks, will remove some barriers but will not automatically give the U.S. larger shares of the markets for processed and high-value agricultural products. World trade challenges to U.S. companies include: (1) becoming more cost-competitive, (2) increasing the efficiency of marketing systems, (3) identifying consumer desires throughout the world, (4) producing products desired by global consumers, (5) improving international language skills, and 6) becoming attuned to ethnic and cultural food preferences around the world. In summary, current policies have harmed the developing nations. Many of these nations rely on agricultural exports for the bulk of their revenue. They would benefit greatly from the access to markets the Uruguay Round proposal would allow.

Recognizing the negative effects which national agricultural policies have on the stability of world agricultural markets and the efficient allocation of world resources, one remedy is to work towards free trade in all agricultural products. However, with the social, political, and economic forces which form the basis of domestic agricultural policies, it appears virtually impossible for governments to convince their agricultural population that free trade has advantages. Even the concept of free trade is associated with leading to undesirable cycles of surplus and shortages.

If GATT is not an appropriate body for liberalizing world agricultural trade, the question must be asked: Is any organization capable of bringing greater order to agricultural trade? The potential benefits of trade have also not been realized because the vast majority of the world's people do not have adequate incomes to meet nutritional needs or satisfy their food preferences.

SUMMARY

The creation of employment and purchasing power is associated with reliance on marketing and food distribution. The lack of demand for food may aggravate a food-deficit situation by inducing outflow of market surplus to other regions. Some famines have occurred when there was no significant decline in food availability compared with previous periods. Problems occurred because of distribution snafus and lack of consumer purchasing power. In many instances, market mechanisms have failed to move food supplies from surplus to deficit areas in times of crisis. To avoid human suffering, market flows may have to be supplemented by deliberate governmental actions.

Generally, international markets have four inherent challenges: (1) Although the international market supply of food comes from a few sources, demand for that food comes from many sources; (2) Those countries which have a greater purchasing power can preempt food supplies; (3) Those countries which strive to protect their domestic markets from external shocks create large variations in both supplies and prices; and (4) International food supplies and prices are sensitive to domestic food production, food pricing policies, and performance or efficiencies in food producing countries or regions.

All nations desire food security. Food security should not be confused with food self-sufficiency. An open world trading system ensures that ample food supplies will be available to those who need them.

Twenty-five years ago, when TV was introduced, projections were made that it would create the global consumer. When satellites were introduced, the same statements were made. Basically, nobody has ever found this global consumer. Inherent in our global diversity is the fact that we enrich our lives when we become consumers of fine quality food products from other nations.

REFERENCES

Abbott, J. C. 1986. *Marketing improvement in the developing world: what happens and what we have learned*. FAO Economic and Social Development Series No. 37. Rome: Food and Agriculture Organization of the United Nations.

Alsudery, Abdelmuhsin. 1985. The world food problems: assessment and solutions. In *Crop productivity – research imperatives revisited*, eds. M. Gibbs and C. Carlson, 71-80. An international conference held at Boyne Highlands Inn, October 13-18, 1985 and Airlie House, December 11-13, 1985.

Austin, James E. and G. Esteva, eds. 1987. *Food policy in Mexico – the search for self-sufficiency*. Ithaca: Cornell University Press.

Barry, Tom. 1987. *Roots of rebellion: land and hunger in Central America*. Boston: South End Press.

Briskey, E. J., V. W. Hays, and R. L. Mitchell. 1983. Future approaches for meeting nutritional needs. In *Agriculture in the twenty-first century*, ed. J. W. Rosenblum, 118-43. New York: John Wiley & Sons.

Cetron, Marvin and Owen Davies. 1989. *American renaissance – our life at the turn of the 21st century*. New York: St. Martin's Press.

Connor, John M. 1988. *Food processing: an industrial powerhouse in transition*. Lexington and Toronto: D. C. Heath and Company.

deSousa, I. S. F., E. G. Singer, and W. L. Flinn. 1985. Sociopolitical forces and technology: critical reflections on the green revolution. In *Food, politics, and society in Latin America*, eds. J. C. Super and T. C. Wright, 228-245. Lincoln and London: University of Nebraska Press.

Durning, Alan B. 1990. Ending poverty. In *State of the world 1990*, ed. L. Starke, 135-153. New York and London: W. W. Norton & Company, Inc.

Farquharson, John E. 1985. *The western allies and the politics of food*. Dover: Berg Publishers.

Fischer, Lewis A. 1985. *Canada's grain market in the European economic community*. Agricultural Economics Research Council of Canada.

Gever, J., R. Kaufman, D. Skole, and C. Vorosmarty. 1986. *Beyond oil*. Cambridge: Ballinger Publishing Company.

Gregor, Bogdan. 1986. Distribution system of agricultural production means and services in Poland. In *World food marketing systems*, ed. E. Kaynak, 197-205. London: Butterworth & Co. (Publishers) Ltd.

Kaynak, Erdener. 1986. *World food marketing systems*. London: Butterworth & Co. (Publishers) Ltd.

Lee, John E. 1988. Trends in world agriculture and trade in high-value food products. *Food Technology* 42(9):119-27.

Lyng, Richard E. 1988. Food and agriculture in a global economy. *Food Technology* 42(9):115-16.

Mason, J. B., J-P. Habicht, H. Tabatabai, and V. Valverde. 1984. *Nutritional surveillance*. Geneva: World Health Organization.

McMahan, Joseph A. 1988. *European trade policy in agricultural products*. Netherlands: Marinus Nijhoff Publishers.

Nadeau, Bertrand. 1985. *Britain's entry into the European Economic Community and its effect on Canada's agricultural exports*. Montreal: The Institute for Research on Public Policy.

Nestle, Marion. 1985. *Nutrition in medical practice*. Greenbrae, California: Jones Medical Publications.

Pelto, G. H. and P. J. Pelto. 1983. Diet and delocalization: dietary changes since 1750. In *Hunger and history*, eds. R. I. Rotberg and T. K. Tabb, 309-330. Cambridge: Cambridge University Press.

Streeten, Paul. 1987. *What price food?* St. Martin's Press: New York.

Tickner, Vincent. 1986. New directions in food marketing policies in less developed countries. In *World food marketing systems*, ed. E. Kaynak. London: Butterworth & Co. (Publishers) Ltd.

Chapter Four

The Global Food Problem and Foreign Aid

INTRODUCTION

You are now aware that we do have a global food problem. This chapter focuses upon what foreign aid actions we, as an interdependent — global — community, are taking to help alleviate this problem. By studying the information given in this chapter, you will be in an informed position to discuss:

- the conditions which have lead policymakers to the conclusion that we do have a global food problem;
- the components of food aid packages, including the development of special food products for nutrition needs around the world;
- the controversies surrounding food aid programs, and how they may be eliminated for the benefit of recipients.

The international community recognizes the following six interdependent conditions as constituting the global food problem:

1. widespread starvation, chronic malnutrition and prevailing hunger among poor people in developing countries;
2. substantial inequalities in levels of food consumption among and within countries;
3. frequent coexistence of acute food shortages in some countries, or regions or areas within countries, and large food surpluses in others;
4. significant disparities in levels of agricultural productivity

among countries, crop-sectors, and farming groups within
countries;
5. wide fluctuations in food prices on international markets, usually most damaging to countries that are least able to adjust;
6. global depletion of agronomic resources such as arable land,
topsoil, and fresh water.

Together, these six chronic conditions have lead to our global
food situation. Although the previous chapter discussed how foreign trade can deal with some of these situations, in this chapter you
will become aware of the huge level of foreign aid which seeks to
eliminate these, and other, conditions.

With the creation of U.S. Public Law 480 "Food for Peace" in
1954, food aid became an explicit and continuing component of
U.S. foreign policy toward the developing world. In addition to
humanitarian objectives, an objective of the bill was to dispose of
surplus stocks of farm commodities. The different objectives of PL
480 have invited conflicting opinions.

Food aid has changed a great deal during the last decade. Development specialists increasingly consider food aid as a resource
transfer to promote economic growth and enhance food security in
recipient countries. As a vital resource, food aid can be used either
wisely or unwisely. Food aid must be closely managed. Food aid
can be an investment in future food security and components of
development transfer funds. As an international resource transfer,
food aid may contribute to a country's balance of payments, provide a budgetary resource for governments, or transfer income to
selected target populations.

Continued public support for large food aid programs will depend
on its development effectiveness. Food surpluses alone will not
make the case for food aid. Donor agencies are being asked to de-
fend the effectiveness of food aid with assurances that it is not a
disincentive to local farmers, it supports and complements agricultural development activities, it helps to prevent recurring emergencies, and it assists and encourages recipient governments to invest
in their rural areas and maintain policies which stimulate productivity.

National boundaries, ethnic considerations, and distance are reduced when vivid pictures appear on our television screens. One of the most striking examples of a successful collaborative effort among many pop music stars to raise funds for famine relief in Africa were the "Band-Aid" and "Live-Aid" programs in the U.K. and U.S., respectively. The recent Band-Aid/Live-Aid support showed an awareness of the problems of turning relief into development. By necessity, the promoters placed a heavy emphasis on famine relief in their fund-raising appeals. Their funds were allocated as: 20 percent to the emergency itself, 20 percent for the transport of food and supporting materials, and 60 percent to measures designed to prevent a recurrence of the emergency. In the short run, the "bailing out" actions predominate and make news headlines. In the long run, only the developmental considerations can solve the problems.

Food aid averages 9 percent of all overseas development aid from all donors, the equivalent of U.S. $2.5 billion per year. Unfortunately, foreign aid has somewhat negative impacts when the foreign exchange set free by food aid is spent for purchasing the latest and most sophisticated foreign military hardware.

INTEGRATION OF FOOD AID AND DEVELOPMENT

To help themselves, people need knowledge, technology, profitability, and organization. Agricultural development must precede economic development in most parts of the world. Theoretically, as agriculture develops, a nation's economy develops, the standard of living rises, demands increase, and nutritional preferences or requirements change in both quantity and kind, with rising affluence.

There is little available experience covering the ground between the largely uncharted area between relief and development. Funds raised for emergencies are not usually available for development purposes and, consequently, only have a palliative effect without addressing themselves to root causes.

Food aid may be given in the form of loans, credits, sales below normal market prices, or free gifts. Food aid may be offered by governments, international bodies, regional institutions, voluntary groups and agencies, or individuals. Donors of food aid need to know when potential developmental benefits are realized. Further, they need assurance when the potentially harmful effects of food aid, resulting in disincentives to local food production, are avoided.

VIEWPOINTS ABOUT FOREIGN AID

The international community is discussing the establishment of some kind of international social security system. At least two opposing viewpoints are being expressed. Some regard providing any form of charity or social security as a brake on personal or collective initiative and, therefore, a disincentive to development and productivity. Others maintain that deprivation must be remedied in view of the increasing interdependence of all countries and the development of an international social conscience.

In emergencies such as refugee influxes or natural disasters where large numbers of people are fed in camps or settlements, food aid involves the physical transfer of donated food to recipient mouths. These "bailing out" actions account for only 20 percent of food aid donated by industrialized countries. The other 80 percent consists of concessional sales or food donated for purposes of budget support. The latter are intended to provide import substitution.

If aid were only given in financial form, the developing countries would have to spend a considerable amount of money on food purchases on the international market. Recipient countries need commodities for their development projects that cost money: machinery, raw materials for industries, and food for their workers engaged in the projects. The foreign exchange saved by food aid can be wasted by such political acts as: importing armaments or inessential luxury items, supporting capital flight, or establishing banking accounts in Switzerland.

Positive Viewpoints

The objectives of food aid are accomplished when they are well-coordinated among donors, and between donors and recipients. When decisions are made about choosing food aid or money, evidence shows that food is disbursed much more quickly to needy recipients.

Food aid objectives need to be effectively linked with other forms of assistance such as financial, technical and health assistance, and trade efforts. Further, all food aid needs to be integrated with the recipient countries' development plans and policies. Information in Exhibit 4.1 includes information about structural or political and temporary situations where food aid is justified. Once these condi-

Exhibit 4.1. Causes for the need for food aid.

Structural need

1. Application of too rigid economic or political formula.

2. Insufficient availability of arable and productive lands.

3. Human and/or animal overpopulation with accompanying ecological degradation.

4. Land-locked or geographically unfavorable position.

5. Lack of essential natural resources.

Temporary inability

1. Drought.

2. Crop failures.

3. Decrease in producer prices or other disincentives to production.

4. Civil strife.

5. Natural disaster.

Structural and temporary inability

1. Severe unemployment.

2. Malnutrition due to inappropriate use of available resources.

3. Epidemics with long-term complications.

4. Seasonal or temporary rise in food prices, placing staples beyond the means of low income groups.

Adapted from: Singer, H., J. Wood, and T. Jennings. 1987. Food aid the Challenge and the opportunity. Oxford University Press.

tions have been documented, it is obviously hoped by the donors that many of them, i.e., the political decisions to apply too rigid an economic formula, will be temporary ones.

Negative Viewpoints

Information in Exhibit 4.2 includes seven arguments frequently made against the use of food aid. Each of these is rather self-explanatory. For many of them, the introduction of effective management practices can nullify their negative effects. For example, food aid can bring about changes in traditional food consumption habits. When these new food habits can be subsequently maintained through local production, no permanent harm occurs.

Some negative viewpoints about food aid relate to the physical nature of the food itself. For example, the continual challenge for improving the handling of farm produce to avoid loss and maintain quality is immense. In some countries, aid funds have purchased mechanized sorting and packaging machinery for this purpose. Un-

Exhibit 4.2. Seven Arguments Made Against Food Aid.

---

1. Food aid reduces the pressure on recipient countries to make policy reforms, especially those related to food producer incentives and nutrition.

2. Food aid tends to depress domestic farm prices, discouraging domestic agricultural production and to reducing the introduction of agricultural technologies.

3. Food aid is unreliable because it depends on donors' surpluses. When needs are greatest, ie. when prices are high, it is often not available. Since donors make their allocations in terms of money, higher prices buy smaller amounts of foods.

4. If food aid is administered through state agencies, it reinforces state hegemony over people and does not always reach the poorest population.

5. Food aid promotes a shift in food consumption patterns away from staples and indigeneous foods, towards wheat and wheat flour.

6. Food aid disrupts international commercial food channels.

7. Food aid leads to unfair burden sharing between donors, when the prices of food are over valued.

Source: Streeten, Paul. 1987. <u>What price food?</u> New York: St. Martin's Press.

fortunately, some advisers, backed by aid donors and foreign equipment manufacturers, have recommended the construction of unsuitable storage facilities and they have been severely underused. One African study of 70 canning, slaughtering, storage, and related plants found they had all failed because the marketing element of food production had not received serious study before investments were committed.

Similarly, many food marketing systems have been designed too elaborately. Where simple sheds are required for protection against sun and rain, heavy concrete structures have been erected. In addition to wasting money that could have been spent more efficiently, these buildings are hard to modify as needs evolve.

In some developing countries, simple solutions can be found to food transportation problems. For example, improving feeder roads and eliminating specific obstacles such as streams without culverts, coupled with purchasing rubber tires for bullock carts and spare parts for vehicles, can be more effective than purchasing new transportation equipment.

There are physical limits to what a country or region or city can absorb. Large shipments of grain to replenish stocks cannot be accepted without adequate port storage plus transportation to the users. Results from improving crop yields cannot be optimized without ensuring suitable storage, marketing, and transport systems. Without effective instruction and maintenance, expensive equipment can be useless.

Many pastoralists have a fine appreciation for how much their environment can bear. Food aid may lead to an increase in the population in a certain area, leading to undernourishment. Sometimes development cancels the built-in regulatory systems of society.

With rational management practices, solutions are available for many of the concerns given in Exhibit 4.2. For example, to prevent food price depressions, counterpart funds from the sale of food aid at market-clearing prices can be used to make deficiency payments to the farmers. With this approach, supply prices can be restored to their original levels.

Public criticisms can involve statements like "the aid and the rain came at the same time." These can often be refuted by statements about how the onset of rains after a drought does not automatically dispense with the need for food aid. Crops do not instantly sprout and ripen. Rains have to be sufficient to ensure a sustained crop. Furthermore, rains may disrupt roads, etc. Some cereal food aid can be used for planting when no other seed stocks are available.

Food aid may also be supplied in the form of animal or poultry feed. There is frequently a need for seeds, especially following droughts when farmers may have been forced to use their stock for consumption.

SELECTED EXAMPLES OF SOME DONORS

A brief overview of some donors follows.

U.S. In 1986, the U.S. Export Enhancement, Commodity Credit Corporation export credit, and PL 480 food aid programs subsidized over 20 million tons of U.S. farm and food commodities, including over one-half of the wheat, almost one-half of the vegetable oil, and one-third of the rice involved in foreign aid programs.

Canada. The commodities available in the Canadian program are predominantly wheat and maize.

Australia. The commodities available in the Australian program are predominantly rice and sugar.

Japan. In recent years, Japan has been acting more like a regional leader, increasing its foreign aid spending dramatically in the 1980s. It now surpasses the U.S. as the world's largest donor. The commodities available in the Japanese program are predominantly rice. Japan has also been using its cash reserves to procure other cereals from Asian countries for its food aid programs.

EC. The main objectives of the EC's food aid policy are to lend support to the balance of payments of recipients, to improve the nutrition of the recipients, and to lend assistance to development through transfer of resources. These objectives are reflected in four eligibility and allocation criteria established by the EC for food aid:

1. Gross Domestic Product (GDP) per capita based on World Bank data;
2. nutritional requirements, based on FAO's calorie data;
3. capacity to import commercially using export revenue, based on International Monetary Fund (IMF) data
4. foreign exchange reserve position, based on IMF data.

These criteria help ensure food aid is optimally integrated with other inputs and long-term development plans of the recipient governments.

The range of products given by the EC as food aid include cereals, rice, milk products (milk powder and butter oil), sugar, vegetable oils, and other foods. Foods are distributed by four established programs: Food for Work, Provision of Food Security Stocks, Direct Action, and Counterpart Funds.

Examples of Direct Action in India involved targeting school children for an operation involving rural and agricultural development such as the Operation Flood project. The objectives of the scheme included the development of local milk production, the guarantee of stable supplies of milk, and the promotion of self-reliance among rural producers.

Thus, EC aid has been linked with internal initiatives. Until food self-sufficiency is reached, food aid will continue to have a role, particularly through the use of Counterpart Funds. It is also necessary to encourage triangular operations whereby aid involves buying products in developing countries which have an exportable supply and donating it to a country with a deficit. This type of operation stabilizes the market in the producer country, provides the recipient country with a local product, and makes a contribution to regional food security.

The implementation of food strategies involves a reduction in the importance of food aid, although it may still play a role within the confines of the strategy. Food strategy pilot cases have shown there is a need for increased financial, technical, and agricultural cooperation in conjunction with food aid.

Because the U.K. has generally not had food surpluses, it has given cash for food aid. If the U.S. and EC were to give cash as a substitute for food aid, they would need monetary increases of 40 and 25 percent, respectively.

The UN World Food Programme is now buying most of its supply of food commodities from Third World countries rather than traditional suppliers in the North. Thus, the potential for South-South trade and neighbor-to-neighbor alternative programs is enormous and will also enable Third World countries to play a more active role in each other's development.

SELECTED EXAMPLES OF SOME RECIPIENTS

The ultimate aim of food aid is to make recipients self-reliant as buyers and producers of food. In the late 1950s, the sale of surplus commodities to Communist countries signaled that food aid had definite political security potential. If a country has a food deficit and imports food, financial aid for essential developmental imports frees up some of their foreign exchange which can then be used for food imports.

After Asia, Latin America has been the second largest recipient of American food aid. Food aid to Brazil and Colombia ceased in 1973. Food aid recipient countries—India, Korea, Israel, Greece, and most of the EC countries which received large-scale U.S. aid under the Marshall Plan after World War II—have used food aid as a basis for vigorous development of local agriculture and food production. Hopefully, the two countries receiving the most food aid now, Egypt and Bangladesh, will be added to this success list.

The resounding success of agricultural development in Taiwan from 1951 to 1965 owed much to the U.S. decision to allocate aid that provided 58.7 percent of all investment in Taiwan's agriculture in that period. Colombia has also graduated from being a food aid recipient.

Twenty years ago, India had a large food deficit and received considerable amounts of food aid. Pessimistic forecasters doubted her ability to emerge from being totally dependent on food aid. However, by the early 1980s, India had become an exporter of cereals. How was this transformation achieved?

Food aid permitted India to break out of the vicious circle of malnutrition, intermittent famine, crop failures, postharvest losses, and inadequate logistics capacity in rural areas. Technology transfer programs assisted with the development of new crop varieties with high yields and drought resistance. Development projects included: improved marketing and storage facilities, expanded veterinary services, milk bottling and processing plants, fertilizer plants, and dams and irrigation schemes. These projects were accompanied with education in the requisite managerial skills. Note that the population of India is twice that of Europe, the U.S., or the Soviet

Union. Similar results should logically be feasible in other countries.

Egypt and Israel, whose aid packages are linked, together consume 37 cents of every U.S. aid dollar. Egypt is the second largest recipient of U.S. aid, next to Israel. Egypt's problems include a population that increases by 1 million every 9 months. Substantial U.S. food aid to Egypt is part of the price the U.S. pays to help prevent political trouble in the region that could devastate the Middle East peace process. However, by enabling the Egyptian government to subsidize many foodstuffs and services, such aid helps distort the economy by disguising the true cost of almost every commodity, and indirectly encouraging the population explosion.

The development of a food strategy is essentially a political act, requiring the ranking of development priorities. Four African, Caribbean, and Pacific (ACP) countries were chosen by the EC to receive food aid because they had a large food shortfall coupled with both the capacity and the will to conduct valid food strategies. The countries recently chosen were: Mali, Rwanda, Kenya, and Zambia. The objectives of four programs, all successfully implemented, are briefly stated for each nation.

Mali. The purpose of the food strategy was to reorganize the grain market and halt the increasing food deficit in that commodity.

Rwanda. The problem was mounting pressure on the land. The food strategy was to concentrate on improving marketing, storage and processing, and promoting access to agricultural inputs and research in an effort to conserve natural resources.

Kenya. The aim was to restore productivity to the agricultural sector and bring about a return to self-sufficiency and perhaps create a surplus.

Zambia. The aim was to balance the needs of food production, the need to generate foreign exchange, and the requirements of the country's rapidly expanding urban sector.

Refugees

Refugees are also recipients of food aid. People in camps or designated settlement areas have insufficient resources to be productive. Furthermore, they are usually not allowed to integrate into the economic life of the local population. Emergencies of this kind are largely unpredictable. When recognized as international problems, the international community attends to their welfare.

There is a predictable trend to "promote" emergencies. In 1982-83, a drought emergency was declared in the north and central areas of Mozambique and a number of deaths were reported, yet there was still water in the rivers in the affected regions. The emergency was caused by government regulations prohibiting the free movement of produce from one district to another, forced delivery quotas for farmers, and the closing of retail outlets. In this case, the need for food aid did not stem from drought conditions.

Although media pictures of starving children make people feel guilty, donors question the concept of food aid if they are not kept informed about reasons for the needs for food aid. For example, is the need for food aid due to lack of food availability, crop failures, or inability to cope with droughts? Media coverage centers on scenarios of failure rather than on positive aspects of food aid and development. For example, massive reforestation schemes in Algeria designed to stop the encroachment of the desert northwards have met with some successes. When negative public opinions are developed, negative views can resurge, for example, in the case of Algeria, maintaining that irreversible climate damage is occurring without any actions to prevent the ecological damage.

Turning to another example, the serious drought in the Sahel region of Africa in the 1970s was portrayed through scenes of dying cattle, parched earth, and misused food aid. This media coverage was also given to Somalia in the early 1970s and to Ethiopia, Chad, and the Sudan in the late 1980s. Limited coverage was given to successful projects: the development of the Niger River basin; range management and reforestation in Somalia; irrigation and soil conservation in Ethiopia; road building, housing and school construction; and school and hospital feeding programs in many of these affected countries.

A drought does not necessarily cause a famine. A natural disaster does not always require massive external assistance. Pastoralists in many parts of the world inhabit the driest and least productive countries and are able to survive droughts better than their well-sheltered urban counterparts. For example, agricultural students at the University of Missouri-Columbia toured Outback Australia during their extended drought conditions in the fall of 1987. Students commented that the people had adapted to the drought conditions and still received satisfaction from their parched lands. During jeep excursions through dried lands covering huge distances, the landowners pointed out how they could smell some of the native trees, pointing them out to the travellers who were used to experiencing "green" and did not have these same senses. During this extended drought, many landowners showed an acceptance of what it took to wait for the rains to return, and an appreciation for what they had. They had diverted into the tourist industry to receive needed funds but their inherent love for the land, in whatever condition, was obvious.

SOME TECHNICAL DETAILS OF FOOD AID PROGRAMS

The "debt/service ratio" is one indicator of the state of health of a country's balance of payments. The "alpha-value" can be used to analyze the effectiveness of food aid. The alpha-value can be defined as: "the ratio of the value of the commodity to the food aid recipients compared with its acquisition and delivery costs." The value to the recipients depends on what substitutes exist for the food aid in their diet, and how they are priced.

For example, if 1 kilogram of wheat costs 50 cents (20 cents to buy, 20 cents to ship, and 10 cents to distribute), and the substitute for the food aid is to buy sorghum at 15 cents per kilogram, the alpha-value would be 0.3, i.e., 15/50. In this example, recipients would be better off receiving a check for 30 cents (the savings in shipping and distribution costs) rather than the kilogram of wheat in a food aid program.

The higher the alpha-value, the more effective food aid becomes. For low alpha-values, food aid can still be valuable, but either a check or alternative types of food aid, i.e., sugar or oil, would have a better income transfer efficiency.

The true value of food aid for the recipient is measured by comparing the value of the beneficiaries' diet with and without food aid, and adding any income derived from the sale of food by the beneficiaries.

Foods Involved in Food Aid Programs

Within food aid programs, the food basket can be defined as: "the selection of commodities and the scale of rations distributed." Optimal food baskets supply a specific amount of energy and protein derived from cereals, milk, meat, fish, oils, pulses, dried fruit, and sugar. The commodities should be compatible with the normal eating habits of the recipients.

In terms of volume and value, cereals account for 90 and 75 percent of all food aid, respectively. Predominantly, cereal grains are: wheat, rice, and coarse grains such as maize, barley, rye, sorghum, and oats. Details of each of these commodities and other food products will be presented.

Wheat and wheat products. When wheat is bulk-shipped, some form of processing is needed before it can be consumed as bread, pasta, or flapjacks. The greatest proportion of wheat is destined for central government grain stores where it becomes part of the national wheat stock which can be used when required for processing. Wheat destined for rural areas is usually shipped as flour. Depending on the extraction rate, a term used to describe the components of the kernel during processing, there is a loss of at least 15 percent of wheat during milling. Essential nutrients are also lost in milling. When flour is bagged in thin cotton sacks, the shelf life is limited under hot and humid conditions.

Bread is frequently included in school meals and baked from food aid wheat flour. Since wheat is not a staple in most recipient countries, the importation does not have adverse effects on local production. Because bread is associated with status, other side effects occur. Eating habits are initiated which can only be sustained through food aid unless local production becomes feasible. Furthermore, wheat may be purchased at the expense of local products such as maize, sorghum, millet, or rice, disrupting local supplies and prices.

Maize. Maize is a staple in Africa, Latin America, and the Caribbean. Although African maize is white, problems occur because food aid maize is yellow. In the African sub-Saharan region, yellow maize is considered to be animal feed. Its acceptability problems are overcome during starvation periods. One permanent solution to this societal problem would be to introduce high-yielding yellow maize varieties to this region.

Rice. Rice is a status food for the more prosperous families in many developing countries. Food aid rice is shipped parboiled or polished to eliminate parasites and improve shelf life.

Sorghum. Sorghum is grown in the U.S. where the variety is red; that consumed in sub-Saharan Africa is white.

Pulses and tubers. Low-cost varieties of pulses and tubers such as lentils, chick-peas, and cowpeas are used. Because they take a long time to soften in boiling water, they cause high fuel and water use.

Dried fruits. Some EC donors provide dried fruits such as apples, apricots, figs, and pears.

Milk. Milk is supplied in powder form either as dry skim milk (DSM), non-fat dry milk (NFDM), or dry whole milk (DWM). The latter is reserved for intensive care situations and nutritional rehabilitation of severely undernourished children when mothers cannot breast-feed. In societies with high levels of lactose intolerance, cow's milk is not a normal part of the diet, and can cause diarrhea and other rejection symptoms. The reconstitution process for dry milk powders requires clean water, heat, and clean and suitable utensils. Local sanitation problems can be overcome by shipping the milk powder to a central dairy where yogurt and cheese can also be produced from it.

Butter-oil or ghee. Butter-oil or ghee is packed in large round cans holding 5 to 10 kg and costs about twice as much as vegetable oils. It is supplied by EC countries.

Cheese. Canned processed cheese is sometimes available from Scandinavia. Without proper storage, the cans tend to explode under tropical conditions.

Vegetable oils. Vegetable oils are made from maize, rape seed or Canola, soybean, sunflower, ground-nuts, etc. When local hygiene is difficult to ensure and water supplies are limited, frying is considered one of the safest methods of cooking. Packaging and transportation requirements have to be met for its distribution.

Fish. Fish is supplied in dried salted form or canned, the former coming from Scandinavia and Germany. The dried forms must be kept dry during transportation and storage and they require clean water for soaking. Very few taboos exist for the consumption of fish.

Sugar. Sugar is provided for use in children's milk.

Foods Developed for Food Aid Programs

When PL 480 was enacted in 1954, the principal commodities involved in the food donation programs were wheat, feed grains, rice, wheat flour, corn meal, NFDM, and edible oils. In 1966, PL 480 was changed to allow enrichment and fortification of commodities to improve their nutritional qualities. The U.S. is currently providing 2 million metric tons of commodities under Title II of PL 480 to about 90 countries throughout the world. Distributed commodities in four categories—whole commodities, processed foods, fortified-processed foods, and blended food supplements— are listed in Exhibit 4.3. These products are being distributed by the UN World Food Programme, U.S. voluntary agencies, and recipient governments.

Several blended foods have been made available after considerable development by food scientists. As seen in Exhibit 4.3, a popular form of these is corn-soy milk (CSM). Blended food supplements have been used in infant and child feeding programs since the early 1970s. These blends contain up to 73 percent precooked wheat or corn products, 15 to 24 percent defatted toasted soy flour, up to 15 percent NFDM, up to 6 percent soybean oil, and ten vitamins and minerals. Nutritional improvements to these foods have been made as research results have become available. For example, processing conditions to destroy salmonella without adversely changing nutritional qualities have been adopted.

Blended food supplements can be used to make a nutritive gruel or porridge, or as an additive to other dishes. Similar blends under various trade names are available from EC food aid sources. These products are particularly useful in infant nutritional rehabilitation programs.

Wheat has been fortified with Vitamin A and dispersed to recipients who receive the benefits of fortification in their traditional foods. In Bangladesh, about 900,000 children under 6 years old have some form of eye disease, and 30,000 children are blinded

Exhibit 4.3. Commodities Distributed under Title II PL-480, U.S. Food for Peace Program, 1984-1986.

Commodity Group	Metric Tons		
	1984	1985	1986
Whole commodities			
Wheat	640,382	518,048	688,509
Corn	243,942	286,618	136,667
Sorghum	119,884	807,032	61,326
Dry beans	4,717	21,999	9,117
Dry peas	24,948	2,359	7,167
Processed foods			
Bulgur	172,501	211,737	298,464
Vegetable oil	121,200	143,789	155,446
Nonfat dry milk	151,681	107,139	127,369
Wheat flour	122,651	126,598	116,845
Cornmeal	80,785	82,463	67,086
Milled rice	136,803	110,994	57,606
Cheese	1,996	439	1,225
Butter	1,996	---	91
Fortified processed foods			
Soy-fortified bulgur	32,114	41,685	106,005
Soy-fortified sorghum grits	53,705	69,872	59,466
Soy-fortified cornmeal	13,381	34,246	31,797
Soy-fortified bread flour	5,080	227	3,356
Soy-fortified rolled oats	2,359	998	4,490
Instant corn-soya-masa flour	---	227	45

Exhibt 4.3 (continued)

Blended food supplements			
Corn-soy-milk (CSM)	141,158	167,058	170,732
Instant CSM	12,202	32,704	22,725
Wheat-soy-milk	12,474	8,800	11,839

Source: Bookwalter, George N. 1990. Nutritional improvement of foods for international assistance programs. In <u>Trends in Nutrition and Food Policy</u>. Ang How Ghee, ed. 179-184. Paper presented at the 7th World Congress of Food Science and Technology, 28 Sept. - 2 Oct., 1987, Singapore.

each year due to Vitamin A deficiency. The receipt of this wheat can eliminate this tragedy. Calcium, Vitamin A, and other enrichment ingredients are being added in another cereal, bulgur.

NFDM is frequently used as a protein enhancer during local preparation of milled cereals for consumption. NFDM is itself enriched with Vitamins A and D to improve nutritional quality.

The nutritional benefits of combining cereals and soybean meal to increase both protein quality and quantity is well-established. The essential amino acid patterns of cereal and soybean proteins complement each other, demonstrated by higher protein efficiency ratios. Bulgur, sorghum grits, cornmeal, bread flour, rolled oats, and corn masa are fortified with 5 to 15 percent soy protein. To avoid changing physical characteristics, soy flakes, grits, and flour are combined with similar physical forms of the cereals. Their standard enrichment includes added thiamin, riboflavin, niacin, iron, calcium, and Vitamin A.

Distribution problems have been encountered with all food commodities. Given the additional expense of preparing the blended foods, losses of these commodities are particularly devastating. For example, the availability of CSM is limited and costs are relatively high. CSM is packaged in 25 or 50 kg bags consisting of a polyethylene inner envelope and two layers of kraft paper coverings. If the inner plastic is punctured under humid tropic conditions, caking occurs and is accompanied by mold and other contamination. With this damage, its use has to be downgraded to animal food; humans do not receive the nutritional benefits.

Other Costs Associated with Food Aid

Using 1985 prices, the ocean freight for bulk grain from a U.S. or European port to East Africa was about 30 percent of the grain costs. When ports do not have bulk handling, freight costs can be 50 percent. For some landlocked countries, delivery costs can exceed commodity costs. Different commodities have varying shipping rates. Bulk grains, where the container or hull capacity is fully utilized, have the most economical rates. Commodities in round cans or drums occupy more space than their original volume.

Given the perishable nature of food commodities, special consideration must always be given to shipping. For example, engine oil should not be stored on top of bags of maize, dried fish should be stored where there is no risk of humidity, and grains have to be stored away from heat sources. The latter may require special ventilation and temperature control to prevent spontaneous combustion. If cans are not stored properly, they can be subjected to too much pressure causing them to burst and become contaminated.

The air-drop technique is the most economical use of aircraft for food emergencies. Blended/processed foods are suited to this method because of the limited tonnage that can be air-lifted, and because of their good nutritional values.

The recipient government is expected to provide necessary storage facilities. Problems arise because quantities, kind, and even delivery times of food aid supplies are unpredictable. One solution is to have a food security system where reserve stocks can be positioned throughout the country. Ideally, these systems should have long-term and high-quality storage to protect commodities from humidity levels, rodents, birds, insects, and other sources of contamination. Except in the case of special emergency relief, food aid is still costly to recipients. Storage is one important element of these costs.

For example, in Chad from September 1 to October 5, 1982, 88 flights were made with 111 landings or destinations to deliver 1,448 tons of food at a cost of U.S. $2 million. This calculated to be U.S. $1,400 per ton of food delivered, but was necessary because the rainy season had made roads impassable.

Many commodities are bagged in the U.S. where they are handled mechanically on conveyors, stackers, fork-lifts, and pallets. In recipient countries, the same bags are handled with laborers. When bags of flour are dropped 4 or 5 feet, they rupture, become contaminated, and mold and contamination can spread to other bags.

Only 20 percent of the cost of breakfast cereal to consumers in developed countries is attributable to raw materials; 80 percent can be attributed to processing, packaging, publicity, and profit. Most of these additional elements are reduced for food aid. Whenever commodities are bagged or canned, they bear donor marks of origin and carry indications prohibiting their sale.

Packaging costs are reduced since the largest proportion of cereal food aid is shipped in bulk in grain-carrying vessels. Publicity costs are limited to stencilling standard indications of product, quantity, grade, and origin on bags and cans.

The most common processing operation is the conversion of grain into meal. In most developing countries, the extraction rate in wheat milling is about 85 percent as opposed to 72 percent in the U.S. This higher rate produces a coarser and more nutritious flour. The costs of milling and bagging wheat flour in the PL 480 program amounts to U.S. $16 for every ton of wheat milled. The milling process loses 20 to 25 percent of the original volume of grain milled.

With CSM, the raw materials mold easily when exposed to moisture. CSM is packed in two strong paper outer bags plus a polyethylene sealed liner. The average cost of CSM per ton is U.S. $259, with much of the extra cost due to the special bagging requirement.

Bulk soybean oil costs U.S. $450 per ton, while the cost of one ton of soybeans is U.S. $200. Following oil extraction, the marketable residue increases the margin between raw material and processed product prices. The cost of one ton of soybean oil packaged in 1 gallon or 5 liter containers is U.S. $1,000.

Many commodities and supplies have special distribution specifications. Unprocessed rice generally averages around twice the price of wheat. Expensive woven polypropylene fiber bags are recommended for rice after processing. When wheat flour or maize meal is delivered in a processed state, it has to be rapidly distributed and consumed or processed into bread, etc., because of its limited shelf life in hot and humid climates. When fuels such as charcoal supplies are distributed, transportation constraints are required, i.e., charcoal supplies cannot be waterlogged.

Regulations require that food aid be transported in state-owned vehicles. If there are transportation delays, food aid deliveries are late. If too little supplies are shipped to recipients with bulk program aid, national shortages of cereals can result, given a heavy reliance on cereal food aid. Conversely, delivering too many bulk commodities within a given time-frame can cause port or storage congestion. Clearly, effective food distribution programs are needed throughout recipient nations.

Unfortunately, there are numerous examples of failures in using aid to build marketing infrastructures. A few of these involve roads, trucks, and processing facilities.

Roads. Aid and development agencies frequently build roads in less-developed countries to standards of the developed countries. When these roads are not maintained to the same codes, the original investment is wasted.

Trucks. Helping countries maintain a steady supply of spare parts and effective repair facilities gives better returns than supplying successive fleets of new vehicles.

Processing. Any technology that is introduced in a less-developed nation should be compatible. Risk is inherent. Technology may be unsuitable because of contrasting capital-to-labor cost ratios, inadequate supplies of raw materials, differences in consumer demands, problems of equipment maintenance, and inherent quality control abilities. For example, the advantages for using advanced technology in food packing and processing for export marketing have been established. The need to meet standards of quality set by developed countries can be a determining factor in a successful export business, e.g., abattoirs built in Central America have to meet standards in importing countries.

SUMMARY

Unfortunately, statements such as those made by World Development on October 2, 1989 constantly appear in our media: "Famine threatens more than 1.7 million people in Ethiopia's drought-stricken north unless relief supplies reach them soon. . . . This figure does not take into account the requirements of Eritreans and Tigrayans in areas under rebel control. . . . Stocks of relief food in Eritrea have fallen to about 10,000 tons, their lowest level since 1984, when famine in northern Ethiopia killed up to one million people. The UN estimates Ethiopia needs about 242,000 tons of emergency food supplies to avoid famine during the next 12 months. The UN says the drought is as serious as the last one in 1987-88, when a famine was only averted by the prompt response of western donors.''

Food aid remains a highly controversial subject. In a normal year, emergency food aid is no more than 10 to 15 percent of total food aid. Food aid has popular support; financial aid is unpopular. Food aid is vital for the welfare and survival of millions of people in poorer countries, particularly in Africa.

Reducing the barriers of distance and race, modern communication systems, television, and vivid reporting have brought the images of human disaster to millions of people throughout the developed world. Their response to harrowing scenes of malnutrition, starvation, and death continues to be generous.

REFERENCES

Bookwalter, G. N., R. J. Bothast, W. F. Kwolek, and M. Gumbmann. 1980. Nutritional stability of corn-soy-milk blends after dry heating to destroy *salmonellae*. *J. Food Sci.* 45: 975-980.

Bookwalter, George N. 1981. Requirements for foods containing soy protein in the Food for Peace program. *J. American Oil Chemical Society* 51: 455-460.

Bookwalter, George N. 1990. Nutritional improvement of foods for international assistance programs. In *Trends in nutrition and food policy*, ed. Ang How Ghee, 179-184. Paper presented at the 7th World Congress of Food Science and Technology, 28 Sept.—2 Oct., 1987, Singapore.

Hall, Lana L. 1985. United States food aid and the agricultural development of Brazil and Colombia, 1954-73. In *Food, politics, and society in Latin America*, eds. J. C. Super and T. C. Wright, 133-149. Lincoln and London: University of Nebraska Press.

Puchala, Donald J. 1989. The road to Rome: the production and distribution of food. In *Global issues in the United Nations' framework*, eds. P. Taylor and A. J. R. Groom, 177-204. New York: St. Martin's Press.

Singer, H., J. Wood, and T. Jennings. 1987. *Food aid—the challenge and the opportunity*. New York: Oxford University Press.

PART TWO:
AGRICULTURAL PRODUCTION, PROCESSING, AND CONSUMPTION AND YOU

Being familiar with the world food and agricultural situation and attempts to make it more equitable via world marketing systems and food aid, you are probably curious about the scientific principles behind our global food situation. The next five chapters start with the seed and end with food waste that is observed in restaurants. Because a great deal of the food that is grown, transported, stored, processed, stored, transported, stored, cooked, and served is wasted, the concept of food waste will be an important one for you to grasp. Specifically, the focus in agricultural production of plants and livestock is towards efficient production. In the following chapters, you will learn that the limited resources, including land, water, fertilizers, and pesticides need to be used as sparingly as possible. The goal is always to reduce prices that consumers must pay for foods.

Once you are familiar with crop production, animal production, fish and shellfish production, you will learn about food processing, distribution, and consumption which occurs at home and away from home throughout the world. You will observe that the discipline of food processing attempts to maximize the amount of food products that are ultimately available for the consumer, sometimes even turning food waste into useful products. You will learn about the controls that are implemented throughout the world to attempt to reduce food waste. However, in the consumption sector, food, packaging and energy waste occur. Except for your personal food plate waste, other wastes that occur in this sector are largely out of your hands. The end result is that after all of the scientific principles have been applied to growing, processing, and distributing crops and animals, excessive levels of food waste occur.

Having this information, you will be in an informed position to relate the total magnitude of the wasted resources that are reflected in food plate waste that you may observe each day.

Chapter Five

Production of Plants and Crops

INTRODUCTION

Plants, along with animals and microorganisms, contribute to our ecosystem which is defined as: "a network of energy and mineral flows in which the major functional components are the populations of plants, animals, and microorganisms." By studying the information in this chapter, you will become familiar with:

- the life cycle of plants, including the environmental factors that affect both their yield and quality;
- a few of the types of agricultural production systems used to grow crops to meet global food and fuel needs;
- the science of herbal medicine and how it helps humans by taking advantage of the global genetic diversity of plants.

All food throughout the world comes directly, or indirectly, from plants.

THE GLOBAL ECOSYSTEM

About 20 major crops and 10 major livestock types are cultured in agricultural production in the U.S. and Europe. About 200,000 species of wild plants, animals, and microorganisms exist in the U.S. Every year humans in the U.S. alone produce about 100×10^6 tons of organic waste; livestock produce 1500×10^6 tons. The efficient reducing organisms in the natural ecosystem, namely bacteria, fungi, protozoa, arthropods, and earthworms, all help to degrade these wastes. These organisms help recycle essential minerals for reuse by all components of the ecosystem including plants. Other organisms improve soil structure while decomposing organic matter. Others, such as earthworms and soil arthropods, assist with soil formation. Earthworms bring 2.5 to 63 tons of soil castings per hectare to the surface and ants carry up to 10 tons per hectare.

Solar Energy

The collection of solar energy to power the ecosystem depends directly on the plant population. Plants depend on solar energy to meet their energy needs. About 25 percent of the solar energy collected by them is used for their respiration, 35 percent for building and maintaining their structure, and 35 percent for their reproduction.

The amount of energy removed from the plant population by animals feeding on living plants, including humans, is about 5 percent. Because of the biological energy chain, energy from the sun is converted into energy for people.

Genetic Diversity

Because some plant strains are more productive than others, they are grown to the exclusion of other varieties. The narrowing of the genetic base of widely cultivated crops has wide implications. If crops are not resistant to them, unexpected plant pests might devastate the world's food supply. The precipitous rise in numbers of biotypes resistant to pesticides makes the management of this resistance imperative. These and other concerns have stimulated efforts to preserve old varieties and to search for more productive and resistant plant strains.

Genetic Resources

Germ plasm collections contain the genes for future crop improvement. They provide security for future sources of food, feed, and fiber. They are a major resource for solving the fundamental problems of agriculture and biology. Five thousand plant species have been used as human foods. Currently about 150 species meet the world's food needs. Plant products derived from about 30 species provide 90 percent of the material for the human diet.

Of the 5 to 10 million plant and animal species on earth, the rate of extinction of genetic resources is estimated at 1,000 per year and rising. Only 5 to 10 percent of the 250,000 to 750,000 existing species of higher plants have been surveyed for biologically active compounds. Adequate data is only available for 10 percent of the Amazon plants.

The world's primary germ plasm repositories are in Fort Collins, Colorado, U.S.; Vavilov All-Union Scientific Research Institute of Plant Industry, Leningrad, U.S.S.R.; Germ Plasm Center, Beijing, China; and the International Agricultural Research Centers (IARCs). The world's largest seed bank, housed in a three-story building on the Colorado State University campus in Fort Collins, has about 235,000 seed samples in paper and aluminum packets. This germ plasm is needed to breed crops more resistant to drought, pests, disease, salt, and other environmental factors that may be affected by the projected global warming trend. Many of these seeds came from developing countries.

Despite the fact that the U.S. is publicly committed to the free flow of germ plasm among nations, its trade has been banned with six countries considered unfriendly: North Korea, Cambodia, Nicaragua, Libya, Cuba, and Vietnam. Other international conflicts over property rights to genetic material occur.

What have been some direct benefits from research efforts with this germ plasm? American farmers are reaping four times the corn and potatoes per acre than 50 years ago. Wheat and rice yields have doubled. About one-half of these gains can be attributed to higher yielding crop varieties, bred with germ plasm from around the world.

Ethnobotany is the study of the ways tribal people use the plants in their rain forests, particularly as medicine. Given that rain forests are declining, this is a science in a hurry! As their habitats are decimated by landless peasants and timber merchants in the tropics and further eroded by urban and industrial sprawl in developed countries, thousands of species of plants and animals are vanishing every year. One-fifth of all global species of plants and animals may disappear over the next 20 years. Many of them, including hundreds of microorganisms and insects which could have medicinal value, have never been identified. From black rhinos in Africa to bowhead whales in Canada, many species have been driven to the brink of extinction by overexploitation.

Australia has lost 18 species of mammals and about 100 species of flowering plants since the European settlement occurred. Biologists in Australia estimate that about 40 species of mammals are at risk of extinction, as are 3,300 species of rare or endangered plants. As a large island, these data have been easier to obtain than in nations with many borders.

To summarize, at least 100 animal and plant species are disappearing each day. This rate is alarming and could be even higher. Scientists are unsure of how quickly species are actually dying off. Furthermore, they are not sure whether there were 4 million or 40 million species at the beginning of human history.

Forestation

Eight forest trees provide most of the world's wood and timber: eucalyptus, radiata pine, Douglas fir, loblolly pine, black locust, teak, Scotch pine, and aspen. All forests are decreasing in size. Exact figures on the forest clearing are hard to come by, but authorities say the problem is real.

Huge tracts of tropical rain forest have been cleared to make way for crops as well as rubber plantations to supply condoms and rubber gloves to the world trying to prevent the spread of AIDS. There is a lot of truth to the saying: "Central American forests went into hamburgers and the Southeast Asian forests are going into condoms and rubber gloves." The latex used to produce gloves and condoms is the most valued rubber product, so it has a disproportionate impact on the market.

LIFE CYCLE OF PLANTS

The unique ability of green plant cells to absorb light energy and convert it into chemical energy is one of the most important biological processes. The term photosynthesis has been applied to the process in which a pigment system absorbs electromagnetic radiation and converts this into chemical forms of energy which are available for growth in a particular environment.

In higher plants, light absorption is brought about by chlorophyll and carotenoids. These are constituents of the chloroplasts. The unique feature of these two pigments is their ability to absorb light and convert it to chemical energy.

Plant Nutrients

Plants have the ability to take substances from the environment and use them for the synthesis of their own cellular components and their own source of energy needed for growth to occur. The essential nutrients required by higher plants are inorganic in nature and are listed in Exhibit 5.1. They have been grouped according to their biochemical behavior and physiological function.

Exhibit 5.1. Classification of Plant Nutrients.

Nutrient Element	Uptake	Biochemical Functions
1st group C, H, O, N, S	in the form of CO_2, HCO_3^-, H_2O, O_2, NO_3^-, NH_4^+, N_2, SO_4^{2-}, SO_2. The ions from the soil solution, the gases from the atmosphere.	Major constituent of organic material. Essential elements of atomic groups which are involved in enzymic processes. Assimilation by oxidation-reduction reactions.
2nd group P, B, Si	in the form of phosphates, boric acid or borate, silicate from the soil solution.	Esterification with native alcohol groups in plants. The phosphate esters are involved in energy transfer reactions.
3rd group K, Na, Mg, Ca, Mn, Cl	in the form of ions from the soil solution.	Non-specific functions establishing osmotic potentials. More specific reactions in which the ion brings about optimum conformation of an enzyme protein (enzyme activation). Bridging of the reaction partners. Balancing anions. Controlling membrane permeability and electro-potentials.
4th group Fe, Cu, Zn, Mo	in the form of ions or chelates from the soil solution.	Present predominantly in a chelated form incorporated in prosthetic groups. Enable electron transport by valency change.

Source: Mengel, K. and E. A. Kirby. 1987. *Principles in Plant Nutrition*, 4th ed. International Potash Institute, Berne, Switzerland.

Group One includes the major constituents of organic plant material. Carbon is taken up in the form of carbon dioxide from the atmosphere and possibly as HCO_3 from soil solution. These compounds are assimilated by a process known as carboxylation, and are accompanied by the assimilation of oxygen. Hydrogen is taken up in the form of water from the soil solution, or from the atmosphere under humid conditions. Nitrogen comes from the nitrate or ammonium from the soil solution or as gaseous ammonia and nitrogen from the atmosphere. Sulfur is taken up from the soil solution in the form of SO_4^2 and sulfur dioxide from the atmosphere. All the reactions which result in the incorporation of the compounds in Group One into organic molecules are basic physiological processes of plant metabolism.

Group Two compounds are absorbed as inorganic anions or acids. In plant cells, they either occur in these forms or are bound largely by hydroxyl groups of sugars forming phosphate-, borate-, and silicate-esters.

Group Three nutrients are taken up from the soil solution in the form of ions. In the plant cell, they are in the free ionic state or are bound to other compounds, e.g., calcium is bound to a group of pectins; magnesium is chelated and bound to the chlorophyll molecule.

Group Four elements are predominantly present as chelates in the plant.

The exclusive requirement of higher plants for inorganic nutrients distinguishes plants from man, animals, and a number of microorganisms which need some organic foodstuffs. To achieve desired crop yields, all of these nutrients must be available in required concentrations during various life stages of the plants. The chemical fertilizer industry is based upon supplying these nutrients when they are not otherwise available.

Germination

For the process of germination to occur, soil embedded seeds require an optimum temperature and a supply of water and oxygen as well as favorable endogenous factors within the seeds. The endogenous factors are mainly phytohormones such as indole acetic acid. The germination process depends on their synthesis or decomposition. Phytohormones are produced in plants in low concentrations and they regulate all physiological processes within the plant. In recent years, growth regulators or chemicals have been used in agriculture to influence the phytohormone turnover. Such regulators can be focused on influencing different stages of plant growth.

With water uptake, the swollen seeds provide the necessary conditions for respiration. With oxygen uptake, the seed reserves of carbohydrates, fats, and proteins are oxidized to carbon dioxide and water, and energy is released in the form of adenosine triphosphate (ATP) and nicotinamide adenine dinucleotide (NADPH). This form of energy is essential for the growth processes. The storage proteins are hydrolyzed and their amino acids are used for the synthesis of enzyme proteins and nucleic acids.

The first organ to be developed is the root, which is responsible for the uptake of water and nutrients. Next, shoot growth starts and photosynthesis is induced as soon as it breaks through the soil surface. Light and carbon dioxide in the atmosphere now become additional growth factors for the plants. As young leaves develop, they are supplied with carbohydrates and amino acids, thus depleting the storage material of the seed. With the onset of their vegetative stages, characterized by rapid development of leaves, stems, and roots, they receive nutrients from older leaves. The photosynthates assimilated in the older leaves provide the source of nutrients for the younger leaves. Mature leaves export about 50 percent of their photosynthates; the remainder are used for leaf metabolism. As occurred in the seeds, carbohydrates in the leaves are oxidized to carbon dioxide and water, releasing energy as ATP. This development is characterized in Exhibit 5.2.

Reproduction

The reproductive stage begins with flower initiation. The maturation stage begins after pollination or anthesis has occurred. In determinate plants such as cereals, the vegetative and reproductive stages are quite distinct. In indeterminate plants, such as certain tomato varieties, these stages overlap. As plant growth progresses from the vegetative stage to maturity, photosynthates are directed away from the younger tissues to the storage tissues.

Exhibit 5.2. Assimilation and Distribution of Photosynthates at Different Stages in Growth

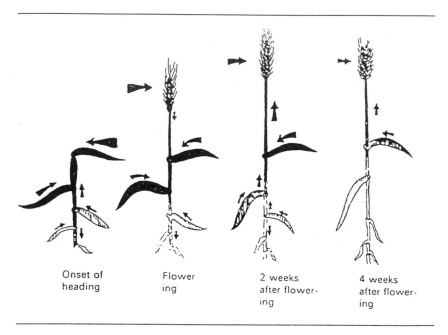

| Onset of heading | Flowering | 2 weeks after flowering | 4 weeks after flowering |

Source: Mengel, K. and E. A. Kirby. 1987. *Principles in Plant Nutrition*, 4th ed. International Potash Institute, Berne, Switzerland.

Pollination is less complex in corn, for example, because the carrier is wind, but is more complex in crops such as cotton because it involves insects as carriers. Much of the pollination is performed by bees. For example, in New York State over 8×10^{12} blossoms may be pollinated in a single day by both wild and tame bees. An individual honeybee may visit as many as 800 blossoms on a bright sunny day, making about 10 trips and visiting 80 blossoms per trip.

Photosynthesis

Without the process of photosynthesis throughout the world, there would be no oxygen, plants, food, or people. In fact, if you study all of the disparities among the human race, the total and absolute reliance upon photosynthesis is one of the features we all share. Plants using photosynthesis are the most important and the only renewable energy resource, the only major source of oxygen, and the basic food manufacturing process. As the world food situation worsens, our supplies of nonrenewable energy will diminish and the entrapment of solar energy through photosynthesis will prove more valuable than all of the energy reserves that will be diminished.

The word photosynthesis means putting together with light. It may be defined as: "the process by which the chlorophyll-containing cells in green plants capture the energy of the sun and convert it into chemical energy." It is the action through which plants synthesize and store organic compounds, especially carbohydrate, from inorganic compounds, carbon dioxide, water and minerals, with the simultaneous release of oxygen.

Photosynthesis is dependent upon the presence of chlorophyll, a green pigment which develops in plants soon after they emerge from the soil. As a chemical catalyst, chlorophyll stimulates and makes possible certain chemical reactions without becoming involved in the reaction itself. By drawing upon the energy from the sun, it converts inorganic molecules, carbon dioxide and water, into energy-rich organic molecules such as glucose, and at the same time releases free oxygen.

Through this process, more than a billion tons of carbon per day are converted from inorganic carbon dioxide to organic sugars (glucose) which can then be converted into the three main groups of organic materials of all living matter: carbohydrates, fats, and proteins. Basic steps of this complicated process are diagrammed in Exhibit 5.3.

Photosynthesis is a series of many complex chemical reactions involving two stages. During the first stage, the water molecule is split into hydrogen and oxygen. Oxygen is released into the atmosphere. Hydrogen is combined with certain organic compounds, and forms energy rich ATP, keeping it available for use in the second step of photosynthesis. Chlorophyll and light are involved in this stage, as indicated in Exhibit 5.3.

During the second stage, which is dependent on temperature,

Exhibit 5.3. Diagram of the Photosynthetic Process.

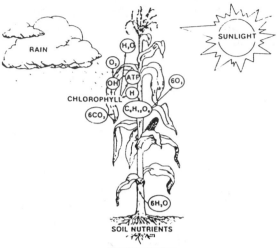

PHOTOSYNTHESIS

LIGHT REACTIONS:	DARK REACTIONS:
WHERE: IN GREEN MESOPHYLL OF LEAVES.	WHERE: IN STROMA OF CHLOROPLAST OF LEAVES.
REQUIRES: CHLOROPHYLL ENERGY FROM SUNLIGHT.	REQUIRES: DOES NOT REQUIRE LIGHT OR CHLOROPHYLL, BUT REQUIRES ENERGY-RICH ATP.
PRODUCES: ENERGY-RICH ATP.	PRODUCES: GLUCOSE-ENERGY-RICH CARBON COMPOUNDS.

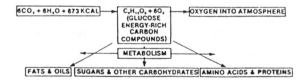

Fig. P-31. Photosynthesis fixes energy. Diagrammatic summary of (1) photosynthesis, and (2) the metabolic formation of organic compounds from the simple sugars. This diagram shows the following:

1. Carbon dioxide gas from the air enters the green mesophyll cells of plant leaves.
2. Plants take up oxygen from the air for some of their metabolic processes and release oxygen back to the air from other metabolic processes.
3. Plants take up water and essential elements from the soil.
4. The energy essential to photosynthesis is absorbed by chlorophyll and supplied by sunlight.
5. For a net input of 6 molecules of carbon dioxide and 6 molecules of water, there is a net output of 1 molecule of sugar and 6 molecules of oxygen.
6. The process is divided into light and dark reactions, with the light reactions building up the energy-rich ATP required for the dark reactions.
7. In the process, 673 Calories (kcal) of energy are used.
8. The sugar (glucose) manufactured in photosynthesis may be converted into fats and oils, sugars and other carbohydrates, and amino acids and proteins.

Source: Ensminger, A. H., M. E. Ensminger, J. E. Konlande, and J. R. K. Robson. 1986. *Food for Health*, published by Pegus Press, 648 West Sierra Ave., Clovis, CA 93612, with the permission of the Ensmingers and the publisher.

dark reactions occur. Carbon dioxide combines with the released hydrogen to form the simple sugars and water. This reaction is energized by ATP, a stored source of energy. Neither chlorophyll nor light are involved in this stage.

The basic equation for photosynthesis is:

$$6CO_2 + 6H_2O + 673 \text{ kcal} \longrightarrow C_6H_{12}O_6 + 6O_2$$

The light phase is also known as the Hill Reaction. Light is responsible for the process of photolysis when water is cleaved to make the energy-rich carbon compounds.

Plants are classified as C3, C4, or Crassulacean acid metabolism (CAM), partially depending on their efficiencies. C3 plants, e.g., soybeans, are inefficient and lose carbon dioxide by a process known as photorespiration. C4 plants, e.g., corn and sugarcane, are very efficient and are able to recapture carbon dioxide. CAM plants are drought-tolerant because they have the ability to fix carbon dioxide in the dark when their stomata are closed. Cacti are CAM plants.

Photosynthesis is limited to plants; animals store energy in their products, i.e., milk, meat, and eggs. All animals depend upon plants to manufacture their energy.

Is photosynthesis efficient? The answer to this question is no. Of the energy that leaves the sun, only 2 percent reaches green plants, and 1 percent is transformed by photosynthesis. Only 5 percent of this plant-captured energy is fixed in a form suitable as food for man. Ruminant animals are the solution to the latter; they can convert inedible plant materials into food for humans. If genetic engineering techniques are ever able to manipulate plants to increase this solar energy conversion, the supply of crops around the world could be increased.

However, with respect to crop yields, the ultimate limit may be photosynthetic efficiency. When specified amounts of nutrients and water are supplied to advanced crop varieties, cereal yields may now be approaching the photosynthesis limit. Photosynthetic efficiency is set by the laws of physics and chemistry. As the genetic potential of high-yielding varieties approaches this limit, their response to the use of additional fertilizer diminishes. Advances in plant breeding, including those using biotechnology, can hasten the goal of reaching the photosynthetic limit. At this point, crop yields will be optimum with the effective use of other supporting factors. There is little hope of altering the basic mechanics of photosynthesis.

Leaf Area Index

In crops, carbon dioxide is being continuously fixed by photosynthesis and released by respiration. The net amount of carbon assimilated is often termed net assimilation. It is measured by the excess carbon gained from photosynthesis over that lost by respiration. The net assimilation rate can be defined as: "the net assimilation of carbon dioxide per unit leaf area."

In the process of respiration, molecular oxygen is taken up by plants and assimilates are oxidized to carbon dioxide and water. In dark or mitochondrial respiration, the oxidation process is accompanied by ATP synthesis. Some green plant cells are capable of light-induced respiration or photorespiration. In this process, ATP is not produced. Photorespiration is absent in C4 crops such as maize and sugarcane. Thus, the compensation point shown in Exhibit 5.4 is different for C3 and C4 plants, with the latter showing a net positive assimilation rate at very low carbon dioxide levels at the leaf surfaces. Both carbon dioxide assimilation and respiration rates increase with temperature. As shown in Exhibit 5.4, a temperature point occurs where the rate of assimilation equals that of respiration. At this point, no net growth can occur.

The higher the density of plants in a particular crop stand, the more they compete for water, nutrients, and light. Mutual shading can increase susceptibility to fungal diseases. In very dense stands, competition for light is often the limiting growth factor, given other optimal conditions. The density of a crop population is expressed as "leaf area index." Some examples of optimal values for various crops are given in Exhibit 5.5.

The degree of utilization of radiation energy by plants is low. Under optimum conditions, the maximum efficiency of utilization of radiation energy for crop production is about 5 percent. The remaining 95 percent of radiation energy is converted into heat. In advanced agricultural systems with intensive cropping, plants of the

Exhibit 5.4. Rates of Carbon Dioxide Assimilation and Respiration in Relation to Temperature.

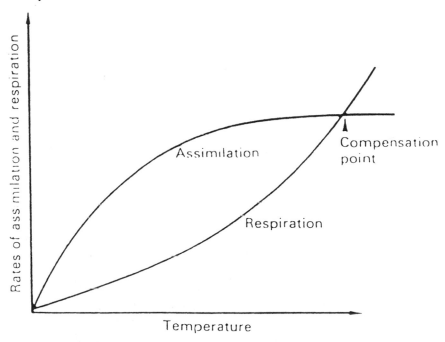

Source: Mengel, K. and E. A. Kirby. 1987. *Principles in Plant Nutrition*, 4th ed. International Potash Institute, Berne, Switzerland.

C3 type use about 2.7 percent of the available radiation energy for their production of dry matter. The comparative figure for C4 plants is 4 percent. In high radiation climates, such as those found around the Mediterranean, both plant yields and the efficiencies of energy conversions tend to be higher than in low radiation climates, such as that found in Finland.

PRODUCT YIELDS OF PLANTS

The biological yield of a crop may be defined as: "the total production of plant material." The economic yield of a crop may be defined as: "the production of the particular plant organs for which

Exhibit 5.5. Optimum Leaf Area Index (LAI) Values for Some Crops.

Soybeans	3.2
Maize	5.0
Sugar beet	3.2 - 6.0
Wheat	6.0 - 8.8
Rice (new varieties)	7
Rice (local varieties)	4

Source: Mengel, K. and E. A. Kirby. 1987. *Principles in Plant Nutrition*, 4th ed. International Potash Institute, Berne, Switzerland.

the crop was grown." The latter definition includes cotton bolls for cotton production, cereal seeds for cereal production, potato tubers for potato production, and so on.

For most crop plants, plant development during the vegetative stage controls both the biological and economic yields. During this period, plant tissues are formed, providing photosynthates for seeds or storage tissues. As vegetative growth consists mainly of the growth and formation of new leaves, stems, and roots, active protein metabolism occurs during this stage. Thus, to a large extent, the nitrogen nutrition of the plant controls the growth rate of the plant. A high growth rate only occurs when abundant nitrogen is available. When the level of nitrogen nutrition is inadequate, the life cycle of the plants is shortened, plants mature earlier, and the economic yield is reduced.

Thus, a balance in the plant is needed between the rate of photosynthate production and the rate of nitrogen assimilation. Under conditions when high photosynthate production can occur, such as high light intensity, optimum temperature, and absence of water stress, the level of nitrogen must be adequate. In species of plants which assimilate carbon dioxide by the C4 pathway, the nitrogen demand is considerable when growth conditions are optimized. In addition to nitrogen, other nutrients are required: Mg^{2+} for the formation of chlorophyll, phosphate for the synthesis of nucleic acids, and potassium for the uptake of nitrates, assimilation into protein, and growth and elongation functions. In summary, when the rate of photosynthate production is high, the amounts of inorganic nutrients must also be correspondingly high in order to convert the photosynthates into the numerous metabolites needed for vegetative growth. As a consequence of selection and plant breeding, yields of plant parts have increased at least ten times more than have wild species. However, the carbon exchange rate per unit leaf area, i.e., the net carbon dioxide assimilation, has not been changed by these man-made changes of domestication.

Grain Yields

Grain yield depends on three main yield components: number of ears per hectare, number of grains per ear, and the single weight of each grain. The number of ears per hectare depends on seed density and tillering capability. Although genetically controlled, the latter is also dependent on environmental factors. Tillering is favored by: short days, high light intensities, low temperatures and adequate nitrogen supplies — the conditions favoring phytohormone activities. In critical growing phases such as heading and flowering, water stress, or water loss from plant tissues, should be reduced. One technique used which has been associated with longer ears, larger grains, and thus higher grain yields of wheat, is to reduce plant densities in arid conditions.

The number of grains produced per ear is affected by nutrition and environmental factors. The grain size or single grain weight is genetically controlled but also depends on environmental factors which influence the process of grain filling during maturation. The diagrams in Exhibit 5.2 illustrate that after the onset of flowering, photosynthates are increasingly used for the grain filling process. The arrows indicate the direction that the photosynthates are translocated. The plant parts shown in black are the most important parts for assimilation. An intensive rate of grain filling is obtained if the level of nitrogen nutrition is high during the grain filling period and the potassium status of the plant is at an optimum level.

Data displayed in Exhibit 5.6 representing the average yields of soybeans in North and Central America illustrate large differences between the two regions, because of the wide variety of growing conditions. Note that the country with the coldest climate and short-

Exhibit 5.6. Yields of Soybeans in North and Central America—1988.

Country	Yield (Kg/HA)
Canada	2180
Costa Rica	1667
El Salvador	1839
Guatemala	1706
Mexico	1176
Nicaragua	1619
U.S.	1803

Source: *FAO Production Yearbook*. Vol. 42. 1988. Food and Agriculture Organization of the United Nations: Rome.

est growing season had the highest yield per hectare. Variations such as these are to be expected whenever average yield data are given for a nation or region.

Maize Yields

Maize can be grown under various climatic conditions given that the temperature is not too low. Good grain yields can be obtained with high temperatures (86-91°F) during the day and relatively cool nights. Maize responds favorably to a high level of nitrogen supply. Maximum grain yields are obtained only if water stress is avoided. Inadequate potassium nutrition favors root and stalk rot and leads to inadequately formed cobs.

Root Crop Yields

For root crops such as potatoes, the factors which influence product yield are: number of plants per hectare, number of tubers per plant, and size of the tubers. Tuber growth is initiated by the phytohormones. Long days restrict tuber initiation and short days with low night temperatures promote their initiation. Tuber growth is closely related to carbohydrate supply, which depends on the intensity of carbon dioxide assimilation of the aerial parts of the plant as well as on the translocation rate of the photosynthates from the leaves to the tubers. For good tuber yields, a high rate of carbon dioxide assimilation during the tuber filling stage is required. During the early stages of development of root crops, they should have sufficient supplies of nitrogen. After flowering, nitrogen supplies should be reduced, promoting the synthesis of dry matter in the tubers instead of leaf material. The economic yield of root crops is closely associated with this accumulation process.

Fruit Crop Yields

A main factor in fruit yield is the quantity of fruits per tree or plant. Fruit setting is related to phytohormone activity and nutrition. Plantation crops such as oil palm, coconut, bananas, and pineapple are not strictly bound to seasons. Their growth and yield depend on an ample supply of nutrients.

Yield Curves

The diagram in Exhibit 5.7 gives a yield curve such as might occur with the addition of nitrogen to wheat. The highest yield increment results from the first unit of nitrogen applied. With successive applications, the yield increment units become smaller, leading to the diminishing response curve diagrammed.

In some cases, yields can be depressed as nutrients are increased. High nitrogen application rates in cereals can increase the susceptibility of the crop to fungal diseases, and physiological disorders may occur. For example, increasing nitrogen nutrition may lead to an excess of soluble amino acids which cannot be used for growth when other nutrients are scarce. Excessive potassium can depress uptake of magnesium, leading to depressed yields. High levels of potassium can reduce the availability of heavy metals, especially copper, further depressing yields.

To summarize, the actual yields achieved during a given season result from numerous physical, chemical, biochemical, and physio-

Exhibit 5.7. Response Curve Showing Diminishing Increments.

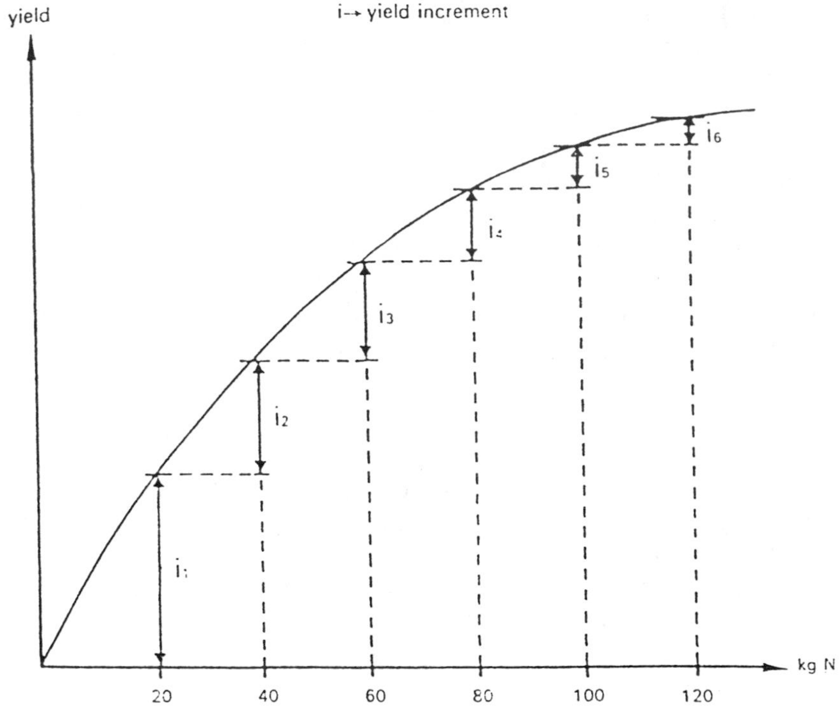

Source: Mengel, K. and E. A. Kirby. 1987. *Principles in Plant Nutrition*, 4th ed. International Potash Institute, Berne, Switzerland.

logical processes, all of which are influenced by other factors which vary throughout the growing period.

PLANT QUALITY

Quality standards are related to the intended use of the plant. For example, very different qualities in barley are required for alternate uses, which vary from malting barley for beer to use as animal feed. Potato tubers used for french fries at McDonald's have vastly different quality requirements than those used for vodka. The major factors controlling crop quality are genetic ones. Potato tuber proteins differ considerably among potato cultivars or varieties. However, exogenous factors can influence the levels of organic compounds in plants, and thus their inherent quality characteristics. The content of carbohydrates or sugars in storage tissues, grains, and seeds is related to the photosynthetic activity of the plant and to the translocation rate of photosynthates to the storage parts of the plant.

Root Crops

Two crop examples, potatoes and sugar beets, serve to illustrate quality parameters affected by plant nutrition. In the case of potatoes, potassium promotes carbon dioxide assimilation and the translocation of carbohydrates from the leaves to their tubers. Although there are excessive limits when the plants have a high level of potassium, their starch content is also high. The sensitivity of potato tubers to damage caused by mechanical harvesting or by transportation is also influenced by nutrition.

The quality of sugar beets depends primarily on sugar content, but it is also affected by the content of soluble amino compounds, and by the content of potassium and sodium. Soluble amino compounds and minerals disturb crystallization during sugar refining, affecting the sugar output. This can be avoided by increasing the potassium nutrition to an adequate level. During the initial period of beet's growth, abundant nitrogen supply is necessary. Later, the supply of nitrogen should decline. If the availability of nitrogen is not decreased, sugar beets have low sugar contents and high concentrations of amino compounds and minerals. Sugar beet quality is also dependent on environmental factors. When water stress occurs, the root growth is poor. Ideal sugar yields are obtained when high light intensity conditions prevail during the last weeks of the sugar beet growth period and when adequate water is available. Thus, the optimum application of fertilizers coupled with irrigation have a direct effect on the quality of sugar beets.

Grain Crops

Grain baking quality is very important to the food processing industry. Wheat cultivars grown under the arid conditions of Canada or southeastern Europe are hard wheat types with high baking qualities. Cultivars grown under more humid conditions are of poorer baking quality. The most important constituent determining the baking quality of cereals is gluten. Nitrogen supplied to cereals at flowering increases the protein content of the grains and improves baking quality, giving greater levels of dough tenacity.

The feeding quality of proteins is mainly determined by the content of crude protein and the proportion of their essential amino acids. The essential amino acids shown in Exhibit 5.8 cannot be synthesized by humans or animals. They must be supplied as constituents of the human and animal diets. Grains low in lysine have poor protein quality. The poor quality grain proteins of wheat, barley, and maize cannot be improved substantially by plant nutrition. Given that these grains have a major role in human nutrition around the world, the improvement of grain proteins is a challenging target for plant breeders. When lysine-rich cultivars have been developed, the increase in lysine content has frequently been offset by a lower grain production.

Barley and Beer

When barley is used for malting during the making of beer, low protein and high starch contents are required. Because large grains are richer in carbohydrates, the kernels of barley should be large. These qualities have been improved by the scientific application of phosphate and potassium fertilizers.

The content of carbohydrates and the content of proteins in grains and cereals depends to a large extent on the nitrogen supply during grain or seed maturation. If the nitrogen supply is low during this stage of growth, a higher proportion of photosynthates is used for

Exhibit 5.8. Essential Amino Acids in Human Nutrition.

Valine	Threonine	Phenylalanine
Leucine	Methionine	Tryptophan
Isoleucine	Lysine	

Source: Mengel, K. and E. A. Kirby. 1987. *Principles in Plant Nutrition*, 4th ed. International Potash Institute, Berne, Switzerland.

the synthesis of carbohydrates. With abundant nitrogen supplies, a larger proportion will be converted to proteins. In cereals, protein synthesis and starch synthesis compete for photosynthates during the grain filling period.

Oil Crops

In oil crops, there is great competition for photosynthates between the formation of crude protein and oils. Seed oils grown at low temperatures are comparatively richer in unsaturated fatty acids than in saturated acids. This is caused by the greater oxygen pressure in the seeds which favors the denaturation of saturated to unsaturated fatty acids since oxygen is required for this oxidation.

Forage Crops

The quality of forage crops such as herbage, i.e., grasses and clover used as pasture or as hay, depends on the digestibility of the fodder. Digestibility decreases as the content of crude fiber, i.e., cellulose, hemicellulose, and lignin, increases. These compounds accumulate as the plant ages. Old forage crops have poorer quality than younger ones. The digestibility of forages is influenced by fertilizer applications. Generally, high nitrogen application leads to an increase in the proportion of grasses. Potassium and phosphorous fertilizers favor the production of quality legumes.

How many cuts can be harvested in a year frequently depends on soil moisture. In arid conditions, water can be the limiting factor to forage growth. Under these conditions, mixed swards of grasses and legumes are more resistant to water shortages and other unfavorable influences.

Forage crops contain energy in the form of carbohydrates, fats, proteins, and the organic constituents required for animal growth and the production of milk, eggs, or wool. Fodder supplies livestock with the essential minerals such as phosphorous, sulfur, calcium, sodium, magnesium, potassium, and heavy metals. Under conditions of intensive production, mineral shortages can occur. For example, for milk production, dairy cows require considerable amounts of sodium, magnesium, calcium, and phosphorous. If they are not provided these nutrients, their milk production will decrease.

Vegetables and Fruits

Taste and flavor of fruits can be influenced by mineral nutrition to a limited extent. Weather conditions and other climatic factors play an important role. Apples grown under high light intensities and temperatures are sweeter and have lower acid contents than the same variety of apples grown under more humid and cold conditions. High light intensity favors the synthesis of Vitamin C and taste and flavor constituents.

ENVIRONMENTAL FACTORS AFFECTING PLANTS

During the discussions about crop yields and qualities, several environmental factors were mentioned which influenced these attributes. Because of the possibility of pending water shortages and increased soil salinity discussed in Chapter Two, the effect of these two environmental factors on the plant structures themselves will be discussed.

Water Stress

Water stress in plants is one of the major factors limiting crop production throughout the world. Research has shown that water stress can bring on many different physiological effects. Water loss from plant tissues causes changes in the spacial relationships of the cellular membranes and influences the metabolic processes. Some changes include: decreased turgor pressure in plant cells, decreased enzyme levels, alterations of some of the phytohormones, inhibition of stomatal opening and photosynthesis, severe reduction in the uptake of carbon dioxide, and so on.

When the water availability in the soil is poor and transpiration is high, i.e., the loss of water by the plant is greater than its uptake, the plants wilt and growth is inhibited. Irrigation is a practical method of avoiding water stress. The water requirement of crops differs between growth stages.

In humid conditions where the soil water capacity is high, water deficits are not common. In arid climates, water stress of crop plants is of major significance. In addition, when nutrients are not sufficient, water is less efficiently used for crop production.

Water Balance

The water potential of the atmosphere is usually lower than the water potential of the soil. Exhibit 5.9 shows the water pathways in plants. The greatest amount of water transpired by crop plants is released through the stomatal pores which are mainly located on the undersides of leaves. Stomata enable gaseous exchange between the leaf and the atmosphere.

Salinity

Soil salinity, a worldwide problem, occurs mainly in arid and semiarid regions when there is an excess of inorganic salts. A physical process known as evapotranspiration causes a rise in the ground water which contains salts, especially in low-lying areas of the world. In these soils, both the yield and quality of crops is poor. For example, sugarcane grown on saline sites is often poor quality because it is low in sugar and contains very high levels of minerals and amino compounds which interfere with the subsequent refining process.

Salinity problems also occur when irrigation is applied to impermeable soils. The irrigation waters contain salts which accumulate in the upper soil layer. In saline soils, plant growth is affected by: (1) high concentrations of specific ions that are toxic and cause physiological disorders, (2) ionic imbalances caused by high salt concentrations, and (3) soluble salts which depress the water potential of the nutrient medium and restrict water uptake by plant roots. Depending on specific conditions, one or more of a number of ions (Na^+, Cl^-, HCO_3^-, Mg^{2+}, SO_4^{2-}, and borate) may be present within the root range in high enough concentrations to affect crop growth.

Great differences occur in salt tolerance among plant species. Some species prevent excess salt uptake and thus protect plant cells against ion concentrations that are too high. Most fruit crops are more sensitive to salinity than are field, forage, or vegetable crops.

Exhibit 5.9. Water Pathways in the Higher Plant.

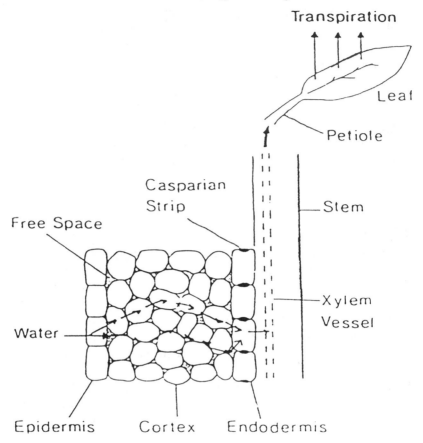

Source: Mengel, K. and E. A. Kirby. 1987. *Principles in Plant Nutrition*, 4th ed. International Potash Institute, Berne, Switzerland.

For crop production, salinity is measured as the electrical conductivity (EC) of a water-saturated soil extract. A high level of conductivity, expressed in mmhos/cm, indicates higher ion concentration in the composition of the extract. Exhibit 5.10 gives information about salt tolerance of various field crops. The extent of the detrimental effects from the EC levels shown in Exhibit 5.10 are also affected by the stage of plant growth; the seedling stage is the

Exhibit 5.10. Salt Tolerance of Various Field Crops at Conductivity at Which the Yield is Reduced by 25%.

	EC		EC
Barley	15.8	Rice (paddy)	6.2
Sugar beet	13.0	Maize	6.2
Cotton	12.0	Sesbania	5.8
Safflower	11.3	Broadbean (Vicia)	5.0
Wheat	10.0	Flax	4.8
Sorghum	9.0	Beans (Phaseolus)	2.5
Soybean	7.2		

Source: Mengel, K. and E. A. Kirby. 1987. *Principles in Plant Nutrition*, 4th ed. International Potash Institute, Berne, Switzerland.

most sensitive. Grain yields are generally less affected than straw yields. For rice, tillering, ear development, and grain production are all affected by salinity levels. As with sugarcane, salinity results in reduced sugar levels in sugar beets.

There is a great need to breed economic crops which are salt tolerant. With salt-tolerant crops, the oceans' water and mineral resources could be used without the expensive process of industrial desalination. There are enormous expenses associated with saline soils.

Soil: Plant Nutrient Medium

Soil is a heterogeneous material which consists of solid, liquid, and gaseous phases which influence the supply of nutrients to plant roots. The liquid phase is actually the soil solution, responsible for the transport of nutrients from various parts of the soil to the plant roots. Nutrients in the three phases are closely interrelated.

Colloidal soil particles are mostly negatively charged. This fact is used for the development of fertilizers with nutrients which will be held by the soil and thus available for the plants.

The solid phase of the soil is made up of inorganic and organic components. The relative proportion of inorganic fractions of different particle sizes determines the texture of the soil.

The higher the clay content of the soil, the more important the soil structure. Clay minerals absorb water which causes swelling of the soil. Both swelling and shrinkage depend on the availability of water. Clay soils such as tropical black earths swell in the wet season and become sticky; in the dry season, they dry out to such an extent that they become rock-hard and severe cracking results. Thus, in spite of their high nutrient content, the poor structure of these soils limits their agricultural potential.

An additional nutrient loss in soil can be caused by erosion. Large quantities of soil are being permanently moved from agricultural land to rivers and lakes. Because this material contains a high proportion of fine soil particles, considerable amounts of plant nutrients can be lost. The degree of erosion depends upon the amount of rainfall, the relief of the land, and the soil cover of the land. Under fallow conditions, the effects of erosion are more pronounced. On soils susceptible to erosion, no-tillage or minimum tillage procedures are recommended.

Policies in the U.S. have provided for 13 million hectares of agricultural lands to be converted to grasslands and woodlands before severe erosion produces a wasteland. With these and other efforts, the U.S. has reduced soil loss by one-fifth since 1985, slowing the depletion of nutrients from the soils.

In many soils, the rate of removal of plant nutrients by crop uptake, leaching, and denitrification exceeds the nutrient release by weathering and mineralization. Fertilizers and manure are applied to reduce the negative nutrient balance.

ENERGY AND FOOD PRODUCTION

Shrinking per capita fuel supplies have put pressure on farmers throughout the world. Nitrogenous fertilizers are made almost exclusively with natural gas; crop drying is done primarily with liquid propane gas; and tractor fuels, herbicides, and insecticides are all petroleum-based products. Coal reserves are almost useless in agriculture. The side effects of industrial agriculture, i.e., increased energy costs per unit of output, may be a significant threat to the system's and society's sustainability.

When expressed in terms of available energy supplies, the quality of the U.S. agricultural resource base is declining. The amount of food produced per unit of energy is declining. Future agricultural policies which emphasize raising production without increasing input/output efficiencies will be expensive. As domestic energy supplies decline, maintaining agricultural production will become a severe problem.

Considerable research is needed in technologies for reducing the energy-intensiveness of agriculture. Research areas include organic and regenerative farming and integrated pest management, to name a few. Nomenclature for some of the new production systems includes such terms as: sustainable, regenerative, alternative, agroecological, biological farming, ecologically healthy systems, holistic, closed-system agriculture, and stewardship. Many of them will focus on the concept of "sustainability" discussed in Chapter Two. Numerous reasons or needs justify focusing on alternative agriculture and food production systems: resource-sparing technologies; environmental constraints; regenerative agriculture; ecologically sustainable production systems; human health and food safety; improved nutrition; and the preservation of land, water, mineral, energy, and genetic resources.

CROP PRODUCTIVITY

Crop productivity may be defined as: "the ratio of the value of all the outputs of crop growth divided by the total of all the inputs for that growth." This definition implies having efficient use and management of resource inputs including land, water, energy, climate, fertilizers, pesticides, labor, and machinery.

Traditionally, six major areas have been identified as affecting crop productivity: nitrogen input; carbon input; water, soil, and mineral input; plant protection from pests; environmental stress; and plant development processes. The potential for biotechnology to provide new products and new plant cultivars has changed this emphasis.

New areas of research proposed in 1985 are summarized in Exhibit 5.11. These areas include: genetic improvement, plant and cell physiology, rhizosphere dynamics, biological constraints, environmental constraints, and production systems. These areas of research demand a reevaluation of social, political, and policy issues to govern the nature and intensity of research efforts. Therefore, sociopolitical research efforts have also been recommended.

Public policies are needed to enhance crop productivity and develop scientific capabilities including human resources, institutions, and government/industry/university interactions.

Information about research activities given in Exhibit 5.11 can be used to summarize the complex nature of crop productivity and its integral relationship with the environment. As worldwide conferences on the environment are held, such as in Bergen, Norway in May 1990, these needs for global agricultural production will undoubtedly be discussed. Courses in Crop Science will be dealing with all of the concepts presented in Exhibit 5.11.

Mixed Cropping Systems

Mixed cropping systems can reduce failures that occur when only a single crop is planted. They provide maximum returns from land, water, and labor resources, optimizing the use of sunlight, moisture, and soil nutrients. Compared to typical monocultures, they reduce the spread and the severity of pests. They may substantially increase food production compared to single crop programs.

Many examples exist which emphasize some of the advantages of selected mixed cropping systems. For example, researchers in Nairobi were surprised to find malnutrition among the families of relatively well-paid sugarcane workers. Upon investigation, they determined that a system of multiple cropping would enable these workers to grow more food for their families. By a marginal widening of the row crop spacing of sugarcane, they found room for two protein-rich, noncash crops, i.e., maize and beans, which could be harvested within 3 months of planting. As sugarcane takes 22 months to mature, it was possible to plant two successive inter-row

Exhibit 5.11. Research Needs for Agriculture Production and the Environment.

DEVELOP A THOROUGH UNDERSTANDING OF THE PHYSIOLOGICAL EFFECTS OF, AND RESPONSES TO, ENVIRONMENTAL STRESS ON PLANTS IN ORDER TO MANIPULATE GENETICALLY CROPS FOR GREATER ADAPTATION TO ENVIRONMENTAL CONSTRAINTS.

1. Understand the mechanisms underlying stress resistance, stress injury and the efficiency with which environmental resources are used in growth.

2. Determine for particular environments the physiological characteristics that help the plant avoid or tolerate stress.

3. Demonstrate the importance of physiological characteristics considered to be adaptive before recommending them as selective criteria.

4. Manipulate the genetic composition of plants to incorporate desired traits, using appropriate technology.

DEVELOP A THOROUGH UNDERSTANDING OF HOW ENVIRONMENTAL MODIFICATIONS CAN MINIMIZE CONSTRAINTS ON CROP PRODUCTIVITY.

1. Determine the way plants reach to environmental constraints and how these affect crop growth in the field.

2. Evaluate the effect of modifying the root and aerial environment to mitigate the impact of stresses.

3. Develop cultural practices and crop management systems that mitigate responses to stress.

DETERMINE IMPACTS OF AGRICULTURAL PRACTICES ON THE ENVIRONMENT.

1. Quantify the rates of erosion and depletion of soil organic matter as a function of agricultural management practice, soil, and landscape.

2. Determine the extent of depletion and contamination of surface and ground waters by nutrients, salinity, pesticides, and trace elements.

3. Quantify gaseous emissions from agroecosystems and their possible adverse effect on the atmosphere and climate.

UNDERSTAND THE IMPACTS OF ANTHROPOGENIC CHEMICALS ON AGROECOSYSTEMS.

1. Determine direct and indirect effects of increasing atmospheric carbon dioxide on agroecosystems.

2. Assess the effects of photochemically produced ozone on agroecosystems.

Exhibit 5.11 (continued)

3. Determine effects of chemicals in surface and ground waters used as irrigation water for agroecosystems.

DEVELOP ALTERNATIVE CROPPING RESOURCE MANAGEMENT STRATEGIES TO MINIMIZE ENVIRONMENTAL CONSTRAINTS.

Source: Davidson, J.M., A.D. Hanson, and D.R. Nielsen. 1985. Environmental constraints. In Crop productivity-research imperatives revisited. Gibbs, M. and C. Carlson, eds. 196-215. An international conference held at Boyne Highlands Inn, October 13-18, 1985 and Airlie House, December 11-13, 1985.

crops before the spreading roots of the cane gave any adverse effects from the competition.

Crops and the Sea

With the sophistication of plant manipulation on land, expanding sea farming throughout the world's oceans and seas now seems possible. In China, genetically improved strains of a brown seaweed, *Laminaria*, are now farmed along the coastline where the plant does not grow naturally. Future genetic studies are expected to produce numerous new crops which can be farmed in the seas and along barren coastlines of continents throughout the world.

Crops and Space

Future National Aeronautics and Space Administration (NASA) research plans include growing crops in space to support crews during extended space journeys. A NASA program called Controlled Ecological Life Support System (CELSS) is charged with developing a biologically based, regenerative life-support system. Preparing for space agriculture will involve very fundamental studies about how plants function on earth. Such investigations will contribute to terrestrial agriculture.

A food production capability in space will use energy and sunlight to convert simple carbon compounds into complex materials for human foods. At least three alternative systems are being proposed.

1. Use energy to drive reactors that chemically synthesize food.
2. Use energy to hydrolyze water to hydrogen and oxygen. The hydrogen and some of the oxygen could be an energy source, allowing hydrogen-oxidizing bacteria, e.g., some species of *Pseudomonas* or *Alkaligewes*, to use carbon dioxide from the atmosphere to build cell materials. After processing to remove possible toxins and nondigestible material, the bacteria could be eaten.
3. Use energy to convert carbon dioxide to methanol on which certain yeasts could be grown, then processed and eaten.

Plants are the most appropriate method of space food production. Although plants respond to their environments in complex manners, they can be controlled. Plants require water, carbon dioxide, oxygen, mineral salts, fixed nitrogen, and light in known quantities and with given qualities at certain times of the day. They also require given ranges of water vapor, some air movement, and specific temperature ranges. These requirements vary significantly with the phases of the plant's life cycle.

The use of secondary sources such as animal protein from insects, chickens, rabbits, or fish would introduce some rather severe complications for space travel. Compared to plants, they have low efficiency in food production.

The chemical synthesis of food is not yet sufficiently reliable to eliminate the possibility of toxic materials entering the food chain. Biological toxins become a problem after extensive periods of human ingestion. All products of space agriculture have value. These products include biomass (food), oxygen, transpired water, and carbon-dioxide-absorbing capabilities. In a space agricultural system, all chemicals must be recycled.

The following description by MacElroy in 1983 of a proposed space system highlights the type of basic questions that need to be answered:

The initial space system will contain humans, food, water, and oxygen for a period of 90 days, plus the equipment necessary to maintain the composition of the space craft atmosphere for this period. During these 90 days, crops will be planted, oxygen will be generated, and carbon dioxide will be absorbed by the growing plants. Bacteria, an inevitable part of the system, will begin to grow around the roots of the growing plants, consuming oxygen and generating carbon dioxide. As the plants mature, the food they have produced will be harvested, separated from inedible portions, and stored or eaten.

Before this can be a successful trip, the following basic questions must be answered:

1. How much oxygen will the plants produce and at what rate?
2. How much carbon dioxide will be required by each kind of growing plant and at what rates?
3. How will carbon dioxide stored in the inedible biomass be released?
4. How much carbon dioxide will be consumed by the root bacteria?
5. What will be the rate of denitrification?
6. Can sufficient quantities of nitrogen be fixed by the plants?
7. What seed germination is likely to occur?
8. How should excess oxygen, carbon dioxide, and nitrogen be removed from the atmosphere and stored?

Further information is needed before the behavior and responses of plants may be manipulated through biological management. For example, if the air temperature is decreased during a certain growth phase, one result may be the initiation of a different growth phase. Decreasing the availability of nitrogen without altering the concentration of carbon dioxide could trigger a metabolic response, preventing fruiting or causing the death of the plant.

Many research activities in the CELSS program will have application to terrestrial agriculture: nitrogen use during growth phases, crop density, hydroponic and aeroponic culture in controlled environments, maximum crop yields, and computer models and control systems. In addition to space travel, research results from space will benefit both the greenhouse and controlled-environment agriculture industries.

FOOD FOR FUEL: THE BRAZILIAN SITUATION

In addition to the nutritional benefits of corn, 4 percent of the total U.S. production of corn in 1986 (300 million bushels) was processed into 780 million gallons of ethanol for nationwide use, primarily as a gasoline replacement. With the elimination of lead as an additive to gasoline, the shortfall in octane supply can be filled by ethanol. This usage has lead to many controversies. Brazil has become a nation committed to the production of ethanol from sugarcane.

Fuel ethanol is a complex market commodity. It begins as an agricultural product where it is produced most efficiently from sugarcane in tropical countries. Costs of producing ethanol from corn in a temperate climate such as the U.S. are currently about 70 percent greater than the costs of producing ethanol from sugarcane in tropical countries such as Brazil.

The availability, cost, and potential supply of ethanol are dependent on the relative productivity of sugarcane, corn, cassava, and other ethanol feedstock sources as they compete with food, feed, and fiber uses for agricultural resources. Levels of productivity and unit costs of production for these crops vary significantly between countries. Every country has a different mix of climate, land, labor, and capital resources devoted to agriculture.

As the principal product from agriculture, food displays a contrasting situation, relative to ethanol, in terms of geographic location and efficiency of production as well as current and projected levels of demand. In the case for ethanol, a comparative advantage argument can be made for food production, especially feed grain production. In this case, temperate regions have the advantage.

Competition between food and fuel uses of agricultural resources in developing countries, however, may be more critical than in developed countries. Thus, while the U.S. has largely satiated its per capita demands for agricultural food products, Brazil will likely double its per capita food demands against agriculture as incomes rise. Brazil is currently the principal supplier of ethanol to international markets while the U.S. is an important user of fuel ethanol and a principal agricultural exporter.

Also, recent technological improvements in Brazilian ethanol production should result in further increased efficiencies and lower future costs. These changes include continuous fermentation, high pressure boilers, by-product use of bagasse, improved sugarcane varieties, and intertilling and rotation of short season crops with sugarcane.

Any analysis of the future Brazilian ethanol market must consider the food needs of the population in addition to their energy needs. Annual per capita food consumption, when measured in cereal equivalents, increases from about 0.3 tons per capita at very low income levels to 2.1 tons at high income levels, as shown in Exhibit 5.12. On this scale, Brazil currently uses about 1.0 tons of cereal equivalents per capita annually. Thus, it is likely that Brazilian food

Exhibit 5.12. Food Consumption and Income 1961-1985.

**FOOD CONSUMPTION IN
CEREAL EQUIVALENTS (TONS/CAPITA)**

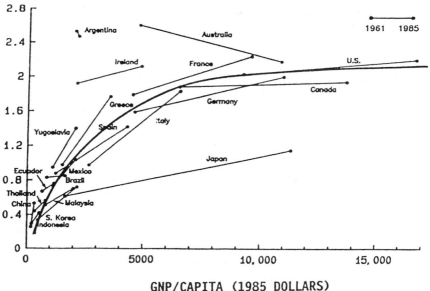

GNP/CAPITA (1985 DOLLARS)

Source: From *National and Regional Self-Sufficiency Goals: Implications for International Agriculture*, edited by Fred J. Ruppel and Earl D. Kellogg. © 1991 by Lynne Rienner Publishers, Inc. Reprinted by permission of the publisher.

needs could at least double on a per capita basis as incomes rise. The most likely consumption increase will be in livestock products, especially feed concentrates for poultry and pork because they are more efficient converters of feed grains to human protein products.

In recent years, U.S. corn exports to Brazil have varied from 0 to 1.7 million metric tons. Given corn productivity levels in Brazil, there should be increased opportunities for U.S. corn exports in coming years. Corn yields in the U.S. are three to four times greater than those in Brazil.

Corn utilization has increased substantially in recent years in Brazil. Future planning to meet food needs should focus on corn and other feed grains as the basic feed inputs for the anticipated expansion in demand for livestock products. Brazil is a large, but not an efficient, producer of corn. Hence, corn becomes an attractive import commodity that can be balanced against exports of ethanol.

On a per hectare basis, alcohol yields from sugarcane in Brazil are almost twice that of U.S. alcohol yields from corn. Since ethanol production costs are substantially lower in Brazil, ethanol can be distributed to U.S. refineries for about 70 percent of the cost of U.S. ethanol.

What are the major differences between producing ethanol from sugarcane versus corn? As a feedstock, sugarcane yields substantially more ethanol per hectare than corn and provides its own energy source or bagasse. In contrast, corn ethanol has a greater need, as well as a more complicated use, for processing energy. With corn ethanol, energy is needed to dry the by-product feeds that form a significant share of the income from ethanol distilleries.

The rather large differences between Brazil and the U.S. in unit supply costs of ethanol and corn, and the projected needs for, and supplies of these commodities, would suggest that the conditions for expanded trading exist. By specializing in those commodities they produce more efficiently and engaging in trade to acquire other commodities, each country would benefit as productive resources are put to their best use.

Comparative advantage may not be a sufficient condition for trade since producers and consumers (and their governments) must have some security of expectations that their excess production will have a market, and that domestic needs for commodities not produced locally will be met on a regular basis through imports. Counter-trade arrangements may be needed. These are agreements between countries or trade groups to provide a measure of security to producers and consumers that specific import and export markets will function.

For example, fuel ethanol production may require multi-year commitments from sugarcane producers and large investments and long-term (at least 20-year) production horizons for ethanol distilleries. At the same time, U.S. corn producers are strong supporters of the U.S. ethanol program and would need some assurance of long-run expanded markets in Brazil to gain their support for a relaxation of tariffs against imported ethanol.

It is apparent that under current agricultural and industrial technology, comparative advantage will be strongly in favor of ethanol produced from sugarcane in tropical resource situations. Many of the developed countries in temperate areas have a comparative advantage in cereal and feed grain production. These commodities are necessary to support economic development in developing countries and to replace food and feed output lost to sugarcane production in ethanol-producing areas.

Negative arguments for the growth of crops for fuel center around several facts. First, when all crop residues are removed from the land for alcohol production, the erosion rate increases ninefold. This fact has serious implications because even a twofold increase in erosion rates would vastly increase the need for energy inputs, thereby reducing some of the benefits. Second, crop land used for fuel production is unavailable for food production. Third, when sugarcane fields are burned, considerable atmospheric pollution occurs.

In summary, given the Brazil-U.S. situation for crop efficiencies, a trade agreement could include ethanol from Brazil and wheat and corn from the U.S. If the U.S. and Brazil proceed to establish a preliminary trade agreement based on these commodities, they would give the world an important first experience in structuring an international supply of fuel ethanol.

PLANTS AND HERBAL MEDICINE

The profession of herbal medicine uses plants, either whole or selected parts, for the preparation of therapeutic tinctures.

The herbs arrive at their destinations in dried form from the locations given in Exhibit 5.13. Either the whole plant or part of the plant, i.e., the leaves, flowers, root bark or roots, are used. They are either macerated in various solvents, percolated with solvent, or a refluxing and distillation system is used. They are left in the solvent for several weeks before they are pressed and vacuum filtered to produce the tincture. There are about 150 different approved tinctures, each one rarely used on its own; in most cases tinctures are combined. When herbal extracts are prepared, there are strict procedures for testing and standardization.

Each of the herbs or plant materials listed in Exhibit 5.13 have different properties and are used in conjunction with one another depending on a person's physical condition. A few examples follow. A person with sinusitis, headaches, and stress would likely be treated with thyme to relieve nasal congestion, feverfew to relieve headaches, and valerian as a relaxant. The medicine (5 mL) would be taken three times per day.

Red clover and wormwood can be used for their tonic and calmative actions in cancer patients. Echinacea and mullein are used for their antibiotic effects for children with recurring ear infections. The bark and berries of prickly ash are used for arthritis pain. Devil's claw, a plant indigenous to southern and eastern Africa, has anti-rheumatic actions. Golden seal from Canada is said to be a powerful tonic for the mucous membranes of the human body.

Many of the plants listed in Exhibit 5.13 are also used for pharmaceutical drugs. For example, the tranquillizer, Valium is made from a small part of the valerian plant with other chemicals added. In herbal medicine, the entire plant is used and side effects can be reduced.

In the U.K. and Europe, herbal medicine is well recognized by much of the medical profession. After training at the School of Herbal Medicine in Kent, U.K., Julia Davidson has her own practice in Marlborough Province located on the far north side of the

Exhibit 5.13. Geographic Source for Plants Used in Medicine.

Country or Region	Common Name of Herbs used in Tincture
North America	Pleurisy Root Black Walnut Bayberry Passion Flower Poke Root Jamaican Dogwood Wild Cherry Scullcap Life Root Sarsaparilla Jamaican Beth Root Guelder Rose Black Haw Bark
North America; Western U.S.	Grindelia Wild Yam Gavel Root Witch Hazel Lobelia Squaw Vine Skunk Cabbage Corn Silk Ginger
U.S.; Northern	Uva Ursi
U.S.; Central	Echinarea Echinacea
U.S.; South Eastern	Gelsen
U.S.; Nebraska	Berberis Bark

Country or Region	Common Name of Herbs used in Tincture
U.S.; Florida	Queen's Delight
Canada	Blue Cohosh Stone Root Black Cohosh Golden Seal Slippery Elm
Canada; British Columbia	Berberis Bark Cascara Sagrada
Mexico	Damiana
Europe	Shepherd's Purse Motherwort Thuga Coltsfoot Violet Leaves Chaste Tree
Europe; Central	Arnica
Europe; Central and South	Gentian
North Atlantic Ocean	Bladderwack
UK	Parsley Piert Hawthorn Eyebright Fumitory Lungwort

Exhibit 5.13 (continued)

Country or Region	Common Name of Herbs used in Tincture
UK (con't.)	English Oak Valerian Vervain
Germany	Marshmallow
Yugoslavia	Horsetail
Russia	Liquorice
Mediterranean Region	Squill
Africa	Cayenne Prickly Ash
North Africa	Myrrh
South Africa	Devil's Claw
South Africa; Cape Province	Buchu
India	Euphorbia
India; West	Guiacum
Australia	Agrimony Pasque Flower

Country or Region	Common Name of Herbs used in Tincture
New Zealand	Couch Grass
	Aloe Vera
	Angelica
	Celery
	Burdock
	Wormwood
	Southernwood
	Mugwort
	Oats
	Calendula
	Feverfew
	Clivers
	Hops
	St. John's Wort
	Hyssop
	Elecampane
	German Chamomile
	Lemon Balm
	Peppermint
	Penny Royal
	Cat Nip
	Plantain
	Rosemary
	Yellow Dock
	Sage
	Elderflower
	Soapwort
	Chickweed
	Comfrey
	Tansy
	Dandelion
	Thyme
	Red Clover
	Nettles
	Mullein

Source: Davidson, Julia. 1990. Personal communication. Blenheim, New Zealand.

southern island of New Zealand. Julia uses 120 tinctures, or herbal extracts in a solution of alcohol, made from the plants listed in Exhibit 5.13. As a member of the New Zealand Medical Herbalist Association, Davidson stresses the importance of her medical education in such fields as anatomy, physiology, pathology, pharmacology, and nutrition and dietetics. Herbal medicine does not replace medical care; it offers people another option for receiving relief from their symptoms and improving their quality of life whenever possible. Through the development of this profession, coupled with international trade in these plant materials (Exhibit 5.13), the life of people in this New Zealand province is being improved. What other plants will become recognized for their therapeutic powers? Will they disappear before we have identified them? Will the discipline of biotechnology enable these substances to be produced more efficiently?

SUMMARY

Adequacy of food supplies, both in terms of quantity and type of food in low- and middle-income countries, is a constantly changing concept. Food needs exhibit a dynamic growth path, reflecting both population increases and changes in diet. Diet changes are the most important and are linked closely to income changes, especially at low levels of income.

As incomes grow, the primary change in food consumption is to improve diets that include greater proportions of higher quality foods such as livestock products which, in turn, are much less efficient converters of agricultural resources. For example, to produce 1 pound of meat requires from 2 to 11 pounds of grain or grain equivalent livestock feed. Thus, grains or cereals that are consumed directly as food are a much more efficient food source than when converted to livestock products. However, as development proceeds, the demands on basic agriculture in many developing countries can increase severalfold, concurrent with the increased desire for more livestock versus plant products.

There are, however, limits to the development-food consumption link. First, development eventually leads to slower population growth, reducing this source of increased food demand. Secondly, with higher levels of income, only a fraction of income is spent on food, and much of this is for convenience and quality factors little related to basic agriculture. Thus, as countries reach mature levels of development, the argument can be made that the demands on agriculture are relatively stable regardless of changes in income.

REFERENCES

Brown, Lester R. 1989. Reexamining the world food prospect. In *State of the world 1989*, ed. L. R. Brown, 41-58. New York: W. W. Norton & Company.

Davidson, J. M., A. D. Hanson, and D. R. Nielsen. 1985. Environmental constraints. In *Crop productivity — research imperatives revisited*, eds. M. Gibbs and C. Carlson, 196-215. An international conference held at Boyne Highlands Inn, October 13-18, 1985 and Airlie House, December 11-13, 1985.

Davidson, Julia. 1990. Personal communication. Blenheim: New Zealand.

Gever, J., R. Kaufman, D. Skole, and C. Vorosmarty. 1986. *Beyond oil*. Cambridge: Ballinger Publishing Company.

Gibbs, M. and C. Carlson, eds. 1985. *Crop productivity — research imperatives revisited*. An international conference held at Boyne Highlands Inn, October 13-18, 1985 and Airlie House, December 11-13, 1985.

Mengel, K. and E. A. Kirkby. 1987. *Principles in plant nutrition*. 4th ed. Berne, Switzerland: International Potash Institute.

Mickelsen, Olaf. 1983. Nutritional considerations in planning for food production. In *Sustainable food systems*, ed. D. Knorr, 394-410. Westport, Conn.: AVI Publishing Company, Inc.

Nestle, Marion. 1985. *Nutrition in medical practice*. Greenbrae, California: Jones Medical Publications.

Pimental, D. and M. Pimental. 1979. *Food, energy, and society*. New York: John Wiley & Sons.

Rask, N. 1987. Economic efficiency and comparative advantage in international fuel ethanol markets. Paper presented at the Copersucar-Journal do Brasil Seminar, Sao Paulo, Brazil, August 1987.

Rask, Norman. 1991. Dynamics of self-sufficiency and income growth. In *National and regional self-sufficiency goals: implications for international agriculture*, eds. F. J. Ruppel and E. D. Kellogg. Boulder and London: Lynne Rienner Publisher, Inc.

Wittwer, Sylvan H. 1983. The new agriculture: a view of the twenty-first century. In *Agriculture in the twenty-first century*, ed. J. W. Rosenblum, 337-67. New York: John Wiley & Sons.

Wittwer, Sylvan H. 1985. Crop productivity — research imperatives: a decade of change. In *Crop productivity — research imperatives revisited*, eds. M. Gibbs and C. Carlson, 1-6. An international conference held at Boyne Highlands Inn, October 13-18, 1985 and Airlie House, December 11-13, 1985.

Yermanos, D. M., M. Neushul, and R. D. MacElroy. 1983. Crops from the desert, sea, and space. In *Agriculture in the twenty-first century*, ed. J. W. Rosenblum, 144-65. New York: John Wiley & Sons.

Chapter Six

Production of Animals:
Livestock, Wildlife, and Insects

INTRODUCTION

Animals, from caterpillars to camels, are produced for their nutrient content, namely: protein, fat, energy, vitamins, and minerals. Their by-products, from cowhides from cattle to silkworm residues, are used to support industrial, agricultural, and national economies. You will hear numerous arguments about the virtues of consuming plants versus animals, with valid arguments made on both sides. One argument in support of animals is that they are completely recyclable, producing a new crop each year and perpetuating themselves through their offspring. By studying the information in this chapter, you will become familiar with:

- the contribution to humanity that animals make throughout the globe, and how they can be effectively managed once all factors of their ecological adaptations are known;
- where different species of animals, including livestock and wildlife and their by-products, are produced and used around the world, contributing to the quality of life of vast human populations;
- small ruminant research programs that are striving to increase the population of these animals throughout developing countries;
- how insects can be used for human food, providing essential nutrients in many developing countries, and their potential for becoming high quality feeds for other animal products such as poultry.

Our basic needs are: food, shelter, clothing, fuel, and emotional well-being. Animals and animal products supply many of these basic needs and contribute to a high standard of living that is sometimes associated with a high consumption of animal products. Animals provide benefits in several areas: food, slaughter by-products used for chemical purposes, slaughter by-products used for animal feeds, manure for fuel, and so on.

About 30 percent of the world human population and 32 percent of the ruminant animal population live in developed regions of the world. Ruminants of these regions produce two-thirds of the world's meat and 80 percent of the world's milk. On a per-animal basis, animals in developed regions are higher in productivity than those in developing countries.

The world meat supply approaches 250 billion pounds with the U.S., China, and the U.S.S.R. leading all other countries. Buffalo meat comes from the water buffalo in Asia and the African Buffalo. Most of the world meat supply comes from cattle, buffalo, swine, sheep, goats, horses, and chickens. Data about the production of some of these animals was given in Exhibit 2.4. About 20 additional species contribute approximately 10 percent of the estimated total protein consumption from meat: alpaca, llama, yak, deer, elk, antelope, kangaroo, rabbit, guinea pig, capybara, fowl other than chicken (duck, turkey, goose, guinea fowl, pigeon), and wild game, exclusive of birds.

Animal products comprise 16 percent of the calories and 31.8 percent of the protein in the total world food supply as shown in Exhibits 6.1 and 6.2, respectively. Developed countries consume 3,377 calories per capita per day; developing ones, 2,464 calories (Exhibit 6.1). Similarly, developed countries consume 58.7 grams of protein per capita per day; undeveloped ones consume 12.7 grams (Exhibit 6.2). Comparing these data with animal versus plant consumption, 30 percent of the calories in developed countries are contributed by animal products versus 9 percent in developing countries (Exhibit 6.1). With respect to total protein consumption, 58.7 percent and 12.7 percent come from animal products in developed and developing countries, respectively (Exhibit 6.2).

Exhibit 6.1. Calories Per Caput Per Day - 1984-86*.

Region/Country	Total (kcal)	Source			
		Plant Products (kcal/day)	%	Animal Products (kcal/day)	%
North and Central America	3370	2403	71	967	29
Europe	3397	2287	67	1109	33
Oceania	3126	2103	67	1024	33
South America	2622	2170	83	452	17
Africa	2299	2120	92	179	8
Asia	2485	2274	92	212	8
USSR	3394	2484	73	911	27
All Developed Countries	3377	2357	70	1020	30
All Developing Countries	2464	2245	91	218	9
World	2694	2274	84	420	16

*Obtained by dividing the food supplies available for human consumption by the country/region population. Data represent only the average supply for the population and do not indicate what is actually consumed by individuals.

Source: FAO Production Yearbook. Vol. 42. 1988. Food and Agriculture Organization of the United Nations: Rome.

ANIMAL CLASSIFICATIONS

Animals are classified as carnivores, omnivores, or herbivores, according to the types of feed they normally eat. Carnivores, such as dogs and cats, normally consume animal tissues as their source

Exhibit 6.2. Protein and Fat Per Caput Per Day - 1984-86*.

Region/Country	Plant Products		Animal Products	
	Protein (g/day)	Fat (g/day)	Protein (g/day)	Fat (g/day)
North and Central America	39.5	60.3	55.2	73.0
Europe	42.7	47.8	58.8	87.6
Oceania	34.4	43.0	57.0	76.8
South America	37.6	31.7	28.6	31.4
Africa	44.8	35.2	12.6	11.8
Asia	48.5	26.9	12.2	16.1
USSR	51.6	33.6	54.0	68.0
All Developed Countries	43.1	48.9	58.1	78.0
All Developing Countries	47.3	28.3	12.7	16.2
World	46.2	33.5	24.1	31.8

*Obtained by dividing the food supplies available for human consumption by the country/region population. Data represent only the average supply for the population and do not indicate what is actually consumed by individuals.

Source: FAO Production Yearbook. Vol. 42. 1988. Food and Agriculture Organization of the United Nations: Rome.

of nutrients. Herbivores such as cattle, horses, sheep, and goats primarily consume plant tissues. Humans and pigs are examples of omnivores, consuming both plant and animal substances.

Both carnivores and omnivores are monogastric animals, having a one-compartment stomach. Herbivores such as cattle, sheep, and goats are ruminant animals having a complex, four-compartment stomach including the rumen, reticulum, omasum, and abomasum. A beef cow's digestive tract is diagrammed in Exhibit 6.3. The rumen is a large fermentation vat in which bacteria and protozoa break down roughages to obtain nutrients for their use. The microorganisms digest cellulose and synthesize animo acids from nonprotein nitrogen and B-complex vitamins. Later, these microorganisms are digested in the small intestine to provide these nutrients for the ruminant animal's use.

The reticulum interacts with the rumen and provides a mixing action and additional fermentation area. The omasum is believed to produce a grinding action for the feed. The abomasum corresponds to the stomach of monogastric animals and has the same functions.

Exhibit 6.3. Beef Cattle Digestive Tract.

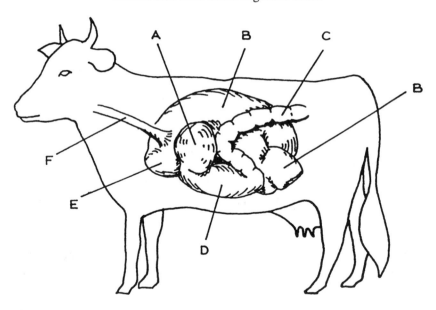

A = Omasum   D = Abomasum

B = Rumen   E = Reticulum

C = Small Intestine   F = Esophagus

Ruminant animals eat forage rapidly and regurgitate it, a process known as chewing their cud.

LIVESTOCK ECOLOGY

Livestock throughout the world are expected to produce under an extremely wide range of environments. Variations in temperature, humidity, wind, light, altitude, feed, water, and exposure to parasites and disease organisms are some of the environmental conditions which they respond to. The diagram in Exhibit 6.4 gives the parameters of livestock management.

Humans' management decisions with farm animals have a role in determining how animals will interact with their environment. Under intensive management, such as in poultry, swine, and dairy operations, many conditions and regimes are controlled: feed, water, balanced rations, health programs, temperature, and humidity, to name a few. When ruminant animals do not have these controls,

Exhibit 6.4. Parameters of Livestock Management.

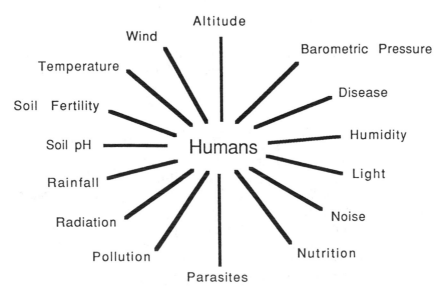

they must graze for forage which can be sparse and changing. Under these adverse conditions, livestock that produce and survive have physiological mechanisms for adaptability.

ANIMAL FEED SOURCES

As with the human diet, animals can have several alternatives for meeting their daily nutrient requirements. These include forage or grazing, crop residues, and feed supplements.

Forage and Grazing

Approximately two-thirds of the world's agricultural land is permanent pasture, range, and meadow. Of this land, about 60 percent is unsuitable for producing cultivated crops that could be consumed directly by humans. However, this land can produce roughage in the form of grass and other vegetation that is digestible by grazing ruminant animals. The most important ruminant animals are cattle and sheep. They are capable of converting vegetation, which is for the most part undigestible by humans, to high-quality protein food.

In the U.S., about 385 million acres of rangeland and forest, representing 44 percent of the total land area, is used for grazing. Although this acreage supports about 40 percent of the total cattle population, it could support twice this much if it was developed and intensively managed. Grassland research in New Zealand is contributing to the productivity of grasslands throughout the world.

Crop Residues

Crop residues are important feed sources. In the semi-arid and sub-humid zones of West Africa, cattle spend 40 percent of their time grazing on crop residues, where they obtain about one-half of their food. Crop residues provide one-half of the feed for sheep in North Africa and West Asia, and more than 70 percent for cattle and buffalo in India.

Four leguminous crops give high grain yield and high biomass production for livestock feed: cowpea, mungbean, peanut, and pigeon pea. Because it reduces the area needed for producing food crops, small land holders rarely grow forage crops. Residues from food crops such as rice straw, peanut hay, wheat straw, barley straw, and sweet potato leaves are their main livestock feeds.

To reduce postharvest losses, effective storage and handling techniques are needed for all crop residues.

Effects of Plant Breeding on Livestock

When crop breeders change the distribution of plant nutrients to achieve increased grain yields, they often grow crops with poorer quality residues for animal feed. Examples from around the globe illustrate resistance to the selection of new crop varieties because of their inferior quality of residue, or stover. Small landholders in North Africa and West Asia have rejected new varieties of barley because the feed value of their residues for sheep is lower than traditional varieties. In Mexico, there is a 50 percent price differential in favor of stover from conventional varieties because of their higher feed value.

In 1984, scientists at the International Crops Research Institute for the Semi-Arid Tropics (ICRISAT) found that small land holders rejected new sorghum varieties because they produced less stover and were less palatable to livestock than traditional varieties.

In Botswana and northern Mali, cowpeas are used as insurance for human food when pasture lands are plentiful and for livestock feed when pasture is poor. When cowpeas are selected for yield, their crop residue decreases, the lignin content of the stalks increases, and leaf drop before harvest increases. Thus, these varieties are seldom used in erratic rainfall areas such as Botswana and Mali.

Farmer resistance to new varieties has been so pervasive that the Centro Agronomico Tropical de Investigacion y Enseianze (CATIE) recommends "new maize" varieties only when farmers are aware of likely changes in stover quality, or when other feed resources can be developed to counter the effects of the low-quality stover.

In Africa, small farmholders are reluctant to adopt new bird-resistant varieties of sorghum because of the lower animal feeding value of both the grain and the stovers from these varieties.

Feed Supplement Example: Poultry Feeds

Energy requirements for poultry feeds are supplied mainly by cereal grains, grain by-products, and fats. Some important grains are yellow corn, wheat, sorghum, barley, and oats. Animal fats and vegetable oils are also incorporated into feeds as energy sources. Most rations contain both plant and animal proteins so that each source can supply amino acids that the other source lacks. Sources of plant proteins include: soybean meal, cottonseed meal, peanut meal, alfalfa meal, and corn gluten meal. Animal protein sources include: fish meal, milk and meat by-products, and blood and feather meal. Vitamins and mineral contents of these rations are also crucial to effective development.

ANIMAL DRAFT POWER

In more than one-half of the countries throughout the world, animals, namely buffalo, cattle, horses, mules, camels, and llamas, are kept primarily for work and draft purposes. More than 20 percent of the world's population depends on animals for moving goods. Animal draft power significantly contributes to the production of major foods such as rice and cereal grains. In India, 200 million cattle and buffalo contribute by providing work energy for fields and milk for people. India would have to spend more than $1 billion annually for gasoline alone to replace the animal energy used for agriculture.

Horses, donkeys (asses and burros), and their crosses (mules and hinnies) have contributed significantly. China is the country with the largest population of these animals. Mules and hinnies have long been used as draft animals in farming operations. They possess several characteristics which make them suitable for draft work: sure-footedness, ruggedness, and endurance for hard work. In addition, mules do not gorge themselves when given free access to grain, avoiding the consequences of overeating. Perhaps some humans in developed countries should determine how mules come by this behavior!

ANIMAL REPRODUCTION

Two developments, artificial insemination and embryo transfer, are greatly increasing the productivity of raising animals.

Artificial Insemination

In the process of artificial insemination (AI), semen is deposited in the female reproductive tract by artificial techniques rather than by natural mating. AI permits extensive use of outstanding sires to maximize genetic improvement. For example, a bull may sire 30 to 50 calves naturally per year over a productive lifetime of 3 to 8 years. In an AI program, a bull can produce 200 to 400 units of semen per ejaculate, with four ejaculates typically collected per week. If the semen is frozen and stored for later use, hundreds of thousands of calves can be produced by a single sire. AI can also control reproductive diseases.

Embryo Transfer

Using sophisticated techniques known as embryo or ova transfer, an embryo in its early stage of development is removed from its own mother's reproductive tract and transferred to another female's reproductive tract. This procedure increases the number of off-spring that a superior female can produce.

The key to the justification of embryo transfer is the identification of genetically superior females. Embryo transfer is usually confined to seed stock herds where genetically superior females can be more easily identified and where high costs can be justified. Recent advances in embryo transfer research have permitted the embryo to be mechanically divided so that identical twins can be produced from a single embryo. Future projections include selecting and freezing an embryo of a desired mate and sex, thawing it, and transferring it into a cow when she comes into heat. Embryo splitting and embryo transfer are areas of biotechnology that continue to advance rapidly.

ANIMAL HEALTH CONSIDERATIONS

Veterinary medicine is crucial to a productive herd of any animal species. Many situations arise when veterinary services are not available. For example, millions of cows and buffalo die each year in developing countries from rinderpest, a viral infection. The mortality rate of infected stock, estimated at 240 million in India, can reach as high as 95 percent with severe economic losses. As part of a global effort to eradicate rinderpest, an emergency vaccination campaign has been organized by FAO. It is sponsored by the Organization for African Unity (OAU) and financed by a $50 million grant from the EC. This vaccination effort involves about 120 million cattle in 29 African countries.

Animal health can be directly related to the condition of the grasslands. For example, grass tetany, a springtime disease that kills cattle, has been linked to a magnesium deficiency. When soils have low phosphorous and ammonium contents, both the calcium and the magnesium uptake by the plants is reduced. Plants deficient in these two elements cause grass tetany in grazing cattle. Cattle ranchers now protect their herds by incorporating magnesium into their feed, using magnesium licking blocks (free choice), and injecting magnesium directly into their cattle. Research is needed to determine how plants absorb magnesium so that this economically costly disease could be eliminated.

Recent research projects have shown that improvements in animal health are feasible once the stockowners receive appropriate educational information. For example, in the Peruvian Andes, the stockowners possess many ideas about reasons for animal health, but they lack the capital, labor, and technology to have healthy herds systematically. With more knowledge, they can take advantage of low- or no-cost controls which will increase the productivity of their herds. For example, low-cost medicines could be developed which are not encumbered with the hidden costs of large pharmaceutical houses. Before this is possible, researchers need to identify the indigenous knowledge base of the population and determine what additional knowledge should be imparted to give them the most benefit. Such tasks involve multidisciplinary research approaches, integrating the social, biological, and educational sciences.

SELECTED GLOBAL ANIMAL SPECIES

Because of the dynamics of the parameters of livestock management (Exhibit 6.4) coupled with societal influences, the location of popular animal species, whether used for meat, food, and/or industrial products, varies around the globe (Exhibit 2.4). Some of the contributions of sheep, goats, poultry, horses, camels, beef, pigs, and selected wildlife species will be presented.

Sheep and Goats

Sheep and goats are important ruminants in temperate and tropical agricultural areas. They provide wool, milk, hides, and meat for people in many parts of the world. Sheep and goats are better adapted to arid tropics than cattle, probably because of their superior ability to use both water and nitrogen. Because sheep and goats produce fibers as well as meat and milk, they offer advantages for small farms in developing countries.

Cattle, sheep, and goats are often grazed together because they use different plants. More than 60 percent of all sheep are in temperate zones, the remaining being in tropical zones of the world. Eighty percent of all goats can be found in tropical and subtropical areas. This production has been influenced by temperature and appropriate forms of vegetation for these animals.

Sheep contribute mutton and lamb for Asia, Oceania, and the U.S.S.R. They also contribute milk to Europe and Africa. Sheep milk is not consumed in the U.S. (Exhibit 2.5).

Goats have a large impact on the economy and food supply for people in tropical countries. In many countries, people consume more goat milk than cow milk (Exhibit 2.5). Goats are also an important meat source. On a worldwide basis, there are more meat goats than dairy goats.

Goats thrive on brushy plants, broad leaf plants, and grass. The choice of plants and plant parts is important to goats; they are more likely to select the most nutritious parts. Goats are less likely to suffer from internal parasites when they browse over a large territory.

Most goats are found in developing countries where they contribute greatly to people's needs. Meat goats are found primarily in Africa and the Middle East where their main uses are for meat and skins. In Africa there has been a preference for the pygmy goat. This animal is small, well-muscled, and agile, feeding mostly on brushy plants and low trees. As many of the areas of goat production are away from cities and towns and thus lack refrigeration, small goats that are slaughtered can be consumed immediately before the meat spoils.

The dairy goat and the dairy cow are about equal in efficiency in converting feed into milk, even though the dairy goat produces much more milk in relation to its size and weight than does the dairy cow. In many parts of the world, including some of the Mediterranean countries, France, and Norway, large quantities of dairy products are made from goat milk. The Norwegian cheese, gjetost, is one example.

Poultry

The term poultry refers to chickens, turkeys, geese, ducks, pigeons, peafowls, and guineas. Poultry meat and eggs are nutritious and relatively inexpensive animal products used by humans throughout the world (Exhibit 2.4). Feathers, down, livers, and other offal are additional useful products and by-products obtained from poultry. Although chickens and turkeys dominate the world poultry industry, in parts of Asia ducks are commercially more important than young chickens. Similarly, in areas of Europe, geese are more important than turkeys.

The U.S. is the leading country in poultry meat production and ranks third, after the U.S.S.R. and China, in egg production. The U.S. exports in excess of 26 million pounds of turkey to West Germany each year.

In some areas of the world, ducks and geese are raised primarily for feathers and down that provide stuffing for pillows, quilts, upholstery, and sportswear. The U.S. imports these raw products from China, France, Switzerland, Poland, and other Asian and European countries.

Goose livers from force-fed geese are a gourmet product in EC countries. These enlarged fatty livers, weighing up to 2 pounds each, are produced by force-feeding geese three times per day for 4 to 8 weeks. The liver is used to make a flavored paste, termed pâté de foie gras, used for hors d'oeuvres and sandwiches.

Horses

Historically, humans have always eaten horse meat. Current production data were given in Exhibit 2.4. Throughout Europe during and after both world wars, as well as during the Great Depression, several prominent French nutritionists advocated eating cheap, abundant horse meat. School cafeterias, along with food charities, used horse meat as a main source of meat. The EC is the world's largest consumer of horse meat, consuming 175,000 horses in 1987. Such cuts as horse Chateaubriand, filet, and rump steak are common. About 65 percent of the horses are imported. The horses have typically reached at least 5 years of age, being work or sport animals, or pets. Many live horses are shipped by truck to EC countries from Eastern Europe. The 1986 Chernobyl nuclear disaster hurt sales because it forced a temporary halt in shipments of live horses from Poland where some were found to be contaminated.

The U.S. has an annual supply of horse meat of approximately 200 million pounds. Although most of it is used in pet foods, shipments are made to Europe (France, Belgium, the Netherlands, Switzerland, and Italy) for human consumption. Frozen or vacuum-packed horse meat comes from the U.S., Canada, and the U.K. The U.S. sold about $82 million of horse meat to Europe in 1988. While horse meat is used widely in American pet food, it is not a significant component of U.S. human food consumption.

Consumer demand for horse meat is decreasing in Belgium, France, Spain, and Italy. The per capita consumption, i.e., the amount calculated to be eaten by each person during one year, of horse meat in the EC has been reduced to about one pound, one-half of the amount that was consumed a decade ago. Marketing efforts are being directed towards increasing this consumption. Recipe promotions include horse spaghetti and horse pizza. Trade associations in the EC are attempting to make horse meat more available by centralizing butchering operations and distributing prepackaged horse meat to stores.

Camels

In areas where the conditions of desert, drought, poverty, and famine are prevalent throughout developing countries, recommendations have been made to make better use of the unique qualities of camels. The camel is the only domestic animal adapted to arid and semiarid lands. Camels survive on desert scrub and little water, continuing to produce milk when cattle are dying. Camel milk is a nutritionally complete food, and a staple diet of thousands of people.

Under normal conditions, a she-camel produces more milk, for longer periods, than cows. Camels are also more efficient, converting fodder into four times as much milk as cows. In addition, as water for camels becomes scarcer, the water content of the milk actually increases. People can live on camel milk when no other sources of food or water are available.

In contrast to cattle, sheep, and goats, camels tend to browse without stripping individual plants bare, digging up roots, or completely clearing grass from the land. Thus, on their soft padded feet, a herd of browsing camels does not destroy the vegetation cover or the soil surface. Camels are not agents of erosion and subsequent desertification; arid cattle lands turn to deserts.

Camels are now extensively bred in Australia for use in countries in the Middle East. A recent pilot project proposal envisioned a camel breeding station in that area. Hormone injections and embryo transplants would be employed to raise the rate of reproduction, lower the age of first pregnancy, and further increase milk yields. Once a high-quality herd is established, the laboratory measures could cease, the herd could maintain itself, and local cattle herders could convert their herds by exchanging cattle for camels.

Recently, scientists at the Sheik Khalifa Genetic Research Laboratory in Abu Dhabi, United Arab Emirates, have successfully removed and artificially fertilized ovules of famous racing camel breeds. Desert camels can now be bred during the cool season from November to April, when desert temperatures cool to 95° F.

Beef

In 1986, these statistics were given about the dominant position of beef production in the U.S.:

1. The U.S. has 5 percent of the world's human population.
2. The U.S. has 8.7 percent of the world's cattle population.
3. The U.S. produces 25.4 percent of the world's beef and veal.
4. The U.S. consumes 28.5 percent of the world's beef and veal.

These statistics attest to the tremendous efficiency of the U.S. cattle industry. Beef continues to be America's favorite food; research continues on both production and processing techniques, to lower its fat and cholesterol contents.

The U.S. demand for beef has impacted several other economies. For example, around 1960 the demand for beef in U.S. fast-food restaurants had a profound impact upon several Central American countries. Guatemalan beef production nearly doubled from 1960 to 1972, but domestic per capita consumption of beef fell by 20 percent. During this period in Costa Rica, beef production rose from 53.3 to 108 million pounds, yet the amount available for domestic consumption remained constant at 34.8 million pounds. This resulted in a reduction in beef consumption of nearly one-third, while exports climbed from 17.5 to 73.7 million pounds.

From 1952 to 1974, the forested area in southern Honduras was reduced from ca. 74,000 to 41,000 hectares to enable beef production. This statistic had three implications for Hondurans: (1) fewer people had access to land for producing subsistence crops; (2) employment opportunities in the local regions declined because raising livestock required less labor than producing crops, and (3) permanent and temporary migration occurred, with socioeconomic-political implications for Central America. As with other marketing and trade conditions, these implications have to be viewed in light of other economic realities made possible because of the influx of foreign funds to Honduras.

When McDonald's recently established a fast food-outlet in Moscow, they searched local beef farms for standards that were acceptable. They found such an operation just outside of Moscow. They pick up the meat from the farm and deliver it to their FoodTown processing operation for deboning and mixing. This operation gives them the capability for serving 32,265 kg of 100 percent local beef on one million buns, every week.

Hogs

The worldwide production of pork meat, the flesh of hogs, is given in Exhibit 2.4. Compared to beef, American consumers eat much less pork. This trend is reversed in numerous countries, especially where hog feed is supplemented with human food scraps. Only about one-third of the pork processed in the U.S. is sold as fresh product; the remainder is cured and smoked. Originally, curing was considered to be a preservative. Today, curing is done to enhance flavor and provide variety and convenience to the pork products.

Wildlife

As a new industry, wildlife ranching may prove to be a more sustainable way of maintaining wild animal stocks than keeping them in game parks. The exotic tastes and lower fat contents of wild game are appealing to widening international markets. Governments in East Africa and other countries are investing in this type of enterprise to increase wildlife populations, protect farmers' crops, and contain poachers. Since 1981, a rancher in Kenya has increased stocks of giraffe, gazelle, ostrich, and zebra by 40 percent despite the culling of 15 animals per week for local restaurants. On 1 acre of land, 14.6 pounds of gazelle were produced, compared with 1 pound of beef reared under traditional stock raising methods.

Zimbabwe has an ample supply of ostriches. Since 1984, the ostrich industry has grown from 1 to more than 20 ostrich farms. The value of ostriches is mainly in the sale of the skin and meat, although the feathers and eggs also command high international prices.

New Zealand, after importing wildlife species from Canada, namely elk and red deer, established a wildlife farming industry.

Considerable research is going into the nutrients that these animals require in their daily diets. In early 1990, deer farmers were selling the velvet antler for its reported aphrodisiac effects for $140 per kilogram on the world market. In addition, venison was being shipped in large quantities to the EC.

Increased wildlife farming is drawing attention to the fact that many animal species are being threatened as civilizations increase the size of their cities. The Canadian province of British Columbia has the widest range of ecological zones in Canada, from bone-dry deserts to temperate rain forests. Almost three-quarters of the nation's bird and mammal species are found there, including some of the world's richest salmon runs, and the nation's largest winter population of birds. However, encroachment and environmental degradation are threatening some plant and animal species. Only 6.6 percent of B.C. lands are now protected.

Because of concerned citizens living in this environment, Greenpeace, now a 3 million-member, $35 million per year, international organization, was established in Vancouver, B.C. Members of this organization strive to protect wildlife throughout the globe.

Numerous examples can be cited of countries which have a high per capita consumption of wildlife. The canning industry in the U.S.S.R. processes more than 50,000 metric tons of reindeer meat per year. This amount has been reduced since the Chernobyl accident that contaminated many reindeer herds. In West Germany, the annual sales of venison exceed $1 million. In Peru, 5 percent of meat sales are derived from guinea pigs.

The 1987 UN report, "Our Common Future," suggested that 12 percent of the world should be protected to conserve a representative sample of earth's ecosystems, including these and other species of wildlife suited for human food.

ANIMAL PRODUCTS

The optimal production of animal species occurs only when all components of the animal are used as food or feed sources, or for the manufacture of industrial products.

Milk and Milk Products

The world's population obtains most of its milk and milk products from cows, water buffalo, goats, and sheep. Horses, alpaca, donkeys, reindeer, yak, camels, and sows contribute a smaller amount to the total milk supply for humans. Data about some of this milk consumption is included in Exhibit 2.5.

Dairy cows produce over 90 percent of the world's fluid milk supply. In the U.S., cattle produce 99 percent of the milk supply. Around the world, the yield of buffalo and sheep milk is increasing, while that from goats is decreasing. Most milk from goats is produced and consumed by individuals or families who raise a few goats.

There are more than 400 different kinds of cheese that can be made from milk. The cheeses made throughout the world have more than 2,000 names, since the same cheese may have two or more different names.

Only a small percentage of the world's milk production enters world trade: butter (4 percent), cheese (4 percent), skim milk powder (18 percent), and casein (80 percent). The EC and New Zealand account for about 80 percent of the total world exports of dairy products. Exports of skim milk powder are used in a variety of recombined products, including those distributed in the U.S. Food for Peace Program.

Meat Quality

All the factors included in the parameters of livestock management (Exhibit 6.4) affect the ultimate quality of the meat. Obviously, meat quality at the point of consumption is also affected by conditions of travel before slaughter, slaughtering and storage conditions, as well as final cooking procedures. In developed countries, there is a strong demand for quality products with adequate variety and consumer services such as convenience. Considerable research activities are being directed to assuring acceptable levels of meat quality, especially as consumer demand for meat products with a lower fat content is increasing.

In developing countries, the same level of quality may not be required as that in developed countries. For example, when people in India eat their meat in stews or curries, they are less concerned about its initial tenderness and juiciness. Because servants do their shopping for them, some of the richer populations in developing countries frequently tolerate crude or inefficient and wasteful retailing operations.

Influence of Religion

Throughout the world, religious communities have taboos and/or special ceremonies about animals and meat products. One-half of the Indian population does not eat meat because of religious conviction. Muslims do not eat pork, and require that animals be slaughtered for meat according to the traditional halal procedure.

Some major societal groups practice vegetarianism for ethical reasons. In the Buddhist philosophy, and in some regions of India, all animal life is considered sacred.

Some religious fasts and festivals introduce major seasonal factors into meat demand. For example, during long religious fasting periods, Christians in Ethiopia do not eat meat. In many Muslim communities, the feast of Id is a peak point for sheep and goat marketing.

Kosher meat for the Jewish population comes from animals that have split hooves, chew their cud, and have been slaughtered in a manner prescribed by the Torah (Orthodox Jewish law). Kosher slaughter, inspection, and supervision are performed by trained people approved by rabbinic authority.

Animal By-Products

By-products are products of considerably less value than the major product. In the U.S., they include hides, fat, bones, and internal organs from animals. However, in other countries, some animals are grown for draft (work), milk, hides, and skins, which are considered to be their primary products. In these countries, once an old, useless animal is slaughtered, the meat is considered to be the by-product. Some pork skins are processed into consumable food items, a favorite food product of U.S. President George Bush. Many pharmaceutical products originate from animal by-products.

In many non-Western cultures, far more types of animals and parts of animals, i.e., viscera, blood, and marrow, are consumed than are consumed in Western societies. Few consumers in the U.S.

have a strong desire for blood sausage, for example, and other products such as the Scottish haggis. Thus, the contribution from animals to the diet of developing countries is high, because of the lack of societal resistance to these by-products. These by-products are not wasted in developed countries, however, since they are used in industry. From the economical viewpoint of a developed country, industrial use is a more efficient one.

Inedible By-Products

Animals contribute a large number of useful products. Tallow, hides, and inedible organs are the inedible animal by-products that are more highly valued. Hides and skins are valued as by-products or as major products on a worldwide basis. Cattle and buffalo hides comprise 80 percent of farm animal hides and skins produced in the world.

A major focal point of by-products is the rendering industry which recycles offal, fat, bone, meat scraps, and entire animal carcasses, with animal fat and protein being the primary products. Many different grades of tallow and semi-liquid feed fat are produced. The major uses of rendered fat are for animal feeds, fatty acid production, and soap manufacture. Fatty acids are used in the manufacture of numerous industrial products: plastics, cosmetics, lubricants, paints, deodorants, polishes, cleaners, caulking compounds, asphalt tiles, and printing inks, to name a few.

Rendered animal proteins are processed into several high-protein feed supplements which are fed to young monogastric animals and pets. These animals, such as swine and poultry, require a high-quality protein with the amino acid lysine. When blood is not processed into blood meal, it is used to produce products for the pet food industry.

SMALL RUMINANT RESEARCH PROGRAMS

Because of the prevalence of ruminants around the world and their contributions to society, several small ruminant research programs have been established. More than two-thirds of the globe's domesticated ruminants are found in the developing countries.

Thus, research findings from these programs will likely have implications for people throughout many developing countries.

In Ethiopia, a milk program was established for small farms in the highlands. The farms (2.8 hectares) were already heavily stocked with an average of one donkey, one cow, a pair of bullocks, one young head of cattle, and seven sheep and goats. Plans were made to lower stock numbers to improve feed sources. Although technicians on the project wanted to forego the donkey and the small ruminants, the women living on the farms refused to work without these animals. Reaching a compromise based on the social implications, the bullock teams were replaced with two cows for work and milk. Although they had wanted the women to have crossbred cows which could yield 10-20 liters of milk per day, the women did not want the task of processing this amount of milk. Further, they liked to keep their crossbred cows constantly tethered because this facilitated manure collection, the dung cakes being used as fuel for both cooking and heating. This milk program was enhanced by providing assistance to the people with improved methods of butter making, home preparation of cheeses, management of tethered animals, and marketing.

In Peru, people value small ruminants for their ability to use high altitude grasslands and other areas not under cultivation. Pastoral peoples in the central Andes rely on herds of alpaca, llama, and sheep for their livelihood. They often follow a rotational fallowing system in which fallow fields are grazed and manured by herds, and crop residues are a critical feed resource for the herds during the dry season. Small ruminants, and the manure they provide, are critical to the continued functioning of this production system.

In Peru, the research mandate of the small ruminant program is to determine techniques for expanding the resource-poor stockowners' herd of sheep, goats, llama, and alpaca. Hopefully, research findings from this program can be applied to other developing countries (with more than two-thirds of the globe's domesticated ruminants). In these countries, animal diseases are prevalent; herds are more susceptible because of climatic and nutritional stress. Thus, veterinary medicine is crucial to the success of any small ruminant program.

In these small ruminant programs, conflicts between biological productivity and social requirements often arise with animal production. For example, if 10 poultry enterprises could produce all the eggs usable in a market at reduced prices, would this be desirable if they diminished income from 100 traditional egg producers? In animal science terms, the program would be warranted. In social terms, it could only be warranted if alternative sources of income were possible in the immediate future.

In another example of this conflict, cattle can be bred to produce milk with over 4 percent protein, but doing so decreases total yields of milk, calcium, vitamins, and lactose by about 50 percent. Further, local markets will not support the high protein milk, and farmers will not tolerate sharp declines in total yields. Multidisciplinary research efforts in ruminant programs should prevent conflicts such as these from reducing the productivity of ruminant production.

INSECT PRODUCTION

Insects make up about 80 percent of the world's animal species. They are the basis of the food chain for most higher animals, being as important to humans as plants are for their oxygen content.

Two types of bugs that can be beneficial are parasites and predators. The parasite bugs require only one host to develop but predator bugs have to eat more than one individual pest to complete their development and go through their life stages. Ladybeetles, also called ladybirds and ladybugs, are predators that were introduced into the U.S. from Australia in the late 1800s, when a scale insect threatened the California citrus crops. The ladybeetle is a voracious predator.

Insects have played an important role in human nutrition. Historical accounts have revealed that hundreds of species have been eaten in Central and Southern Africa, Asia, Australia, and Latin America. Correspondence from former Peace Corps volunteers has attested to the wide use of insects in numerous countries.

In countries or cultures where the use of insects as food is traditional, the insects are highly prized and sought after. They are not merely used as an alternative for staving off starvation. They are incorporated into the regular diet when the insects are in season, and they are frequently sought throughout the year.

Food insects serve as a direct source of essential nutrients, adding to the rural economy and developing greater food self-sufficiency among rural populations at risk of malnutrition. The proportionally small quantitative contribution of insects to the diet, compared with plant foods, has been dictated by limited supplies. The knowledge among indigenous people about the host plants and seasonal history of local food insects has been noted throughout the tropical regions.

Preparing Insects

Current information suggests that more than 30 species are used as food by indigenous populations in many developing countries. Some examples from regions of these countries follow.

Zaire

In the country of Zaire, 35 species of insects are currently used as food, comprising at least 10 percent of their animal protein. Caterpillars are roasted on heated sheet metal, cooked in boiling water, or fried in oil. Salt and red peppers are sometimes added. To preserve a portion of the harvest, caterpillars are either smoked or boiled in salt water, drained, and dried.

Mexico

In Mexico, more than 200 species have been consumed as human food. In southern Mexico, food insects are sold in the finest restaurants in the largest cities, and are also exported to Europe and the U.S.

South Africa

In South Africa, caterpillars known as "mopanie worms" are a special favorite. When available for sale, they seriously affect the sale of beef. A mopanie cannery is in operation. The South African Bureau of Standards estimates annual sales of about 40,000 bags, each containing 40 kg of traditionally prepared dried caterpillars. This amounts to 1,600 metric tons. This official volume, travelling through food marketing channels, is only a fraction of the actual number of mopanie that are consumed. In South Africa, food insects are also served as a relish with cereal meal porridges, providing flavor to the bland porridge.

Japan

In Japan, in spite of a degree of Westernization in its society, insects are widely consumed and appreciated, particularly in rural areas. Some are consumed as a snack to accompany alcoholic beverages.

Zimbabwe

In Zimbabwe, dried caterpillars of saturniid moths are sold in local markets, and large quantities of termites, locusts, and tettigoniids are eaten by the majority of the population in spite of the growing presence of Western cultures. The introduction of electricity has increased the insect population in towns at night, sometimes leading to traffic jams that suddenly occur as streets are blocked by rural people coming to collect insects that have been attracted by the vast number of lights.

Asia

In parts of Asia, pupae of the silkworm are available as a by-product of the silk industry and have been used both as human food and as a high protein supplement for poultry. Insects could be "farmed" to produce low-cost feed for pond fish on small farms in Asia.

Thailand

The cooking technique for some grasshoppers in Thailand is simple. Their wings, heads, and tails are removed before they are cleaned and thrown into a frying pan.

Colombia

Developments in this country illustrate another use for insects. Silkworm culture has been introduced to southwestern Colombia as a diversification for small coffee farms. In that country, the lack of inexpensive, high-protein feed sources is a major problem confronting poultry, swine, and pond fish producers. The pupal by-product from this industry could represent a major new resource for the farmers, either for local use or for export. In addition, the silkworm frass and other residues could be used as fertilizer in the mulberry plots or for pond fish food.

U.S.

The Mormon cricket, incredibly numerous during the spring of 1990, is a potential U.S. candidate for mass harvest. Being a large wingless insect weighing approximately 1 gram (dry weight), it travels in bands throughout the western U.S. states. It received its name after the Mormons imported seagulls to curb its population around the Salt Lake area of Utah. At cricket densities of 10-20/m^2, a 1 km^2 band totals 11-22 metric tons of high protein powder, an excellent feed source for broiler chickens.

Nutrient Content of Insects

How does the caloric value of grains and insects compare? A 100 gram serving of corn contains between 320 and 340 kcal. When 100 gram servings of nine Mexican insect species were analyzed, they contained from 377 to 513 kcal. Further, they were rich sources of iron and riboflavin. Some insects with high fat contents have been found to contain 613 kcal per 100 g serving. Some insects are high in both calcium and phosphorous, others are good sources of trace minerals.

Insects are being used as high-protein replacement for expensive fish meals imported for poultry production with good results. Studies have been conducted on fly pupae or larvae as a high-protein source for poultry, generally with the aim of using the fly larvae to recycle animal wastes. During recycling, the muscid larvae convert poultry manure to a loose, crumbly texture. The substance is nearly odorless and can be dried for use as a feedstuff or soil conditioner, supplying organic matter and trace minerals. Problems that must be overcome before mass production is possible include: moisture control, aeration, and regulation of the larval density.

Agricultural Potential of Insects

The Food Insects Research and Development Project (FIRDP) was organized at the University of Wisconsin in Madison in 1986. Its objectives include stimulating a wider awareness among food and agricultural scientists, government agencies, and the public that insects are a food resource that warrants serious investigation. In 1988, the University of Wisconsin in Madison offered a course entitled "Use of Insects as Food and Animal Feed."

Insects offer a number of attributes:

1. high food conversion efficiency compared with conventional meat animals;
2. the ability to use a wide array of organic substances not efficiently used in conventional agriculture;
3. productivity without the need for additional arable land, irrigation, fertilizers, herbicides, pesticides, or expensive equipment;
4. the possible adaptability for incorporation into a pest management program that would help reduce the need for insecticides for crop protection before they are harvested for human food and/or animal feed. Each year in the U.S., farmers spend about $3.5 billion for the chemical war on bugs.

Several factors are threatening to reduce the availability of insects as food in the developing world. First, there is an acculturation to Western attitudes which do not have a high level of acceptance for eating "unsanitary" and "crawly" bugs. Second, the ecology is deteriorating in terms of tropical forest destruction and water pollution. For example, as Mexico City has expanded, several species of aquatic Hemiptera have disappeared because of lake pollution and the increased need for landfills. For centuries, these insects were the basis of aquatic farming there. Third, there is a lack of governmental recognition and support for this concept. Such government recognition of traditional insect foods would help provide respectability for this practice, and could provide legitimacy for the research and extension services needed to enhance their use.

In a Mexican project, the larva of the "white agave worm," derived from a species of caterpillar, are considered a delicacy throughout the country, being served in some of the finest restaurants. Although formerly exported, the larva is now relatively scarce because of over-collection procedures. Research is investigating reasons for the problems with mating that occur when they are reared in captivity.

Food insect harvest methods are, for the most part, as primitive as they were generations ago. Some species will continue to be obtained by labor-intensive collecting; others could be significantly increased in number by some rather simple innovations in small-scale harvest or culture. Other species should lend themselves to sophisticated methods of large-scale harvest. These species have characteristics that make them suitable for controlled mass production, extending their period of seasonal availability. For insects that are attracted to light such as the tettigoniid grasshopper and the winged termite, light or lantern traps represent a simple technology with potential for greatly increasing their harvest.

It is anticipated that many of the insects now considered candidates for improved harvesting will become candidates for controlled year-round production as more is learned about their biology that is relevant to sustained culture.

Practically every substance of organic origin, including cellulose, is fed upon by one or more species of insect. Eventually, successful recycling systems will be developed. In El Salvador, efforts are being made to recycle coffee pulp waste using the larvae of some of their indigenous insects. Because the cricket takes in food and water ad lib, it appears to be an excellent candidate for recycling under-used agricultural organic matter such as banana and pineapple wastes. Studies are needed to determine precisely the cricket's dietary requirements.

From properly loaded terminal lagoons for human wastes, it may be possible to harvest the biomass for animal feeds. The high nutrient content of the biomass comes mainly from aquatic insects.

Insects are eaten in foods in developed countries although it is done unknowingly. Regulations for individual food items frequently include allowances for "animal parts" from production insects such as aphids and other herbivores associated with the growing crop, and processing insects such as ants, cockroaches, and flies. Food scientists inspect processed foods to ensure that the regulations are not exceeded. This raises an interesting point: since the diet of developed societies already includes insect parts, which is preferable for consumption, insect parts or the pesticide residues developed to reduce them? Entomologists, scientists who study all aspects of insects, from their biological and biochemical processes to their social behavior, argue that it is safer to consume "cooked" insect parts than insecticide residues in our foods.

Escargot, or snail, sales in the U.S. amount to $300 million per year. Given the similar "status," similar markets may open up for certain edible insects. This would create markets for farmers dedicated to low-input specialty crops as part of sustainable agriculture systems. In contrast to the rationale for enhanced food insect use in developing countries because of high labor costs, insect snacks and hors d'oeuvres in the U.S. would probably be priced as luxury foods and advertised for the "upscale" consumer.

NASA has considered insects among possible foods for space travel. The use of insects to reduce the quantity of waste materials to a minimum is being investigated. A small beetle is being investigated for its recycling capability.

Research is needed by food scientists and food engineers to develop processing procedures that extend shelf life or improve nutritional qualities, shape, texture, and flavor, thereby increasing the desirability of insects to a broad range of consumers. In Canada, when the pupal fraction or honey bee brood was deep fat fried in vegetable oil, consumers said that it compared to such foods as walnuts, pork crackling, sunflower seeds, and Rice Krispies.

SUMMARY

Today, nutrition, health, and management needs of animals are well known and scientifically based. The demand for meat products will likely continue in developed countries and likely increase in some developing ones. In spite of these two trends, arguments will continue to be made about whether or not we have the right to produce animals. Now that you are aware of the benefits that livestock, wildlife, and insects offer society, arguments from both sides will be summarized.

More acres of cropland are required per person for a diet high in foods from animals than for a diet including only plant products. As ruminant animals, the original advantage for producing cows was that they could thrive on grass, shrubs, and other plants nonedible for humans. The conversion ratios for beef are about five times poorer than those for chickens and swine. Thus, this argument is made against cattle production: Whenever cattle feeds are grown on land that could otherwise support crops for humans, or when the feed grains are also edible for people, the original advantage of producing cattle is lost.

Another argument is this: Much of the impetus to make heavy use of fertilizers, irrigation, and pesticides comes from consumers' preference for animal products. That is, they satisfy the demand for the production of feed grains. However, even with slight changes in eating habits towards reduced meat consumption, population growth, and the 15:1 lever effect of animal products in the diet, the demand for animal feeds will probably continue to increase.

Some opponents of animal production credit some deforestation rates with it. For example, 40 years ago, 75 percent of Costa Rica was forested. Two-thirds of this bounty has been destroyed, in large part to make way for cattle ranches. Once the forest soil becomes depleted or exhausted, these animal-production efforts are halted because of inadequate pasturelands. Such depletion of resources may result in Costa Rica becoming a net importer of both lumber and meat by the year 2000.

The argument is frequently made that livestock and poultry compete with humans for food. As the production of poultry is increasing in many developing countries, data is becoming available that grains going to feed poultry may stimulate total grain production. For example, in India, a positive correlation has been found between increases in grain and livestock production, mainly because of increased feed from more crop residues.

Livestock sales provide the capital for improving crop-production. The cash can be used for inputs such as fertilizers, seeds, pesticides, and so on. Thus, cash from selling livestock products serves as a catalyst for the farm system. There is a need to recognize mixed farms as having two major subsystems, crops and animals. Both contribute to family welfare.

For range and small-scale systems, animals and livestock are often a vital and necessary part of crop-production systems. World-wide, 40 to 80 percent of the livestock are associated with mixed crop/livestock farming systems. In warm climates, animals provide 150 million horsepower per year. Most of this energy is used for cropping. Global needs for animal power will increase by 100 percent by the year 2000.

To summarize, animals provide manure for fertilizer, solid fuel, and biogas. Worldwide, animals contribute more than 56 million tons of edible protein and more than 1 billion megacalories of energy each year. Their quality protein is equivalent to more than 50 percent of that produced from cereals grown throughout the world.

REFERENCES

Abbott, J. C. 1986. *Marketing improvement in the developing world: what happens and what we have learned*. FAO Economic and Social.

Carlisle, Hildred. 1990. Personal communication. Agritour Associates Ltd, Hamilton, New Zealand.

Cullen, Lorol. 1990. From Russia with love. *Foodservice and Hospitality* 24(1):19-26.

DeFoliart, Gene R. 1989. The human use of insects as food and as animal feed. Bulletin of the ESA, Spring: 22-35.

Ensminger, A. H., M. E. Ensminger, J. E. Konlande, and J. R. K. Robson. 1986. Food for health—a nutrition encyclopedia. Clovis, CA: Pegus Press.

FAO Production Yearbook. Vol. 42. 1988. Rome: Food and Agriculture Organization of the United Nations.

Food and Agriculture Organization of the United Nations. 1983. *Changing patterns and trends in feed utilization*. FAO Economic and Social Development Paper 37. Rome.

Gever, J., R. Kaufman, D. Skole, and C. Vorosmarty. 1986. *Beyond oil*. Cambridge: Ballinger Publishing Company.

Harwood, R. R., R. J. Battenfield, B. D. Knezek, and J. L. Davidson. 1985. Production systems. In *Crop productivity—research imperatives revisited*, eds. M. Gibbs and C. Carlson, 216-238. An international conference held at Boyne Highlands Inn, October 13-18, 1985 and Airlie House, December 11-13, 1985.

Jamtgaard, Keith A. 1989. Targeting production systems in the small ruminant CRSP: a typology using cluster analysis. In *The social sciences in international agricultural research*, ed. C. M. McCorkle, 195-212. Boulder & London: Lynne Rienner Publishers.

McCorkle, Constance M. 1989. Veterinary anthropology in the small ruminant

CRSP/Peru. In *The social sciences in international agricultural research*, ed. C. M. McCorkle, 213-227. Boulder & London: Lynne Rienner Publishers.

McDowell, R. E. 1989. Social sciences in agricultural research: an animal science perspective. In *The social sciences in international agricultural research*, ed. C. M. McCorkle, 242-248. Boulder & London: Lynne Rienner Publishers.

National Research Council. 1988. *Designing foods – animal product options in the marketplace*. Washington, DC: National Academy Press.

Pelto, G. H. and P. J. Pelto. 1983. Diet and delocalization: dietary changes since 1750. In *Hunger and history*, eds. R. I. Rotberg and T. K. Tabb, 309-330. Cambridge: Cambridge University Press.

Taylor, R. E. and R. Bogart. 1988. *Scientific farm animal production*. 3rd ed. New York: Macmillan Publishing Company.

Wittwer, Sylvan H. 1983. The new agriculture: a view of the twenty-first century. In *Agriculture in the twenty-first century*, ed. J. W. Rosenblum, 337-67. New York: John Wiley & Sons.

Yermanos, D. M., M. Neushul, and R. D. MacElroy. 1983. Crops from the desert, sea, and space. In *Agriculture in the twenty-first century*, ed. J. W. Rosenblum, 144-65. New York: John Wiley & Sons.

Chapter Seven

Global Fish and Shellfish Production

INTRODUCTION

As vertebrate animals which live exclusively in water, breathe through gills, and have limbs which take the form of fins, fish comprise one-half of all known species of vertebrates. Scientists have named and documented more than 20,000 kinds of fish. Shellfish are hard-covered, edible, mostly marine animals from two groups: the mollusks (oysters, clams, mussels) and crustaceans (crabs, lobsters, shrimp). Other foods taken from the sea, depending on the area and the culture, include octopus, squid, and sea turtles. Although the fishing industry is rapidly evolving today largely in response to declining supplies of fish, the fishing industry has been an important industry throughout civilization. Seafood, with its perceived healthfulness and culinary attributes, is increasingly the protein choice of people throughout the world.

By studying the information contained in this chapter, you will become familiar with several topics:

- the dynamic nature of fish ecosystems, and how they are being affected by the human population;
- global developments in the aquaculture or fish-farming industries producing human foods, animal feeds, and sources of biomass, a renewable energy source;
- scientific fisheries management approaches, including developments within the multidisciplinary approach, termed cooperative management, of local fisheries.

More than 60 percent of the fish consumed in the U.S. is imported, causing a trade deficit of more then $2.5 billion, or about 28 percent of the U.S. trade deficit, exclusive of petroleum products. In the U.S., trout have been farmed for a hundred years. U.S. aquaculture accounts for only 3 percent of the total fisheries landings. The Sea Grant Program was established in the U.S. in 1966 to develop and conserve the nation's marine resources. One recent USDA study estimated that seafood expenditures would increase 27.4 percent between 1980 and 2005, well above the projected increases for beef, pork, and poultry.

THE DYNAMIC FISH ECOSYSTEM

Perpetual species of fish possess feedback mechanisms that regulate their population numbers in accordance with the environmental favorableness. Annual variation in food supply is a primary attribute of an aquatic environment's favorableness. A strong food supply in a given year signals that the environment can support greater populations of a given fish species.

New opportunities exist to examine how altering aquatic environments affects the fish populations. Recent advances in techniques for estimating food consumption, i.e., energy intake rates, in fish populations have improved the capacity to measure mechanisms of energy flow through fish populations.

The measurement of energy flow through ecosystems is a standard basis for their evaluation. The relative amount of energy flowing through a population within an ecosystem documents a great deal about its role and environmental adaptation.

Human Effects on Fish Populations

Humans affect fish populations through direct exploitation caused by recreational, commercial, and subsistence fishing, as well as indirectly through impacting the aquatic environment. Anthropogenic stresses on fish populations have increased as a direct function of human population growth and are significantly related to human technological developments.

Although humans have exploited marine fish stocks for hundreds of years, demands on these resources have been so high throughout this century that they have caused significant stock depletions. Efficient fishing technologies such as trawling have accentuated the impact of an expanding human population upon fish stocks.

Since the late 1800s, phosphorous loading into aquatic ecosystems has increased in response to the building of shoreline communities. This action has altered or degraded numerous fish communities by grossly shifting the complexion of aquatic environments. The process of eutrophication has accelerated. Technological developments leading to the use of phosphorus detergents in the late 1940s significantly intensified eutrophication problems.

Humans disturb aquatic environments, reducing rates of fish production and the availability of desired fish species. Common anthropogenic impacts on aquatic ecosystems involve nutrient loading, acidification, sedimentation, modification of flow rates, addition of oxygen-demanding substances, and the alteration of thermal regimes. Each of these may substantially reduce optimal conditions for fish populations. Each of these impacts has a degrading potential exhibited by toxicity-related disturbances.

Toxicity impairs populations in ways that are more subtle than direct lethality. For example, concentrations of selenium below levels that are directly lethal to bluegill adults or their young cause anatomical abnormalities in the progeny of exposed females, leading to low survival rates. Some changes in fish behavior associated with metal toxicity actually impair their population-regulating mechanisms. As a result of the Chernobyl nuclear accident, fish in contaminated waters have grown very large, and they are also exceptionally weak. The affects of these levels of radiation on future fish populations are virtually unknown.

One of the largest salmon runs in the world has long been associated with the Thompson and Fraser River systems in western Canada. A recent Canadian study stated waste-water discharge into the Thompson River system in B.C. had increased 12 times to 228,100 cubic meters per day between 1965 and 1985. One pulp mill is responsible. When the river levels drop during the winter season, waste-water discharge accounts for about 2 percent of the total river flow. Juvenile chinook salmon which remain in the Thompson River during the winter are subject to the "sub-lethal effects" from raw and biologically treated bleached kraft pulp mill effluent. This can have a harmful effect on salmon stocks in the river. Other complaints from this pollution include: coloring in the water, growth in algae, reduction in some fish species, and a physical deterioration in other species.

More than 1,000 kilometers of shoreline on the Atlantic and Pacific coasts of Canada, worth millions of dollars to the fishing industry, have been closed to shellfish harvesting because of pollution. Only 500 kilometers were affected 20 years ago. Untreated human sewage is dumped into waterways from almost 40 percent of Canadian municipalities, making a large contribution to polluted waters.

COMMERCIAL FISHERIES INDUSTRY

One sign of the pressure on commercial fishing is the growing number of harvesting restrictions being placed on species around the world. Another factor is the growing consumer concern about pollution of ocean and fresh water resources. This should strengthen aquaculture's position as an alternate source of seafood.

"Free-for-all" fishing has lead to resource depletion, economic waste, and inefficient government regulation. Such regulations should specify the catch and assign well-defined rights. Fishermen should employ the most efficient way to harvest catch, as well as cooperating with resource management. In New Zealand, transferrable fishing rights have resolved many of the problems in the commercial fishery industry.

One of the most dramatic changes in property rights over fish took place in the mid-1970s when coastal fishing nations began extending their jurisdiction over most living marine resources to 200 nautical miles from shore. Although daily efforts prevail within the 200-mile fishing limits adopted around the world, the sea is extremely hard to police. Once an area is overfished, an extremely long recovery time is required. Entire fisheries have collapsed, i.e., Californian sardines and Peruvian anchovies.

Data for the 1986 commercial fish catch around the world are given in Exhibit 7.1. Overfishing has turned the oceans into the world's slaughterhouse. Many scientists believe the 203.2 billion

Exhibit 7.1.   Commercial Fisheries Catch - 1986.

Country	Fish Catch[1] (billions of pounds, live weight)	Country	Fish Catch[1] (billions of pounds, live weight)
U.S.	10.9	North Korea	3.7E
Canada	3.2	Norway	4.2
Chile	12.3	Peru	12.4
China	17.6	Phillipines	4.3
Denmark	4.1	South Korea	6.8
Iceland	3.7	USSR	24.9
India	6.4	Spain	2.9
Indonesia	5.6	Thailand	4.7
Japan	26.4		
Mexico	2.9	World, Total	203.2

[1]Refers to catch of fish, crustaceans, mollusks (including weight of shells) and other aquatic plants and animals, except whale and seals.

E = estimated.

Source: Statistical Abstract of the United States.   1989.   109th ed.
U.S. Department of Commerce.   Washington, DC: U.S.
Government Printing Office.

tons of fish hauled out of the ocean each year have surpassed the critical point for replenishing stocks.

Cod stocks are dwindling off the Atlantic Coast; the North Pacific driftnet fishery is taking too many salmon, steelhead, porpoises, and seabirds; the tuna fishery in the eastern Pacific is killing an estimated 100,000 dolphins per year. Oil spills, incinerator ships, human waste, toxic chemicals, and plastic debris impact fish stocks. Throughout Canada, 83 of 149 pulp mills are dumping more toxic chemicals into Canadian waters than national pollution standards allow. Do humans know the rate at which they can safely harvest biological resources without depleting them?

AQUACULTURE

Although aquaculture's contribution to the world seafood supply is less than 12 percent, it is becoming an increasingly important industry. World seafood demand is growing much faster than wild seafood production. Aquaculture will be the source of the increased seafood production needed to meet growing demands. Aquaculture is believed to be the only hope for substantially increasing world seafood production.

Aquaculture is a large international business worth billions of dollars each year. A high percentage of the world's farmed seafood production is targeted at U.S. markets. However, there are problems, challenges, and research needs throughout the aquaculture industry. For example, U.S. catfish farmers have boosted production so rapidly that demand can lag behind supply.

In 1985, farmed seafood began to have a major impact on the world seafood market. The FAO of the UN is the central clearinghouse for all seafood statistics. However, data are not yet being collected for all of the industry. For example, the U.S. does not report its trout production and China does not report its carp production. A few examples follow of the species being farmed.

Examples of Species

Shrimp

Shrimp is the biggest business in aquaculture. More than 300,000 metric tons of shrimp are now farmed worldwide compared to 100,000 metric tons 5 years ago.

China has undertaken an ambitious development program to farm a white shrimp, *Penaeus chinensis*, along the Bohai Gulf in northeastern China. Shrimp can be farmed at a production cost of about $1 per pound for shell-on tails. Their delivered market price to U.S.

importers is more than $3 per pound. In 1988, China became the leading shrimp supplier to the U.S. market, exporting about 50,000 metric tons. China is the world's largest producer of farmed shrimp with annual harvests in excess of 100,000 metric tons. Possessing enough land for this industry that also requires extensive labor, China plans to double its output of this shrimp species every 3 years.

Ecuador farms about 100,000 metric tons of shrimp per year. Compared with China, Ecuador has the next lowest shrimp production costs about $1.50 per pound for shell-on tails.

Unlike China and Ecuador, the shrimp farming business in Taiwan used highly technological, specialized methods. The shrimp species farmed in Taiwan is *Penaeus monodon*, the black tiger.

Indonesia, Thailand, and the Philippines are currently experiencing a boom in shrimp farming. Major Japanese investments have been made in these countries, supporting this increase.

Salmon

Salmon farming is the second most valuable aquaculture endeavor. The total farmed salmon production is about 200,000 metric tons. Norway, the world's leader in this sector, had salmon exports worth $1 billion in 1989. The Norwegians produced 120,000 metric tons of Atlantic salmon in 1989, followed by Scotland which harvested 30,000 metric tons.

Other important salmon farming countries include Canada, which harvests about 20,000 metric tons per year from farms on both coasts; Japan, which net pens about 15,000 metric tons of coho salmon per year; and Chile, which plans to harvest 10,000 metric tons each year. Other countries actively farming salmon include: Iceland, Ireland, the Faeroe Islands, New Zealand, Australia, and the U.S. The U.S. production is projected to level off at about 10,000 to 15,000 metric tons per year.

With the exception of Chile, which can produce coho salmon for about $1.75 per pound, salmon cannot be farmed for less than $2 per pound.

Catfish

Catfish production in the U.S. has plateaued at about 150,000 metric tons. With production costs about $.60-$.70 per pound, catfish is one of the cheapest fish to farm.

Crawfish

Crawfish production is the second in size to catfish farming in the U.S. Like catfish, these species are easy to farm. In Australia, crawfish are grown in ponds lined with old Japanese automobile tires to give them a desired habitat for their 1-year growth period. When plated and served, these large crawfish can often be mistaken for rock lobster tails. No significant U.S. expansion in crawfish beyond 35,000 metric tons per year is expected until new markets are developed.

Trout

Trout farming is well established in Europe. The state of Idaho accounts for 80 percent of the total U.S. production, growing about 20,000 metric tons per year. Farmers are attempting to increase their stock densities by using liquid oxygen and improving genetic selection procedures.

Oysters

Oysters are the largest shellfish industry in the U.S. In 1988, the Pacific oyster harvest exceeded 30,000 metric tons. The west coast state of Washington has the world's largest oyster hatcheries, in Quilcene.

Mussels

Mussel farming is a huge industry in Holland, France, and Spain. In these countries, hundreds of thousands of tons of mussels are farmed each year by a variety of methods including bottom culture, longlines, and poles. New Zealand has developed a significant industry around the green mussel which is farmed on longlines on both the south and north islands. New Zealand 1988 harvests approached 15,000 metric tons. Blue mussels have developed into a fairly profitable small industry. U.S. mussel farmers gross annual sales of about $5 million.

Clams

Though still a modest industry, clam farming should grow rapidly in the near future as the technology becomes more widely available.

Abalone

Although farming abalone is a slow process, it is a popular shellfish. The slow-growing limpets support a significant industry in Japan. Farms in California and Hawaii harvest the red abalone whose meat is worth about $20 per pound.

Scallop

Japan has a scallop farming industry with annual harvests of 200,000 metric tons. Considerable effort is being expended in Europe to develop a scallop farming industry.

Other Species

Three other finfish species, tilapia, hybrid striped bass, and white sturgeon, are being farmed in the U.S. on a small scale. Tilapia may be the easiest fish to farm in the world; hundreds of thousands of tons are farmed in Asia and Africa each year. Hybrid striped bass, a cross between striped bass and white bass, is receiving considerable attention in the fish farming industry.

White sturgeon is a quality fish in demand by fine restaurants. It is being farmed in California by a number of farms including Sea Farm, Inc., a large aquaculture company with operations in Europe, the U.S., and Canada.

Japanese and Chinese Innovations

The world's leaders in aquaculture are Japan and China. In the Orient, support from the Chinese Institute of Oceanology and the Ocean Engineering Association of Japan is leading to the development of novel marine farming techniques. Research efforts related to the domestication and genetic improvement of new marine crop plants is also in progress.

When the 200-mile fishing zone was established, Japan initiated plans to reduce dependence on fishing in foreign waters. Note in Exhibit 7.1 that Japan had the largest commercial fish catch in 1986.

Japan has created benthonic farming areas. The sea floor has been cleared of existing vegetation, encouraging the settlement and growth of selected plant and animal species. The Japanese have experimented with digging coastal channels to be used as farms, treating the intertidal region with caustic soda to clear away existing vegetation, and sandblasting rock to encourage the growth of desirable species.

They have experimented with many kinds of floating rafts, nets, and longlines for off-the-bottom cultivation of seaweeds and invertebrates. They have developed floating fish pens which can be pulled down below the sea surface for protection during storms. These nets are used to cultivate tuna and yellowtail in unprotected offshore regions where normal floating pens cannot be used.

Japan plans to create 2,500 artificial reefs and develop one-fifth of their coastline into fishing zones. They are developing seaweed farms in deep offshore waters for the production of biomass energy. Seaweed biomass will be converted into biogas by anaerobic bacterial digestion.

The Chinese have been farming since before Christ was born. Fifty percent of the world's cultivated fish are produced in China. Chinese fishermen harvest 3.1 million tons of marine fish per year and aquaculturalists grow and harvest 17.5 million tons of freshwater fish.

Future of Aquaculture

The forests and grasslands of the sea have not yet been fully exploited as food sources for livestock and humans. Global aquaculture will become more important, especially in tropic and subtropic regions. Although U.S. catfish farming is expected to increase, specialty luxury species such as shrimp, lobster, oyster, and salmon will continue to dominate the U.S. industry. One possibility of increasing yields of catfish is to raise the temperature of ponds by covering them with layers of plastic sheeting.

In the warmer climates of Taiwan, Japan, and China, fish culture will continue to be combined with hog and duck production. Their integrated systems of pigs, ducks, and tropical fish produce 250 pigs or 2,500 ducks per hectare and provide sufficient waste for the production of 6 tons of Chinese carp and tilapia per hectare per year.

A number of forces will contribute to the continued growth of U.S. aquaculture. First, the interaction of worldwide population growth and the biological limits of ocean and lake fish production should increase the demand for farm-raised fish. As the commercial fisheries industry for "wild" fish approaches the maximum harvest rates for more and more species, aquaculture will receive added pressure to become a major source of seafood production.

DEVELOPMENT OF MARINE FARMS

Projections are being made that world fishing grounds will be transformed into sites for marine farms in the twenty-first century. These will be unmodified ecosystems and the marine farmer will experiment mostly with undomesticated plants and animals. Several research areas are crucial to the success of this industry. First, the biological features of the plants and animals need to be identified. Second, methods are needed for seedstock production and genetic selection. Third, all parameters of the marine ecosystems need to be precisely defined.

Two U.S. farms have been proposed. One would be an open-sea planktonic farm in offshore waters where fish could be grown. The site for this farm would be southern California which is influenced by the California Current and has the seasonal upwelling of cold, nutrient-rich deep water. It is now a source of anchovy. The other farm would be a near-shore, on-the-bottom benthonic farm where seaweeds could be grown. The near-shore farm could be modified for kelp.

Along with other economic factors, the questions of crop ownership and control of harvesting activities need clarification. With benthonic farming, the sea floor can be leased from the government and the cultivated organism can be planted in rows and harvested.

"Farming" Biomass from the Oceans

Kelp beds off the Pacific coast were first harvested for potash. Now they are used to produce algal gums and mucilages used as thickening and emulsifying agents in food products.

Natural kelp beds serve as models of what large-scale, near-shore marine farms might be like in the next century. They are productive and stable. The bed in Goleta Bay, California, has ranged in size from 650 to 1,160 acres since 1955. It has a standing crop of ca. 44,000 metric tons of which about 5,700 tons of material are dislodged during storms and beached annually. One-quarter to one-half of the plants are lost and replaced each year. This bed could produce about 3.7 tons of dry ash-free biomass per acre per year.

A near-shore marine biomass farm could show self-renewing capabilities. High biomass yields could be achieved with appropriate planting, cultivating, and harvesting. Under ideal experimental conditions, yields of 10 to 15 ash-free tons per acre have been realized. Projected yields of 20 to 30 tons may be feasible, with optimal marine farm management procedures.

Marine farming will undoubtedly lead to future conflicts between farmers and fishermen. Kelp beds are good nursery grounds for fish. Thus, fishermen could have greater catches if kelp farms were planted in areas where kelp does not traditionally grow.

SCIENTIFIC FISHERIES MANAGEMENT

While the objectives of fishery management have varied over time, "conservation" is the most universally accepted goal. Biblical teachings include cautions against waste of natural resources. Fishery managers have traditionally perceived their role to be that of defenders of fish populations against depletion by the harvesters. Where the fishery industry is based on highly migratory fish stocks and there is more than one group of fishermen utilizing the stock, government-level management becomes a necessity.

Scientific fisheries management approaches have significantly curbed the decimation of many exploited marine fish populations. Wastewater treatment technologies, applied throughout the 1970s and 1980s, have reduced some of the rates of phosphorus loading into the aquatic ecosystems. Some dramatic recoveries have occurred. Thus, while human population growth has intensified the stresses placed on fish communities, some key technological and scientific advancements have reduced this pressure.

While fishery management thinking may have changed considerably over the years, the actual day-to-day practice has changed very little in North American communities. Single-species population dynamics models are still being used, even when ecological interactions are known to be highly important. Rather than dealing with the dynamics of the situation, i.e., fish populations subject to year-to-year changes and varying over long periods of time because of unknown or poorly understood ecosystem processes, scientists recommend estimates of maximum sustainable yields.

Management for maximum sustainable yield results in the development of fish harvest objectives for one type of fish at a time without regard to the fact that fish do not exist independently of their ecosystems. Complex conditions such as competition, predation, and parasitism, between target fish species and others, have to be taken into account. In addition, other changes such as year-to-year changes in the physical environment have to be considered.

Indirect fishing controls include such policies as: seasonal and area closures, minimum landed fish size, and gear regulations. These standard approaches are being challenged. In fishing forums, recurring themes are being discussed, incurring new approaches to fisheries management:

1. New, alternative approaches need to be investigated.
2. No commitments or limitations should be established until local fisherman have been thoroughly consulted. Further, fishery managers should involve local communities and groups of fishermen in the management process in a meaningful way.
3. Fishermen should be continuously consulted to permit effective responses to unanticipated problems.

In many cases, the fishermen are on the ocean with the fish problems and opportunities, and the policymakers are on the land, attempting to give meaningful interpretation to data. To the extent that use of fishermen's information can reduce the amount of field research needed, savings in research budgets may be realized.

Changes are being recommended because traditional fishery management tools are not always effective. For example, closing fishing seasons for a given species for 1 month or 2 may have been acceptable when fishermen were tired or had been neglecting their vessel repairs. However, annual fishing seasons lasting only a few days or even a matter of hours, as found in Pacific halibut and herring roe fisheries, have led to absurd and dangerous pressures on fishermen as well as high prices and low quality for the consumer.

Standard fishery regulations in Canada and the U.S. are being subjected to an ever-increasing amount of criticism. Observers from industry, government, and academia all agree that new approaches should be carefully considered and attempted on an experimental basis. Such approaches will only be successful if fishermen are involved in very direct and substantive ways.

Cooperative Management of Local Fisheries

In recent years, concern over the mismanagement and depletion of our natural resources has grown. Innovative responses are developing in the form of multidisciplinary research projects that are investigating cultural, scientific, and governmental aspects of these challenges. People who are involved include: anthropologists, environmental planners, biologists, economists, lawyers and mediators, community planners, fishery managers, civil service workers, and tribal and governmental leaders.

It is sometimes assumed that aboriginal peoples are by nature, and under all conditions, conservationists. While this assumption contains some truth, it requires qualification. Under fairly stable preindustrial conditions, small-scale societies tended to develop ways of exploiting the natural environment without eliminating the resources on which they depended. Knowledgeable chiefs and elders had use rights over fishing areas and the authority to limit the extent of fishing in that area. Religious beliefs about the dire consequences of wasteful practices, or harvesting more than was needed, gave support to the conservational thrust. It is possible that overfishing occurred in the past. However, when it did, it is apparent that the groups involved learned from their experiences. All evidence suggests that conservation practices were thoroughly institutionalized in North America, by secular and spiritual authority, before the Europeans invaded.

Small-scale, localized segments of industrialized societies can also conserve resources under the right conditions. Probably this is more likely to happen when the society is "traditional" in the sense of having a long history in the area. Further, its local culture could generate norms and values independently from national culture. These norms, such as those to conserve fish populations, will likely be easier to establish if the boundaries of the community are clearly defined. When sociologists have identified these conditions, cooperative management procedures are easier to implement.

Fishery regulation is a very costly process both for the regulators and the regulated. Developing biological information such as estimates of stock size is very expensive. In an effort to improve communications, many groups of fishermen are making greater efforts to document their collected information using scientific procedures. Local knowledge of natural history and fishermen's day-to-day experiences while fishing can provide an inexpensive and useful kind of information that complements scientific data.

The planning process for fisheries management is also costly. Saving short-term costs by failing to hold meetings or hearings in or near fishing communities may lead to greater long-term costs when the fishery policies turn out to be ineffective or unenforceable.

There is a renewed interest in the idea of resource-dependent regions and communities achieving greater control over their own development. This shift comes at a time of global economic change which has shown the limited ability of governments to buffer communities against change. Community planners, development workers, anthropologists, biologists, geographers, and environmental scientists have worked with such communities to develop both the theory and the practice of community-based development.

In Canada, a policy shift occurred in 1976. The federal government stated that, instead of regulating the fishing industry in the interest of the fish, the industry should be regulated in the interest of people who depend upon the fishing industry.

In Canada, particular attention has been given to Native communities, partially because of their extreme dependence on the natural resource base. Fishing communities have an opportunity to influence their own development and to prevent the destruction of the resource base, i.e., fish species population, which can allow community-based development. Perceiving their fate as linked to the health of local watersheds, local marine waters, and local stocks, fishing communities are often willing to contribute to stock rehabilitation efforts, especially if they can gain influence in the harvesting decisions for these stocks.

The Native hunting/fishing groups in the Canadian North, which have had long-term stable relationships with fish and game, view their dependence on these natural resources as the secure portion of their economy, able to carry them through the vagaries of commodity and labor markets. By having a mechanism to recirculate some of the increased wealth back into fishing-dependent communities, and by having some decision making and control exercised by local people, the incentives to enhance and protect the resource are perpetuated.

SUMMARY

Considerable research is needed to achieve the full potential of using fish and seafood for human foods. Species of fish should be acceptable to humans; culturing species is just one of the areas that merits further study. Research is needed about the type of fishing vessels used. Humans have to learn how to control the fish harvests. For example, in 1989, only 70 "wild" salmon were caught off Norwegian waters. As a conservation measure, fishing for "wild" salmon was banned for 1990 in that country.

During the next 50 years, scientific and technological advances that will allow optimal harvesting of fish without further stressing their populations will be critical. Globally, the total fish harvest appears to have stabilized despite increasing fishing efforts, suggesting that maximum yields may have been reached under current fisheries management practices. Even if fish production could be substantially improved around the globe, the rapid population growth rate could tend to negate the effect of greater yields.

REFERENCES

Brown, E. Evan. 1983. *World fish farming: cultivation and economics*. 2d. ed. Westport: The AVI Publishing Company, Inc.

Ensminger, A. H., M. E. Ensminger, J. F. Konlande, and J. R. K. Robson. 1986. *Food for health — A nutrition encyclopedia*. Clovis, Calif.: Pegus Press.

Pimental, D. and M. Pimental. 1979. *Food, energy, and society*. New York: John Wiley & Sons.

Pinkerton, Evelyn, 1989. Introduction: attaining better fisheries management through co-management — prospects, problems, and propositions. In *Cooperative management of local fisheries*, ed. E. Pinkerton, 3-33. Vancouver: University of British Columbia Press.

Potter, Norman N. 1986. *Food science*. 4th ed. Westport, Conn.: The AVI Publishing Company, Inc.

Redmayne, Peter C. 1989. World aquaculture developments. *Food Technology* 43(11): 80-81.

Rettig, R. B., F. Berkes, and E. Pinkerton, 1989. The future of fisheries co-management: a multi-disciplinary assessment. In *Co-operative management of local fisheries*, ed. E. Pinkerton, 273-289. Vancouver: University of British Columbia Press.

Rothschild, B. J. 1986. *Dynamics of marine fish populations*. Cambridge: Harvard University Press.

Wittwer, Sylvan H. 1983. The new agriculture: a view of the twenty-first century. In *Agriculture in the twenty-first century*, ed. J. W. Rosenblum, 337-67. New York: John Wiley & Sons.

Yermanos, D. M., M. Neushul, and R. D. MacElroy. 1983. Crops from the desert, sea, and space. In *Agriculture in the twenty-first century*, ed. J. W. Rosenblum, 144-65. New York: John Wiley & Sons.

Chapter Eight

Food Processing Industries

INTRODUCTION

The geographical distribution of food sources (Exhibit 1.5), and its frequent remoteness from populated areas, has challenged agronomists, agricultural economists, food technologists, and those concerned with food shipments. Nutritional quality and safety of the food supply have to be ensured from the point of food production to its delivery to the consumer. Preservation methods have been introduced to store foods for long periods, ensuring freedom from decomposition, insect infestation, and bacterial contamination. Such methods have reduced famines in many areas of the world.

In developed countries of the world, we do not depend upon locally produced foods for our food supply. Supermarkets typically carry more than 15,000 food items, most of which are brought in from outside the local area. Modern food technology has greatly expanded our options.

The food processing industry may be defined as: "the branch of manufacturing that starts with raw animal, vegetable, or marine materials and transforms them into intermediate foodstuffs or edible products through the application of labor, machinery, energy and scientific knowledge." Various processes are used to convert relatively bulky, perishable, and typically inedible food materials into ultimately more useful, concentrated, shelf-stable, and palatable foods and/or potable beverages.

Heat, cold, drying, and other preservation techniques are applied to enhance storability. Containers and packaging materials confer portability as well as extend shelf life. Except for some egg shells, nature does not provide food which is commercially sterile and/or packaged in a form to guarantee extended shelf life.

Changes in product forms often reduce preparation time for consumers. Increasing palatability, storability, portability, and convenience are all aspects of "adding value." Food processors use factory systems to add economic value by transforming products grown on farms or fished from the sea. To illustrate, through food processing operations, beef steers become meat, wheat becomes flour, corn becomes fructose, and fresh tuna becomes canned tuna.

By studying the information contained in this chapter, you will be in an informed position to discuss:

- the scope of the U.S. food industry and how it impacts upon food availability and the nutritional status of the population;
- some aspects of the evolution of the food processing industries in developing countries, particularly Africa and Latin America;
- the food safety role of the food processing industry, particularly as developments occur in biotechnology.

As an example of the food processing industry, the milling of wheat and the production of alternate products will be described, illustrating some of the diversity of the industry for you. Throughout this chapter, the U.S. food processing industry will be emphasized, also giving you a perspective about how this industry is organized in other developed countries.

Information in Exhibit 8.1 lists 41 food processing industries in the U.S., along with the value of their shipments in 1985. The industries are ranked according to how much value is added to the commodities during processing. The baking industry adds the most value; the butter industry, the least. The value-added component can also be classified as the marketing cost component. Value is added because of the following expenditures: labor, packaging material, transportation, fuels and electricity, processing, wholesaling, and retailing and foodservice operations. Seventy percent of the U.S. consumer's food dollar is spent on services after the product leaves the farm gate.

Important U.S. food processing developments began in the 1830s. Prior to 1900, commercial companies sold a few specialized items such as coffee, sugar, spices, tea, salt, and alcoholic bever-

Exhibit 8.1. The Size of the U.S. Food Processing Industry, Ranked by Value Added - 1985.

Industry	Measure of Industry Size	
	Value Added	Value of Shipments
	(Million dollars)	
1. Bread, rolls, cakes	8,811	14,389
2. Soft drinks bottling	7,587	19,358
3. Miscellaneous prepared foods	7,027	13,708
4. Meatpacking	5,859	42,554
5. Confectionary	5,883	11,514
6. Beer	5,681	12,216
7. Fluid milk	4,953	19,679
8. Canned fruits and vegetables	4,418	10,999
9. Cookies and crackers	4,184	6,446
10. Breakfast cereals	3,995	5,718
11. Meat processing	3,705	12,406
12. Flavorings	3,108	4,840
13. Pet foods	3,074	5,305
14. Frozen specialists	2,985	6,508
15. Poultry dressing	2,859	10,340
16. Coffee	2,446	6,677
17. Frozen fruits and vegetables	2,355	5,803
18. Animal feeds	2,276	10,410
19. Canned specialities	2,161	4,802
20. Sauces, pickles	2,116	5,123
21. Cheese	1,910	11,060
22. Spirits	1,691	2,763
23. Prepared milk	1,628	5,288
24. Wet corn milling	1,363	4,190
25. Cooking oils and margarine	1,190	5,608
26. Flour	1,159	5,205
27. Frozen fish	1,070	3,947
28. Wine and brandy	1,063	2,763
29. Ice cream	1,041	3,477
30. Cane sugar	1,035	3,785
31. Dried fruits and vegetables	840	1,788
32. Soybean oil	712	8,629
33. Flour mixes	700	1,635
34. Other fats and oils	653	2,386
35. Pasta	629	1,155
36. Poultry processing	535	1,839
37. Beet sugar	524	1,789
38. Rice	389	1,581
39. Canned fish	227	697

Exhibit 8.1 (continued)

| | Measure of Industry Size | |
Industry	Value Added	Value of Shipments
40. Cottonseed oil	219	881
41. Butter	98	1,571

Source: Reprinted by permission of the publisher, from Food
Processing: An Industrial Powerhouse in Transition
by John M. Connor. (Lexington, Mass: Lexington Books,
D.C. Heath and Company, copyright 1988, Lexington Books.)

ages. From 1964 to 1972 in the U.S., the number of new products introduced each year ranged from 500 to 600. From 1972 to 1982, new product introductions increased by 7 percent. In the 1970s, 5,000 to 7,000 new grocery items were introduced per year in the U.S. Some of these items only represented minor changes, such as a 1-ounce reduction in packaging size. Because introductory promotion costs are high, less than one-third of new products become profitable within 1 or 2 years.

In 1980, there were over 250,000 warehoused grocery items in the U.S. The proliferation of brands and types of processed foods is a rather ambiguous indicator of technological progress. Many new products are of doubtful novelty, and some could be considered frivolous. The development of the food processing industry has had important societal consequences. For example, the practice of strangers adopting infants was not common in the U.S. until the 1920s when infant formula was invented.

Within the food processing industry, each commodity undergoes a series of processes leading to desired characteristics in the final product. The examples of food processes given in Exhibit 8.2 are classified according to six major types of processes: physical, chemical, thermal, drying, freezing, and chemical additions. Although not a complete list, information in Exhibit 8.2 illustrates the complexity of operations within the food processing industry. In order to process most food products, many of the processes listed in Exhibit 8.2 are performed in sequence. The following description of the processing of wheat products offers one example.

Exhibit 8.2. Selected Examples of Types of Food Processes.

Classification	Example
Physical Processes	Cracking, crushing, flaking, grinding, pressing, chopping, dicing, grating, mashing, mincing, slicing, trimming, peeling, scraping, homogenizing, deboning, cutting, separating fat/lean.
Chemical Processes	Solvent extraction, refining, agitation, bleaching, deodorization, winterization, hydrogenation (hardening), fermenting, curing.
Drying Processes	Sun, hot-air, drum, spray, freeze-drying, puff-drying.
Freezing Processes	Air-blast, plate, liquid.
Thermal Processes	Heat (air or oil), heat and air velocity, heat and air velocity and r.h., heat and pressure, microwave, pasteurize, heat and pressure and vacuum.
Chemical Additions	Salt, acidification, salts of fatty acids, antioxidants, vitamins/minerals.

A FOOD PROCESSING EXAMPLE: WHEAT PRODUCTS

Cereals provide most of the energy and vital nutrients consumed by humans throughout the world. Grains are either eaten directly, processed, or eaten by meat-producing animals.

A diagram of the wheat kernel is given in Exhibit 8.3, with the location of its nutrients shown in Exhibit 8.4. Wheat is a single-seeded fruit with three primary parts:

1. bran (fiber and minerals);
2. endosperm (starch granules in a protein matrix);
3. germ (lipid).

The aleurone layer separates the bran from the endosperm. The process of milling separates these three layers.

Flour Production

Milling ranges from rudimentary crushing or cracking to sophisticated separation and refining. The purpose of milling is to isolate the starch/protein from the high-fiber and high-lipid components. The advantages of milling include improving palatability, digestibility, and usefulness of the whole cereal grains. The objective of the milling processes is to produce flours with high levels of desirable quality, a uniform color, and a stable shelf life.

Wheat Cleaning

During wheat cleaning operations, the extraneous materials such as sticks, stones, soil, chaff, and mixed grains, are removed. Any product variations will affect the level of acceptability and the baking performance of flour.

Selective Sizing

During the sizing processes, wheat moves over sieves which remove grains larger than wheat kernels.

Aspiration

During the aspiration stages, high-velocity air currents are directed over the wheat to remove low-density materials such as chaff.

Metal Removal

Magnets are run over the wheat to remove all fragments of metals such as those from nails or bolts that entered the wheat bins during transportation.

Secondary Selective Sizing

During this stage, all grains other than wheat seeds are removed. Other grains which have contaminated the wheat during storage and transportation may include barley, oats, corn, soybeans, and weed seeds.

Exhibit 8.3. Cross Sections of a Kernel of Wheat.

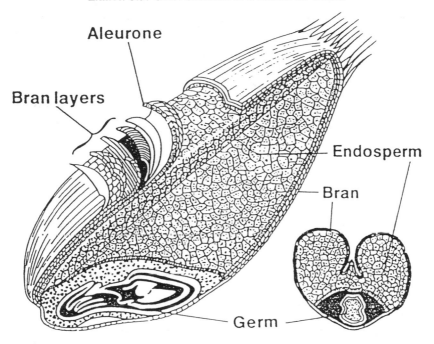

Aleurone

Bran layers

Endosperm

Bran

Germ

Source: Leveille, G. A. and M. A. Uebersax. 1980. Fundamentals of food science for the dietitian: wheat products. *Dietetic Currents* 7(1): 1-8. Used and reprinted with permission of Ross Laboratories, Columbus, OH 43216.

Friction

Friction is applied so that all of the surface dirt can be removed by rotating abrasive discs.

Water Wash

Finally the wheat kernels are washed and centrifuged to remove residual soil and microbes.

Exhibit 8.4. Distribution of Nutrients in the Wheat Kernel.

Nutrient	Distribution (Percentage of Volume)*		
	Endosperm (83%)†	Bran (14.5%)†	Germ (2.5%)†
Protein	73	19	8
Pantothenic acid	43	50	7
Riboflavin	32	42	26
Niacin	12	86	2
Pyridoxine	6	73	21
Thiamine	3	33	64

* Numbers in columns show what percentage of the total amount of each nutrient is located in each part of the wheat kernel.
† Percentage of total kernel volume.

Source: Leveille, G. A. and M. A. Uebersax. 1980. Fundamentals of food science for the dietitian: wheat products. *Dietetic Currents* 7(1): 1-8. Used and reprinted with permission of Ross Laboratories, Columbus, OH 43216.

Tempering

Tempering involves adjusting the moisture content by spraying the kernels to achieve a 14-19 percent moisture level depending on the type of wheat. This phase of the milling process requires about 18 to 72 hours. Water is added to the wheat kernels for three reasons:

1. The initial moisture level affects the uniformity of the flour separation.
2. The milling efficiency is improved by toughening the bran and softening the endosperm.
3. Better control of the milling process is possible, including heat generation during milling.

Conditioning

During this stage, wheat is held at about 115°F for 8 to 18 hours to accelerate the tempering process. The endosperm becomes softer during this conditioning process.

Exhibit 8.5 gives a schematic diagram of the air and mechanical purification of the middlings from the wheat kernel. Throughout the milling process, care is taken to avoid the generation of heat which would damage the starch and functional properties of flour.

The milling process can be simple or complex. The former is usually found more frequently in developing countries and involves smashing the whole grain into meal, pounding until the correct particle size is reached. An inferior flour product results. There are many particles which are smaller than the size desired. In addition, the heat and friction from the smashing process damage the starch and protein molecules.

Exhibit 8.5. Schematic of Air and Mechanical Purification of Middlings.

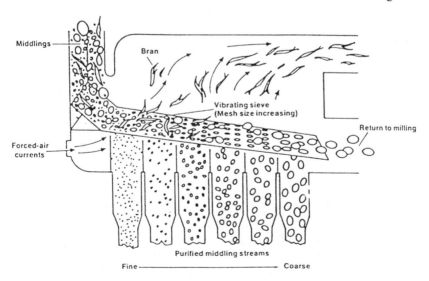

Source: Leveille, G. A. and M. A. Uebersax. 1980. Fundamentals of food science for the dietitian: wheat products. *Dietetic Currents* 7(1): 1-8. Used and reprinted with permission of Ross Laboratories, Columbus, OH 43216.

With modern and more complex milling operations, kernel components are separated into different mill streams after each size reduction, enabling efficient and complete separation of components under conditions that do not cause heat and mechanical damage. There are three features to this process:

1. A series of break rollers (cylinders) are used to shear flakes of bran, with pieces of bran adhering to the endosperm and large pieces of endosperm adhering to the kernel.
2. Sieves are used between the break rollers and air is used to separate the components. The middlings, i.e., the endosperm and fine bran, pass through the sieves. Bran and germ are removed as nonflour streams.
3. Reduction rollers reduce the size of the middlings. Particles of the correct size are removed as flour; others are returned for further reduction.

During this process, heat is controlled to reduce any damage of the starch granules and to increase the levels of reducing sugars which would subsequently promote browning reactions to occur.

The extraction rates for flours generated by the complex milling operations are given in Exhibit 8.6. The term "flour extraction" refers to the proportion by weight of flour obtained from wheat. No bran has been removed if the extraction rate is 100 percent. Straight flours are blended to produce commercial flour grades. Major flour protein classifications are given in Exhibit 8.7.

Baked Products

Gluten proteins account for 75 percent of the total flour proteins. A gluten protein network is developed during mixing when flour, water, yeast, and other ingredients are blended to produce dough. During baking, starch granules swell by absorbing water and help stabilize the loaf. All ingredients have a function. Dough conditioners or emulsifying agents are used to develop less tacky, more extensible dough that will pass through machinery without tearing or sticking.

The two methods of commercial bread production are the straight dough process and the sponge dough process. When the loaves have

Exhibit 8.6. Extraction Rates of Flours.

Name of Flour	Extraction Rate (%)	Composition of Flour (Color)
Straight	75	Endosperm portions (white)
Clear	80-90	Endosperm and nonendosperm portions (creamy)
Whole wheat	100	Whole kernel (brown)

Source: Leveille, G. A. and M. A. Uebersax. 1980. Fundamentals of food science for the dietitian: wheat products. *Dietetic Currents* 7(1): 1-8. Used and reprinted with permission of Ross Laboratories, Columbus, OH 43216.

been formed and proofed, the baking process causes physical and chemical changes to occur in the dough. The properties of the product at the end are drastically different from those of the raw ingredients at the beginning of the breadmaking operation. During baking, because of the high moisture content, the interior of the loaf cannot exceed 212°F even though the oven temperature is above 400°F.

The irreversible process of staling is the cause of one of the industry's major losses. Stale products represent a loss of agricultural and processing energy and a loss of nutrients from the human food chain. Staling is caused by chemical changes involving hydrogen bonding of the starch molecules which excludes water and forms harder crystalline structures. Staling is not reversible. Although some stale bread can be softened when exposed to microwave energy, this effect is extremely temporary.

Breakfast Cereal Products

Breakfast cereals have been produced in the U.S. since the late 1800s. Three processes, flaking, shredding, and puffing, will be described briefly.

Exhibit 8.7. Classification of Major Flour Proteins.

Nonglutens (15%) (Non-Dough-Forming)	Glutens (85%) (Dough-Forming)	
Albumins (60%) (Water-soluble, heat coagulable)	Gliadin (Soluble in 70% ethanol) Extensible, low elasticity*	Glutenin (Insoluble in alcohol, soluble in dilute acids and bases) Elastic, low extensibility
Globulins (40%) (Soluble in neutral salts)		
Peptides, free amino acids		

* Extensibility is the degree to which dough can be stretched without breaking; elasticity is the resilience of the dough.

Source: Leveille, G. A. and M. A. Uebersax. 1980. Fundamentals of food science for the dietitian: wheat products. *Dietetic Currents* 7(1): 1-8. Used and reprinted with permission of Ross Laboratories, Columbus, OH 43216.

Flaking

Tempered grain is steamed, rolled, and pressure-cooked for 90 minutes at 20 PSI in the presence of water, maltose, and optional ingredients. This mass is dried to about a 20 percent moisture content. It is then flaked by passing it through flaking rollers, toasted at high temperatures to obtain crispness and about a 3 percent moisture level, cooled, sprayed with an emulsion of vitamins and minerals, and packaged.

Shredding

To make shredded wheat biscuits, whole grain wheat is boiled for 60 minutes, formed into strands, stacked into 20 layers, cut into biscuits, dried, and toasted. A diagram for the production of shredded wheat biscuits is given in Exhibit 8.8.

Exhibit 8.8. Schematic for Production of Shredded Wheat Biscuits.

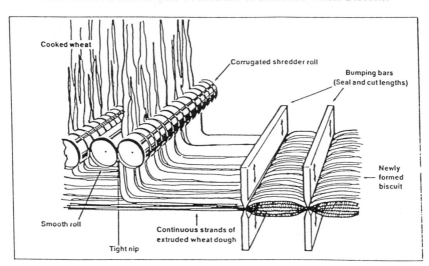

Source: Leveille, G. A. and M. A. Uebersax. 1980. Fundamentals of food science for the dietitian: wheat products. *Dietetic Currents* 7(1): 1-8. Used and reprinted with permission of Ross Laboratories, Columbus, OH 43216.

Puffing

Puffed breakfast cereals are either made from whole kernels or from a formulation of many flours. For the process known as explosion puffing, whole kernels are pearled to remove the bran, conditioned, and steamed. During this process, pressure builds up inside the kernel. The pressure is suddenly released, expanding the product by at least 10 times its original volume. To promote a stable shelf life, the cereal product is dried to achieve a moisture level of about 3 percent.

Puffing operations can also be achieved by a process known as extrusion which is used when a formula is prepared of different flours and ingredients. The extruder is a continuous screw that rotates in a steam-jacketed cylinder. The formulation enters one end of the extruder, passes through, and exits via a small-diameter orifice or die. The spacing of the screw threads compresses the product as it proceeds through the cylinder. Pressure and temperature are maximum at the end of the screw. The hot, pressurized product is extruded through the die and instantly expands when exposed to atmospheric pressure. A knife positioned over the die cuts the pieces into the desired length as the product is expelled from the die. The die can be modified to yield a variety of shapes: circles, stars, letters, or spheres, and so on. Finally, the cereal is dried to attain about a 3 percent moisture level and the desired amount of crispness.

Pasta Products

A hard wheat, called Durum, is used to make pasta. The wheat is milled to produce large chunks of endosperm called semolina. Next a pasta paste is formulated, which includes semolina, water, and egg yolks. The subsequent processing steps include: blending, mixing under a vacuum, extruding through dies to desired shapes, and drying the surface. Too rapid drying causes surfaces to crack, giving the product poor cooking characteristics. Therefore, the drying process occurs for 12 to 36 hours to reach a 10-12 percent moisture level required for shelf stability.

FOOD REGULATIONS

The example of the processing of wheat products did not include any of the quality assurance and food safety procedures which occur at each type of processing operation. Because of improvements in food handling and preservation, prices of many foods have decreased in many countries during the last several decades. Numerous foods, considered to be expensive delicacies only 20 years ago, are now commonly available in some countries. Improvements in food preservation and production have been made possible by improved agricultural practices including the use of pesticides, fungicides, growth-promoting agents, and veterinary drugs. Because of these developments, the field of food regulation has become increasingly important to evaluate and control the multifactorial health impacts resulting from the use of these ingredients.

In 1986, there were 2 million cases of food-related illnesses caused by *Salmonella* and *Campylobacter* in the U.S.; the number appears to be drastically rising. The U.S. Center for Disease Control (CDC) estimates that in more than 50 percent of the disease outbreaks attributed to foodborne pathogens, the specific microbial agent responsible is not identified. An episode of *Salmonella* in the Chicago area affected 16,000 persons.

The possible worldwide economic impact of foodborne illness at $20 billion/year is a figure which demands attention. Both industrialized and developing countries jointly will need the expertise of food scientists and technologists to win the fight against outbreaks of foodborne diseases and the presence of contaminants and to search for safer food products free of toxicants and even more nutrients.

The major U.S. federal regulatory agencies, encompassing more than 350 programs, are listed in Exhibit 8.9. Many other developed countries have established agencies with similar functions. Because of the sophistication of the food processing industry, the long distances for food transportation, the extended food storage requirements, and new technological developments, activities of these agencies will only increase in the future.

THE U.S. FOOD PROCESSING INDUSTRY AND EXPORTS

In the late 1970s, the U.S. had a small trade surplus in processed foods and beverages. This trend was reversed in the mid-1980s. U.S. food exports consist primarily of undifferentiated, low value-added products, whereas imports tend to be packaged consumer products with a relatively high intensity of added value. The U.S. has a higher share of world trade in semi-processed food products, about 28 percent in 1985. In the highly processed category, the U.S. share of world trade is 14 percent. The reverse situation is found in EC countries.

In the 1980s, foreign firms controlled about 10 percent of the U.S. market for processed foods; four-tenths of that control came through imports into the U.S., and six-tenths through foreign direct investment in U.S. subsidiaries.

Although 4 percent of domestic food shipments are exported, considerably more sales abroad are made by U.S. subsidiaries. Sales abroad by foreign affiliates of U.S. food processors were over 37 percent of domestic sales or 27 percent of worldwide sale values.

Exhibit 8.9. Federal Regulatory Activities in Food, Nutrition, and Agriculture.

Agency	Regulatory Activities
Food and Drug Administration (FDA)	Inspects food samples Regulates food additives Investigates consumers' complaints Assists the food industry in setting standards Regulates food package labels Supervises recall of unsafe food products Establishes standards of identity, quality, and contents
U.S. Department of Agriculture (USDA)	Inspects plant, animal, and poultry production Supervises meat processing Conducts voluntary quality grading Controls animal and plant food pests
Environmental Protection Agency (EPA)	Regulates quality of drinking water Regulates pesticides and chemical contaminants in food
U.S. Public Health Service (USPHS)	Advises on control of infectious diseases transmitted through food Investigates outbreaks of food-borne disease
Federal Trade Commission (FTC)	Regulates food advertising

Source: Nestle, M. 1985. Nutrition policy and politics. In Nutrition in Clinical Practice. 310-317. Jones Medical Publications, Greenbrae, CA.

Over 31 percent of worldwide sales of U.S. food processors occurred in international markets in the early 1980s.

Many U.S. exports are assisted by export subsidies or other government programs, and several product classes with net imports are protected by U.S. quotas or other barriers to trade.

In addition to trade barriers, food processing companies give several reasons why they produce finished consumer products in foreign plants rather than export them from U.S. plants. One reason is to reduce transportation costs. Second, it can be easier to deal with local governments and regulatory agencies if the food product is produced in the host country. Third, for consumer value-added products, being on location makes it is easier to keep familiar with local tastes and demands and opportunities for new product development or reformulations. Fourth, firms that initially export to a market can decide to switch to foreign production once the export market becomes large enough.

Information included in Exhibit 8.10 gives the labeling information for one product, Diet Coke™, produced in both the U.S. and Holland. Respective regulations in each country are followed when information is printed on the label. When food products are made in foreign countries, local regulations are adhered to. Coca-Cola accounts for 40 percent of the soft-drink market; PepsiCo, 30 percent; and 7-Up and Dr. Pepper, 14 percent of the market.

As we enter an era of global economics, more and more quality standardization of imported foods will be necessary as well as constant vigilance with novel foods and foods new to the industrialized world.

U.S. Food Consumption Pattern

The mix of foods in the U.S. diet has changed in the last two decades. Consumer life-styles and new food production, processing, and storage technologies have changed selection priorities. The net effect has been a decrease in the caloric contribution of the meat, poultry, and fish group, from 23 to 21 percent of total calories. The cereal/legume/nut group of foods has stabilized at 23 percent of total calories, supplying the largest amount of thiamin, riboflavin, niacin, folacin, iron, magnesium, and copper. The role of each of these nutrients will be discussed in Chapter Ten.

All income groups show a reduction in the meat, poultry, and fish group of foods, with middle and high income households showing the greatest decrease. Dairy products supply 10 percent of calories and a large share of riboflavin, calcium, and phosphorus. Higher income groups consume higher amounts of low-fat milk, natural cheeses, and dairy desserts. Vegetable consumption has remained stable at 7 percent of total calories since 1970, although the intake of some fresh and frozen vegetables, i.e., broccoli and cauliflower, has doubled during this 20-year period. Reasons for this increase include improvements in the production and transportation

Exhibit 8.10.   Label information for Diet Coke: Europe and U.S.

Information	Europe	U.S.
Name	Coke Light	Diet Coke
Label Language	English and German	English
General	Low calorie soft drink with vegetable extracts	Diet Coca-Cola Very low sodium
Ingredients	Carbonated water Color (E 150) Aspartame Saccharin Acidulants E 336 Citric acid Natural flavorings Preservative: E 21L Caffeine	Carbonated water Caramel color Aspartame Phosphoric acid Citric acid Natural flavors Potassium Benzoate (Preservation) Caffeine
Nutritional	Saccharin (1.1 kilojoule 0.27 kilocalories) 0.02% absorbable carbohydrates Contains phenylalanine	Serving size: 6 ozs. Servings per container: 2 Calories per serving: 0 Protein: 0 Carbohydrate: less than 1 g Fat: 0 Sodium (milligrams): 35 or less Percentage of U.S. recommended daily allowances (U.S. RDA): contains less than 2% of the U.S. RDA of protein, vitamin A, vitamin C, thiamine, riboflavin, niacin, calcium and iron.
Manufacturer	Canned under authority of the Coca-Cola Co. by Liko B.V. Bodegraven, Holland.	Canned under authority of 1986 The Coca-Cola Co., Atlanta, GA. by Johnston Coca-Cola Bottling Group, Inc. General Offices - 2750 Eagandale Blvd., Eagan, MD 56121.

of fresh vegetables as well as increased popularity of salad bars, contributing to the making of lettuce into a staple of the U.S. diet.

The consumption of fruits has been increased because of the evolving popularity of juice drinks. Sugars supply about 20 percent of the diet's energy. The increased use of high fructose corn syrup in soft drinks affects this percentage. Fats and oils supply nearly 20 percent of diet calories, with margarine and salad dressing being the most commonly consumed sources.

FOOD PURCHASING POWER

The purchasing power of a country's population is the determining factor in the kind of food products demanded and consumed within the limits of production potentials. Data given in Exhibit 8.11 illustrate drastic differences in the amount of income that is expended for food. Note that people in India spent 53.1 percent of their total private consumption expenditures on food, but U.S. consumers spent only 11 percent. The latter figure attests to the efficiency of the U.S. food processing industry.

In most of the developing countries, the richest 20 percent of the people have 50 to 60 percent of the total income. The gap between rich and poor people seems to be widening every year.

The contrast in life-styles is quite evident when diets are analyzed in developing countries. The large majority of the population spends an average of 60 to 70 percent of their income for basic foods. The privileged are able to buy, in up-to-date supermarkets and food stores, the most sophisticated food products produced locally or imported from abroad.

Exhibit 8.11. Food Expenditures as a Per Cent of Total Private Consumption Expenditures - 1984.

Country	Per Cent
India	53.1
Mexico	31.7
Israel	23.1
Denmark	17.2
U.S.	11.0

Source: Statistical Abstract of the United States. 1989. 109th ed. U.S. Department of Commerce. Washington, DC: U.S. Government Printing Office.

FOOD PROCESSING IN DEVELOPING COUNTRIES

In the majority of the developing nations, relatively high amounts of research in food science at the laboratory level have been carried out during the past 50 years, but very little of it has been used in food technological processes. The agricultural production capacity of the countries must be reinforced to be able to develop stronger food industries.

In most countries, there is an inability of the agricultural sector to provide the raw materials of the quality and in the quantity required by the food industry, with the possible exception of conventional agro-industrial crops such as sugarcane. The same may be true for the edible oil industry. These two crops are controlled by the component of the agricultural sector with a high capacity, i.e., with sufficient economic resources and knowledge, to invest in technology. On the other hand, cereal grains, fruits, and vegetables are in the hands of farmers with a low capacity to invest, absorb, and utilize technology.

In most developing countries, some food processing industries use very modern processes to produce high-quality, sophisticated products; the majority use routine processes and technologies to make products which are affordable to those with medium or low income.

Dairy products; processed meats; aseptic and frozen fruit juices and pulps; frozen, canned, and dehydrated vegetables; coffee and tea products; and cocoa and its derivatives are examples of products that are manufactured using up-to-date technologies in some developing countries. They contribute to progress and the improvement of the GNP and per capita income.

Living in suburban areas where large supermarkets are nonexistent, the low-income population usually pays higher prices for their basic food staples than those with high incomes. The latter population has the means to pay cash for what they buy in food chain stores. Improved marketing strategies are needed to make better distribution channels possible for food commodities in developing countries.

Because of such facts as large populations, low and variable agricultural production, poor economies, low food availability, higher costs, poor-quality foods, and the effects of adverse environments, diseases, and low socioeconomic conditions, the possibilities for rapid improvements have been very slim.

Adoption of more advanced techniques such as genetic engineering, irradiation sterilization, freeze-dehydration preservation, refrigerated distribution systems, etc., to the production, processing, distribution, and storage of food products in the developing countries will come slowly. Ironically, it is these advanced activities that contribute to the efficiencies of food processes and, thus, to the lowering of the food costs.

In developing countries, when it has been realized by food scientists and other professionals that foods, particularly the basic staples, were not being produced in sufficient quantities, numerous recommendations have been made:

1. increase agricultural production;
2. reduce postharvest losses;
3. reduce wheat imports;
4. develop the composite flour concept;
5. develop efficient food technologies;
6. reduce seasonal variation in food availability;
7. introduce the grain quality concept;
8. improve food quality through fortification, supplementation, and complementation;
9. develop new sources of foods;
10. develop a demand for specific food items, such as oils.

The low agricultural production of basic staple foods prompted the establishment of the International Agricultural Research Centers (IARCs) in developing countries in Asia, Africa, and Latin America. This event was fundamental to the recognition of the Green Revolution, and undoubtedly they have made significant contributions to increased food production throughout the world.

These institutions introduced into their objectives concepts in the area of food science, particularly grain quality characteristics of the staples and other foods of their particular mandate. The institutions also promoted food processing and utilization research activities, for example, research by the International Rice Research Institute

(IRRI) on rice, research by Centro Internacional de Agricultura Tropical (CIAT) on the use of cassava as a substrate in biotechnology, and research by the International Potato Center (IPC) on potatoes as a component in high-quality foods. Food legumes also came into focus as potential sources of complementary protein. These research activities not only induced increased research efforts for these foods, but also stimulated the national and international agricultural sectors to increase their processing and utilization research efforts in food product development.

Numerous surveys of foods consumed in developing countries indicated that wheat, as wheat flour, was being consumed in increasing quantities. Since most developing countries located in the tropical belt of the world do not produce wheat, which must therefore be imported, the composite flour concept was born, i.e., milling flours from more than one type of grain. It received much publicity.

In the early 1970s, cassava flour became better known as a product that could be combined with wheat flour to make bread. Although much was done in the developing world, very little of that was placed into actual use. When wheat prices became lower in comparison with costs of locally produced grains, the program on composite flours lost interest. However, it is still very important and probably much more significant today because of the developing countries' poor economic situations and increasing populations.

Food Purchasing in Developed versus Developing Countries

When the Institute of Food Technologists (IFT) celebrated its 50th anniversary with a special issue of *Food Technology*, a food scientist, Ricardo Bressani, described some differences between food shopping in developed and developing countries. Because these findings are direct results of the food processing industries, some contrasting excerpts follow:

> For those people not familiar with them, it is simply fascinating to walk, aisle after aisle, admiring the variety of attractive cartons, cans, and many other fancy containers with all kinds of foods. Aside from the beauty, diversity, and abundance of

food items, the supermarket has many implications not evident to the consumer. It implies very efficient agricultural production, to be used for feeding people, and as raw materials for the food industry or other production systems. It implies making seasonal production available throughout the year. It implies many years of research in food science, nutrition, and other allied disciplines. It implies the use of food science research results to develop and implement food technology activities, also the result of research and a close association between research centers and the food industry. It implies the availability of knowledge in packaging, marketing, and quality control. It implies food security and food safety to the consumer. And it implies a receptive population with the knowledge to appreciate the foods, and with the economic capacity to purchase it.

It is also fascinating to walk through the narrow passages of the colorful open markets typical of developing countries. There, however, the variety of foods is low, mainly cereal grains and food legumes in burlap bags. Occasionally, baskets full of foods, mainly vegetables and fruits, are also to be found, but their availability is dependent on seasonal production. These foods come from poor and inefficient agricultural production systems, not good enough to supply the demand, deteriorating under the sun, dust, or rain, with flies and other insects as constant visitors. Those foods not sold by the end of the day go to waste. Food products such as meat and eggs are in short supply and expensive. Only dry staples are sold, mostly cereal grains. The full benefits of processing, of engineering, and of food science and technology are still not reaching most people in the developing countries.

Efforts which were initiated some 50 years ago must be increased substantially if the developing countries are ever to have supermarkets with the quantity, quality, and variety of foods that exist in the industrialized countries. Food science and technology is increasing in the developing countries, and it is certainly expected that this trend will continue in the future. The important activity now and in the future is the transfer of the great many research findings into practical applications.

Food Scientists in Developing Countries

It is difficult to obtain statistics on the number of trained people in food science and technology in developing countries. Local students trained in industrial countries have, upon returning to their own country, been organizing food science and technology associations which are helping create this very much needed discipline.

The development of new professional disciplines, including food science, technology, and engineering, is slowly creating a critical mass which, together with the needs of the industry and those of the countries, will result in developments of food technology in the developing world. With the hope that the problems in the developing countries could be solved by training local scientists to find local solutions, several training programs have been established. Such training facilities include great diversity, and together with foreign teams visiting from developed countries and postgraduate training in developed countries, several have been creating the critical mass of scientists needed in the different areas of food science, technology, and engineering.

As a consequence, a number of events have taken place. First, local universities have started building up academic programs to award professional degrees in food science and technology. Governments have created special institutes to undertake developmental and adaptive food research to serve the food industry, and have created laboratories for quality control with trained personnel. Institutes in nutritional sciences have incorporated into their structure technical groups in food science and technology to work on food problems with a nutritional content not greatly appreciated previously by the food industry or government food research institutes.

FOOD PROCESSING IN AFRICA

Manufacturers of import-substitution products are an important part of the African food industry. The foreign debt of African countries is compelling them to increase the contents of local materials when formulating their products. This situation is stimulating research and development efforts for new food products. For example, many African countries market a good quality beer in which a substantial part of imported barley has been replaced by locally grown crops.

Africa's food supply is vulnerable because of low technology levels. In addition to having low agricultural yields per hectare per farm worker, there are high postproduction losses resulting from poor processing and handling practices.

Selected Food Products

Wheat Products

Because Africa is not a wheat producing region, manufacturing bread and bakery products has necessitated the importation of wheat and flour. Because of the high rates of population growth, African economies will not be able to meet the considerable demands of foreign exchange required for this importation. Therefore, research is progressing with the use of composite flours, i.e., mixtures of flours in known proportions from wheat and locally grown crops such as millet, maize, rice, sorghum, cassava, plantain, and non-wheat flours. Composite flours have been used for bread, biscuits, cookies, and pasta products. The absence of gluten in nonwheat flours limits their uses.

Flour formulations for the production of breads contain at least 70 percent wheat. The supply of alternative crops for composite flours appears to be adequate. However, the costs associated with conversion of mills to enable processing of the alternate crops can be prohibitive.

Dehydrated Vegetables

Vegetable dehydration for export to soup and processed food manufacturers has attracted much attention among African countries. Lightweight dehydrated products are packed in airtight plastic bags and placed inside metal drums. Packing material and transport costs are low in relation to the value of the product.

Indigenous Protein Foods

In African countries, weaning foods have had limited success because of the use of poor protein-quality foods as well as traditional food preparation practices that reduce nutrients. Protein quality of weaning foods can be improved by complementing the essential amino acid profile of the cereals with those from the legumes. Thus, they have been improved by blending cereals with locally available legumes such as cowpea, groundnut, pigeon pea, soybean, and others.

In addition to being a major protein source for African diets, cowpeas can be used as ingredients in processed foods in similar ways that cereal grains and oilseed meals are used in industrialized countries. Cowpea extracts can be extruded to produce texturized vegetable protein products, ready-to-eat cereal blends, and snack foods. Industrially exploiting the cowpea would provide immense economic benefits to many African nations.

Because of an inadequate milk supply from cows, goats, or camels (Exhibit 2.5), vegetable sources are being explored as African milk substitutes. Liquid milk has been extracted from a combination of groundnuts and agushie. The product, supplemented with vitamins and minerals, is being evaluated in nutritional studies in Ghana.

Pearled dura, dehulled and polished sorghum, that is boiled for 40 minutes, is beginning to replace rice in the diet in certain areas of Africa.

Beer

A traditional drink of the African Bantus is homemade beer that is brewed in large iron kettles. During the brewing process, the alcohol produced dissolves iron from the kettle and adds about 80 mg of highly absorbable iron to each quart of beer. Some of the tribesmen who regularly drink this beer develop hemosiderosis, a disease related to excessive levels of iron in the body.

Role of Food Scientists

One of the greatest challenges to advances in the African food industry is the serious shortage of highly qualified and experienced manpower in both technical and managerial areas. In many countries, government administrators have not fully recognized the role of the food scientist who is usually trained abroad.

Political administrations are not easily influenced by scientists who are isolated and unrecognized for their talents. Their expertise is quickly diluted in government-controlled institutions where scientific research and objectivity are not always understood. Thus, many researchers tend to lead a migratory, unfulfilled professional life. Many research projects are abandoned without the exploitation of useful findings.

FOOD PROCESSING IN LATIN AMERICA

While industrialized countries have grown by an average of 3.0-3.5 percent per year in GNP in the past decade, the average economic growth in Latin American countries was zero. The 1980s are being called the lost decade for Latin America. In all countries of Latin America, the number of people migrating to cities is greater than the number of people living in the rural areas. A change in food quality is evident in the development of a higher middle class which, with a higher income and greater knowledge, is beginning to demand better-quality foods.

In almost all the countries in Latin America, well-nourished people live side-by-side with the hungry. Countries with both high technological and living standards are struggling to find the ways and solutions to diminish these insupportable conditions.

Role of Food Scientists and Engineers

Science and technology are some of the tools that government and entrepreneurs are trying to use to minimize these circumstances. In the mid-1960s, there was a rush in Latin American countries, as well as in other parts of the world, to organize research institutions. Since food was always a first priority, emphasis was given to this area. As a result, food science and technology research organizations flourished.

There is no automatic harvest of benefits just because a research and development organization becomes established. Further, hiring competent people does not ensure sufficient technical productivity. Effective management must be continuously provided to ensure success throughout the food research institutions.

Many developing countries have established research institutes in the hope that such attempts would automatically bring about effective technology transfer in a short time, but the results have often been disappointing. In Latin America, research and development organizations in the field of food science started with a bright future ahead. After a relatively short period, many constraints were imposed on these organizations. They were unable to improve recruiting ability and selectivity of staff. Losing their attractiveness, they minimized their chances to hire top graduates and people from competing organizations. In spite of these growing pains, progress is being made.

In Latin American countries today, groups of food scientists are carrying out projects at the most advanced frontier of modern technology. Biotechnology in many countries has been given a top priority, not only to improve existing raw materials but also to develop better and new plants or animals through genetic engineering.

Interregional programs in biotechnology are also being started, fostered by the initiative of government-sponsored research organizations associated with private groups in the participating countries. Laboratories are also doing research to produce recombinant insulin locally and studying the synthesis of many organic and inorganic components such as amino acids, vitamins, and various hormones.

Robotization and the use of computers in industry and some universities are commonplace in Latin America. Also, part of the locally manufactured computer production is exported. Computer science is a compulsory discipline in most universities in Brazil.

Throughout Latin America, improvements are being made in manufacturing techniques and labeling. Further, foods are being engineered to meet dietetic requirements, providing the consumer with alternatives with desired nutritional composition, taste, and dependability.

ROLE OF TECHNOLOGY IN FOOD SCIENCE

Food problems do exist in today's world, and both past and present technologies have failed and are still failing to reduce human misery, not because they are inadequate technologies but because the technological factor is only part of the solution. Scientific principles are usually transferable; many technologies are not. Technologies based on biological principles, whether they relate to the cultivation, raising, transformation, preservation, or distribution of plant and animal products, are intensely influenced by the physical, social, cultural, and economic environment.

During the past 50 years, food science and technology in developing countries has advanced and made some contributions. These could have been more important and effective if other factors had concomitantly existed.

Postproduction systems need to be studied comprehensively and in their entirety before change is proposed. New or improved postharvest technologies that are tied to sound scientific principles should be developed in areas where they are to be used. Competent food scientists are fully aware of the existing constraints and the needs of both the agricultural producers and the food industries, and thus will produce more feasible technologies.

The loss-reduction activities, particularly those using postharvest technologies, are basically dependent on well-trained technical personnel. Food science and technology courses in both academic and extension institutions are the most important instruments for bringing knowledge to those who have the responsibility to improve communication among farmers, government, educational agencies, and planning organizations, and thus help to disseminate information and learning materials.

In general, industrialized countries spend 2 to 3 percent of their GNP on science and technology while, in developing countries, the average expenditure is 5-6 times smaller. Thus, education is overlooked. The subsequent high level of illiteracy greatly impairs the efficiency of the people engaged in food production as well as their knowledge regarding improved diets.

Role of Biotechnology in Food Science

Genetic engineering will produce nutrients, colors, flavors, sweeteners, and preservatives. As plants and animals are genetically modified to attain specific ratios of macronutrients and fiber and specific amounts of micronutrients, societies will be increasingly faced with both scientific and ethical questions. The scientific questions may be easier to answer since they will be directed by research data. The potential uses of biotechnology will create great consumer concerns. This innovative research area will be discussed in Chapter Twelve.

NUTRITION AND FOOD SCIENCE

Many food industry leaders have accepted the nutrition challenge, convinced that solutions to malnutrition problems can be partially provided by private enterprise. The search for high-quality food proteins still occupies the time and effort of scientists all over the world, including the developing countries. The development of fish protein concentrate to be used as a supplement was a significant contribution.

Technology has contributed not only to the quality, safety, convenience, and reduced cost of food, but also to the nutritional status of the industrialized world. Techniques have been developed to reduce or eliminate natural anti-metabolites and anti-nutrients. Restoration, enrichment, and fortification procedures have contributed to the demise of many nutritional deficiency diseases. Changes in the basic chemical nature of food ingredients have allowed the formulation of low- or modified-fat foods for the population that requires them.

Several health changes can be attributed to research conducted by U.S. food scientists:

1. Life expectancy is increasing.
2. The death rate from heart disease over the past two decades is down by 20 percent, and from stroke, by more than 30 percent.
3. Fewer people are dying of cancer.

4. Infant mortality is decreasing.
5. Childhood infectious diseases have nearly disappeared.

Recent nutritional products include Procter & Gamble's fat substitute, Olestra™, projected to have a $1 billion market by the mid-1990s. NutraSweet's left-handed sugars, as sweet as natural sugar and indigestible by humans, marketed under the name Simplesse™, will also be a $1 billion product. The obsession with the calorie content of food is a recent one, and geographically limited to certain segments of the industrialized world.

The greatest impact on the health of human beings, which is reflected in the facts numbered above, has come from food technology. The discovery and utilization of scientific principles in food technology, culminating in the preparation, packaging, and distribution of processed food, have provided a supply of safe, wholesome, and nutritious foods unknown before in history.

Although between 75 and 80 percent of a total world population of more than 5 billion live in the developing nations, their nutritional status definitely is only slightly better than 50 years ago. The challenge for food scientists is immense.

Food science and nutrition research areas are closely related. For example, a problem now receiving worldwide attention is the hard-to-cook condition in some beans, which has not as yet been resolved. This condition induces difficulties in cooking beans, causing large expenditures in fuel energy and, as a consequence of the prolonged cooking times, losses in nutritive value and acceptability to consumers. This problem is useful to indicate that, besides nutritive value, other attributes of commodities are also being recognized such as functionality.

SUMMARY

New food technologies in the future will have to be instituted with great care. For instance, does the demand for ever-lower levels of salt for the entire population produce health benefits that justify increased microbiological risks? In many products, salt is either a major factor or a co-factor in food preservation.

As a society, we may have to conclude that we cannot recommend one diet for all people of all ages. Flexibility will be the key to providing many foods with differing proportions of fats, proteins, and carbohydrates, along with appropriate fortification of vitamins and minerals, in a biologically available package.

We have reached the point where it has become feasible to foresee widespread genetic testing to establish those at risk for cancer, heart disease, and other disorders, who would benefit from a particular diet high or low in specific nutrients. "Customized mass production" could be our aim in the twenty-first century. This will place greater responsibility on the food technologist to ensure that added nutrients will be of known bioavailability that is maintained throughout processing and storage.

The multifactorial nature of food is considered in the production of high-quality, safe, and nutritious food. Food technology has been an integral part of society. The contribution of food scientists to the global world food supply is immense. The real challenges are in the future where the food scientist must develop and utilize new techniques ranging from molecular biology to sophisticated communications systems, to create the flexibility and innovation required in the twenty-first century.

REFERENCES

Ames, B. N., R. Magaw, and L. S. Gold. 1987. Ranking possible carcinogenic hazards. *Science* 236:271.

Anonymous. 1987a. Soviet bread. *Science* 236:25.

Boeh-Ocansey, Osei. 1989. Developments and challenges in Africa's food industry. *Food Technology* 43(5):84-92.

Bressani, Ricardo. 1989. Food science and technology in developing countries during the past 50 years. *Food Technology* 43(9):108-132.

Brown, Judith E. 1990. *The science of human nutrition*. San Diego: Harcourt Brace Jovanovich, Publishers.

Cetron, Marvin and Owen Davies. 1989. *American renaissance–our life at the turn of the 21st century*. New York: St. Martin's Press.

Clydesdale, Fergus M. 1989. Present and future of food science and technology in industrialized countries. *Food Technology* 43(9):134-146.

Connor, John M. 1988. *Food processing: an industrial powerhouse in transition*. Lexington and Toronto: D. C. Heath and Company.

Gorgatti-Netto, Agide. 1989. Present and future of food science and technology in developing countries. *Food Technology* 43(9):148-168.

Hood, Lamartine F. 1988. The role of food science and technology in the food and agriculture system. *Food Technology* 42(9):131-34.

Lee, John E. 1988. Trends in world agriculture and trade in high-value food products. *Food Technology* 42(9):119-27.

Leveille, G. A. and M. A. Uebersax. 1980. Fundamentals of food science for the dietitian: frozen foods. *Dietetic Currents* 7(4):21-24.

Leveille, G. A. and M. A. Uebersax. 1980. Fundamentals of food science for the dietitian: wheat products. *Dietetic Currents* 7(1):1-8.

McGovern, R. Gordon. 1988. Worldwide consumer trends and the competitive position of the U.S. food industry. *Food Technology* 42(9):128-9.

Middlekauff, R. D. and P. Shubik. 1989. Introduction. In *International food regulation handbook*, eds. R. D. Middlekauff and P. Shubik, 1-5. New York and Basel: Marcel Dekker, Inc.

Ouellette, Robert P., N. W. Lord, and P. N. Cheremisinoff. 1980. *Food industry energy alternatives*. Westport, CT: Food & Nutrition Press.

Pelto, G. H. and P. J. Pelto. 1983. Diet and delocalization: dietary changes since 1750. In *Hunger and history*, ed. R. I. Rotberg and T. K. Tabb, 309-330. Cambridge: Cambridge University Press.

Todd, E. C. D. 1987. Impact of spoilage and foodborne diseases on national and international economics. *Intl. J. Food Microbiol.* 4:83.

Chapter Nine

Food Distribution, Consumption, and Losses

INTRODUCTION

Food is either directly or indirectly consumed by humans, or it is lost. Given all of the substantial resources expended to deliver food to consumers throughout the world, food losses are disastrous for global consumers. By studying information in this chapter, you will become familiar with several concepts:

- food consumption patterns and projections for developed countries;
- the magnitude of, and reasons for, preharvest and postharvest losses which occur throughout the world;
- the magnitude of the losses associated with food waste, including energy, water, and packaging materials;
- the controlled use of enzymes on food processing wastes to produce useful food products from waste resources.

When you read about food consumption in the U.S., you will be able to visualize foodservice establishments in many other parts of the developed world. Many countries give similar types of establishments different names. For example, Poland refers to local restaurants as "milk bars." In developed countries, going out for a pizza on Friday nights may be part of your weekly entertainment. In countries with a per capita income of $400, such eating dignities are not feasible.

FOOD DISTRIBUTION

Lack of awareness of the importance of marketing, including food distribution activities, was reflected in the way national development plans were formulated in the 1950s and early 1960s. A 1970 review of government attitudes toward marketing in Asia showed that government officials possessed little marketing knowledge. Thus, major decisions were frequently made without adequate information.

The growth of commercial food distribution networks has been intricately related to the development of food processing technologies. Most developing countries need an improved food transportation system to reduce the time lag between departure from the production site and arrival at the market. This would reduce food losses that occur in transit.

FOOD CONSUMPTION

Information in Exhibit 9.1 gives the places where food was purchased for consumption in the U.S. during 1984. Retail stores are the largest markets for food distribution, followed by foodservice outlets. In 1987, U.S. consumers spent $162.6 billion for food consumed at home and $120.6 billion for food eaten away from home. Data in Exhibit 9.2 give projected expenditures for food for the next 30 years. Food purchased in grocery stores is expected to rise at a rate of between 1.2 and 1.4 percent per year, up to the year 2000. Food for away-from-home consumption will increase at 1.4 to 2.0 percent per year. In future years, the decelerating population growth rate in the U.S. reduces these growth rates (Exhibit 9.2). To a great extent, these statistics affect the products that are produced by the food processing industry. Generally, restaurants and other foodservice establishments purchase in larger quantities, thus receiving inherent economies of scale.

Consumption and Energy Waste

Data in Exhibit 9.3 were compiled in response to the challenge to answer the question: "Is energy expended within foodservice establishments being wasted? If so, how large is the problem and can it

Exhibit 9.1. Total U.S. Food and Beverage Demand - 1984.

Demand Sector	Place Consumed	Distribution Channel	Places Purchased	Retail Value of Purchases
				$ billion
Households	At-home	Retail	- Retail stores (food, liquor, department)	$274
Households	Away-from-home	Foodservice	- Separate eating and drinking places	146
			- Hotels and motels	13
			- Retail hosts	7
			- Vending machines	5
			- Recreation and entertainment places	4
			- Clubs and associations	2
			- Mobile on street	1
			Total foodservice	176
Business	Away-from-home	Institutional	- Nursing homes and residential care	9
			- Plant and office cafeterias	8
			- Hospitals	7
			In-transit feeding	3
			- Elderly feeding	1
			Total business	28
Government	Away-from-home	Institutional	- Educational facilities	13
			- Military services	3
			- Correctional facilities	1
			Total government	17
Rest of the World	Outside	Export	- Free on board ships	11
TOTAL				$505

Source: Reprinted by permission of the publisher, from Food Processing: An Industrial Powerhouse in Transition by John M. Connor. (Lexington, Mass: Lexington Books, D.C. Heath and Company, copyright 1988, Lexington Books.)

be reduced?'' Although the foodservice sector cannot affect major changes in energy supplies or prices, they can effect energy usage while striving to use their energy sources efficiently. To show the recent energy situation in the hospitality industries of various nations, economic and energy data were summarized (Exhibit 9.3).

Exhibit 9.2. Predicted U.S. Real Household Expenditures for Food, 1980 to
2000, 2010, and 2020.

Category	Year					
	2000		2010		2020	
	Low growth	High growth	Low growth	High growth	Low growth	High growth
	Percent increase					
Food at-home	26	32	39	48	49	62
Food away-from-home	31	49	46	79	62	112
	Percent per year					
Food at-home	1.2	1.4	1.1	1.3	1.0	1.2
Food away-from-home	1.4	2.0	1.3	2.0	1.2	1.9

Note: Prediction based on 1.9 births per woman and resulting shifts in
regional, racial, and age distributions. High growth scenario assumes 2
percent increase in annual real household disposable incomes; low
growth assumes 1 percent growth rate. It assumes no change in
preferences, relative prices, or female labor participation rates.

Source: Reprinted by permission of the publisher from Food Processing: An
Industrial Powerhouse in Transition by John M. Connor. (Lexington,
Mass: Lexington Books, D.C. Heath and Company, copyright 1988,
Lexington Books.)

These data can be used to help interpret the importance of the industry to a nation's economy, and thus recommend incentives for increasing energy efficiencies within this sector. These data indicate orders of magnitude rather than precise quantifications. Precise data about energy expenditures for the preparation of food in foodservice establishments are not collected on a global basis.

When food is consumed away from home, consumers do not have any control over how energy is expended or wasted to prepare their meals. Whether they are dining at the Ritz in London or grabbing a taco from a street vendor in Mexico, the seller has total control over how energy required to store, prepare, cook and serve

Exhibit 9.3.   Energy and Expenditure Data for the Hospitality Industry in
Selected Nations - 1981.

Nation	Total Expenditure		Total Energy Consumption
	Millions of dollars	Dollars per capita	Kg of coal equivalent per capita
Belgium	2,597	263	5,329
Canada	10,832	447	10,070
Denmark	1,466	286	5,653
Finland	1,639	341	4,761
France	24,313	450	4,081
Greece	1,307	135	2,013
Ireland	134	39	3,206
Italy	16,323	285	3,273
Netherlands	4,000	281	5,652
Norway	1,029	251	5,950
Portugal	1,418	143	1,250
Sweden	1,542	185	5,156
United Kingdom	32,267	578	4,641
United States	107,337	467	10,204

Source: Unklesbay, N. and K. Unklesbay. 1985. Energy waste: how large is
the problem and can it be reduced?   In Advances in Catering
Technology-3, ed. George Glew, 167-180.   London and New York:
Elsevier Applied Science Publishers.

menu items is expended. According to a UN study, substantial energy losses are caused by human decisions.

For the data given in Exhibit 9.3, wasteful examples of energy usage include: partial oven loading, imprecise scheduling of energy-intensive equipment, and little or no enforcement of energy-conserving policies. Unfortunately, energy wastage associated with such managerial decisions is tolerated by society, including food-service customers who pay for it "on the bottom line." Five energy managerial policies, documented in Exhibit 9.4, were developed to reduce energy wastage when food is consumed within this industry.

Consumption and Food Waste

The reduction of food waste in foodservice facilities could contribute to a better utilization of our food resources and lead to cost savings for the customers. Information in Exhibit 9.5 gives information obtained from a U.K. study in different types of facilities. Note that the pubs had the largest amounts of total waste expressed as MJ of food energy per customer. This food waste was about equally attributed to actions of the kitchen employees and those of the pub customers. Alcoholic beverage waste was not included in this study! The low wastage level in schools was attributed to close managerial controls.

From this study, the researchers concluded that there was potential scope for the caterer or foodservice operator to save food if it was found to be desirable. The objectives of the caterer are varied, many being concerned with customer satisfaction and finance. Thus, the saving of food can only be beneficial to the operator if it

Exhibit 9.4. Energy Management Policies for Foodservice Establishments.

1. Energy sources: Include projected costs and availability of alternative energy sources as inputs to the decision-making process when procuring energy consuming equipment.

2. Energy efficiency: Investigate the energy efficiency of alternative methods of using direct and indirect energy when procuring energy consuming equipment.

3. Utility rates: Operate energy-consuming equipment so that energy can be purchased at cost-effective rates.

4. Operating procedures: Operate energy-consuming equipment in energy-effective modes.

5. Maintenance requirements: Ensure that the specified energy efficiency rating of all energy consuming equipment is maintained through appropriate maintenance procedures.

Source: Unklesbay, N. and K. Unklesbay. 1985. Energy Waste: How large is the problem and can it be reduced? In Advances in Catering Technology-3, ed. George Glew, 167-180. London and New York: Elsevier Applied Science Publishers.

Exhibit 9.5. Food Waste From U.K. Catering Establishments.

Category	No. of Units	Waste[a]			
		Total	Kitchen	Service	Customer
Schools	12	0.22	0.003	0.06	0.167
Place of Work	9	0.44	0.036	0.27	0.138
Restaurants, hotels, pubs	7	1.24	0.559	0.13	0.562
Cafes, snack bars	6	0.13	0.037	0.01	0.082
Hospitals	3	0.82	0.099	0.30	0.424
Welfare	2	0.37	0.003	0.23	0.136
Overall average	39	0.49	0.123	0.140	0.236

[a]Refers to amount of MJ per person per meal.

Source: Collison, R., G. H. Banks, and J. S. Colwill. 1985. Food waste: its size and control. In Advances in Catering Technology-3, ed. George Glew, 157-165. London and New York: Elsevier Applied Science Publishers.

enhances the managerial objectives. Customers pay for food whether it is eaten or wasted. As such, food waste becomes one component of doing business. However, this study identified many areas where food wastage could be reduced, especially by paying attention to portion sizes and management controls.

FOOD LOSSES

Estimates of worldwide preharvest losses include: grains, 10 percent; oil seeds, 12 percent; vegetables, 14 percent; and meat, eggs, and milk, 17.5 percent. Significant quantities of our food supply are lost because of pests such as insects, pathogens, weeds, birds, and rodents. World crop losses due to pest infestations are about 35 percent. These losses include destruction by insects, 13 percent; pathogens, 12 percent; weeds, 9 percent; and mammals and birds, 1 percent.

After harvesting, insects and rodents are as important as microbial agents. In developing countries, 25 percent of dried fish is destroyed by insects. The overall world spoilage of stored food is 30 percent. Fungi are important microorganisms, causing postharvest losses. Primary and secondary reasons for food losses are listed in Exhibit 9.6.

Postharvest losses of the food supply range from 9 percent in the U.S. to 20 percent in developing countries. When postharvest losses are added to preharvest losses, total food losses due to pests alone can rise to 48 percent in some countries. Thus, pests are consuming and/or destroying nearly one-half of the potential world food supply. When faced with an increasing need for food, can we afford a loss of such magnitude?

In developing countries, in-home losses are low. Because food accounts for a large portion of the family budget (Exhibit 8.11), it is usually of very poor quality before it is discarded.

Defining postharvest food losses and determining their extent is both location- and culture-specific. Human perception of what constitutes food, and food loss or food waste, is very subjective. Food loss can be defined as: "any change in the availability, edibility, wholesomeness, or quality of food that prevents it from being consumed by humans." A direct food loss is the disappearance of food by spillage or consumption by rodents or birds. An indirect food loss is the lowering of quality below standards for human consumption. The presence or absence of legal standards can also affect the eventual retention or rejection of a food for human use.

Converting edible food into another form more acceptable or convenient to consumers through processing is another source of food loss. For example, losses occur when making bread from wheat, beer from barley, sausages from meat, instant coffee from coffee beans, and so on. These losses are planned and thus not included in Exhibit 9.6.

In light of the statistics of food losses and our chronic need for additional food sources, more knowledge about economic cost-benefit factors in postharvest food loss reduction is required. Based on the information given in Exhibit 9.6, a major emphasis in developing countries' postharvest loss-reduction activities should be given to food preservation methods. Diseased animals, failed crops, and

Exhibit 9.6.   Summary of Food Losses.

Primary

Biological and microbiological damage

- consumption or damage by insects, mites, rodents, birds, and large animals and by microbes such as molds and bacteria.

Chemical and biochemical losses

- undesirable reactions between chemical compounds that are present in the food, enzyme-activated reactions, or accidental or deliberate contamination with harmful substances.

Mechanical losses

- arise from abrasion, bruising, excessive polishing, peeling, or trimming, puncturing of containers, or defective seals on cans or other containers.

Physiological losses

- caused by sprouting of grains and tubers, aging of fruits and vegetables, and changes caused by respiration and transpiration.

Secondary (lead to conditions in which a primary cause of loss can occur)

Inadequate drying equipment or a poor drying season.

Inadequate storage facilities to protect the food from insects, rodents, birds, rain, and high humidity.

Inadequate transportation to move food to the market before it spoils.

Inadequate refrigeration or cold storage of perishables.

Inadequate marketing system.

Source: Pariser, E. R. 1987. Post-harvest food losses in developing countries. In Food policy integrating supply, distribution, and consumption, eds. J. P. Gittinger, J. Leslie, and C. Hoisington, 309-25. Baltimore: The John Hopkins University Press. "A World Bank Publication."

spoiled food can have disastrous effects on communities and nations.

Research carried out in developing countries on various aspects of the food system has focused attention on the problem of developing postharvest technology, particularly to reduce losses of staple foods. When the grain storage practices conducted in developing countries have been analyzed, solutions to the problems have been provided. Although some solutions have been implemented, the problem of postharvest food losses still prevails, particularly with small farmers who, to a very large extent, are responsible for production of the basic staple foods.

Losses of Highly Perishable Foods

In developing countries, the main perishable staples are cassava, yam, sweet potato, white potato, taro, banana and plantain, and breadfruit. These foods comprise two-fifths of the food crops consumed in these nations. Perishable foods have a moisture content of at least 50 percent. They are difficult to dry and their dried products are often not acceptable.

The extended storage periods for these perishable goods are limited. They comprise the storage and reproductive parts of plants. Even those that are organs of dormancy, such as yams, are metabolically much more active than cereals and seldom have prolonged dormant periods. They are more susceptible to mechanical injury than grains. If they are exposed to undue heat, cold, or other unsuitable environmental conditions, the reduction of their moisture content may be abnormally high. During storage, losses occur mainly because of fungal and insect damage, and sprouting.

Refrigeration

As a preservation technique to reduce food losses by keeping perishable foods chilled, refrigeration has some severe limitations. The unit cost of many perishables is too low to support the expense of mechanically refrigerated storage. Many valuable tropical horticultural products are liable to low-temperature injuries, that is, physiological deterioration that occurs at temperatures near, but above, freezing. When refrigeration units do not have sophisticated thermostat systems to precisely control temperatures, additional losses of these valuable products will be realized.

Fish Losses

The commercial fisheries industry has serious food losses at every stage from harvest to consumption. Postharvest loss of fish is significant because 17 percent of the animal protein for worldwide human consumption comes from fish and fish products. About 20 percent of the total fish catch intended for human consumption is lost. Fish losses occur at sea when fish are discarded as by-catch in the harvest of other species such as shrimp. Dried fish products, such as those distributed in food aid programs, are fragile products. If they are roughly handled or vibrated on overloaded trucks on poor roads, they will be reduced to powder form.

Fish, although usually healthy when caught, are frequently damaged or spoiled before they are landed. About 4 to 5 million tons of trawled fish are dumped overboard before docking because of spoilage. About 5 million tons of shrimp, representing five times the catch sold at the docks, are destroyed, mainly because of poor storage at sea for this fragile product.

Some of the fish losses cannot be avoided. For example, ciguatera poisoning may affect 50,000 persons worldwide each year. Most of these are inhabitants of tropical or subtropical coastal areas where large reef fish such as barracuda, grouper, amberjack, and red snapper are eaten. The toxin originates from dinoflagellates associated with algal growth on coral, and passes up the fish food chain because it is fat soluble.

Water Losses

In many localities, water requirements of the food processing industry compete with those of residences. Of the water used in an average household, 45 percent goes for toilet flushing, 30 percent for bathing, 20 percent for laundry and dishes, and 5 percent for cooking.

In their first waking hour, an American family of four flushes close to 100 liters of water down the toilet (20 liters per flush), and at least another 200 liters down the shower drain. The average 5-minute shower uses 135 liters of water. This family has used more fresh water and energy than the average family in Bangladesh uses in one month.

Food Packaging Losses and Opportunities

Food processing companies can reduce costs by cutting back on elaborate packaging for their products. Paper, glass, metal, and plastic packaging constitute 50 percent of U.S. garbage by volume and 30 percent by weight. To help reduce wasted material, manufacturers are beginning to concentrate on using recyclable packaging materials. Convenient food packaging means that forests are levelled and waterways polluted to produce such articles as paper plates.

Canadians consume about 77 kilograms of plastic products per year compared to 11 kilograms for the average Brazilian. Expressed in another manner, Canadians buy more than their own weight in bottles, containers, plastic bags, appliances, and plastic construction materials each year. Much of it ends up in solid waste landfills and garbage dumps.

The "Seven billion served" statistic that the well-known fast-food chain proudly displayed on its golden arches also means that close to seven billion bags, cups, and wrappers have been placed in the continent's landfill sites and garbage dumps. Fast food chains are now initiating recycling programs. The price of disposing of packaging should be reflected in the cost of fast food.

As a result of day-to-day living, each American and Canadian generates 60 tons of garbage in a lifetime. That includes bulky packaging, "disposable" containers, food waste, and recyclable materials that never make it to the recyclers. The U.S. creates twice as much garbage per person as other industrialized nations in the EC, and the total is expected to grow by 20 percent in the next 10 years. Only 10 percent of U.S. trash is recycled. Western Europe, in contrast, recycles nearly one-third of its trash, Japan more than one-half.

On the other hand, effective food packaging reduces food losses by prolonging the shelf life of many products until they can be consumed. Many innovative techniques are being investigated throughout the food processing industry. For example, tests at the University of British Columbia (UBC) for modified atmosphere packaging technology on a variety of foods showed blueberries were still fresh after 8 weeks; asparagus, after 4 weeks; and peaches, after 8 weeks. Pacific Asia paid UBC for research and development and a percentage of revenues in return for holding worldwide rights to this modified atmosphere packaging technology. This technology, which can also be applied to flowers or seafood, has also been used to maintain freshness in snack foods, processed meats, and bakery goods. The packaging residues generated from such technologies as this one can be judged on a much sounder basis than those packages which serve only a "convenience" need for society.

Foodborne Diseases and Food Losses

Food- and waterborne disease is one of the major causes of diarrhea with up to 100 million cases every year in children under 5 years of age, resulting in 5 million deaths. The economic impact of foodborne disease in developing countries has never been estimated, but is probably much greater than in industrialized countries. The social costs have to be considered in terms of high infant mortality, malnutrition, chronic diarrhea, lost work, and child care. In other words, when foods of questionable safety are consumed, the resulting foodborne diseases cost society more than if the food had been wasted.

Air Canada would like to recycle its garbage but the federal government will not allow it. Agriculture Canada requires garbage from international flights to be incinerated. This is believed to be the most effective way to destroy bacteria and viruses foreign to Canada. More than 500 tons of international flight refuse are incinerated monthly from flights landing in Canada, adding to the level of air pollution. Air Canada is examining the possibility of irradiating international food refuse.

Numerous examples exist of expending resources to distribute foods around the world which are subsequently destroyed because of various types of contamination. For example, in the U.K., several incidents of food poisoning were traced to South American canned corned beef. One 6-pound can of Argentinean beef that was mixed with other ingredients and used in a catering establishment was found to be responsible for 507 cases of typhoid fever. The can had been contaminated after processing when it was placed in heavily contaminated river water for cooling. A ban was subsequently placed on the importation of Argentinean corned beef, with severe economic consequences for South America.

ENERGY LOSSES

From tilling soil to baking bread, every step in producing food requires energy. To feed rapidly expanding populations, most developing nations need to move beyond the limitations imposed by human and animal muscle to the scale of mechanized agriculture. Fuel is expensive. Thus, throughout the food industry, from production to consumption, energy-saving practices should be studied and developed to achieve economical processes.

Energy in one form or another, i.e., solar, human, animal, fossil, or biomass, is a component of every step in food production and processing. Fertilizer represents a large energy expenditure, and when it is imported by a nation, it depletes the amount of foreign exchange available for other food products. When energy and fertilizers were cheap, there was little incentive for energy-saving technologies.

Rising energy costs, predictable for the next decades, may again exacerbate this issue. Thus, there is a desperate need to ensure that the highest percentage of all food produced on a raw or processed basis reaches the stomach of the consumer. The situation cannot continue to be accepted that, after all the effort spent in labor, equipment, fertilizers, chemicals, and energy to produce food crops, a large part is wasted because of a lack of proper technology for harvesting, handling, transportation, and storage. We have available procedures and technology for reducing food losses (Exhibit 9.6).

ENZYMES AND FOOD PROCESSING WASTES

Enzymes can be used to reduce food processing wastes in four main areas. First, they decrease food waste because they enable a thorough or more complete utilization of raw materials or commodities. Second, they decrease food waste through enzymatic processing of waste streams to give higher value by-products such as fish processing wastes. Third, they aid by improving the processing efficiency of raw materials. Finally, they assist in the clean-up of food wastes in by-product streams created during processing.

Fish Wastes and Proteases

Protease enzymes have been successfully used in fish waste processing. In the form of trash fish and stickwater, fish waste can be recycled and upgraded as fish meal. A commercial protease preparation can be used to prepare fish pellets (Exhibit 9.7). The enzyme solubilizes the proteins of comminuted whole fish. The solubilized proteins are recovered and used in either a liquid concentrate or dry solid form to add nutritional value to fish food. In addition, proteases have been added to the liquid phase in fish meal production, or stickwater, to reduce viscosity and increase the final solids content.

Protease enzymes have also been used during processes which recover fish oils. The recovery of fish oils improves the efficiency of the evaporator tubes and decreases the deposition of sludges in centrifuges. These desirable features serve to reduce processing costs.

SUMMARY

Rates of food losses vary among countries. Traditionally, the U.S.S.R. has written off one-quarter of its harvests to transportation losses, rodents, mildew, and thievery. Within the U.S., postharvest losses range from 1 to 8 percent, being reduced by good management practices. A 1 percent increase in yield, through waste reduction by better process control in the U.S. food processing industry, would produce a value in excess of $1 billion. The review questions listed in Exhibit 9.8 ask some hard questions that global societies should soon answer.

Exhibit 9.7. Commercial Preparation of Fish Food Pellets from Trash Fish.

Fish Waste - to - Fish Food

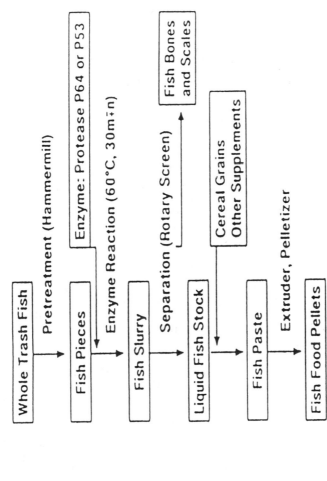

Source: Shoemaker, S. 1986. The Use of Enzymes for Waste Management in the Food Industry. In *Biotechnology in Food Processing*, eds. S. K. Harlander and T. P. Labuza, 259-269. Park Ridge, NJ: Noyes Publications.

Exhibit 9.8. List of Review Questions.

1. In attempts to reduce world food shortages, what is the significance of the quantity of food lost and willfully wasted?

2. Under what conditions is it fair to say that if losses could be reduced, more people could be fed adequately?

3. Assuming that members of a certain community are malnourished because they are unable, for economic or any other reasons, to gain access to sufficient food, does the reduction of food losses in that community mean that those in need can obtain more food or will it simply enhance the consumption of those already meeting their food needs?

4. What are the conditions that will make it possible for a food loss reduction in one locality to permit people in that or another locality to consume more food?

Source: Pariser, E. R. 1987. Post-harvest food losses in developing countries. In Food policy integrating supply, distribution, and consumption, ed. J. P. Gittinger, J. Leslie, and C. Hoisington, 309-25. Baltimore: The John Hopkins University Press. "A World Bank Publication."

REFERENCES

Abbott, J. C. 1986. *Marketing improvement in the developing world: what happens and what we have learned*. FAO Economic and Social Development Series No. 37. Rome: Food and Agriculture Organization of the United Nations.

Cetron, Marvin and Owen Davies. 1989. *American renaissance – our life at the turn of the 21st century*. New York: St. Martin's Press.

Hood, Lamartine F. 1988. The role of food science and technology in the food and agriculture system. *Food Technology* 42(9):131-34.

Knorr, Dietrich. 1983. Recycling of nutrients from food wastes. In *Sustainable food systems*, ed. D. Knorr, 249-278. Westport, Conn.: AVI Publishing Company, Inc.

Pariser, E. R. 1987. Post-harvest food losses in developing countries. In *Food policy integrating supply, distribution, and consumption*, ed. J. P. Gittinger, J. Leslie, and C. Hoisington, 309-25. Baltimore: The Johns Hopkins University Press.

Pimental, D. and M. Pimental. 1979. *Food, energy, and society*. New York: John Wiley & Sons.

Streeten, Paul. 1987. *What price food?* New York: St. Martin's Press.

Todd, Ewen, C. D. 1987. Impact of spoilage and foodborne diseases on national and international economies. *International Journal of Food Microbiology* 4:83-100.

PART THREE:
NUTRITION AND YOU

The two chapters of this section address the two contrasting situations that you are facing with respect to world nutrition, namely, overnutrition and undernutrition. The first chapter focuses on the role of the essential human nutrients. This information will assist you in at least five areas for your daily life. First, you will become informed about your personal need for nutrients. Second, you will become informed about how nutrition is linked to behavioral problems such as bulimia and anorexia. Third, you will have information to enable you to make food selections, recognizing that the legal requirements for nutritional labels on food packages in the U.S. are in transition. Fourth, information presented in this chapter will help equip you to deal with the media bombardment of food advertisement. Although you will realize that you need much more information, you will be on your way to becoming an informed consumer of food products. And finally, once you are aware of the role of nutrients in the human body, coupled with the food production, distribution, and consumption issues previously discussed, you will be in a good position to understand the serious ramifications of malnutrition throughout many countries of the world.

This basic scientific information will be included in a discussion of two major efforts in the U.S. to reduce the societal effects of overnutrition, namely, the U.S. Surgeon General's report of 1988 on Nutrition and Health and the new U.S. Recommended Dietary Allowances (RDAs). When studying this section, you will become aware that you would need at least one comprehensive course in the science of human nutrition before you could be familiar with how nutrients are absorbed and the accompanying physiological and bio-chemical concepts of human nutrition.

By studying the chapter on malnutrition, you will be able to inte-grate all of the factors associated with malnutrition around the world. You will be introduced to a diagram which shows the physi-cal human outcomes resulting from the interrelated factors of agri-culture, society, diet, food uses, and nutrition. You will be intro-duced to the indicators used to determine the extent of malnutrition in societies. As you were previously exposed to the body functions of nutrients, you will now become aware of the physiological and biochemical consequences when one or more of the essential nutri-ents are deficient in the human diet. Finally, using a case study approach, you will be introduced to the evolving technique termed nutritional surveillance, with the goal of reducing human suffering from malnutrition around the world.

Societies which suffer from overconsumption of foods have health problems, and have begun the long effort to reduce them through the application of sound nutrition research. Developing countries suffer from severe malnutrition, an extremely compli-cated and, admittedly, depressing situation. Although other sugges-tions have been given in the previous sections and will be included in the last section on current issues, management techniques such as effective nutritional surveillance programs are enabling many ex-perts to strive for a reduction in the effects of malnutrition.

Chapter Ten

Essential Human Nutrients

INTRODUCTION

Nutrition is the study of how substances in food affect human bodies and health. The study of nutrition may be defined as: "the science of food, the nutrients and other substances therein, their actions, interactions, and balance in relation to health and disease; and the processes by which the organism ingests, digests, absorbs, transports, uses, and excretes food substances." By studying information in this chapter, you will become familiar with the complex nutrition issues, namely:

- the functions of the essential energy sources, i.e., carbohydrates, fats, and proteins, and vitamins and minerals required to support human health;
- two prevalent human behavioral and nutrition disorders, anorexia nervosa and bulimia, which are affecting a portion of young adults in the U.S.;
- ten recommendations made by the U.S. Surgeon General to improve the health of Americans and reduce the effects of, and the death rates from, several diet-disease associations;
- how recent nutrition research has lead to the establishment of the Recommended Dietary Allowances (RDAs), designed to improve the nutritional health of the U.S. population.

If you have had courses in physiology and biochemistry, sections in this chapter about the functions of nutrients will be much easier for you to understand. Perhaps studying this condensed information may interest you to take an entire course in nutrition where information can be presented at a more leisurely and thorough pace. In any case, by being at least aware of the complex role of nutrients in human growth, maintenance, and metabolism, you should be in an informed position to understand the devastating effects of malnutrition around the globe.

At least 2 billion chemical reactions occur inside the human body, each one playing a role in how food ultimately affects human health. The complexity of nutrition and health relationships and the present limitations of research into human nutrition still cause large gaps in our knowledge. However, sufficient scientific knowledge is available about food and nutrition to lead to significant improvements in human health throughout the world.

GOOD HEALTH: A DEFINITION

Good health is a product of complex interactions among environmental, behavioral, social, and genetic factors. What people eat in developed countries affects their risk for several leading causes of death: coronary heart disease, stroke, atherosclerosis, diabetes, and some forms of cancer. These disorders account for two-thirds of the deaths in the U.S. each year. The grim statistics for this fact are included in Exhibit 10.1.

The modern concept of nutrition is that human life depends on a steady intake of a variety of specific dietary substances in defined amounts.

OVERVIEW OF NUTRIENTS

To sustain normal growth, development, and health, the human diet must contain adequate energy, all essential nutrients, and certain other dietary factors. The macronutrients include carbohydrates, fats, and proteins, as sources of energy; essential fatty acids; and amino acids that either cannot be synthesized in the human body or are synthesized in too small amounts to meet physiological needs. The micronutrients include vitamins and mineral elements which are required in small amounts. Although fiber does not fall into either category, it is beneficial for good health. Each nutrient, plus the role of water, often termed the "forgotten nutrient," will be discussed.

Exhibit 10.1. Estimated Total Deaths and Percent of Total Deaths for the Ten
Leading Causes of Death in the U.S. — 1987.

Rank	Cause of Death	Number	Percent of Total Deaths
1[a]	Heart diseases	759,400	35.7
	(Coronary heart disease)	(511,700)	(24.1)
	(Other heart disease)	(247,700)	(11.6)
2[a]	Cancers	476,700	22.4
3[a]	Strokes	148,700	7.0
4[b]	Unintentional injuries	92,500	4.4
	(Motor vehicle)	(46,800)	(2.2)
	(All others)	(45,700)	(2.2)
5	Chronic obstructive lung diseases	78,000	3.7
6	Pneumonia and influenza	68,600	3.2
7[a]	Diabetes mellitus	37,800	1.8
8[b]	Suicide	29,600	1.4
9[b]	Chronic liver disease and cirrhosis	26,000	1.2
10[a]	Atherosclerosis	23,100	1.1
. . .	All causes	2,125,100	100.0

[a]Causes of death in which diet plays a part.
[b]Causes of death in which excessive alcohol consumption plays a part.

Source: U.S. Department of Health and Human Services. 1988. *The Surgeon General's Report on Nutrition and Health.* DHHS (PHS) Pub. No. 88-50210. Washington, DC: U.S. Government Printing Office.

Energy Sources

Adequate human diets contain sufficient energy to support growth and development, maintain basic physiological functions, support muscular activity, and repair physical damage caused by injury or illness. In the U.S., energy intakes and expenditures are measured in kilocalories (kcal), and commonly referred to as calories. In other countries, the term kilojoules (kJ) is used, with 1 kcal = 4.184 kJ.

The human body obtains chemical energy from food from the oxidation or chemical burning of protein, fat, carbohydrate, and alcohol. In pure form, the oxidation within the body of one gram of each of these substances yields about 4, 9, 4, and 7 kcal, respectively. Body weight depends on complex physiological controls of the balance between energy intake and energy expenditure.

Exhibit 10.2 gives selected information of food available from McDonald's fast food restaurants. Note that a gram is a measure of weight — 1/28th of 1 ounce, or the weight of one small paper clip. Tables are compiled in this way to enable you to sum together nutrients from different menu items.

Carbohydrates

Carbohydrates are the leading source of energy for most people around the globe. Rice, beans, millet, cassava, breads, and pasta are all rich sources of carbohydrates. Carbohydrates are produced in plants from carbon dioxide, water, sunlight, and chlorophyll. They are composed of three elements in different amounts and configurations: carbon, hydrogen, and oxygen. Alcohol (ethanol) is the only other important source of energy for some adults.

In addition to being sources of energy for vital metabolic processes, carbohydrates are also cellular components of nucleic acids, glycoproteins, and enzyme cofactors. They are structural components of cell walls and membranes of plant foods. They are classified as either simple or complex carbohydrates.

Monosaccharides and disaccharide sugars are simple carbohydrates; polysaccharides such as starches and fibers are complex carbohydrates. Each type of carbohydrate has a given chemical structure which determines how it is digested and used within the human body.

Monosaccharides. Three important monosaccharides — glucose, fructose, and galactose — are simple sugars that are absorbed in the body without further digestion. Glucose and fructose are found in fruits, vegetables, and honey and they are the digestive products of sucrose, commonly called white sugar. When glucose is obtained from corn starch, it can be enzymatically converted to fructose, producing high-fructose corn sweeteners, commonly used to sweeten soft drinks.

Disaccharides. Sugars formed from two monosaccharides are termed disaccharides. Examples include: sucrose or white sugar, composed of glucose and fructose; maltose, found in beer and cere-

Exhibit 10.2. Selected Nutrient Information About Food Available at McDonald's.

Nutrient	Menu Item		
	Egg McMuffin	Big Mac	Chef Salad
Serving Size (g)	135	215	265
Calories	280	500	170
Protein (g)	18	25	17
Carbohydrate (g)	28	42	8
Fat (g)	11	26	9
Mono-Unsaturated Fatty Acids (g)	6	16	4
Poly-Unsaturated Fatty Acids (g)	1	1	1
Saturated Fatty Acids (g)	4	9	4
Cholesterol (mg)	235	100	111
Sodium (mg)	710	890	400
Vitamin A (% U.S. RDA)	10	6	100
Vitamin C (% U.S. RDA)	*	2	35
Thiamin (% U.S. RDA)	30	30	20
Riboflavin (% U.S. RDA)	20	25	15
Niacin (% U.S. RDA)	20	35	20
Calcium (% U.S. RDA)	25	25	15
Iron (% U.S. RDA)	15	20	8

* Contains less than 2% of the U.S. RDA of these nutrients.
Source: McDonald's Nutrition Information Center, Oak Brook, IL. 1991.

als, composed of two glucose molecules; and lactose, found in cow's milk, composed of glucose and galactose.

Most simple sugars have a sweet taste. Their order of magnitude of sweetness is: fructose, glucose, galactose, and disaccharides. When adding sugars to processed foods, combinations of sugars are frequently used to achieve the specified level of sweetness at the desired price. This fact can be observed by noting more than one type of sugar on some food ingredient labels.

Polysaccharides. High molecular weight polysaccharides include starch, glycogen, and most types of fibers. Starch and glycogen are composed of glucose molecules. Fiber includes a variety of carbohydrates and other components.

Polysaccharides differ from each other in the way that their monosaccharide units are linked to each other. Thus, they differ in their ability to be digested to sugars in the body. In starch and glycogen, the chemical linkages are split by human intestinal enzymes. The polysaccharides found in fiber are indigestible. However, some fiber components can be broken down by enzymes, being released by bacteria in the digestive tract to short-chain fatty acids that can be reabsorbed to provide food energy.

Fiber

Dietary fibers are mainly indigestible complex carbohydrates in plant cell walls, i.e., cellulose, hemicellulose, and pectin, and a variety of gums, mucilages, and algal polysaccharides. Lignin is a noncarbohydrate component of dietary fiber in plant cell walls.

Two basic types of dietary fibers come from plants. Insoluble fibers include the fibrous components of plant cells, including the plant cell walls. Primary sources of insoluble fibers are seeds and the bran that covers whole grains such as wheat, rice, and rye. Soluble fibers are nonfibrous components of plant cells. They are primarily found within the cell, and form a gel-like solution when combined with water. Good sources of soluble fibers include the pulp of fruits and vegetables, oat bran, and dried beans.

Data in Exhibit 10.3 for soybean hulls or seed coats reveals that some fibers can absorb up to 6.59 times their weight in water. The particle sizes of fine, medium, and coarse refer to granular sizes of

Exhibit 10.3. Maximum Absorption of Water by Soy Hulls for Experimental Conditions.

Conditions Temperature (°C) Grind Size	Water Absorbed (g/g Soy Hulls)	Conditions Temperature (°C) Grind Size	Water Absorbed (g/g Soy Hulls)
(25°C)		(50°C)	
Fine	4.18	Fine	4.80
Medium	4.93	Medium	5.43
Coarse	5.76	Coarse	5.85
(75°C)		(95°C)	
Fine	5.01	Fine	6.04
Medium	5.83	Medium	6.42
Coarse	5.82	Coarse	6.59

Source: Muzilla, M., N. Unklesbay, Z. Helsel, K. Unklesbay, and M. Ellersieck. 1989. Effect of particle size and heat on absorptive properties of soy hulls. J. of Food Quality 12:305-318.

0.84, 1.65, and 2.36 mm, respectively. When food products are cooked, the level of absorption of fibers is partially dependent on temperatures achieved.

Although dietary fibers are not directly absorbed into the body, they affect digestion and absorption. Cellulose, a fibrous component of cell walls, facilitates the movement of food through the digestive tract. On the other hand, gel-forming pectins slow down the passage of food through the intestinal tract, enabling more absorption of nutrients to occur. Some gel-forming fibers, such as oat bran, have been associated with decreasing the absorption of glucose and cholesterol.

In summary, the effects of various fiber types on intestinal functions differ. Insoluble fibers reduce blood cholesterol, enhance glucose tolerance, and increase insulin sensitivity. Although research with dietary fiber is continuing, the Food and Nutrition Board of the National Research Council (NRC) recommends that a desirable fiber intake be achieved by consumption of fruits, vegetables, legumes, and whole-grain cereals.

Lipids

Lipids are organic compounds with limited solubility in water, being present in biologic systems mainly as energy stores within cells or as components of cell membranes.

Dietary fats or lipids include a variety of substances that are insoluble in water. Food lipids include triglycerides, composed of fatty acids and glycerol; phospholipids; and cholesterol. Triglycerides are the principal lipid component of foods and enhance palatability by absorbing and retaining flavors and influencing food texture.

Excess chemical energy in the body that is derived from carbohydrate, fat, protein, or alcohol can be converted to fatty acids and stored in adipose tissue. Dietary fat is essential because it supplies linoleic acid, an essential fatty acid, and is a vehicle for the absorption of fat-soluble substances such as Vitamins A, D, E, and K.

Lipids are concentrated sources of energy as well as structural components of cell membranes. They are molecular precursors for the synthesis of hormones and other substances. Furthermore, fats impart characteristic mouth-feel and flavors to foods and increase the feeling of satiety after meals by delaying the passage of food from the stomach to the small intestine. The reservoirs of stored fat protect the body's organs, provide insulation from heat loss, and maintain energy production during periods of reduced food consumption.

Fatty acids. Fatty acids are molecules containing carbon, hydrogen, and oxygen with chain lengths ranging from 4 to about 25 carbon atoms. Most fat in food occurs as triglycerides, or three fatty acid chains attached to a glycerol molecule, as shown in Exhibit 10.4. The fatty acids commonly found in food are usually composed of an even number of carbon atoms, from 12 to 22, and contain from 0 to 6 double bonds or sites where additional hydrogen atoms can be attached. The number of double bonds determines the degree of saturation of fats. Fatty acids with no double bonds are termed saturated; those with one double bond, monounsaturated; and those with two or more double bonds, polyunsaturated. The distinctions are diagrammed in Exhibit 10.4.

Although all dietary fats consist of a mixture of saturated, mo-

Exhibit 10.4. Basic Chemical Structure of Fats and Oils.

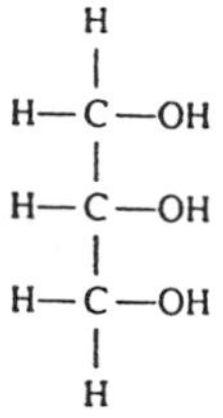

Glycerol

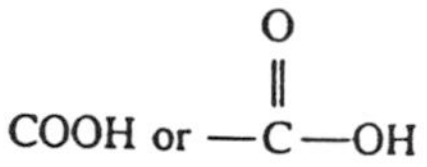

Carboxyl Group

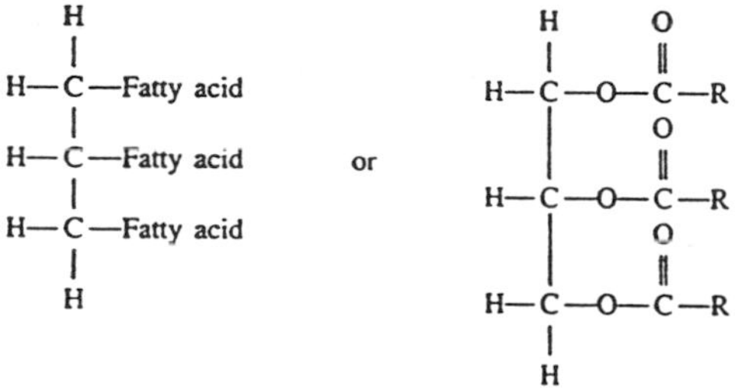

Triglyceride

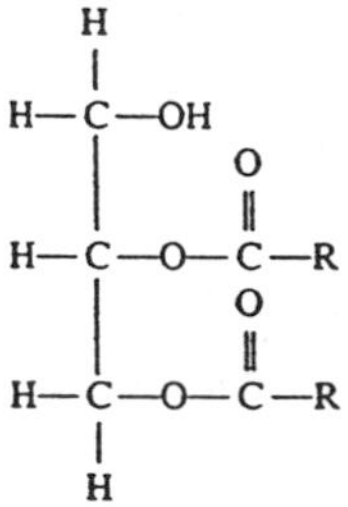

Diglyceride

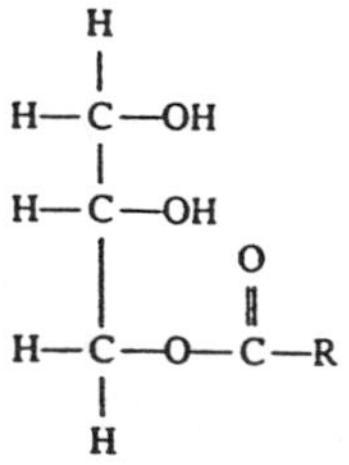

Monoglyceride

Exhibit 10.4 (continued)

$$
\begin{array}{c}
\quad\ \ \ \mathrm{H}\ \ \ \mathrm{H}\ \ \ \mathrm{O} \\
\quad\ \ \ |\ \ \ \ |\ \ \ \ \| \\
\mathrm{R-C-C-C-OH} \\
\quad\ \ \ |\ \ \ \ | \\
\quad\ \ \ \mathrm{H}\ \ \ \mathrm{H}
\end{array}
$$

Saturated Fatty Acid

$$
\begin{array}{c}
\ \ \ \mathrm{H}\ \ \ \mathrm{H}\ \ \ \mathrm{H} \\
\ \ \ |\ \ \ \ |\ \ \ \ | \\
\mathrm{R-C=C-C-COOH} \\
\ \ \ \ \ \ \ \ \ \ \ \ | \\
\ \ \ \ \ \ \ \ \ \ \ \mathrm{H}
\end{array}
$$

Unsaturated Fatty Acid

$$
\begin{array}{c}
\ \ \ \mathrm{H}\ \ \ \mathrm{H}\ \ \ \mathrm{H}\ \ \ \mathrm{H}\ \ \ \mathrm{H}\ \ \ \mathrm{H} \\
\ \ \ |\ \ \ \ |\ \ \ \ |\ \ \ \ |\ \ \ \ |\ \ \ \ | \\
\mathrm{R-C=C-C-C=C-C-COOH} \\
\ \ \ \ \ \ \ \ \ \ \ \ |\ \ \ \ \ \ \ \ \ \ \ \ | \\
\ \ \ \ \ \ \ \ \ \ \ \mathrm{H}\ \ \ \ \ \ \ \ \ \ \ \mathrm{H}
\end{array}
$$

Polyunsaturated Fatty Acid

nounsaturated, and polyunsaturated fatty acids, fatty acids in foods of animal origin are more often saturated. Plant fatty acids are more frequently monounsaturated and polyunsaturated. However, coconut oil and palm kernel oil contain a high proportion of saturated fatty acids even though they are derived from plants. Certain fish are good sources of polyunsaturated fatty acids.

The location of the double bonds along the carbon chain is physiologically important. The site of the double bonds is used to categorize unsaturated fatty acids into three groups: the omega-3, omega-6, and omega-9 fatty acids. The end of the carbon chain containing the methyl group has a carbon atom known as the omega carbon. When fatty acids are metabolized, the end of the carbon chain containing the methyl group tends to remain unchanged. Enzymes can add or subtract carbon atoms or double bonds starting from the end of the molecule that contains the carboxyl group. Thus, the chemical features of fatty acids are usually described in terms of the structure at the methyl end of the chain.

Oleic acid has nine carbon atoms between its methyl omega carbon atom and its closest double bond, so it belongs to the omega-9 classification of fatty acids. Linoleic acid, an omega-6 fatty acid, cannot be synthesized by the human body and must be consumed in the diet. Although linoleic acid is widely distributed in the fatty portion of both plant and animal foods, vegetable seed oils are especially rich sources. Given that linoleic acid deficiency can be avoided by consuming 3 to 5 g of linoleic acid per day, fatty acid deficiencies are rarely reported in the U.S.

The role of omega-3 fatty acids, particularly eicosapentaenoic acid and docosahexaenoic acid in nutrition is under investigation. Recent data suggest that omega-3 fatty acids may have important physiologic effects that cannot be met by omega-6 or omega-9 fatty acids. The consumption of fish and other marine animals may offer special benefits for the reduction of coronary heart disease. The fatty acids in these species are rich in long-chain polyunsaturated fatty acids of the omega-3 series, particularly eicosapentaenoic and docosahexaenoic acids.

Studies in Greenland indicated that Kalatdlit who consumed large quantities of fish and marine animals had a low incidence of coronary heart disease in spite of their high fat and cholesterol intakes. It has been assumed that the low incidence of atherosclerosis and thrombosis in this indigenous population is partly attributable to the high proportion of omega-3 fatty acids in their traditional diets. As with numerous other nutritional findings, further studies are still in progress.

Food supply disappearance data suggest that per capita consumption of fat in the U.S. has increased since the late 1970s. Although animal fats still predominate, this greater consumption can be attributed to vegetable products such as margarine, shortenings, and edible oils. Factors affecting the increased use of edible oils include the rapid evolution of fast food establishments where foods are cooked in oil, as well as the increased use of convenience foods that are either fried or contain added oil.

A note of caution about food supply disappearance data is in order. These data cannot indicate the amount of fat actually consumed unless they are adjusted for waste, spoilage, trimming, and cooking losses. The latest U.S. Department of Agriculture (USDA) survey indicates that the fat intake of adults represents 36.4 percent of their total caloric intake. The Food and Nutrition Board of the NRC recommends that the fat content of the U.S. diet should not exceed 30 percent of caloric intake, and less than 10 percent of calories should be provided from saturated fatty acids.

Cholesterol. Cholesterol has figured in extensive controversies regarding its possible contribution to the etiology of atherosclerosis and coronary heart diseases. The structure of cholesterol (Exhibit 10.5) is composed of four interlocking rings of which three contain 6 carbon atoms each and the fourth contains 5 carbon atoms. An alcohol, hydroxy group (OH) is attached to carbon number 3 of the first ring and a chain of 8 carbon atoms is attached to carbon number 17 of the fourth ring.

During a recent survey of U.S. consumers, more than 50 percent could not distinguish between fatty acids and cholesterol. As shown in Exhibits 10.4 and 10.5, their chemical structures are totally different!

Although the role of cholesterol in disease is being debated, there

Exhibit 10.5. Chemical Structure of Cholesterol.

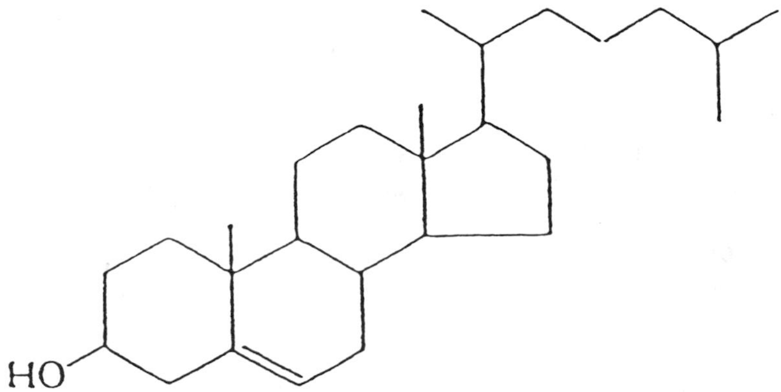

is no question about the necessity for this lipid in human bodies. Cholesterol is essential as a precursor of several important compounds, particularly the steroid hormones, including cortisone and testosterone. Cholesterol is required for the human body's production of Vitamin D and bile acids. It is an important constituent of all cell membranes.

Cholesterol is both synthesized in the body (endogenous) and obtained from the diet (exogenous). Cholesterol is needed metabolically but is not an essential nutrient. The human liver manufactures cholesterol at the rate, perhaps, of 50^{15} molecules per second. The raw material that the liver uses to make cholesterol is acetoacetate which can be taken from glucose or saturated fatty acids.

After manufacturing, cholesterol either is transformed into hormones or it leaves the liver for three possible destinations: excretion from the body, depositions in body tissues, or accumulations in arteries. In normal individuals, endogenous synthesis of cholesterol is reduced when blood cholesterol levels are high. When the physiologic mechanisms that regulate this feedback mechanism are insufficient, blood cholesterol levels can rise and increase the risk for coronary heart disease. The Food and Nutrition Board of the NRC recommends that dietary cholesterol should be less than 300 mg/day.

Proteins

Both animal and plant proteins are made up of about 20 amino acids. The proportion of these amino acids varies as a characteristic of a given protein. With the exception of gelatin, all food proteins contain some of each of these amino acids.

Proteins serve many functions in the human body. These include structural components of cells and tissues, enzyme catalysts of biochemical reactions, peptides and hormone messengers, and immune system components. Some amino acids are needed for the synthesis of special compounds. For example, the amino acid, tryptophan, is required for the synthesis of both serotonin and niacin.

Proteins are formed from various combinations of amino acids that are linked together in chains ranging from several to hundreds in length. Each plant and animal species has its own characteristic proteins that are distinguished by the sequence of amino acids. Plants synthesize their amino acids from carbon, oxygen, hydrogen, nitrogen, and sulfur.

Humans lack the ability to synthesize nine essential amino acids and must obtain them from the diet: histidine, isoleucine, leucine, lysine, methionine, phenylalanine, threonine, tryptophan, and valine. The remaining amino acids are termed nonessential. The amino acid, cystine, can replace part of the requirement for methionine. Tyrosine can replace part of the requirement for phenylalanine.

Proteins in different foods vary in their biological value according to their content and balance of amino acids. When the concentration of one amino acid is low relative to the others, that amino acid is considered to be limiting and the protein is incomplete. Limiting amino acids can be compensated for, at least partially, by having a dietary intake of complementary proteins, those with different limiting amino acids. The addition of even a small amount of protein from animal foods can improve amino acid intake.

To adjust for the amino acid composition, a score is calculated according to the most limiting amino acid, i.e., the one in greatest deficit for the age group involved.

$$\text{Amino acid score} = \frac{\text{Content of individual essential amino acid in food protein (mg/g of protein)}}{\text{Content of same amino acid in reference pattern (mg/g of protein)}}$$

The amino acid score is based on the appropriate pattern for age. Five amino acids affect the protein quality of mixed human diets: lysine, threonine, tryptophan, methionine, and cystine.

The protein efficiency ratio (PER) represents a protein's ability to promote growth in laboratory animals. Increases in muscle mass, bone, and other lean tissues of growing animals decline when only incomplete proteins are consumed. PER values determine the extent to which different types of food products will promote growth in humans and animals.

Vitamins

Vitamins are organic compounds that are essential in very small amounts for health, growth, and reproduction. They must be obtained from the diet either because they cannot be synthesized by the human body, or because the amounts made in the body are insufficient to meet body requirements. They are classified according to their solubility in fat or water. Their property of solubility affects their occurrence in foods as well as their absorption, transport, storage, and metabolism in the human body. Like other organic substances, vitamins are destroyed when their molecular structures are broken down. This destruction happens during transportation, storage, processing, and cooking as well as during digestive processes. Many handling and packaging procedures are designed to minimize vitamin losses in foods.

Fat-Soluble Vitamins

The fat-soluble vitamins are Vitamins A, D, E, and K. They are transported in the body by the same mechanisms as fat, bound to lipoprotein or specific transport proteins, and stored in liver and fat tissue. Because excretion is minimal, excess intake can lead to toxicity. Deficiencies are found in children who are rapidly growing and who lack adequate fat stores.

Vitamin A. Vitamin A is present in the diet both as the vitamin and its precursor, retinol. Preformed Vitamin A is found in foods derived from animals, i.e., milk, butter, egg yolks, and liver, and is bound to a fatty acid when used to fortify foods. Retinol occurs in foods primarily in the ester form. Certain carotenoids, i.e., pigments found in many dark green, yellow, and orange vegetables, fruits, and egg yolks, can be converted by the body into retinol. The conversion of beta-carotene into retinol occurs mainly in the intestinal mucosa.

Excessive intake of foods rich in beta-carotene causes the skin to take on an orange hue that disappears when the carotene consumption declines. Vitamin A is essential for visual processes, for the normal differentiation of epithelial tissue, for the regulation of cell membrane structure and function, and for the maintenance of immunocompetence.

The richest sources of preformed retinol are liver, fish liver oils, whole and fortified milk, and eggs. Biologically active carotenoids are abundant in carrots and dark green leafy vegetables.

Vitamin D. Vitamin D3 (cholecalciferol or calciol) is synthesized from a precursor (7-dehydrocholesterol) in skin that becomes activated by exposure to ultraviolet light from the sun. It is essential in the diet when exposure to sun is inadequate. The vitamin is converted by the liver to 25-dihydroxyvitamin D (calcidiol) and then further converted by the kidney to 1,25 dihydroxyvitamin D (calcitriol), the metabolically active form. Excess Vitamin D can be toxic, especially to children and adults who have kidney disease or certain metabolic disorders. Another form, Vitamin D2 (ergocalciferol), is the product of the ultraviolet light-induced conversion of ergosterol in plants.

In the U.S., the major food source of Vitamin D is fortified foods. Processed cow's milk contains 10 ug of cholecalciferol (400 IU) per quart. Solid food sources include eggs, butter, and fortified margarines.

Vitamin E. Two groups of compounds found in plant materials have Vitamin E biological activity in varying degrees. The most important group, the tocopherols, is characterized by a ring system and a long saturated side chain. There are four members of this group: the alpha, beta, gamma, and delta tocopherols, which differ only in the number and position of methyl groups on the ring. The other group, the tecotrienols, differ from the tocopherols by having an unsaturated side chain. The most active form of Vitamin E, alpha tocopherol, is the most widely distributed in nature.

Vitamin E functions as an antioxidant. Its principal dietary sources are vegetable seed oils such as soybean, corn, cottonseed, and safflower, and margarines and shortenings made from them. Wheat germ is high in Vitamin E, as are green leafy vegetables.

Vitamin K. Vitamin K refers to a group of compounds all of which contain the 2-methyl-1,4-naphthoquinone moiety. In plants (phylloquinone), the substituent at C-3 is a 20-carbon phytyl group; in bacteria (menaquinones), it is a polyisoprenyl side chain with four to thirteen 5-carbon isoprenyl units. Animal tissues contain both phylloquinone and menaquinones.

Vitamin K functions as an activator of blood-clotting proteins, proteins in bone and kidney, and the formation of other proteins that contain gammacarboxyglutamin acid (GLA). It is synthesized by intestinal bacteria, establishing the bacterial flora in the jejunum and ileum as a potentially important source of Vitamin K.

The Vitamin K content of commonly consumed foods is not known with precision and, therefore, is not included in food composition tables. Green leafy vegetables, milk, dairy products, meats, eggs, cereals, and fruits are believed to be some of the best sources.

Vitamin toxicity. With Vitamin A, signs of toxicity appear with sustained daily intakes, including both foods and supplements, exceeding 15,000 ug of retinol (50,000 IU) in adults. Spontaneous abortions have been observed in the fetuses of women ingesting therapeutic doses (0.5 to 1.5 mg/kg) of 13-cis retinoic acid (isotretinoin) during the first trimester of pregnancy. Large daily doses of retinol (20,000 IU) may cause similar abnormalities. Although excessive, prolonged ingestion of carotenoids may cause skin to appear yellow, they are not toxic. The Food and Nutrition Board of the NRC recommends that nutritional labeling of food products should distinguish between retinol and carotenoids, the former being toxic.

Although the toxic level for Vitamin D has not been established for all age groups, 45 ug (1,800 IU) of cholecalciferol per day has been associated with hypervitaminosis D in young children. As the sunlight-stimulated production of the vitamin is active throughout the warm months, dietary supplements may be detrimental to children drinking Vitamin D-fortified milk.

Extreme cases of toxicities have not been established for Vitamins E and K.

Water-Soluble Vitamins

The water-soluble vitamins include Vitamin C (ascorbic acid) and those of the B-complex group: biotin, folate, niacin, pantothenic acid, riboflavin, thiamin, Vitamin B6, and Vitamin B12. These vitamins are generally found in whole grain cereals, legumes, leafy vegetables, and meat and dairy foods. The two exceptions are Vitamin C which can be obtained in adequate amounts only from fruits and vegetables, especially citrus fruits; and Vitamin B12 which is synthesized by bacteria and found in foods of animal origin.

Water-soluble vitamins are absorbed from the intestine, and most are stored in a form that is bound to enzymes or transport proteins and excreted in the urine. Although tissue depletion may take as long as several weeks or months, they should be supplied in adequate amounts in the daily diet.

Water-soluble vitamins are essential components of enzymes and enzyme systems that catalyze a wide variety of biochemical reactions in cellular energy production and biosynthesis. The B-complex vitamins are prevalent throughout the U.S. food supply.

Vitamin C. Unlike most animals, humans cannot convert glucose to Vitamin C. Vitamin C or ascorbic acid promotes iron absorption by changing the ferrous form of iron to the ferric state, giving it an additional electron. Thus, Vitamin C converts a poorly absorbed form of iron into one that is readily absorbed. As an antioxidant, Vitamin C protects molecules from oxidation because it is highly susceptible to oxidation itself. Oxidative reactions in foods can cause off-flavors. The addition of Vitamin C to some foods prevents these reactions, including the formation of nitrosamines in bacon if it has been preserved with nitrates.

Vitamin C is abundant in citrus fruits and some other fruits and vegetables. The world's richest source of Vitamin C, containing as much as 880 mg per ounce, is the Australian green plum. Potatoes supply about one-sixth of the U.S. consumption of Vitamin C.

Thiamin (Vitamin B1). Thiamin plays a role in energy metabolism. Its coenzymes, along with those of riboflavin and niacin, are involved. Thiamin activates enzymes involved in the formation of energy from glucose. Thiamin is involved in the formation of energy from alcohol.

Riboflavin (Vitamin B2). The two coenzyme forms of riboflavin activate enzymes involved in the formation of energy from the breakdown of carbohydrates, proteins, and fats.

Niacin (Vitamin B3). The two coenzymes of niacin accept energy that is released during the breakdown of glucose and transfer it to a storage form. They are used in fatty acid synthesis and in biochemical processes leading to the formation of water, a major end-product of energy metabolism.

Vitamin B6 (pyridoxine). The coenzymes of Vitamin B6 activate a large number of enzymes which are involved in protein metabolism.

Folacin (folic acid). Folacin's coenzymes have key roles as activators of enzymes involved in DNA replication and the synthesis of proteins from amino acids. Folacin influences cell division. Thus, it is a particularly important vitamin for growth.

Vitamin B12 (cyanocobalamin). The coenzymes of Vitamin B12 are involved in the metabolism of fatty acids and amino acids that lead to the formation and maintenance of components of nerve, blood, and other cells. Together, the coenzymes of Vitamin B12 and folacin function to activate the enzymes involved in cell division. Also, Vitamin B12 is involved in a series of reactions that precede the use of folacin in DNA replication.

Within the body, the absorption of Vitamin B12 is facilitated by the intrinsic factor, a protein produced by the stomach which combines with Vitamin B12. In the U.S., Vitamin B12 is supplied by the coenzymes found in meats, milk and milk products, and eggs.

Biotin. The biotin coenzyme plays a major role in energy production and in the synthesis of nonessential amino acids and fatty acids by activating enzymes involved in splitting and rearranging glucose, amino acids, and fatty acid molecules.

Pantothenic Acid. Pantothenic acid or pantothenate is the main component of "coenzyme A," a pervasive enzyme involved with the release of energy from glucose, the formation of glucose from amino acids, and the synthesis of fatty acids.

With the exception of Vitamin B12 which is found in meats, milk and milk products, and eggs, the other B vitamins are widely distributed in foods. A varied diet is almost guaranteed to provide enough of them. Recent discussions of changes in the U.S. regulations for nutrient labeling of foods have included removing thiamin, riboflavin, and niacin from the labels. The prevalence of these vitamins throughout the U.S. food supply has virtually eliminated their deficiency diseases throughout the nation.

Minerals

Minerals perform a number of roles in the human body. They function as inorganic components of enzyme systems that catalyze the metabolism of protein, carbohydrates, and lipids. Some minerals act to regulate fluid and electrolyte balance, to provide rigidity to the skeleton, and to regulate the function of muscles and nerves. Minerals also work together with vitamins, hormones, peptides, and other substances to regulate the human body's metabolism.

Essential minerals are often classified as macrominerals, required in amounts from several hundred milligrams to 1 or more grams per day. The essential minerals for humans include: calcium, phosphorus, magnesium, sodium, potassium, and chloride. The trace elements are: iron, zinc, iodine, copper, manganese, fluoride, chromium, selenium, molybdenum, and cobalt which is a component of Vitamin B12. Minerals such as lead and mercury are potentially toxic to man.

Minerals are distributed in a variety of foods, but are usually present in limited amounts. Brief functional information about the essential minerals and one trace mineral, namely iron, will be discussed. Being prevalent throughout the food chain, only a few of the richest sources will be given. Tables which include food composition data will give you precise levels of all nutrients contained in your foods.

Calcium

The primary function of calcium, currently associated with osteoporosis, is building and maintaining bones and teeth. Other functions are associated with: blood clotting, muscle contraction and relaxation, nerve transmission, cell wall permeability, enzyme activation, and the secretion of several hormone and hormone-releasing factors. The richest calcium food sources include cheeses, wheat-soy flours, and blackstrap molasses.

Phosphorous

Also essential to bone and teeth formation and maintenance, phosphorous is essential for milk secretion and is important for building muscle tissue. As a component of both RNA and DNA, it is important for genetic transmission and the control of cellular metabolism. It assists with the maintenance of osmotic pressure and the acid-base balance in the body, and performs other metabolic functions. The richest phosphorous food sources include cocoa powder, rice bran, soybean flour, sunflower seeds, and wheat bran.

Magnesium

Magnesium is a constituent of bones and teeth, and an essential element for cellular metabolism, activating enzymes involved in phosphorylated compounds such as ADP and ATP. In addition, magnesium is involved in protein metabolism and the functioning of nerve impulses. The richest magnesium food sources include some instant coffees, cocoa powder, sesame seeds, soybean flour, some spices, and wheat bran and germ.

Sodium

Sodium ions help to maintain the balance of water, acids, and bases in the fluid outside of cell walls. Sodium is a constituent of pancreatic juice, bile, sweat, and tears. Sodium is associated with muscle contractions and nerve functions and plays a specific role in the absorption of carbohydrates. Some high-sodium foods include Canadian bacon, green olives, canned shrimp, caviar, corned beef, and pretzels and some other snack products.

Potassium

Potassium is involved with maintaining the proper acid-base balance and transferring nutrients in and out of body cells. It relaxes the heart muscle and is required for the secretion of insulin by the pancreas. It is involved with numerous enzyme reactions involving phosphorylation of creatine, carbohydrate metabolism, and protein synthesis. Rich food sources for potassium include dehydrated fruits, molasses, rice bran, seaweed, soybean flour, and some spices.

Chloride

Chloride plays a major role in regulating osmotic pressure and in the water and acid-base balances. It is required for the production of hydrochloric acid in the stomach and is necessary for the absorption of both Vitamin B12 and iron. Its actions assist with the breakdown of starch. Finally, it is associated with suppressing the growth of microorganisms that enter the stomach with food and drinks. Table salt (sodium chloride) is the main source of chloride in the diet.

Iron

Iron (heme) combines with protein (globin) to make hemoglobin, the compound in red blood cells. It is involved with transporting oxygen throughout the body and it is a component of enzymes which are involved in energy metabolism. The richest sources of iron include many spices, liver, wheat-soy blend (from the U.S. Food for Peace Program), molasses, kidneys, oysters, and eggs.

Diet Supplements

An estimated 40 percent of the U.S. population unnecessarily consumes supplemental vitamins, minerals, or other dietary components at an annual cost in excess of $2.7 billion. There are no known advantages to healthy people consuming excess amounts of any nutrient, and amounts greatly exceeding recommended levels can be harmful.

Water

Water is the largest single component of the human diet as well as the human body. In spite of its importance, it is often termed the forgotten nutrient. An important new source of water in the U.S. diet is the wide assortment of imported and domestic bottled waters. In the 1960s, drinking "Perrier" chilled and served with lemon slices became popular in France.

Physically inactive adults living in moderate climates need about 10 cups of water per day to replace that lost in urine, perspiration, stools, and exhaled air. People who are physically active, live in hot climates, or have illnesses that produce vomiting, diarrhea, or fever, need to drink more than 10 cups of water to replace their daily losses.

Water is sufficiently scarce in some parts of the U.S.S.R. that drinking water dispensers are coin-operated. In the Middle East, decorative outdoor fountains are status symbols and drinking water is sampled, judged, and celebrated there, just as fine wines are in France.

HUMAN BEHAVIOR AND NUTRITION

The disciplines of nutrition and behavior overlap in several areas. Although behavioral factors determine the choice of foods in the diet of people in developed countries with an adequate food supply, any attempt to alter dietary patterns involves changes in behavior. Given that eating is a behavior controlled by the brain, all eating disorders inherently involve the central nervous system and may be associated with personal mood changes. Eating-related problems such as anorexia nervosa (self-starvation) or bulimia (binge/purge syndrome) most often occur in females aged 13 to 20 years from upper and middle social classes. Estimates of the incidence of bulimia vary from 2 to 19 percent among U.S. college women, and about 5 percent for men.

Anorexia Nervosa

Anorexia nervosa is a condition characterized by extreme weight loss. It is a behavioral disorder afflicting young female adults in developed societies. The condition either consists of a single episode with full recovery or it involves unremitting episodes until death is caused by starvation unless therapy and counselling are successful. Ranging from 15 to 21 percent, mortality is among the highest for psychiatric disorders.

Anorexia nervosa tends to occur in intact families with model children and is frequently precipitated by seemingly minor events during adolescence. The clinical features include personality characteristics such as rigidity or perfection, fear of obesity, and symptoms of starvation. These symptoms are manifested by a lack of recognition of the severe body emaciation that has occurred, plus a belief that one is "fat." For this disorder to progress, a serious distortion of personal body image occurs. Individuals are usually overly preoccupied with food. They often engage in extensive physical exercise and have a pervasive sense of personal ineffectiveness. They typically continue to deny their weight-losing behaviors and avoid treatment until they become severely emaciated.

Most persons admitted to treatment resist therapy because of their fear of weight gain. When patients are 35 to 40 percent below normal weight, hospital treatment includes the provision of enteral nutritional support. This treatment isolates the person and provides an opportunity to instill behavioral rewards for weight gain. Successful treatment is a combination of a nutritious diet, medication, and family therapy.

Bulimia

Bulimia is a behavioral disorder characterized by recurrent episodes of binge eating in which large amounts of food are consumed over a short period of time. These episodes are usually terminated by abdominal pain, self-induced vomiting, sleep, or an excessive dose of laxatives. The severity of the binge ranges from occasional episodes of morbid overeating at a party, say, to a severe form of the disorder, termed bulimia nervosa, in which vomiting or purging follows frequent episodes of binge eating.

Although both anorexia nervosa and bulimia occur in young women, the latter occurs in slightly older women. Both are related to the preoccupation with thinness and dieting and both usually begin with a period of dieting. In addition to an adequate diet, treatment includes modification of the behavioral program designed for obese patients and a combination of psychological approaches.

THE SURGEON GENERAL'S REPORT ON NUTRITION AND HEALTH

In 1988, the U.S. Surgeon General's Report on Nutrition and Health reached the conclusion that overconsumption of certain dietary components was a major concern for Americans. While many food factors were involved, emphasis was given to the disproportionate consumption of foods high in fats, often at the expense of foods high in complex carbohydrates and fiber that may be more conducive to health. A key list of their recommendations is given in Exhibit 10.6.

These recommendations promote a dietary pattern that emphasizes the consumption of vegetables, fruits, whole grain products (rich in complex carbohydrates and fiber and relatively low in calories) and fish, poultry prepared without skin, lean meats, and low-

Exhibit 10.6. A List of Key Health and Nutrition Recommendations.

Issues for Most People:

● *Fats and cholesterol:* Reduce consumption of fat (especially saturated fat) and cholesterol. Choose foods relatively low in these substances, such as vegetables, fruits, whole grain foods, fish, poultry, lean meats, and low-fat dairy products. Use food preparation methods that add little or no fat.

● *Energy and weight control:* Achieve and maintain a desirable body weight. To do so, choose a dietary pattern in which energy (caloric) intake is consistent with energy expenditure. To reduce energy intake, limit consumption of foods relatively high in calories, fats, and sugars, and minimize alcohol consumption. Increase energy expenditure through regular and sustained physical activity.

● *Complex carbohydrates and fiber:* Increase consumption of whole grain foods and cereal products, vegetables (including dried beans and peas), and fruits.

● *Sodium:* Reduce intake of sodium by choosing foods relatively low in sodium and limiting the amount of salt added in food preparation and at the table.

● *Alcohol:* To reduce the risk for chronic disease, take alcohol only in moderation (no more than two drinks a day), if at all. Avoid drinking any alcohol before or while driving, operating machinery, taking medications, or engaging in any other activity requiring judgment. Avoid drinking alcohol while pregnant.

Other Issues for Some People:

● *Fluoride:* Community water systems should contain fluoride at optimal levels for prevention of tooth decay. If such water is not available, use other appropriate sources of fluoride.

● *Sugars:* Those who are particularly vulnerable to dental caries (cavities), especially children, should limit their consumption and frequency of use of foods high in sugars.

● *Calcium:* Adolescent girls and adult women should increase consumption of foods high in calcium, including low-fat dairy products.

● *Iron:* Children, adolescents, and women of childbearing age should be sure to consume foods that are good sources of iron, such as lean meats, fish, certain beans, and iron-enriched cereals and whole grain products. This issue is of special concern for low-income families.

Source: U.S. Department of Health and Human Services. 1988. *The Surgeon General's Report on Nutrition and Health.* DHHS (PHS) Pub. No. 88-50210. Washington, DC: U.S. Government Printing Office.

fat dairy products. These foods should be selected to minimize the daily consumption of total fat, saturated fat, and cholesterol.

These conclusions were reached even after the fact that nutrition has received considerable media coverage in the U.S. for about 10 years. Although the "yuppies" of the 1980s have apparently learned how to adopt a healthier diet, there are many target groups which have not yet been reached such as the blue-collar work force, ethnic groups from other countries, "latch key" children, and the elderly.

A disproportionate burden of diet-related disease in the U.S. is borne by population subgroups. For example, Afro-Americans have higher rates of high blood pressure, strokes, diabetes, and other diseases associated with obesity. They have lower rates of os-teoporosis than the overall population. Some groups of Native Americans exhibit the highest rates of diabetes in the world. Many older persons suffer from chronic diseases that can reduce functional independence; many take multiple medications that may adversely interact with nutrients.

In most developed societies, deficiency diseases have been eliminated because of abundant food supplies, fortification of some foods with critical trace nutrients, and better methods for determining and improving the nutrient content of foods. These recommendations are aimed at reducing the incidence of diet-influenced causes of death in the U.S. population (Exhibit 10.1).

RECOMMENDED DIETARY ALLOWANCES (RDAs)

The RDAs are defined as: "the levels of intake of essential nutrients, considered in the judgment of the U.S. Food and Nutrition Board, on the basis of available scientific knowledge, to be adequate to meet the known nutritional needs of practically all healthy persons." With the exception of the RDA for energy, each RDA is deliberately set higher than the actual requirement for that nutrient in most people. The RDAs are estimates of the nutrient requirements for populations rather than for individuals. They may need to be modified for people who are ill or injured. The RDAs are amounts intended to be consumed as part of a normal varied diet.

They take into consideration factors that influence absorption and the efficiency of their utilization within the human body.

Although the initial application of developing the RDAs was to assist with food planning and food purchasing for group feeding situations, the use of the RDAs has expanded with varying degrees of appropriateness and precision.

Generally, the RDAs are used to assure the safety and quality of the U.S. diet, analyze dietary survey data, evaluate the adequacy of diets, educate the public, guide food selection, and document reasons for additional research. The American Dietetic Association (ADA) has stressed that information is needed for macrocomponents of the diet other than protein, i.e., fat, fatty acids, carbohydrate, and fiber.

The RDAs are recommended allowances for nutrients intended to be consumed as part of a normal diet. When the RDAs are met by diets composed of a variety of foods derived from diverse food groups rather than by supplementation or fortification, such diets will likely be adequate in all other nutrients for which RDAs have not yet been established.

The RDAs are safe and adequate levels of nutrients, reflecting the state of current knowledge of nutrition, including nutrient bioavailability and variations in nutrients required among the U.S. population. As such, they can be considered neither as minimal recommendations nor as optimal intake levels.

Although the RDAs are most appropriately applied to groups, they do enable comparisons among individual intakes given that consumption is averaged over a sufficient time period. In this manner, the RDAs enable individual estimates of probable risks of deficiencies. The RDAs were reviewed by Elaine Monsen in 1989.

Three physical conditions require immediate adjustment of the RDAs for individuals. First, prolonged conditions of extreme exposure to high temperatures reduce physical activity, energy expenditures, and the need for food intake. Do you consume as much on a hot summer day as a cold winter day? Second, increased activity increases the need for energy and some nutrients. In hot climates, excessive sweating increases water and salt losses, and can lead to measurable losses of other nutrients. Specially formulated beverages for sports activities address this concern. And finally, the

RDAs do not cover special nutritional needs arising from metabolic disorders, chronic diseases, injuries, premature birth, other medical conditions, and drug therapies. Daily requirements for people with any of these situations can be determined by dietitians.

Registered dietitians are nutrition experts who can separate facts from fads and translate the latest scientific research findings into dietary food requirements and practical food choices. In the U.S., the letters "R.D." after a dietitian's name signify that a minimum of 4 years of education and training in dietetics or a related area has been completed at an accredited college or university and competency has been demonstrated in a national registration examination. Many registered dietitians also hold advanced degrees.

When planning meals or food supplies, it is technically difficult and biologically unnecessary to design a single day's diet that contains all the RDAs for all nutrients. The RDAs are goals to be achieved over time, i.e., at least 3 days for nutrients that metabolize rapidly; 1 or more months for those that are slowly metabolized.

MEALS AT SCIENTIFIC MEETINGS: ONE GOOD EXAMPLE

Scientific meetings are often held to consider what is a healthy diet. The food, however, provided at such meetings often departs from these recommendations. This even applies to meetings on nutritional problems. Such bad practices by health personnel form a negative example for the general population. At an International Symposium on Diabetes and Nutrition held in Sorrento, Italy, in 1987, the menu was designed to show that a healthy diet based on traditional Mediterranean cuisine was appetizing and digestible, even for non-Mediterranean Europeans. The traditional Mediterranean diet approximates very closely the usually accepted guidelines for healthy eating. The results showed that the quality of the meals was high and acceptable to all the delegates.

In recent years, many authoritative national and international organizations have recommended the types of diets that are associated with a lower incidence of cardiovascular as well as other so-called Western diseases such as obesity, diabetes, hyperlipidemia, hypertension, cancer, and disease of the bowel.

All these organizations agree on the need to prevent or correct obesity by adjusting the energy intake to the level of physical exercise. Furthermore, they agree on the benefits derived from a reduction in saturated fat and cholesterol which are the most important dietary determinants of plasma cholesterol levels. The reduction in saturated fat should be compensated for by an increase in polyunsaturated (not more than 10 percent of total calories) and especially in monounsaturated fats. Furthermore, they emphasize the importance of vegetables, legumes, and fruits, usually high in soluble fiber, as partial substitutes for foods of animal origin which tend to be rich in cholesterol and saturated fat. Another factor in all dietary recommendations is reduction in the intake of salt and alcohol (Exhibit 10.6).

These recommendations describe a diet similar in many aspects to the diet typical, at least until recently, of the Mediterranean countries, i.e., low in unsaturated fat and high in monounsaturated fat and complex carbohydrates. In these countries, the prevalence of coronary heart disease (CHD) and plasma cholesterol levels were, and still are, low in comparison with other populations: the 15-year CHD mortality rate per 10,000 of the male population is 284.0 in Mediterranean countries as opposed to 655.1 in non-Mediterranean European countries.

The Mediterranean diet can therefore be considered as a useful model for a natural "healthy diet." One of the main objections, however, to the promulgation of this model for healthy nutrition is the difficulty that people from northern Europe and North America might encounter in trying to change their dietary habits in this way.

A social dinner (Exhibit 10.7) was planned especially to demonstrate that it is possible to follow a healthy diet without foregoing the pleasures of excellent cuisine. Its nutritional composition made it clearly evident that it is possible to really enjoy a high standard of eating while keeping the calorie intake at a satisfactory level as well as the total and saturated fat contents to 25 and 4 percent, respectively. Furthermore, the amount of dietary fiber was at a level considered appropriate according to current dietary guidelines, 57 g/day with roughly 45 percent of the soluble type, which has been shown to have a beneficial effect on glucose and lipid metabolism.

The diet was not only accepted by all the delegates, but it also provoked considerable enthusiasm among those from northern Europe who were able to discover new ways to prepare and serve

Exhibit 10.7.   Dietary composition of the social dinner.

Menu Item	Portion size (oz)	Energy (Kcal)	Total fat (g)	Saturated fat (g)	Fiber (g)
Pizza Napoletana	1-3/4	120	6	0.8	1
Bruschetta	1-3/4	160	5	0.7	3
Fisherman Linguine	1-3/4	220	3	0.4	2
Gnocchi alla Sorrentina	1-3/4	200	6	2.0	2
Grilled Fish	3-1/2	90	1	0.3	-
French beans and potatoes	7	150	5	0.7	5
Carrots alla scapece	7	90	5	0.7	5
Mixed salad	8-3/4	100	5	0.7	7
Brown bread	1-3/4	114	1	---	3
Lemon sorbet	2-1/2	70	-	---	-
Total		1314	37	6.3 (25%)	28 (4%)

Source: Rivellese, A., Giacco, A., Pacioni, D., DeMartinis, M. and G. Riccardi. 1989. Experience of a healthy diet during a scientific meeting on diabetes and nutrition. Catering and Health 1:183-187.

different kinds of pasta, pulses, and other vegetables and fresh fish dressed only with olive oil.

NUTRITION RESEARCH

After World War II, the major focus of nutritional research in the United States shifted away from acute nutrient deficiency diseases. The introduction of good transportation, refrigeration, and frozen foods expanded the availability of fresh foods. In addition, food fortification helped to increase the availability of previously scarce nutrients.

How are all the recommendations made in the Surgeon General's Report on Nutrition and Health, and inherent in the RDAs, established? Scientists can draw inferences about the relationships between dietary factors and disease from either laboratory animal studies or human metabolic and population studies that approach the issues indirectly. Human studies include data from clinical measurements of the physiological indicators of nutritional status or risk factors as well as dietary intake estimates for the population or individuals being studied.

Although clinical, laboratory, and dietary intake studies provide useful information, each has limitations. Laboratory measurements reveal only a portion of the complex physiological responses to diet, and they may reflect past, rather than current, nutritional conditions. Dietary surveys depend on accurate recall of the types and portion sizes of foods consumed as well as upon the assumption that the food intake during any one period actually represents the typical intake. Even when an association or correlation between a dietary factor and a disease is found, it is often difficult to prove that the dietary factor is an actual or sole cause of that disease.

REFERENCES

Behrman, J. R., A. B. Deolalikar, and B. L. Wolfe. 1989. Nutrients: impacts and determinants. *World Bank Economic Review* 2(3):299-320.

Brown, Judith E. 1990. *The science of human nutrition*. San Diego: Harcourt Brace Jovanovich, Publishers.

Gibson, Rosalind S. 1990. *Principles of nutritional assessment*. New York and Oxford: Oxford University Press.

Monsen, Elaine R. 1989. The 10th edition of the Recommended Dietary Allowances: what's new in the 1989 RDAs? *J. Amer. Dietet. Assoc.* 89:1748-1752.

Muzilla, M., N. Unklesbay, Z. Helsel, K. Unklesbay, and M. Ellersieck. 1989. Effect of particle size and heat on absorptive properties of soy hulls. *J. Food Quality* 12:305-318.

National Research Council (U.S.). 1989. *Recommended dietary allowances*. 10th ed. Subcommittee on the Tenth Edition of the RDAs, Food and Nutrition Board, Commission on Life Sciences. Washington, D.C.: National Academy Press.

Nestle, Marion. 1985. *Nutrition in clinical practice*. Greenbrae, CA: Jones Medical Publications.

O'Neil, Carolynn. 1990. Communicating the concepts of good nutrition in the 1990s. *J. Amer. Dietet. Assoc.* 90:373-374.

Rivellese, A., A. Giacco, D. Pacioni, M. DeMartinis, and G. Riccardi. 1989. Experience of a healthy diet during a scientific meeting on diabetes and nutrition. *Catering and Health* 1:183-187.

Schiller, M. R., M. Rosita, M.S. Breese, R.S. Hurley, and C. Agriesi-Johnson. 1985. *Basic and applied nutrition review*. Norwalk: Appleton, Century, Crofts.

U.S. Department of Health and Human Services. 1988. *The Surgeon General's report on nutrition and health*. DHHS(PHS) Pub. No. 88-50210. Washington, D.C.: U.S. Government Printing Office.

Chapter Eleven

Ramifications of Malnutrition

INTRODUCTION

The prevalent term malnutrition refers to an impairment of health resulting from a failure of the diet, or from a failure of the physiologic processes of the body itself, to provide body tissues with the correct proportions of nutrients. Malnutritive states involve nutrient deficiencies and/or excesses of nutrients such as carbohydrates leading to obesity. In this chapter, malnutrition will be emphasized as it is seen throughout the developing world, being chiefly caused by nutrient deficiencies attributed to both diet and diseases. Through studying information presented in this chapter, you will be in an informed position to discuss:

- reasons for malnutrition throughout the globe, how it is measured, and how nutrient deficiencies affect the human body;
- how the management technique termed "nutritional surveillance" has significant potential for alleviating malnutrition in developed and developing countries.

As recently as the early 1970s, malnutrition was widely classified as only a medical problem and health-related solutions were prescribed and considered to be appropriate for its reduction. Using this simplistic approach, it was assumed that the solutions, namely protein foods and health education, could both be delivered through the health system.

Fortunately, in the late 1980s, academics, political leaders, administrators, and other professionals have been paying increasing attention to malnutrition, hunger, starvation, and famine. One major consequence of this multidisciplined approach has been that complete ramifications of the serious conditions associated with malnutrition are now becoming recognized. However, in spite of radical advances made by science and technology in many different spheres of life, little progress seems to have been made in eradicating signs of malnutrition and starvation from the face of the earth.

Hunger and chronic undernutrition today are at least as much of a political, economic and social challenge as they are a scientific or technological challenge for agriculture. Malnutrition is a silent killer. In many nations, earlier progress in fighting hunger, malnutrition, and poverty has come to a halt or is being reversed. For example, in Peru, the number of malnourished preschoolers increased from 42 percent in 1980 to 68 percent in 1983. Further, infant deaths, an important indicator of malnutrition, have risen in Brazil during the 1980s.

According to the World Health Organization (WHO), at least 1 billion people are suffering from disease, poor health, and malnourishment throughout the world. Complicating matters, the burden of suffering is unevenly distributed among different regions of the world, different classes of people, and different age groups within each region and/or class. The acute and chronic conditions of poverty are generally accepted as the major cause of malnutrition throughout the world. Three major causes of poverty are:

1. inadequate food availability to, and within, households;
2. unsanitary living conditions;
3. inadequate access to systems which can lead to conditions of good health and nutritional status.

Adequate nutrition is a basic human need and a prerequisite to good health. One of the eight essential elements of primary health care is the promotion of adequate nutritional states. Public policy decisions on nutrition require extensive and reliable data about the extent to which people consume sufficient food of adequate quality, and the effects of infectious diseases and how they relate to human health and well-being. For example, with respect to food quality, protein foods with high PER (protein efficiency ratio) values which promote growth must be consumed. Knowledge of nutritional problems, their causes, and how they are evolving and affecting a particular sector of society can assist with the formulation of relevant public policy decisions.

WORLD HISTORY AND MALNUTRITION: A DEMOGRAPHIC EXAMPLE

Throughout world history, conditions favoring malnutrition have influenced demographics around the world. For example, the location of Afro-Americans today is believed to be related to famine conditions in parts of Africa. Most people recruited in Africa for the Atlantic slave trade were previously believed to be recent captives of war, political prisoners, or persons who were judicially condemned. Comparatively few were believed to be domestic slaves whose owners sold them for cash. Additional evidence suggests that famines may also have been a major source of slaves. Whenever famine occurred in most parts of tropical Africa, lineage heads could sell lineage members into slavery to save the lives of the remaining society. This included the sale of domestic slaves or other dependents including children.

In both the Senegambia and the southern savannas of Angola, the distribution of water was uneven so populations began starving in some places before others. Between 1746 and 1754, statistical correlations made between prolonged periods of droughts and increases in the slave trades are very high. Thus, when a drought became severe enough to threaten food supplies, the excess people were sold down the Senegal River to the European posts on the coast, and were eventually transported to the U.S.

An interesting conclusion can be drawn from such situations: Malnutrition is not an independent variable but rather a mediating element in humanity's relationship to its environment. Is the African slave trade an example of how human creativity was able to manipulate the environment for human benefits?

AN INTEGRATED APPROACH TO MALNUTRITION

Information contained in Exhibit 11.1 clarifies the relationships among nutrition, disease, and social conditions. As a model, it illustrates the dynamic linkages among agricultural, social and

Exhibit 11.1. An Integrated Approach to Malnutrition.

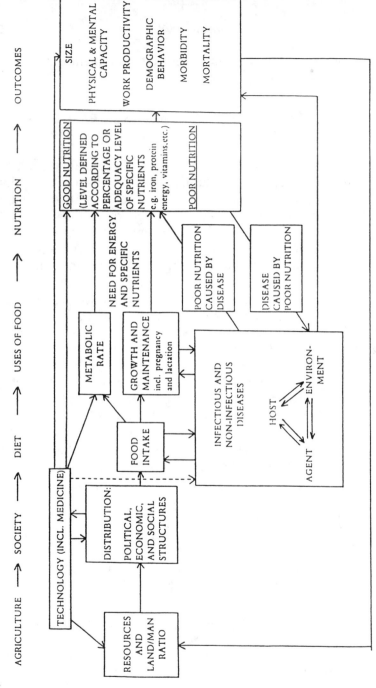

AGRICULTURE → SOCIETY → DIET → USES OF FOOD → NUTRITION → OUTCOMES

Source: Rotberg, R. I. and T. K. Rabb. 1983. *Hunger and History.* Cambridge: Cambridge University Press.

physical activities, food, and nutrition. Each stage of the model is affected by technological developments. There is an obvious reciprocal influence from the health, energy, and productivity of a population to its agriculture systems and food resources.

Any society's prospects are first determined by its resources and the ratio of its population to productive land. Resources are influenced by the global trade of food and agricultural inputs, as well as by the dynamics of food aid. Japan is an example of a country which has used world trade to increase its resources drastically.

Activities associated with all of the interrelated boxes in Exhibit 11.1 are subject to the effects of technology including medical developments and the health and capacity of the population. Along with technology, people help to determine the political, social, and economic structures that promote technological advances and, also, the distribution of food and nutrients.

Whether diets lead to good nutrition or malnutrition is determined by: the nutritional quality of the foods as preserved and modified by processing; the effective distribution and consumption of quality foods; the level of physical activity; and the effects of all human, plant, and animal diseases. Nutrition and disease are strongly affected by a reciprocal influence referred to as "synergy." The level of nutrition, combined with the effects of diseases, establishes the health, capacity, and productivity of a population. Note in Exhibit 11.1 that the outcomes or characteristics of the society such as their work productivity are linked to the society's resources.

Society and Malnutrition

If malnutrition is to be alleviated throughout the globe, all of the synergistic interactions between social factors and the consequences of malnutrition need to be considered. Agricultural developments and the industrial revolution, plus other technological developments, have had profound effects on human nutrition and its role in a nation's health. The demographic characteristics of these periods of development were largely determined by the nutritional status of the people. Today, population growth and population density are not limited to the quantity of people; they should be studied for their effects on the actual quality of people's lives.

In 1974, the FAO and WHO proposed a strategy of three parts to combat pervasive malnutrition throughout the world. First, they recommended establishing broadly based rural development that would improve agricultural production and income distribution. Second, they recommended that improvements be made in both the combination of foods produced and in their processing and distribution systems. Finally, they recommended that specific programs should include specific targeted intervention measures determined by societal needs. Although opportunities may exist for tackling the immediate causes of malnutrition, direct societal interventions may be counter productive if they impede long-term, recommended changes for that nation, region, or society.

Basic human needs include two elements: (1) minimum requirements of a family for private consumption including adequate food, shelter, clothing, household equipment, and furniture; and (2) essential services provided by, and for, the community at large such as safe drinking water, sanitation, public transport, and health and educational facilities. These two basic elements recognize that health and nutrition programs or services alone cannot provide long-term or sustained solutions to malnutrition problems.

Economic shifts within families and societies can have devastating effects upon good nutritional health. For example, income sources change when farmers shift from food to cash crops. If purchased food does not adequately replace that previously obtained from the farm, the entire family's nutritional health may deteriorate.

Designed to offset some of these imbalances, food subsidies and food distribution programs may positively impact nutrition in households. However, additional measures may be needed to ensure that an increase in real income leads to greater household food availability. In addition, data is needed to determine if an increase in food availability actually leads to improved nutrition for everyone concerned. Specifically, programs should reach vulnerable groups of societies including mothers, infants, and preschool children who have specific nutritional requirements at different growth stages.

To summarize, the level of health and nutrition itself is a direct indicator of the quality of life, and an indirect indicator of overall socioeconomic development.

Some Physiological Effects
of Malnutrition

In Exhibit 11.1, the middle boxes concerning diet, food uses, diseases, and nutrition are linked largely because of the physiological responses of nutrients. Such responses are quantified into specific measurements and used to assess nutritional status. For example, although growth is determined mainly by genetics and is influenced by many factors other than diet, attained height and weight measurements can be taken fairly easily and accurately. These measurements do not cause much inconvenience or discomfort to the individual. As such, these indicators become one measurement of the physiological and biochemical response to nutrients consumed in the food supply.

Other indicators of nutritional status measuring such parameters as physical growth and development, physical capacity, work output, cognitive performance, morbidity and mortality from infectious disease, and energy available for social development are more difficult to measure. However, they should be available to assist with public policies and any judgments of the significance of food consumption patterns of all societies.

Entire populations of numerous countries are currently consuming an average of 10 to 20 percent fewer calories than their requirements. Within these societies, many individuals consume much less than the average data for the country or region suggest. However, all of the people in these populations are not wasting away and dying of starvation. Entire populations have adapted physiologically, mainly by reducing their physical activity, and have an overall positive energy balance. The model in Exhibit 11.1 includes this as the effect of the reduced metabolic rate. However, the social cost for this adaptation is high. Because work activities must be maintained for human survival, especially when appropriate animal draft power is not available, the discretionary activities are sacrificed first.

The stereotype of a peasant sleeping in the shade describes this survival mechanism. For children, this adaptation means less interaction with their environment at a critical age, with resulting permanent cognitive deficiencies. Since metabolic adaptations to low energy intakes are limited, most of the necessary adaptation is a reduction in physical activity.

When individuals consume 50 percent below their recommended energy levels, personal activities become limited to sleeping, dressing, eating and digesting food, and attending to personal hygiene. Consuming 1.5 times above the basal metabolic rate (BMR) is not sufficient for productive activity or for long term health maintenance.

Survival during periods of starvation extracts both biological and psychological costs. When food deprivation extends beyond a certain point, human adaptive mechanisms are not sufficient to maintain survival. Healthy adults can survive the longest without food; children and those who are ill or in poor nutritional health are most vulnerable.

In all countries, major increases in life expectancy have come to be expected. Medical information and food supplies, facilitated by computers, telecommunications, and information transfer, will likely add substantially to the longevity of people throughout the world. Elderly people consume far more than children under 5 years of age. The latter are greatly affected by malnutrition and have high incidences of mortality. Thus, as a group, young children in many countries contribute little to current food use. Therefore, in addition to economic status, the age distribution of future populations will be an important factor in determining nutritional needs.

Infections and Malnutrition

Good health and nutritional status are totally interdependent. Sufficient food, containing the essential energy and nutrients, is needed for good health; freedom from disease is needed for good nutritional status.

Exhibit 11.2 lists some diseases that definitely influence nutritional status under most physiological conditions, and others having variable or minimal effects. The transmission of these diseases includes both food and water supplies. Thus, public health measures

Exhibit 11.2. Diseases that Influence Nutritional Status.

Definite Effects	Variable Effects	Minimal Effects
Measles	Typhus	Smallpox
Diarrhea	Diphtheria	Malaria
Tuberculosis	Staphylococcus	Plague
Most Respiratory Infections	Streptococcus	Typhoid
Pertussis	Syphilis	Yellow Fever
Most Intestinal Parasites	Systemic Worm	Encephalitis
Cholera	Infections	Poliomyelitis
Leprosy		
Herpes		

Source: Rotberg, R.I. and T.K. Rabb. 1983. <u>Hunger and History</u>. Cambridge: Cambridge University Press.

are also required to deal with water, sanitation, immunization, health services, and health education issues.

Infections worsen nutritional status by several mechanisms including, but not limited to, reduced appetites, poorer quality of diets ingested, increased metabolic loss of nutrients, increased metabolic needs, and decreased absorption, especially when gastro-intestinal tracts are affected. In addition, infections can precipitate clinical manifestations of deficiencies of nutrients when they are being consumed at borderline levels in the diet.

In excess of four million children die each year from diarrhea. One-half of all cases of severe child malnutrition are precipitated by such illnesses as diarrhea, measles, chicken pox, tuberculosis, or intestinal parasites that depress appetite and reduce both energy levels and body weight.

Unfortunately, societal customs that lead to withholding nutritious foods during the course of some of the diseases listed in Exhibit 11.2 further aggravate illnesses, malnutrition, and the risk of death. Further, conditions within poor households may prevent the best nutritional use of the available food and can certainly cause high rates of infection. As illustrated in Exhibit 11.1, inadequate nutrition retards normal growth, lowers resistance to infectious disease, impairs maternal and child health, and may adversely affect the ability to function at peak physical and mental capacities.

Nutrient Deficiencies

Nutritionists and dietitians view the problem of hunger not only as the consequence of a deficit in food energy relative to need, but also as an inadequate intake of any essential nutrient, including amino acids, vitamins, fatty acids, and minerals. Much of this hunger is hidden, and the individual is unaware of it. However, the functional consequences of hidden hunger in the development of human societies has probably been at least as important as the drastic consequences of overt hunger or famine.

A deficient intake of energy or nutrients can lead to protein-energy malnutrition, or to deficiency diseases. Protein-energy malnutrition and diseases due to deficiencies of various nutrients are prominent causes of premature death and disability in developing countries. Major vitamin and mineral deficiency diseases are described in the following paragraphs; in conditions of malnutrition, few are observed alone. Together, these deficiencies, largely under control in developed countries, present a rather gruesome realization of emaciated human bodies and severe suffering throughout developing countries.

Vitamin Deficiency Diseases

Vitamin A deficiency. Vitamin A deficiency, through adverse effects on eye epithelial tissues, is a major cause of blindness among children in many developing countries, and it is also responsible for substantial additional illness. Estimates have been made that as many as 250,000 new incidences of blindness develop each year in developing countries due to this deficiency. Malnourished adults and children who eat mostly starchy foods, and those who have chronic infectious diseases, problems with absorbing fats, and liver disease, are at risk for developing the Vitamin A deficiency disease.

Before vision loss occurs, the ability to see dim lights is impaired, the surface of the eyes dry out and thicken, and the cornea of the eye is damaged. Retinol supplementation may improve the survival of children. Retinol is hazardous to pregnant women and should only be taken under medical supervision.

Vitamin D deficiency. When Vitamin D deficiency occurs, the bones become soft and fragile. In children, this condition is called rickets; in adults, it is called osteomalacia. Without Vitamin D, the bones do not mineralize properly because calcium and phosphorous are poorly absorbed.

The condition of infants and children in the U.K. since World War II has been remarkably satisfactory, partly as a result of the special measures taken by the government to protect their nutritional status. However, Vitamin D deficiency diseases reappeared among the immigrant populations of both adults and children in the U.K. in the 1960s and 1970s. This problem was eliminated by fortifying margarine, infant formula and other foods which provided supplements of Vitamin D. In addition, the affected Asian population was educated about the importance of sunlight in the synthesis of Vitamin D.

Vitamin E deficiency. Vitamin E deficiency has been associated with hemolytic anemia in premature infants and neurologic symptoms in adults. When premature infants have not been able to build up a store of Vitamin E, this deficiency can occur. With this disease, red blood cell membranes break down easily when they are exposed to oxygen or an oxidizing agent, causing changes in the cell membranes. People who cannot readily absorb fat, such as those with cystic fibrosis, are prone to Vitamin E deficiency.

Vitamin K deficiency. People with Vitamin K deficiency bruise and hemorrhage easily because the clotting process is interfered with. Newborn babies should be given an injection of Vitamin K after birth to avoid this deficiency. Long-term antibiotic therapy kills most of the bacteria in the gut, thereby removing the human source of Vitamin K.

Scurvy. Scurvy, the Vitamin C deficiency, includes the progressive symptoms of abnormal collagen formation, poor bone and teeth development, weakening of blood vessels, delayed healing of wounds, small hemorrhages which produce black and blue marks under the skin, sore and bleeding gums, hair and teeth loss, internal bleeding, and sudden death. Psychological signs at advanced stages of scurvy include hysteria and depression.

Beriberi. The thiamin deficiency disease is termed beriberi. The first symptoms are behavioral changes such as mental confusion, loss of appetite, irritability, and the expression of fears. These changes are followed by physical ones including a loss of sensation in the arms and legs, irregular heartbeat, muscular weakness, and eventually, paralysis and heart failure. Beriberi is found among people who consume refined, unenriched grains as staple foods, and among alcoholics who only absorb low levels of thiamin.

Ariboflavinosis. Ariboflavinosis is the riboflavin deficiency disease. Because riboflavin plays a broad role in energy metabolism, a deficiency in riboflavin causes decreased growth, cracks around the nose, reddening of the eyes, inflammation and soreness of the lips and tongue, and greasy, scaly skin eruptions. Most diets that are deficient in riboflavin are also deficient in protein and some other vitamins and minerals. Alcoholics and people who consume only small amounts of milk, cheese, and meats are at risk of developing ariboflavinosis.

Pellagra. Niacin deficiency can lead to pellagra, a problem in many countries where the population relies on corn as their staple food. Although corn contains niacin, it is in a bound form that cannot be absorbed by the human body. Thus, cornmeal is frequently treated with lye to liberate the niacin from its bound form. The three major symptoms of pellagra are dermatitis, diarrhea, and dementia, followed by weight loss. Without treatment, death is inevitable.

Vitamin B6 deficiency. Vitamin B6 deficiency involves mental changes of depression and confusion followed by protein metabolism disturbances leading to convulsions and severe disturbances of the nervous system.

Megaloblastic anemia. The folacin deficiency disease is termed megaloblastic anemia. Without folacin, DNA does not replicate and body cells cannot divide. Thus, large, irregularly shaped red blood cells are found throughout the body. Body cells that line the cheeks and gastrointestinal tract are also affected by folacin deficiency.

Folacin deficiency also produces psychological symptoms such as irritability and paranoid behavior. About one-third of pregnant women throughout the world develop megaloblastic anemia. Poorly nourished children, women taking oral contraceptive pills, and alcoholics are also at risk.

Pernicious anemia. Pernicious anemia, a progressive and fatal disease, results from an inadequate intake of Vitamin B12 or the lack of production of the intrinsic factor in the stomach. Progressive symptoms include numbness and tingling in the hands and feet, enlarged red blood cells, psychological disturbances, irreversible nerve damage, and death.

Biotin deficiency. Biotin deficiency is rare. Its symptoms include mental changes, muscle pain, nausea, and appetite loss.

Pantothenic acid deficiency. Pantothenic acid deficiency is generally observed when people are starving. Symptoms include headache, fatigue, reduced growth, burning feet, and a wide range of other symptoms.

Major Mineral Deficiencies

Calcium deficiency. Diets deficient in calcium affect the human body's functions of bone formation and maintenance, transmissions of nerve impulses, muscular contractions, and abilities for blood coagulation. Tetany develops when nerve impulses are affected and when contracted muscles fail to relax, leading to severe muscle spasms and uncontrollable nerve impulses. When blood calcium is inadequate, the body uses the calcium deposited in bones. Calcium deficiency is affiliated with Vitamin D deficiencies.

Phosphorus deficiency. Diets deficient in phosphorus occur among alcoholics, people with kidney disease, and people who consume regular doses of stomach antacids, particularly those containing aluminum hydroxide. Low blood levels of phosphorus lead to feelings of weakness and confusion, followed by painful bones and joints.

Magnesium deficiency. Deficiencies of magnesium occur in alcoholics and people with gastrointestinal disorders. Symptoms of this deficiency include muscle spasms, irregular heartbeats, convulsions, and personality changes such as a general sense of confusion. Because magnesium is needed for the effective use of calcium, magnesium deficiencies are also manifested by those symptoms discussed in calcium deficiencies.

Iron deficiency. Iron deficiency, the most common nutrient deficiency in the U.S., affects at least 20 percent of the world's population. Iron deficiency is first diagnosed when iron stores are depleted, leading to increased infections, sluggishness, poor appetite, and short attention spans. When the available iron is insufficient for normal hemoglobin production, anemia develops.

With this condition, the body cells do not receive enough oxygen, and people become pale, tired, weak, and have rapid heartbeats. Both iron deficiency and anemia can develop from body injuries or diseases when a great deal of blood is lost. A seemingly lethargic person may be iron-deficient and will change their whole pattern of behavior after only a few days of supplementary iron.

Zinc deficiency. Zinc deficiencies occur throughout the world, having profound effects on growth, susceptibilities to infections, and the onset of sexual maturation. In both Iran and Egypt, zinc deficiencies have caused isolated populations of dwarfed persons.

Iodine deficiency. Iodine deficiencies have severe human ramifications. Goiters, or enlarged thyroid glands, develop when insufficient amounts of thyroid hormones are produced, resulting in abnormally slow growth and development. Pregnant women with iodine deficiency may deliver infants with cretinism, a condition which causes permanent reductions in physical growth and mental development.

Cases of goiter tend to cluster in areas where the soil content of iodine is very low and where iodine-fortified products are not used. For example, over 40 million people living in areas of India which have a poor soil content of iodine, and where the people do not have access to iodized salt, have iodine-deficiency goiter. India has instituted a program for iodizing all salt produced in the country by 1992.

Iodine has been known to leach from the soil in one area, being deposited in other areas, with accompanying reductions in the incidence of goiter in the enriched area. In developing countries throughout the world, 330 million cases of endemic goiter have been estimated.

Copper deficiency. Severe copper deficiencies cause anemia, reduced growth rates, and other symptoms associated with other mineral deficiencies throughout the body. Critically ill adults and children with protein-calorie malnutrition are susceptible to this deficiency.

Fluoride deficiency. Fluoride deficiencies are manifested by increased susceptibilities to tooth decay. Tooth decay, although still a serious health problem, is declining in the U.S., Sweden, Scotland, the Netherlands, England, New Zealand, and other countries. Switzerland has a national education program that has helped to reduce its tooth decay. A "happy tooth" emblem is located on food labels that have been found to be safe for teeth. As a result, a majority of candies sold in Switzerland contain sweeteners that do not promote tooth decay.

The opposite problem is being observed in developing countries when soft drinks, candy, and sugary snacks are widely available. These countries generally do not have the added benefits received from fluoridated water supplies.

Some dentists admit to having a different view of China. With a population of one billion persons, with 32 permanent teeth per person, the possibility of being paid for treating 32 billion teeth exists. Numerous pictures of the population in China reveal that dental care is not prevalent among much of the population.

Chromium deficiency. Chromium deficiencies produce elevated blood glucose levels with the associated diabetic-related problems. In addition, chromium deficiencies are related to elevated levels of cholesterol and associated increased risks of heart attacks.

Selenium deficiency. Selenium deficiencies are associated with causing a type of heart disease and contributing to an increased risk of developing cancer. The latter risk occurs because selenium functions as an antioxidant in every body cell. This deficiency has been found in parts of China where almost no selenium exists in the water or soil.

Sodium deficiency. Sodium deficiency causes diarrhea, vomiting, and kidney disorders, causing people to feel very weak. Environmental and work conditions leading to excessive sweating can cause immediate symptoms of sodium deficiencies. In developed countries, liquid products such as Gatorade™ are formulated to rapidly replenish sodium and other minerals, especially during sport activities. A 16-ounce serving of Gatorade™ contains 220 mg of sodium.

Potassium deficiency. Potassium deficiencies can occur after prolonged use of some diuretics or after prolonged periods of vomiting and diarrhea. Immediate effects of low potassium levels include a feeling of weakness and irregular heartbeats.

Chloride deficiency. Chloride deficiencies occur when severe vomiting and diarrhea are accompanied by the loss of the secretion of stomach juices, including hydrochloric acid needed to assist with digestion.

FOOD USES AND MALNUTRITION

Another factor affecting the information diagrammed in Exhibit 11.1 is the actual food usage, influenced by the diets chosen by individuals, when food choices are available to them. Food demand is dependent on, and interrelated with, many factors in the vast human social and ecological system. Basically, this demand depends upon human population numbers and the desired standard of living.

Two-thirds of the world's population consumes primarily a vegetarian-type diet. In these areas, about 182 kg of grain products are consumed yearly per person. Grains are consumed directly and little food of animal origin is eaten. People in the remaining one-third of the world consume about 115 kg of animal foods yearly per person. To produce this amount of animal food in the U.S., about 605 kg of grain per person are raised and then fed to animals. Although meat, poultry, and dairy products are popular, they are not efficiently produced. For example, 6 to 8 kg of cereal grains are required to produce 1 kg of beef.

Many scientists argue that, in the not-too-distant future, it will become increasingly difficult to provide foods from animal sources, so our dependence on cereals will increase. These beliefs and statements are based on inputs from many parameters, including our world supplies of nonrenewable energy.

Are some diets more conserving of fossil energy than others? When given a choice, people seldom eat just one or two foods, making dietary choices from a variety of available foods. Nearly twice as much fossil energy is expended for the food in a lacto-ovo vegetarian diet (i.e., a diet which includes dairy products and eggs) than for the pure vegetarian. For the nonvegetarian diet, the fossil energy input is more than three times that of the pure vegetarian diet. When faced with considering options for the future, producing plant food is significantly more energy-efficient than producing food from animal sources. This deserves consideration in agricultural policy as well as in personal dietary choices.

Energy, land, and other biological resource limitations make it impossible to provide the present world population with a U.S. daily per capita diet of 73 g of animal protein. The standard of living in the world will have to be reduced to accommodate the rapidly growing numbers of people. To avoid severe levels of malnutrition throughout the world, less meat will have to be consumed while more grain, potatoes, beans, and turnips will be eaten. Thus, to achieve a goal of eliminating malnutrition, people in the developed world will have to join the other two-thirds of the world's population in eating a more vegetarian-type diet such as that consumed in India and China.

Three Major Processes of Dietary Change

When malnutrition is analyzed with respect to actual food use, dramatic changes are revealed in food availability to populations throughout the world. Although hard to catagorize, three major processes are responsible for current changes observed in dietary behavior:

1. a worldwide dissemination of domesticated plant and animal varieties;
2. the rise of increasingly complex international food distribution networks, and the growth of food processing industries;
3. the migration of people from rural to urban centers and from one continent to another, on an unprecedented scale, with a resulting exchange of culinary and dietary techniques and preferences.

In a local community, these changes are obvious because of the following changes that become apparent and/or necessary:

1. New plant and animal varieties are introduced to the community for local production, or locally produced foods are removed from the community for sale elsewhere.
2. New foods are made available through commercial or governmental channels.
3. The people move to a new area, or they receive immigrants, resulting in cultural exchange of culinary/dietary preferences.

Other changes deal with local developments of new food production or preparation techniques. These changes lead to a process known by sociologists as delocalization. Other terms for this slowly evolving process are: modernization, development, progress, or acculturation.

Whatever it is called, the process of delocalization may result in the reduction of local autonomy of energy resources. This occurs when a total dependence develops for gasoline-driven equipment for transportation, local industry, and other essential processes. In remote areas of the globe, such as the Arctic regions of North America for example, Inuit have become dependent upon motor-driven boats, snowmobiles, and other equipment.

In more complex urban centers, delocalization is evidenced in the increased sensitivity of prices and costs to political fluctuations in any sector of the world energy and food network. Examples of this phenomenon include effects from such diverse world events as: Soviet grain-purchasing policies, OPEC manipulations, coffee and sugar production levels, and the beef consumption demands of the international fast food industry.

The effects of delocalization are also found in developed countries. For example, in the U.K. from 1950 to 1973, total fruit as a component of household consumption increased from 18 to 25 ounces per week per person, while bread dropped from 56 to 34 ounces. Diversification of protein resources was evident in the rise in poultry consumption. Increased obesity, problems of food sensitivities, and other more subtle nutrition-related problems may be related to delocalization of food patterns in the industrialized countries.

Dietary Changes in Small Communities

Hunter-gatherer societies, such as those of the Inuit, usually had rather small population densities, seldom exceeding 10 persons per 100 square miles.

In the Alaskan Inuit community of Napaskiak, in recent years, everyone has come to regard store goods such as sugar, salt, flour, milk, coffee, tea, tobacco, and cooking fats as essential necessities. Other foods frequently purchased include: various canned meats and fish, crackers, candy, carbonated beverages, canned fruits, potatoes, onions, and rice.

The emphasis on the increased availability of modern foods in the local stores such as sugar, flour, canned goods, soda pops, potato chips, etc., has had a powerful effect on diets. In the northern hospitals in Labrador today, most of the Inuit patients are served diabetic diets. This prevalent physiological disorder has appeared in the population as their diets have included more sources of carbohydrates. In-breeding in small communities is another cause of diabetes.

In Nicaragua, the Miskito Indians purchase 30 percent of their foods, including sugar, flour, beans, rice, and coffee, from stores. By 1973, these foods had captured two-thirds of the Miskito food economy, mainly because of the depletion of green sea turtles which are sold to international food companies rather than consumed locally. Since the high-carbohydrate, purchased foods are quite different in nutrient content from the wild foods that they replace, the Miskito, like virtually all small-scale societies, are undergoing rapid dietary changes.

In addition to the effects of delocalization, food supplies are influenced by such factors as arable land, water, climate, fertilizer, fossil energy, public health, losses due to pests, availability of labor, environmental pollution, and the life-styles of the people, to name a few. All of these factors can be catagorized under agriculture and society in Exhibit 11.1.

NUTRITIONAL SURVEILLANCE

In developing countries, the balance between an adequate level of nutrition and severe malnutrition is fragile. Relatively minor changes in the economic situation or in environmental factors can alter this balance and precipitate widespread protein-energy malnutrition. National surveillance programs have been established to monitor the nutritional status of the population, ensure timely warning of impending shortages in food consumption, and instigate long-term and short-term measures to prevent or alleviate such crises.

Nutritional surveillance programs can be concerned with everything that affects nutrition, from food production through food processing, distribution, and consumption to the health status of the targeted population. Effective nutritional surveillance programs give priority to focusing on data acquisitions that are necessary for making crucial decisions, i.e., those that support public policies and programs designed to ensure adequate nutrition throughout the population.

Nutritional surveillance programs are established with three interrelated objectives:

1. to plan for national health and development;
2. to provide effective program management and evaluation;
3. to offer timely warning and intervention strategies when needed to prevent short-term food consumption crises.

These three objectives are not mutually exclusive. Together, these activities lead to the gathering of knowledge that is needed to ensure adequate nutrition. Their success depends on numerous considerations, many of which are political.

Some nutritional surveillance programs function within the programs that have already been established in the region or nation. For example, decisions may be made to enhance the positive effects of nutrition on established development policies and programs such as those being planned primarily for economic and political reasons.

Development programs require effective decisions leading to informed choices for targeting by area and socioeconomic group as well as for the possible effects of different activities upon nutrition. Health and nutrition programs need similar decisions.

Data Collection and Nutritional Surveillance

Timely warning and intervention programs that are designed to handle acute food shortages need data to trigger appropriate interventions. Information included in Exhibit 11.3 includes some selected indicators that are used for national health and nutritional status. These data are selected because they are quantifiable. Note that they would have to be collected from several different agencies.

Measurements used in nutritional surveillance, also listed in Exhibit 11.3, include many of those defined as socioeconomic and health status indicators, particularly with respect to the nutritional status of children and mortality data. The same measurements can be used for assessing the effects of development programs—thus, the recommendation that nutritional surveillance programs be closely coordinated with some development ones.

Breaking down the population into defined groups that may have

Exhibit 11.3. Selected Indicators used in Nutritional Surveillance Programs.

NATIONAL HEALTH STATUS INDICATORS:

1. Nutritional status and psychosocial development of children.
2. Infant mortality rates.
3. Child mortality rate (ages 1 - 4 years).
4. Life expectancy at birth or other specific ages.
5. Maternal mortality rate.

NUTRITIONAL SURVEILLANCE INDICATORS:

1. Nutritional status of preschool children.
2. Infant and child mortality rates.
3. Prevalence of low birth weight.
4. Height of children at school entry.

Source: Mason, J.B., J-P. Habicht, H. Tabatabai and V. Valverde. 1984. Nutritional surveillance. Geneva: World Health Organization.

different risks or prevalences of malnutrition is important. People with the worst nutritional problems merit priority and should receive prompt benefits from government policies.

Distinctions about what data can and cannot be used for in nutritional surveillance programs are important. Fundamental knowledge about cause-effect relationships of nutrition and health is investigated by scientists doing nutritional research. Their research is directed towards answering specific scientific questions, and they cannot use any general data collection procedures to efficiently collect data, proving any cause-effect relationships. Their specific research findings have led to recommendations presented in Exhibit 10.6. Data from these types of research studies are not included in nutritional surveillance.

In addition, decisions about patient diagnosis and management are important for the individual, but they fall outside the scope of nutritional surveillance as they are not directly related to decisions about populations. However, data used for individual patient identification and treatment can be included in nutritional surveillance programs. Nutritional surveillance methods provide regular information about nutrition in populations. They draw data from the most suitable sources that are already available, including surveys and administrative data. The undertaking of ad hoc investigations can also be included in nutritional surveillance activities.

The relevance of dietary surveys and feeding trials is direct and obvious, but the diets consumed by population groups, families, and individuals are difficult and expensive to measure accurately. Furthermore, the measurements are even more difficult to interpret in terms of nutritional adequacy. Thus, this form of nutritional research is also excluded from nutritional surveillance programs.

Administrative Structure
for Nutritional Surveillance

As management programs, nutritional surveillance requires an administrative structure. The diagram in Exhibit 11.4 includes one example of such an administrative structure. Given the complexity of nutritional surveillance programs, several ministries, or areas of the national government, are involved. Obviously, such programs

Exhibit 11.4. Administrative Structure for Organization of a Nutritional Surveillance System.

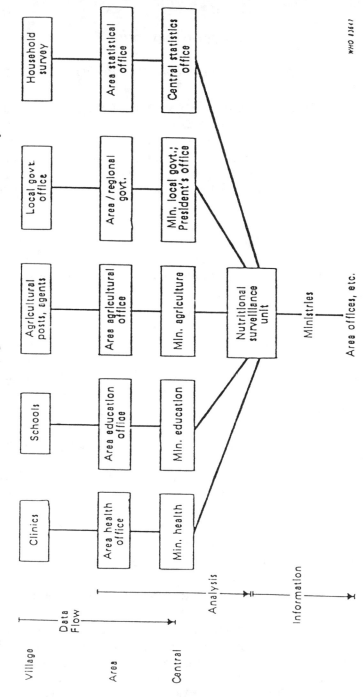

Source: Mason, J. B., J-P Habicht, H. Tabatabai, and V. Valverde. 1984. Nutritional surveillance for health and development planning: uses and organization. In *Nutritional Surveillance*, 59-81, Geneva: World Health Organization.

cannot even be initiated without support of the national government.

At the village or local level, data such as those given in Exhibit 11.3 are collected from clinics, schools, offices, or household surveys. In the latter case, workers may physically have to collect the data themselves. The data are then centralized in area offices related to health, education, agriculture, and statistics. As with any reliable and valid survey, the statistical office plays a major role in synthesizing the data for interpretation.

The nutritional surveillance unit then coordinates the data analysis and interpretation with all of the involved ministries. This analysis requires a massive commitment on the part of each of the agencies involved. Traditionally, ministries of health and agriculture have functioned separately in many countries, largely because of the problems of "turf" and budget matters. For nutritional surveillance to be effective, agencies must openly share their expertise using a multidisciplinary problem-solving approach. Each ministry must have an appreciation for the other areas, and understand that solutions cannot be reached in isolation. Finally, when decisions are made, they are translated back down to the area offices where local public policies are changed.

Establishing an administrative structure such as the one presented in Exhibit 11.4 requires considerable effort and evaluation as well as a long-term financial commitment. Decisions are required in the context of both national policies and particular programs. Decisions about national policies concern resource allocation by area and sector and legislative measures such as prices as well as recommendations for specific programs. When organized effectively, nutritional surveillance can lead to informed decisions in these vital areas.

In low-income countries, nutritional surveillance is relevant to a number of different sectors of government. The overall health of the population depends on social and economic development. The causes of malnutrition are extremely complex and pervasive throughout society. The range of possible actions to prevent and alleviate malnutrition is extensive, and clearly extends beyond the health sector. Development of primary health care requires efforts between sectors, and the managerial planning process requires adequate and relevant information support (see Exhibit 11.4).

Decisions based on nutritional surveillance indicators mediate through bodies that coordinate sectors. They relate to resource allocations, policies, and program designs in economic planning, agriculture, social welfare, and health. It is rare when the health sector alone can have direct influence on the activities of ministries who can affect food availability to malnourished families. Pressure for action for a policy to ensure health for all must come from a higher political level than the ministry of health.

Some Implementation Actions

Nutrition interventions can include such activities as supplementary feeding, rehabilitation, nutrition education, and fortification or enrichment of foods. Nutrition programs have a less established role than health programs because their impact has been disappointing. When health services do not reach the poor, nutritional services do not reach them.

Some inappropriate nutrition interventions have been adopted which were either inappropriate or unadaptable to the local conditions. The level of resources applied is often not sufficient. Implementation can deviate significantly from the planned actions. For these and other reasons, nutritional surveillance programs include the evaluation of both the implementation and the outcomes. In this process, data analyses are used to make decisions about any modifications, extensions, and terminations of programs.

The recommendation of nutritional surveillance programs does not imply that other short-term nutritional assessment endeavors that do not require long-term commitments are never successful. On the contrary, some of these short-term efforts can accomplish improvements in nutritional status in spite of a lack of government interest. On occasions, these programs have led to policy changes and the support of local governments. For example, several legislative actions could be adopted which could have a profound affect upon nutrition:

1. setting prices paid to producers or charged to consumers;
2. regulating the flow of commodities;
3. establishing minimum wage levels.

How are nutritional considerations introduced into national planning? While the purpose of nutritional surveillance may not be to provide data to support price policy analysis itself, tracing the effects of price policies on nutritional conditions in the country concerned could be an important function of a nutritional surveillance system.

Nutritional Surveillance: Two Case Studies

Although generally used in developing countries, the management techniques of nutritional surveillance have been successfully used throughout developed countries. Nutritional surveillance is relevant to both undernutrition and overnutrition, and to both industrialized and low-income countries. A brief example of each follows.

In 1971, the U.K. government announced changes in the provision of welfare milk for pregnant women and preschool children, school milk, and school meals. Members of Parliament were concerned that these changes might be detrimental to the nutritional status of children. Thus, a committee was established with the charge of considering the best method of assessing these changes and making any necessary recommendations.

Initially, the committee stated that measurements of attained height and weight were the most reliable means of assessing nutritional status. They designed studies to provide baseline information against which changes in growth rate could be compared over a 5-year period.

Results of the study showed that the legislative changes in the price and availability of milk in 1971 had little effect on milk consumption in families. The committee concluded that the social habits relating to the purchase of milk were very stable so that changes in cost had relatively little direct effect on consumption and, thus, nutritional status. In this example, feedback about new policies such as diagrammed in Exhibit 11.4 was not necessary.

Turning to an example in a developing country, the 1981-1987 drought was the worst in Botswana's recorded history. During the drought, when some countries in Africa were suffering from massive famine, people in Botswana were not reported to have died from starvation. The reason for this finding was related to President Masire's drought-relief program, coupled with nutritional surveillance and an early warning system, which ensured that adequate food supplies were distributed across the country. Botswana actually emerged from the drought with less malnutrition than in previous years.

SUMMARY

Since questions of nutrition do not have clear-cut answers, renewed concern for growth, foreign exchange, and political issues often shifts attention away from their ill-defined problems and still farther away from any obvious set of conclusions. Planning, including nutritional surveillance programs, can help governments efficiently realize their nutritional goals and policies. Nutritional surveillance is most effective when it follows some governmental policy commitment to nutritional objectives.

REFERENCES

Achaya, K. T. 1984. *Interfaces between agriculture, nutrition and food science.* Tokyo, Japan: The United Nations University.

Alsudery, Abdelmuhsin. 1985. The world food problems: assessment and solutions. In *Crop productivity – research imperatives revisited*, eds. M. Gibbs and C. Carlson, 71-80. An international conference held at Boyne Highlands Inn, October 13-18, 1985 and Airlie House, December 11-13, 1985.

Bell, D. E. and M. R. Reich. 1988. *Health, nutrition, and economic crises. Approaches to policy in the third world.* Dover, Mass.: Auburn House Publishing Company.

Briskey, E. J., V. W. Hays, and R. L. Mitchell. 1983. Future approaches for meeting nutritional needs. In *Agriculture in the twenty-first century*, ed. J. W. Rosenblum, 118-43. New York: John Wiley & Sons.

Brown, Judith E. 1990. *The science of human nutrition.* San Diego: Harcourt Brace Jovanovich, Publishers.

Brown, Lester R. 1989. Feeding six billion. *World-Watch* 2(5):32-40.

Committee on Medical Aspects of Food Policy. 1981. *Second report by the subcommittee on nutritional surveillance.* London: Her Majesty's Stationery Office.

Curtin, Philip D. 1983. Nutrition in African history. In *Hunger and history*, eds.

R. I. Rotberg and T. K. Rabb, 173-209. Cambridge: Cambridge University Press.

Ensminger, A. H., M. E. Ensminger, J. F. Konlande, and J. R. K. Robson. 1986. *Food for health—a nutrition encyclopedia*. Clovis, Calif: Pegus Press.

Falcon, W. P., C. T. Kurien, F. Monckeberg, A. P. Okeyo, S. O. Olayide, F. Rabar, and W. Tims. 1987. The world food and hunger problem: changing perspectives and possibilities, 1974-84. In *Food policy integrating supply, distribution, and consumption*, eds. J. P. Gittinger, J. Leslie, and C. Hoisington, 15-38. Baltimore: The Johns Hopkins University Press.

Mason, J. B., J-P. Habicht, H. Tabatabai, and V. Valverde. 1984. *Nutritional surveillance*. Geneva: World Health Organization.

Pelto, G. H. and P. J. Pelto. 1983. Diet and delocalization: dietary changes since 1750. In *Hunger and history*, eds. R. I. Rotberg and T. K. Rabb, 309-330. Cambridge: Cambridge University Press.

Pimental, D. and M. Pimental. 1979. *Food, energy, and society*. New York: John Wiley & Sons.

Pomeranz, Y. 1987. Bread around the world. In *Modern cereal science and technology*, 258-333. New York: VCH Publishers.

Rotberg, R. I. and T. K. Rabb, eds. 1983. *Hunger and history*. Cambridge: Cambridge University Press.

Scrimshaw, Nevin S. 1983. Functional consequences of malnutrition for human populations: a comment. In *Hunger and history*, eds. R. I. Rotberg and T. K. Rabb, 211-13. Cambridge: Cambridge University Press.

PART FOUR:
CURRENT FOOD ISSUES AND YOU

In recent years, you have been bombarded with sensational media topics related to agriculture and food such as biotechnological developments, genetic engineering, chemicals in the food supply, and global warming. The emerging issues of these topics will be briefly discussed in this section. In previous chapters, the role of science and technology in food and agriculture has been stressed. In this section, some aspects will be presented to you in sufficient detail that you will be able to discuss them from a scientific viewpoint. For example, the physical process of genetic engineering manipulations of a tomato plant will be presented.

Previous sections have presented you with the facts about the food and agricultural situation throughout the world. In this section, you will be exposed to ideas for solving some of the problems that you have become familiar with. Due to the inherent uncertainty of scientific research, some of the conclusions made in the next four chapters may not materialize. Conflicting opinions exist among scientists themselves, and among policymakers dealing with political, economic, social, and scientific issues. For example, we do not yet know if the warnings being made about global warming are factual. Thus, in the chapter dealing with global warming, you will be presented with the major issues and selected opinions of informed professionals.

As you study these current issues and become aware of others that are not presented here, you should get a sense of optimism about the world food problem. Your optimism should come from your realization that research and development efforts are being made to increase the food supply and decrease the wastage of the current food supply. When you acknowledge that people throughout the world are concerned about achieving a healthy world population, you should feel encouraged. Solutions to complex issues only come after problems, and their inherent causes, have been identified.

Chapter Twelve

Biotechnology and Agricultural Production

INTRODUCTION

Throughout this chapter, you will be introduced to the complex techniques and issues of biotechnology in agriculture which have been referred to in previous chapters. After studying material in this chapter, you will be in an informed position to:

- discuss the role of biotechnology in agricultural production and food processing;
- discuss how biotechnology firms are emerging in both developed and developing countries, with legal, political, and societal ramifications.

This chapter provides some details of genetic engineering techniques so you will become aware of some of the complexity and sophistication of these multidisciplined research techniques. For the remainder of your life, you will hear discussions about biotechnology in the media; some will be extremely positive and some will be drastically negative. Studying this information and its likely contributions to agriculture may stimulate you to learn more about how you could play either a scientific or a political role in future biotechnological developments.

Biotechnology may be defined as: "the collection of industrial processes that involve the use of biological systems." Biotechnology is difficult to understand because it is made up of several disciplines: biology, chemistry, biochemistry, and food science. Biotechnology includes any technique that uses either live organisms or parts of organisms to make or modify products, improve plants or animals, or develop microorganisms for specific uses.

In some instances, these techniques or processes involve recombinant DNA technology in which the hereditary apparatus of an animal, plant, or bacterial cell is altered, enabling it to produce more or different chemicals or perform new functions. Biotechnology encompasses areas other than genetic engineering such as enzyme and protein engineering, plant and animal tissue culture technology, biosensors for biological monitoring, and bioprocess and fermentation technologies.

Biotechnology is an integrated, multidisciplinary field with a profound impact on several industries including agriculture, food, pharmaceutical (for both human and veterinary health care), chemical, and energy. In all of these industries, biotechnology creates exciting opportunities for new product development and differentiation, cost reductions, and the creation of novel processing methods.

While the ability to combine genes from one organism to another became a reality in the early 1970s, the theories behind genetic engineering extend back to research findings of the 1930s and 1940s. Once recombinant DNA techniques were achieved in the 1970s, attention focused on the environmental and safety concerns of research.

The combining of electronics with biotechnology and the application of engineering methods to the study of live organisms are resulting in new possibilities for humans throughout the world. For example, in agriculture, productivity has been substantially increased and plant species have been grown in new environments. Through genetics, new proteins are being created and others are being reprogrammed. The ability to unlock the genetic code has dramatic implications for world population growth, medicine, and health.

The impact of technology on agriculture is profound. Genetic engineering promises to revolutionize future agricultural methods. Genetically engineered seeds and the development of highly drought- and herbicide-resistant species are likely to lead to rapid and continuing improvements in productivity and total output. These developments could lead to eventually making countries that have been traditional food importers largely self-sufficient. Also, they could either eliminate, or at least sharply restrict, many of the current markets for temperate-zone agricultural goods. Further advances in enhancing agricultural productivity, crop varieties, and animal breeding techniques appear to continue causing shifts in the balance of world demand and supply.

As discussed in previous chapters, technology has affected agricultural output and productivity and created new substitutes for primary goods. The rise of multinational companies with their ability to take advantage of recent technological developments, without any necessary regard to frontiers, has changed international trade. Clearly, biotechnology has created new imperatives which nations must learn to accept.

PLANT BREEDING

Classical plant breeding is a long, tedious, and demanding exercise in which scientists seek to introgress specific genetic characteristics. Plants which retain the desirable characteristics are selected, as they are gradually being freed of undesirable traits, by repeated backcrossing techniques. This is an extremely complex and demanding process. A target characteristic (for example, a high-amylose, low-gelatinization temperature starch in a hybrid or variety of corn) must be accompanied by all of the required agronomic characteristics of yield, disease and insect resistance, and uniformity. Further, the issues of crop residues need consideration.

Information in Exhibit 12.1 outlines the steps involved in the typical procedures for developing new inbred lines of corn. The two stages in Exhibit 12.1 briefly depict the steps needed to develop an inbred line. When two such inbred lines are crossed, the result is an F1 hybrid, hopefully with the desired agronomic and functional attributes. Molecular biology procedures hold the promise of being able to do this in a more direct manner instead of taking many generations and discarding lots of combinations.

There are important differences between crossbreeding programs and genetic engineering. When selecting progeny from crosses made with parents with known mutations, breeders must go through several generations in the belief that the genes being selected for are in the F1, F2, and F3 progenies. Because these are recessive traits, they will not be phenotypically detectable in the first few generations. These efforts, such as depicted in Exhibit 12.1, are generally

Exhibit 12.1. Traditional Procedures for Developing New Inbred Lines of corn.

STAGE ONE: GROWTH OF THE PLANT

The corn plant has a male organ, the tassel, which is a source of pollen. The female organ, the silk is located in the ear just below the tassel. Just before the emergence of the silk from the ear, the ear is physically bagged to protect it from unwanted and random pollination. Sometime later, when the tassel is ready to drop pollen, it is also bagged.

STAGE TWO: POLLINATION

The pollen is shaken into the bag and can then be dusted on the silks of specific plants to complete the cross. The pollinated ear is then covered with a pollinating bag which is secured around the ear and the kernels are permitted to develop as the ear matures.

Source: Moshy, Raymond. 1986. Biotechnology: its potential impact on traditional food processing. In Biotechnology and food processing. ed. S.K. Harlander and T.P. Labuza 1-14. New Jersey: Noyes Publications. "With permission".

conducted in environmentally controlled greenhouses. However, years can be involved in accomplishing these tasks. Any problems with growing conditions and harvesting can cause even further delays. With biotechnological procedures, a new tomato can be bred in 2 years instead of 10 years by conventional crossbreeding techniques.

Luther Burbank performed research experiments for years in order to crossbreed plants to produce the billion-dollar Idaho potato industry. Bioengineers have set out to duplicate that feat, both scientifically and commercially, with new life forms.

GENETIC ENGINEERING TECHNIQUES

Several techniques will be briefly presented; further information may be found in the references cited at the end of this chapter. In this discussion, more attention is paid to genetic engineering techniques with plants than with animals. Although techniques with animals and livestock are vitally important, those with plants have considerable applications throughout the world for both humans and livestock.

Virtually no techniques used by molecular biologists involve using only chemical or physical techniques. All of their most important techniques depend on exploiting the naturally occurring activities of a number of enzymes. The contribution of the scientist involves controlling a series of enzyme reactions in test tubes.

An important result of these manipulations is an amplification of specific genes and genetic elements so that they can be studied in detail. After a few months of work, a researcher can take a gene out of a complex genome where it might be just one of several hundred thousand genes and produce millions of copies of that gene. The isolated gene can then be sequenced and used in molecular studies to determine how its expression is controlled, and how it performs within cells.

Recombinant DNA (rDNA)

In 1953, James Watson and his colleagues unlocked the double helix of deoxyribonucleic acid (DNA), the genetic key to heredity. Twenty years later, two California academics, Stanley Cohen and Herbert Boyer, made "recombinant" DNA (rDNA) by transplanting a toad's gene into bacteria which then reproduced toad genes. They hold the first patents for making rDNA.

All life uses nucleic acids, generally in the form of DNA, to store and transmit genetic information. Chemically, the DNA from any one organism is identical to that from any other. The informational differences between different DNAs lie in changing the order of the four monomer units that are used to construct the long polymeric DNA molecules.

The code used to change this information into active biological molecules or proteins is also highly conserved. The chemical conservation of DNA has two important consequences. First, once a piece of DNA is introduced into the genetic material of a host cell, it can be properly replicated and passed to daughter cells regardless of whether it expresses any genetic information in the host cell. Second, biochemical techniques can be developed to manipulate any DNA molecule regardless of the details of the information it contains.

In practice, rDNA technology consists of a set of techniques that allow researchers to cut DNA molecules in defined and reproducible ways, join different pieces together in a controlled manner, and identify the individual coding properties of particular DNA fragments. The single common factor in all of these techniques is that they all rely on using naturally occurring enzymes.

Gene Mapping

Used first in medical research for detecting genes responsible for hereditary diseases, gene mapping allows the identification of the precise locations of genes on chromosomes. In plant research, genes of interest are those responsible for the color, size, sweetness, taste, aroma, and other features pertinent to the quality of the specific plant. Recent focus has been placed on salt and drought tolerance. Molecular biologists and plant breeders work together towards developing genetic maps. Gene mapping may also be used to produce such products as varieties of corn from which higher yields of sweetener can be obtained.

Genetic engineering techniques make extensive use of molecular probes. The use of molecular probes with radioactively labeled genes such as sugary-1 or amylose extender in the F2 population can be detected at the earliest plantlet stage. Therefore, only those plantlets will be retained and grown out; all others will be discarded. Obviously, this can save time previously required to grow at least two or three generations in the field.

Plant Cell Cultures

The biotechnology tools of clonal propagation, somaclonal variation, gametoclonal variation, and protoplast fusion permit new variety development on an accelerated schedule, making them attractive for food industry applications. Information in Exhibit 12.2 very briefly lists the main actions of these techniques and gives one plant example for each. Clonal propagation is used for the scale-up of special parents for breeding programs, the mass propagation of elite plants, and the multiplication of virus-free germ plasm.

Biotechnology permits the use of the micropropagation technique, which is a form of tissue culture with the ability to produce clones of more uniform planting materials. An example with palm

Exhibit 12.2. Bioengineering Techniques for Plant Cell Cultures.

Name	Action
Clonal Propagation	Produces genetic carbon copies of plants. Used when a unique combination of traits would be lost in seed production and when methods of asexual propagation are inefficient. Example: Fruit trees.
Somaclonal Variation	Regenerates plants from callus, leaf tissue explants, or plant protoplasts to recover genetic variants. Used to introduce new useful characteristics into plant varieties. Example: Potatoes.
Gametoclonal Variation	Regenerates plants from cultured microspore or pollen cells contained within the anther. Example: Rice.
Protoplast Fusion	Permits the combination of different plant cells and produces new hybrid plants. Example: Tomatoes.

Source: Evans, D. and W. Sharp. 1986. Potential applications of plant cell culture. In Biotechnology in food processing, ed. S. K. Harlander and T.P. Labuza. 133-43. New Jersey: Noyes Publications. "With permission".

trees will be discussed. The process begins with a tiny root cutting which has been induced to form a callus. A callus is a proliferation of undifferentiated cells. The callus is first induced to differentiate. When embryogenesis has occurred, embryos can be separated and each can result in a plant which can be propagated to produce a larger plant in stages. Once large enough, plants that possess the desired characteristics can then be placed into the plantation. As all the palm trees are identical, their resulting oil yields will be similar. Because projections are always needed about the productivity of a given acreage of palm trees, having identical oil yields is a very desirable characteristic.

Both somaclonal variation and gametoclonal variation are used to develop new breeding lines for variety development. Protoplast technology is used predominantly in the research laboratory. However, during the next few years, regeneration procedures will be developed to allow plantlet regeneration from protoplast fusion products on a large scale, enlarging the portfolio of food crops amenable to protoplast fusion, mediated improvement.

Plant Hybrids

Researchers in Belgium have developed a genetic engineering technique for creating hybrid plants for a number of key crops, including corn. Researchers have isolated a plant gene that prevents the production of pollen. The gene can prevent a plant from fertilizing itself. Such male-sterile plants could be fertilized by pollen from another strain of the plant, thereby producing hybrid seed. The new generation of plants will possess the flourishing, high-production trait known as "hybrid vigor," similar to that now seen in hybrid corn.

On a commercial scale, the sterilization of the pollen-producing male part has only been achieved in corn and sorghum feed grains. This technique has been limited to these plants because the male part, the tassel, and the female, the silk, are some distance apart on the corn plant, as was stated in Exhibit 12.1. In a labor-intensive process, the tassels of each plant are removed, making it male-sterile. A row of male-fertile plants is sowed nearby. They pollinate the male-sterile plants. The first hybrid corn seeds produced using this mechanical approach were introduced in the 1930s. They produced yields as much as 20 percent more than corn plants that were naturally pollinated. The vast majority of the U.S. corn crop is now grown from hybrid seeds.

A similar technique is almost impossible to apply to other crops such as cotton, soybeans, and rice. The male part of the plant, the anthers, and the female, the pistils, of the same plant are located within a fraction of an inch from each other or are even attached to each other. The anthers in these plants are difficult to clip off. In China, a great number of workers are engaged in pulling out the male organs of rice plants using tweezers, and one-third of rice produced there is grown from hybrid seeds.

Using genetic engineering techniques in Belgium, researchers have isolated a pollen-inhibiting gene that can be inserted into a plant to confer male sterility. This gene was successfully introduced in oil-producing rapeseed plants, a major crop in Europe and Canada, using a "promoter gene" as a carrier. The sterilizing gene is expressed just before the pollen is about to develop and it deactivates the anthers of every flower on the plant.

For herbicide resistance, a second gene is attached to the pollen-inhibiting gene. Both genes are then inserted into a few greenhouse plants that are pollinated and allowed to mature and produce seed.

The laws of heredity dictate that half of the plants springing from these greenhouse-produced seeds will be male-sterile and herbicide resistant and half will be male-fertile and herbicide susceptible. The application of herbicide kills off the male-fertile plants, leaving male-sterile plants that can be cross-pollinated to produce hybrid seed. The hybrid rapeseeds created with this genetic engineering procedure yield 15 to 30 percent more output than the commercial strains developed with traditional techniques.

Thus, a company in Belgium is experimenting with the technique on alfalfa, with plans to include similar research with cotton and corn among other crops. This genetic approach will obviate the need for mechanical emasculation of anthers which costs U.S. seed producers alone about $70 million each year.

In a related genetic engineering research study, a company in California is developing a spray containing a gene that spreads from cell to cell and interferes with the genes that are responsible for producing pollen. This gene, called "gametocide," is carried into the plant by a virus that remains active for a few days.

BIOTECHNOLOGY AND FOOD PROCESSING

There are numerous applications for biotechnology and food processing including, but not limited to, screening and making selective improvements of microorganisms and their mutations, controlling fermentation and enzymatic processes, and using soluble and immobilized enzymes for numerous chemical reactions. Most food processors establish a level of end-product quality as a goal; quality is the final result of the regulation of microbial and enzymatic processes. Since all food processes commence with raw products or commodities, applying genetic engineering techniques to them has a direct effect upon subsequent food processes.

Food Product Development

Formulation is a key component of food product development. The myriad of food products found in supermarkets attest to the advanced state of product formulation throughout the food industry. Formulated processed food products start with one or two basic commodities such as cereal grains that are then modified for human digestion. This modification involves either processing or a bioconversion procedure producing a cereal mass. Flavors, sweeteners, colorants, or antioxidants may then be added. The next step is some form of process engineering, the second component of food technology. For example, to produce a ready-to-eat cereal, the mixture could be extrusion-cooked, baked, puffed, toasted, and dried. The final step is packaging to keep the product at as high a quality as possible and reduce losses through ineffective storage procedures.

Tremendous potential exists for the application of biotechnology to food product development. One key aspect that has been missing in product development is the ability to custom-produce basic food raw materials. Raw materials with uniform and predetermined functional properties are needed to achieve better formulation, processing, and stability after packaging. Today, the development of agricultural commodities with properties tailored to meet end-product requirements lags behind the advances in food formulation, processing, and packaging.

Typically, first-stage agricultural raw materials such as orange juice concentrate, cornmeal, tomato paste, or wheat flour have to be manipulated to produce desired functional properties. For example, if they lack texture, they are texturized; if they lack stability, they are stabilized; it they have a tendency to become rancid because of the presence of oxygen, antioxidants are added and effective package designs are used. All of these processing operations add to both the complexity and the cost of the formulated processed foods.

Biotechnology could assist with producing a wheat variety which results in a flour that does not stale. Biotechnology could produce a variety of peas that, when canned, would give equivalent quality to that of frozen peas, or when blanched and frozen, quality equivalent to that of fresh peas. Biotechnology could produce a variety of corn that contained starch with a high-amylose content and low-gelatinization temperature. Biotechnology could produce a variety of corn which was devoid of lipoxygenase and, thus, did not require blanching prior to freezing. The possibilities for improving the basic food commodities used in food processing are endless. Some will be briefly discussed.

Genetically Modified Varieties of Corn

Many South American varieties of corn or maize are available which could serve as rich source material for introducing new characteristics into commercial U.S. corn lines. For example, one South American variety, Teosinte, is perennial, which may be a desirable trait for the annual crops grown in the U.S. However, without assistance from biotechnology, classical breeding techniques would be overwhelmed with the attempt to access specific genetic characteristics buried among the millions of genes represented in the large corn population.

Because of advances in genetic engineering such as those given in Exhibit 12.2, possibilities exist for sweet corn to have two new functional attributes: enhanced sweetness and creaminess. These would be achieved by manipulating some of the carbohydrate-determining genes. Corn kernels could also have improved texture and

frozen storage life attributes by deleting the enzyme lipoxygenase.
These changes would have consumer and economic benefits. Procedures for these genetic engineering procedures will be briefly described.

Synthesis of Starch in Corn

There are about 24 mutants in maize that affect starch synthesis.
Studying the biochemical pathways which lead to a specific carbohydrate end-product reveals the enzyme systems involved. Once the
enzymes have been identified, this can lead to the identification of
the gene sequences that are responsible for the expression of these
enzymes. In corn, the endosperm mutants, dull [du], sugary-2 [su-
2], waxy [wx], and amylose-extender [ae], all affect the relative
proportions of the two types of starches, amylopectin and amylose,
produced in the final product.

The waxy endosperms do not produce any amylopectin. The
other mutations all increase the amylose content. The sugary-1 [su-
1] mutant affects the production of the water-soluble phytoglyco-
gen which contributes to the creamy texture of sweet corn. Two
shrunken mutants, sh-1 and sh-2, and a brittle-2 [bu-2] mutant limit
reducing sugars and sucrose availability for starch synthesis. Thus,
endosperms with these mutants will have an increased level of those
sugars, enhancing their sweetness. Double, triple, or quadruple
gene mutations can occur in corn.

Coupled with molecular or genetic probe techniques, these materials offer substantial assistance in the acceleration and precision of
a breeding program. Scientific developments related to tracking
these genes using molecular probes in a crossing program provide a
rapid procedure for the development of corn hybrids with predetermined carbohydrate composition and functionality.

Increasing the Shelf Life of Corn

Frozen shelf life is another trait that can be selected for by using
genetic engineering techniques. Lipoxygenase is the enzyme system which catalyzes the oxidation of unsaturated fatty acids and
decreases the storage life of corn. Blanching in water at 205-212°F
for about 10 minutes is required to inactivate lipoxygenase, and

consequently minimize the development of oxidative rancidity which causes off-flavors to develop during frozen storage. However, blanching has a deleterious effect on the texture of the rehydrated frozen cob corn, making it too pasty and soft.

The reaction of oxygen with linoleic acid produces aldehydes such as cis-3-hexenal and cis-nonadienal which cause rancidity in the frozen corn. These carbonyls may be reduced to alcohols and also isomerized to the trans form by the actions of ADH and isomerase, respectively. One solution is to develop a mutant of corn which does not produce lipoxygenase.

This might be done by supplementing the classical breeding and selection approach with lipoxygenase probes. Soybean lipoxygenases have been cloned. If they were to cross-hybridize with corn lipoxygenase, they could then be used as molecular probes. If this technique is not successful, corn lipoxygenase would have to be isolated and used as the probe. This example reveals that molecular biotechnology involves aiming a particular piece of DNA or gene into a cell. Its source does not matter as long as it contains the desired genes. This is an important issue.

Genetically Modified Varieties of Tomatoes

Whenever food and genetics are discussed, the desired characteristics of tomatoes are delineated. Two desirable characteristics under consideration are high-solidity tomatoes with less moisture and enhanced flavor. The fresh notes or qualities of tomatoes may be restored or enhanced in processed tomato products by the use of lipoxygenase activity. Oxidation products which have been catalyzed by lipoxygenase have positive flavor and aroma impacts. Since the tomato is a dicotyledon and more amenable to transformation, a lipoxygenase gene from another source might be inserted into the tomato genome and interesting flavor results could occur.

The tomato industry could significantly reduce overall processing costs by using tomatoes with higher solids contents. The average solids content of a tomato is approximately 5 percent; the remaining portion is mainly water. Thus, water must be removed to give processed tomato products a solids content as high as 32 percent.

Biotechnology techniques have the capability of increasing the solids content of tomatoes by at least several percentage points, thereby reducing processing costs. The higher the tomato solids, the shorter the time required to move raw product through a processing plant. For every 1 percent increase in tomato solids, the U.S. tomato processing industry would save $80 million per year.

The U.S. domestic varieties of tomatoes are round and red. In South America there is a wild variety that is small, skinny, and green. A U.S. variety of tomato weighs up to 13 times as much as this South American variety. However, the wild southern fruit has proportionately twice as much sugar, nutrients, and soluble solids as its U.S. counterpart. Scientists have developed a genetic map of about 400 fragments of tomato DNA, representing the plant's entire genetic blueprint. With a new method of locating the gene clusters responsible for desirable qualities, the researchers hope to combine the greater nutritive value of the wild species with the robust bulk of the common variety, thereby creating a better tomato.

Wheat Varieties and Bread Staling

Throughout the world, the staling of bread is a major problem and cause of food losses. However, staling can be controlled by altering the starch composition of wheat using different varieties of wheat. Furthermore, the staling problem of bread could actually be solved by developing varieties of wheat that produce loaves of bread having these desired qualities. This would enable the baking industry to reduce drastically their use of chemical anti-staling agents used in their current bread formulas.

Yield and Characteristics of Palm Oil

Turning to another example, receiving the optimal yield of oil from plants is a desired agronomic characteristic. Within one tree, the production of oil from palm fruit is uniform. However, wide variations in yield occur among trees. Thus, when seeds from different trees are planted, wide variations in palm oil yields are observed. Planting palm trees which would give products with optimal agronomic characteristics without diversity would have obvious advantages.

There is a need to reproduce and use only planting materials representing palms with an optimal oil yield. Similarly, palm trees having disease resistance, ideal physical stature, and specific fatty acid compositions are desirable. The latter are needed to control precisely the nutrient content of formulated food products.

Developments with Cocoa

Biotechnology techniques developed for the pharmaceutical industry show great promise in the food industry. The *Theobroma cacao* is essentially a primitive agricultural plant. A tropical perennial, it is not well suited to the standard methods of genetic improvement. In the Cacao Biotechnology Program with Pennsylvania State University and the American Cocoa Research Institute, tools of biotechnology and food science are being applied in a systematic way to improve the productivity, disease resistance, and climate tolerance of cacao varieties.

The complex subjects of quality and flavor characteristics of cocoa and chocolate are being considered during this research effort. A reliable micropropagation system for the cacao plant would be a major enhancement to breeding programs throughout the world. Research is underway to define a system which would be able to produce hundreds of complete clones of a desirable individual plant from in-vitro proliferation of plant tissue. Success in this endeavor will speed the process of genetic improvement greatly over traditional root-cutting propagation methods.

Complementing this research is work characterizing the *T. cacao* genome. Understanding the cell's total complement of genetic material, and how it functions in a coordinated way, is essential to any long-term breeding success and to a thorough understanding of the complex subject of cocoa quality.

Direct manipulation of the genetic material in the cacao plant is an integral goal of this program. One phase involves research to apply the technique of Agrobacterium-mediated gene transfer to the cacao plant. This research involves evaluating individual strains of *Agrobacterium* for their ability to transfer genetic material to cacao. In addition, gene mapping using restriction enzymes is being actively developed into a tool for cacao germ plasm identification.

Cacao breeders will then have a fingerprinting technique for identifying the genetic status of seeding plants. This could save substantial time and expense when evaluating individual plants.

Research activities also include studying the biosynthetic pathways of cocoa butter production in the plant. The quality and quantity of cocoa butter in the bean is largely determined by four enzymes. It is postulated that beans with higher amounts of specific enzymes produce more cocoa butter. Knowledge of the genetic control of these pathways, combined with gene mapping, offers good prospects of advancing the inherent genetic productivity of a primitive agricultural species. Further, this will be able to be accomplished much more rapidly than ever before while monitoring, or even enhancing, the quality of the final product. Additional studies are determining the exact chromosomal count of T. cacao, and are exploring the genetic basis for widely varying resistance to Phytophthora pod rot, a disease of the plant that causes major economic losses.

This research involves the simultaneous development of species productivity and quality in an extremely complex product. Wide variation in product quality because of fermentation practices and inherent quality differences led to the recommendation for cocoa research that included breeding programs and incorporating quality assessment techniques. In summary, the biotechnology techniques used in this project are providing the tools for the modification of a species, and will also lead to a better understanding of the genetic component of product quality.

To summarize, biotechnology offers the tools to remake archaic and modern agricultural plants, so product quality, production efficiencies, and economic factors are more manageable and predictable.

Future Applications

Numerous projections are being made about the future of biotechnology and the food processing industry. Many products that will be marketed will be replacement products, e.g., the enzyme rennin used in cheese manufacture. Genetically engineered rennin may replace natural calf rennin now widely used throughout the industry. Advantages include cost reductions for the manufacture of cheese.

One approach to engineering low-calorie fats and oils would be to induce the production of shorter chain fatty acids in commonly used vegetable oils such as soybean or rapeseed.

Biotechnology will continue to play a major role in the nonnutritive sweetener market. A new class of compounds called taste active proteins will likely be targets of biotechnology research. These compounds act as sweeteners and/or flavor modifiers, and include compounds such as aspartame, thaumatin, monellin, and stevioside. Thaumatin, a sweetener known under the trade name of Talin™, is the sweetest compound in the world, being 2,500 times as sweet as sucrose. The isolated gene that codes for thaumatin can be used in the production of Talin™ or engineered into plants to give new and unique foods.

Some low-calorie beers are produced by the addition of enzymes designed to cleave dextrin, a complex starch structure, into units that can be acted upon by amyloglucosidase and degraded into alcohol. Biotechnology techniques are also being used to develop specialized yeasts and enhanced enzymes to aid in the production of low-calorie beer.

Information given in Exhibit 12.3 was excerpted from a day in the life of a Canadian woman in the year 2060. By the middle of the next century, many of the food items sold in supermarkets will be the same ones that people now eat and enjoy. However, as a result of genetic engineering, future fruits, milk, meats, and cereals may

Exhibit 12.3. Genetic Engineering: A Futuristic Case Study.

Describing a day in the year 2060 for a Canadian woman, her raw vegetables were placed on a plate under a sonic dome until the tone was heard telling her they were ready. She guessed that genetic engineering -- which had led to the development of new strains of green beans and mushrooms and dozens of other things that heated themselves in response to sound -- was truly one of the marvels of the mid-21st century. She thought about her childhood in the second decade of the 21st century and could vaguely remember her mother actually having to boil water to cook vegetables.

Source: Tomorrow's World. Maclean's 102(37):36-49, 1989.

be vastly superior to those currently available. For example, these future products could be richer in amino acids and proteins, having higher PER values while possessing superior quality characteristics.

Foods in the future will be altered by gene splicing to protect them from bacteria and insects. As a result, pesticides and some herbicides will no longer be necessary. Biotechnology could also ensure that food stays fresher for longer storage periods, both chilled and frozen. Since scientists have already identified a gene in tomato plants that causes the fruit to deteriorate, there may be hope that other developments could produce peaches that do not go mushy, lettuce that does not wilt and chickens that resist *Salmonella*.

BIOTECHNOLOGY AND LIVESTOCK

Humans have always stated their claim for ownership of animals; scientists have made extensive use of traditional methods of animal husbandry to develop breeds with desirable traits. Genetic engineering techniques give scientists alternatives for substantial species alterations. Gene-splicing techniques enable scientists to pick and select among qualities of one animal, insert those qualities into the genetic code of another animal, and produce a living thing never before imagined. This is an amazing development.

Bovine growth hormone (BGH) is a naturally occurring bovine hormone that increases lactation in dairy cows. It can be commercially manufactured by splicing the BGH gene into bacteria which can be grown in large quantities in fermentation tanks. The BGH manufacturers say the hormone is a tool to reduce farmers' production costs. The same amount of milk can be produced by fewer cows, reducing feed and overhead costs.

The U.S. Food and Drug Administration (FDA) has established that research studies have demonstrated that the consumption of BGH in cows' milk has no effect on humans. Their findings were based on daily doses equivalent to 2.3 million times the amount humans would be exposed to in five 8-ounce glasses of milk per day. However, due to political forces in the U.S., final policies for the use of BGH have not been established.

Additional technologies and methods derived from biotechnology that increase milk output are being researched. These include improved genetic manipulation in breeding, the creation of new types of animal feed in which bacterial additives help expedite the animals' digestion, and improved treatment of mastitis, an inflammation of the udder which is a common ailment responsible for reducing cows' milk output.

THE EMERGING BIOTECHNOLOGY INDUSTRY

Given all the examples discussed, the commercialization of some of the fascinating results of biotechnological applications, as well as the research techniques developed, was inevitable.

Developed Countries

Exhibit 12.4 provides a list of U.S. food companies that were concentrating upon genetic engineering research in 1986. The food and beverage companies of Japan began to enter the biotechnology field aggressively in 1980. Japan leads the world in the production of amino acids and fermented food products.

The Japanese government has pledged to make that country the leader in biotechnology, putting tremendous pressure on their scientists. To achieve this goal, Japan has policymakers and academic scientists in both the government and the food companies, all working together on a very focused path. They can have major impacts on the world food industry; information is being developed at an intense rate. By the 1980s, research scientists in many developed countries were setting up biotechnology companies to exploit knowledge about genetic discoveries that they and their colleagues had made just a few years previously.

Environmental concerns and economic issues necessitate the better utilization of raw materials and the further reduction of food processing waste, defined as low-value by-products and residuals from food processes. The tools of plant biotechnology which shorten the time for crop improvement offer the food industry opportunities to modify their raw materials or commodities such as those listed in Exhibit 12.4.

When new varieties are developed through applying the complex

Exhibit 12.4.   U.S. Food Companies and Genetic Engineering Efforts: 1986.

Food Product	Companies Involved in Research
Tomatoes	Campbell Soup, Del Monte, Hunt, Heinz
Palm oil	Unilever, United Fruit
Soybeans	Nestle
Popcorn	American Home Foods
Vegetables	Kraft
Potatoes	Frito-Lay
Cacao	Hershey, General Foods
Carrots	Campbell Soup
Spices	McCormick
Flavors	W.R. Grace
Onions	American Basic
Garlic	American Basic

Source: Evans, D. and W. Sharp. 1986. Potential applications of plant cell
culture. In <u>Biotechnology in food processing</u>, ed. S. K. Harlander
and T. P. Labuza, 133-43. New Jersey: Noyes Publications.   "With
permission".

techniques of biotechnology, they offer food companies the opportunity to have proprietary raw material for use with specific brand names. Genetic engineering makes it possible to breed the raw plant material according to specifications prescribed by the processor or to develop fresh market products geared to the consumer. In summary, the food processing industry is playing an expanded role in genetic development of new and better natural compounds to meet consumer desires for natural foods. Other possibilities include increasing the yields of cereal grains by making them more tolerant of salt, drought, and heat.

Legal Developments

Several U.S. states, led by Minnesota, have taken or have begun to take legislative action to regulate field tests of genetically engineered organisms. The Minnesota law requires that permits be obtained for the proposed release of any genetically engineered organisms. Wisconsin law requires state agency notification prior to the release of genetically engineered organisms. North Carolina has passed legislation to regulate environmental releases.

A permit was issued by the Minnesota Department of Agriculture for a field test by Crop Genetics International at the Northrup King research facility in Stanton, Minnesota. The permit enables the production of a sweet corn variety that is engineered to contain a gene from *Bacillus thuringiensis*. This gene produces a protein that is toxic to the European corn borer, the cabbage moth, and other lepidoptera larvae. A second field test at the Northrup King facility will assess herbicide resistance of genetically engineered alfalfa. Both permits are designed to reduce costs associated with agricultural production.

Exhibit 12.5 provides a list of biotechnological developments recently approved by the U.S. Animal and Plant Health Inspection Service (APHIS). This agency has determined that no significant impacts will result from testing these items. This is not a complete list, nor is it intended to be completely understood by readers of this chapter. It is presented to show the complexity of genetic engineering. Although they are not food products, tobacco plants are included in Exhibit 12.5. The research with tobacco plants, either the methods used or the results, can probably be applied to other food and feed plants in the future.

By stating that these tests have "no significant impacts," the APHIS has made a determination that scientists believe that the item in question will not present a risk of introducing or disseminating a plant pest, and will not have a significant impact on the quality of the human environment.

The process for approving testing sites for genetically engineered material has met with considerable resistance. For example, a plant pathologist for the University of California, Berkeley, discovered a procedure for snipping a particular gene from bacteria so the rede-

Exhibit 12.5. Examples of Biotechnological Tests Approved by the U.S. APHIS.

Tobacco Plants

- genetically modified to increase their tolerance to insect pests (Test Site: Yolo County, California; Calgene, Inc.).

- genetically modified to express a bacterial chloramphenicol acetyl transferase enzyme in order to confer resistance to the antibiotic chloramphenicol (Test Site: Iowa; Iowa State University).

- genetically modified to express a dihydropicolinic acid synthase gene (DHDPS) which provides increased nutrient value to the plant (Test Site: Wisconsin; Bio Technica Agriculture, Inc.).

- genetically modified to express a mouse metallothionein gene, for use as a model system to investigate the possibility of lowering concentrations of toxic metals in leaf tissue (Test Site: Kentucky; University of Kentucky).

Alfalfa Plants

- genetically modified to express a gene from Streptomyces viridochromogenes, which provides resistance to the glufosinate-class of herbicides (Test Site: Minnesota; Northrup King Co.).

- genetically modified to express a gene which provides resistance to the glufosinate-class of herbicides (Test Site: California; Northrup King Co.).

Rice Plants

- the bacterium Clavibacter xyli subsp. cynodontis, designed to express the deltaendotoxin gene of Bacillus thuringiensis var. kurstaki, another bacterium, in rice (Test Site: Maryland; Crop Genetics International).

Tomato Plants

- genetically modified to be tolerant to tobacco mosaic virus, tomato mosaic virus, or both (Test Site: Jerseyville, Illinois; Monsanto Agricultural Co.).

Cotton Plants

- genetically modified for tolerance to the herbicide Bromoxynil, and to initiate crosses between genetically engineered plants and nontransformed cotton varieties and lines (Test Site: Mississippi; Calgene, Inc.).

Source: The Ag Bioethics Forum. 1989. Regulatory News 1(5):4.

signed microbes resisted frost formation down to 24°F. Theoretically, if crops were sprayed with these microbes, they could be protected from cold snaps. In 1983, permission was received from the National Institute of Health (NIH) to test these bugs, called ice-minus, on a small plot of potatoes in northern California.

These bugs were to be the first genetically altered bacteria released into the environment. Although there was strong evidence that the microbes were benign, biologists at Berkeley and the NIH had failed to consider fully the experiment's environmental impact. The oversight allowed a lawsuit to block the experiment. The courts agreed and testing was postponed for three years while the NIH, the USDA, and the Environmental Protection Agency (EPA) determined how to establish rules under which genetically engineered products could move from laboratory research to field tests.

The ice-fighting bacteria, developed into a commercial product called Frostban™, was sprayed on a test field in 1987. As predicted, it proved harmless. Although severe time delays were observed, this test case led to the formation of precise regulations for genetic research with the goal of protecting the health of individuals and the environment.

Consequences of genetic manipulation have focused renewed public attention on animal welfare. The issue must be taken seriously; the animal protection movement has increased its membership at least fivefold in the last 10 years. In 1988, the U.S. Patent and Trademark Office (PTO) issued the first patent on a vertebrate animal named the "Harvard mouse." In 1987, the PTO Board of Patent Appeals and Interferences ruled that a polyploid Pacific oyster was patentable. New animal patents are being continually issued.

There have been genetic engineering "accidents" which may or may not have impacts upon the environment. For example, a biochemist was recombining the genes of sea organisms while working in his beachfront home in Massachusetts. His goal was to create a new type of building material. When his house collapsed, microorganisms escaped. The scientist claimed that they were not harmful. Because he was using only private funds for this research, no laws were violated. Because he was not using public research funds, he was not obligated to follow any federal guidelines. This incident led to the conclusion that the likelihood of unintentional releases becomes greater with increases in the production of genetically altered organisms.

Before a new organism can be safely released to the environment, it must be tested in a microcosm, and the dynamics of the ecosystem for which it is targeted must be carefully modeled. This strong recommendation is necessary. Introductions of genetically engineered organisms (GEOs) might create new human diseases, spawn new plant or animal pests, or otherwise disrupt delicate ecological balances. This has happened in the past when exotic species such as the gypsy moth and the citrus canker were introduced to the environment for targeted purposes.

Would corn planted at the edge of a forest take over the forest? Occasionally, natural organisms that have been introduced from different environments have caused widespread damage. Kudzu, for example, was imported into the southwestern U.S. for forage and erosion control. It has since become a major weed problem in forests and along roadways.

By 1993, the USDA expects to receive over 200 applications for release of GEOs, including plants and animals. The U.S. regulatory system governing the release of GEOs is modeled after the same controls that apply to the chemical industry. Critics state that it is ineffective because it does not take into account the unique properties of microorganisms such as their ability to reproduce and mutate.

The U.S. National Institute of Science and Technology was recently established to promote the transfer of new technology from the laboratory to usage, especially in such fields as synthetic materials, biotechnology, and factory automation.

Scientists have not yet developed standard tests for genetically novel strains, similar to those used to determine whether a new chemical will cause mutations. Environmental safety is a global concern. An accidental release of GEOs could harm food crops or human health worldwide.

Developing Countries

The potentially large opportunities of advanced technologies, such as nitrogen fixation of nonleguminous crops; increased photosynthetic efficiency; pest and disease resistance; and salt, heat, and drought tolerance, have major implications for developing countries. However, for a number of reasons, biotechnological advances will likely occur only in developed countries, at least initially.

In the late 1960s, the inquiries launched by the Pearson Commission revealed that expenditures committed to research and development in Latin America, Asia, and Africa lagged far behind the outlays in the industrialized countries. Of all funds committed to research and development on a worldwide basis, less than 3 percent are expended in the developing countries. In general, the size of the indigenous scientific communities is inadequate even to identify problems. They have trouble effectively dealing with problems across the entire spectrum of natural and social sciences. They will unlikely be in a financial position to make numerous biotechnological breakthroughs.

However, biotechnological findings will likely address the food production requirements of many developing countries. In addition, biotechnological research studies will utilize, for the benefit of the entire world's food supply, the rich genetic biomass resources that are cultivated in the tropical regions and have immense potential in the agricultural sectors of many countries.

Presently, many of the developed nations of the world are racing to develop biotechnologies. Japan and Western Europe have committed themselves to developing biotechnology research centers and industries. Concerns have been raised about the impacts of biotechnology on developing countries, especially in terms of the control of their agricultural inputs.

Scientists emphasize that the U.S. should prohibit U.S. multinational corporations from conducting field tests or other procedures abroad that have been prohibited in the U.S. Further, scientific data about environmental safety must be widely shared to deter nations, especially developing ones desiring immediate short-term economic gains, from allowing unapproved testing procedures within their borders.

Political and Societal Ethics

Technologies should add to, rather than deplete, the earth's resources. They should be nonpolluting, environmentally benign, applicable to all agricultural production systems, and sparing of capital, management, and nonrenewable resources. They should result in stable food production at acceptable levels.

The sheer complexity of biotechnology, as a process which enables applications in areas such as medicine, agriculture, energy, defense, and industry, surrounds this vital field with controversies and wide-ranging debates.

Advances in genetic engineering are rearranging some institutional relationships and forging new ties between social institutions and the physical sciences. The extremely high capital investment requirements of this research coupled with the intense social implications of the control and use of the new technologies are attracting the attention of sociologists.

Our society is encountering unprecedented, deep, and continual technological changes, including those associated with biotechnology. There is a fundamental lag between the current rate of technological change and the rate of adjustment to these changes among decision-makers. While annual investment in U.S. biotechnology innovation from private, state, and federal sources totals about $5 billion, investment in expanding our knowledge of how these innovations affect the environment and public health is only one-thousandth of that figure.

Some critics oppose biotechnology because it provides what they perceive to be a radically new and dangerous method to alter life. Some opponents justify their position by claiming that the introduction of new biotechnologies will erode genetic diversity. They also fear that a genetically altered organism may become a vector for diseases which could harm natural life forms.

Within the political parties of Europe, the party known as the German Greens has a position on genetic engineering. They regard it as the final stage in a process of selling nature to commercial interests, and oppose animal experimentation and the patenting of animals and other life forms. They support terminating all animal experiments. In addition, they support the total banning of genetic engineering and biotechnology, and government promotion of biotechnology.

The biotechnology industry produces a new form of waste that can live and multiply in the environment. Because it consists of living organisms, biological waste has the potential to spread disease. Another major concern about genetic engineering is the dilemma over the potential for accelerating genomic change and destroying the ecosystem's delicate balance. Techniques of biotechnology could also transfer genetic material to organisms of different species, genera, and families, fostering the creation of new pathogenic strains or compromising the ability of humans, animals, or ecosystems to protect themselves.

Proponents of biotechnology argue that genetic engineering techniques are only improvements for established practices in medicine and agriculture. When an industry designs a new product for release into an environment where it could pose discernible risks, several hard questions need meaningful answers: What does society gain? What could society lose? What is being displaced? Does the new product meet societal needs?

FUTURE PROJECTIONS FOR BIOTECHNOLOGY

The market for bioengineered medical products is nearing $1 billion a year, but bioengineering applications have had much more difficulty in penetrating other fields. Projections are being made that in the late 1990s, this situation will change dramatically. Researchers have already developed bacteria that can protect crop plants from frost damage, new plant varieties that can grow in areas unsuited to natural strains of those same plants, and synthetic hormones that will help cattle produce more milk or beef on the same amount of feed. These, and many other developments, are projected to be in widespread use by the turn of the century.

In the early years of the next century, the first genetically engineered crops are projected to reach U.S. farmers. Some will be plant varieties that grow in regions too hot or cold or dry or saline for their natural ancestors, while others will offer better nutrition or processing advantages. One potential example is a genetically modified variety of corn that is rich in lysine and tryptophan, two nutrients found in only low levels in the corn that is now a staple for about 200 million people. Given that one-half of those people are chronically malnourished, this one variety could have tremendous nutritional implications.

Significant projections are being made that, by the year 2005, biotechnology companies will have plants available that capture their own nitrogen fertilizer from the air, resist insects and plant diseases, and yield more food per acre.

REFERENCES

Blumenthal, W. Michael. 1988. The world economy and technological change. *Foreign Affairs* 66(3):527-50.

Brown, Lester R. 1989. Reexamining the World Food Prospect. In *State of the world 1989*, ed. L. R. Brown, 41-58. New York: W. W. Norton & Company.

Cantarelli, C. and G. Lanzarini. 1989. *Biotechnology applications in beverage production*. London and New York: Elsevier Applied Science.

Cetron, Marvin and Owen Davies. 1989. *American renaissance – our life at the turn of the 21st century*. New York: St. Martin's Press.

deSousa, I. S. F., E. G. Singer, and W. L. Flinn. 1985. Sociopolitical forces and technology: critical reflections on the green revolution. In *Food, politics, and society in Latin America*, eds. J. C. Super and T. C. Wright, 228-245. Lincoln and London: University of Nebraska Press.

Evans, D. and W. Sharp. 1986. Potential applications of plant cell culture. In *Biotechnology in food processing*, eds. S. K. Harlander and T. P. Labuza, 133-43. New Jersey: Noyes Publications.

Gibbs, M. and C. Carlson, eds. 1985. *Crop productivity – research imperatives revisited*. An international conference held at Boyne Highlands Inn, October 13-18, 1985 and Airlie House, December 11-13, 1985.

Harwood, R. R., R. J. Battenfield, B. D. Knezek, and J. L. Davidson. 1985. Production systems. In *Crop productivity – research imperatives revisited*, eds. M. Gibbs and C. Carlson, 216-238. An international conference held at Boyne Highlands Inn, October 13-18, 1985 and Airlie House, December 11-13, 1985.

Hood, Lamartine F. 1988. The role of food science and technology in the food and agriculture system. *Food Technology* 42(9):131-34.

McGovern, R. Gordon. 1988. Worldwide consumer trends and the competitive position of the U.S. food industry. *Food Technology* 42(9):128-9.

Moshy, Raymond. 1986. Biotechnology: its potential impact on traditional food processing. In *Biotechnology and food processing*, eds. S. K. Harlander and T. P. Labuza, 1-14. New Jersey: Noyes Publications.

Shoemaker, Sharon. 1986. The use of enzymes for waste management in the food industry. In *Biotechnology and food processing*, eds. S. K. Harlander and T. P. Labuza, 259-69. New Jersey: Noyes Publications.

State of the U.S. food industry. *Food Engineering*, June 1989.

Tomorrow's World. 1989. *Maclean's* 102(37):36-49.

Wittwer, Sylvan H. 1983. The new agriculture: a view of the twenty-first century. In *Agriculture in the twenty-first century*, ed. J. W. Rosenblum, 337-67. New York: John Wiley & Sons.

Wittwer, Sylvan H. 1985. Crop productivity — research imperatives: a decade of change. In *Crop productivity—research imperatives revisited*, eds. M. Gibbs and C. Carlson, 1-6. An international conference held at Boyne Highlands Inn, October 13-18, 1985 and Airlie House, December 11-13, 1985.

Yermanos, D. M., M. Neushul, and R. D. MacElroy. 1983. Crops from the desert, sea, and space. In *Agriculture in the twenty-first century*, ed. J. W. Rosenblum, 144-65. New York: John Wiley & Sons.

Chapter Thirteen

Chemicals in the Food Supply

INTRODUCTION

Most foods contain hundreds to thousands of chemical components. There are about 40,000 edible plants and most contain unidentified chemical components. Given this knowledge, we have an enormous task to protect humans from a harmful food supply. On October 26, 1989 when U.S. President George Bush introduced his proposed Food Safety Plan, he said: "We have the safest food supply in the world. I'm absolutely convinced of that. And we're going to keep it that way."

The improved conditions in food preservation and production have been made possible by agricultural practices which include the use of pesticides, fungicides, growth-promoting agents, and veterinary drugs. By studying the information given in this chapter, you will be in an informed position to discuss:

- the issues involved with the use of chemicals in agricultural production and food processing;
- some of the physiological effects, in humans and other mammals, from the consumption of unintended chemicals, particularly benzene;
- the intention of the international regulations designed to both ensure and protect the world food supply.

Information given in Exhibit 13.1 classifies some of the naturally occurring toxicants, environmental contaminants, and intentional and unintentional food additives potentially found in foods that you consume on a daily basis. Partially because of these compounds, recommendations are being constantly made that you should eat a

Exhibit 13.1. Examples of Naturally Occurring Toxicants, Environmental Contaminants, and Food Additives.

Substance	Examples of Sources
Naturally Occurring Toxicants	
Allergens	Wheat gluten, cow's milk protein
Avidin	Raw egg whites
Goitrogens	Cabbage, turnips, kale, brussels sprouts, rutabaga
Oxalic Acid	Spinach, Swiss chard, beet greens, rhubarb
Tryramine	Aged cheese and wine, some chocolates, tofu, soy sauce
Environmental Contaminants	
Aflatoxin	Moldy grains, beans, peas, and peanuts
Lead	Lead-base-paint flakes, car exhaust, plants grown in contaminated soil
Mercury	Industrial pollution of water and fish
Radioactive Particles	Fall-out from nuclear plant accidents, leakages of stored or discarded radioactive materials
Pesticides, Herbicides	Fruits and vegetables
Food Additives, Intentional	
Flavoring agents: sugar, salt, herbs, sweeteners, more than 1,000 natural and artificial flavors	Beverages, breakfast cereals, snack products, desserts, candy, bakery products
Flavor enhancers: MSG (trade names: Accent, Ajinomoto, Vestin)	Oriental foods, some processed meats
Coloring agents: blue #1 and #2, green #3, red #3 and #40, yellow #5 and #6, carrot oil, dehydrated beets, caramel and other natural coloring agents	Margarine, soft drinks, fruit drinks, candy, bakery products, ice cream, orange peel, cheese, and many other products
Fortifying nutrients	Refined flour and rice, bakery products, breakfast cereals, dairy products, beverages

Exhibit 13.1 (continued)

Preservatives: BHA/BHT, salt, citric acid, gamma radiation, sulfites (sulfur dioxide), sodium nitrite, sodium benzoate, vitamins C and E	Breakfast cereals, bakery products, beverages, fruits, vegetables, bacon, sausage, ham, snack foods, salad dressings
Texure enhancers: mono- and diglycerides, alginates, agar, gelation, gums, carrageenan, lecithin, starches	Margarines, ice cream, frozen desserts, puddings, cheese spreads, gravies, bakery products

Food Additives, Unintentional

Iodine (iodide)	Milk and bakery products
Estrogen	Meats
Antibiotics	Meats
Vitamin B_{12}	Microorganisms in food

Source: Brown, Judith E. 1990. The science of human nutrition. New York: Harcourt Brace Jovanovich, Inc. Reprinted by permission of the publisher.

varied diet. For example, if you had a low thyroid condition and you ate cabbage twice daily, you could likely destroy the ability of your thyroid gland to produce an adequate amount of thyroxin for your bodily functions. You cannot avoid all the chemical compounds listed in Exhibit 13.1. Further, legal and scientific actions are being taken to ensure that they are offered to you at safe levels, assuming you have a varied diet.

Pesticides, herbicides, and fertilizers are the three major classifications of agricultural chemicals that have been accused of causing the arable lands to become "chemical soups."

PESTICIDES AND AGRICULTURAL PRODUCTION

Pests destroy about one-third of the world's food crops every year. Without the use of pesticides, world production of food would be further reduced by at least 30 percent. This would mean that the data given in Exhibit 1.5 would have to be reduced by 30 percent. Can the human population afford this reduction?

Further, insect damage can result in food which is lower in nutritional content and contaminated with natural toxicants. Without pesticides, there would be less variety, less availability, poorer quality, and higher prices.

Pesticides significantly reduce pest problems in agriculture and protect human health by eliminating disease-spreading pests. When used improperly, they are also responsible for serious environmental and health problems. Some chemicals used in pesticides have been found to cause birth defects, sterility, tumors, organ damage, and injury to the central nervous system in laboratory animals. Pesticide use in the world has caused 200,000 to 300,000 human poisonings annually; about 5 percent of these are fatal.

Commercial Pesticides

The application of commercial pesticides has several disadvantages for agricultural production. Pesticides destroy beneficial insect species along with many pest species. Natural enemies of pests are often eliminated during routine pesticide applications. When outbreaks of other pests occur because their natural biological control has been exterminated, additional pesticides can be applied to control the new pest. Treated pest populations soon evolve resistance to the pesticide or pesticides being applied. About 367 species of pests are considered resistant to pesticides.

Pesticides can have a potent effect when they invade soil and waterways. Where insecticides have been heavily applied to control agricultural pests, the malaria vector *Anopheles* mosquitoes that lived in contaminated water have evolved high levels of resistance to the insecticides. Thus, the level of insecticide has had to be increased two to three times the initial recommended dosage.

The cycle of pesticide application, destruction of beneficial species, increased environmental pollution, increased pest resistance, and increased pesticide application is continuing throughout agricultural production today. Because nonrenewable energy sources are used to manufacture pesticides, the ultimate effect on crop production and food supplies will be greater inputs of energy for pest control.

The federal government estimates that more than 250 different pesticides are used in Canada. They kill insects, fungi, microorganisms, and weeds. They help ripen produce, enable better color development in produce, and can prevent some tissue bruising from occurring.

LD_{50} Values and the HERP Index

One way to describe the short-term or acute effects of exposure to pesticides is with the LD_{50} value which may be defined as: "the dose that will kill 50 percent of the subjects, typically mice or rats, tested in a short-term trial." LD_{50} values are expressed in milligrams of poison per kilogram of the test animal's body weight. Lower LD_{50} values correspond to greater toxicity. LD_{50} values describe the toxicity of the product's active ingredient at full strength. LD_{50} values indicate the dose that will kill the average test animals; individuals, whether rodents or humans, differ in their susceptibility to poisoning.

The world-renowned biochemist, Bruce Ames, at the University of California in Berkeley, attempted to quantify and thereby compare the possible hazards from various carcinogens ingested by humans. He and his colleagues developed a measure of potency called the TD_{50}, which is the daily dose rate (mg/kg/day) required to halve the percentage of tumor-free animals by the end of a standard lifetime. The lower the dose that achieves the same number of tumors, the more potent is the carcinogen. They then used the TD_{50} to calculate an index of possible hazard by expressing each human exposure (daily lifetime dose in mg/kg/day) as a percentage of the TD_{50}. They called this percentage the Human Exposure dose/Rodent Potency dose (HERP) index. A higher HERP value indicates a greater hazard. A few arbitrarily chosen examples are shown in Exhibit 13.2.

Pesticide Labels

Each pesticide has active and inert ingredients. The latter are used to dilute or deliver the pesticide and do not have any pesticidal activity. Concerns are being expressed about the potential effects of inert ingredients on human health and the environment. Many of these compounds, e.g., aerosol propellants, are being investigated.

Pesticide labels do not list LD_{50} values, but they do indicate

Exhibit 13.2. Comparison of Selected Human Exposure X Rat Potency (HERP) Values for Various Materials.

Compound	HERP Value
Tap water (liter)	0.001
Well water (liter) contaminated with TCE, Silicon Valley	0.004
Well water (liter) contaminated with TCE, Woburn	0.0004
Swimming pool, 1 hr	0.008
Home air	0.6
Mobile home air	2.1
PCB	0.0002
EDB	0.0004
Comfrey herb tea	0.03
Brown mustard	0.07
12 oz. beer	2.8
250 mL wine	4.7
Phenobarbitol (one)	16
Formaldehyde (worker)	5.8

Source: Reprinted from Food Technology. 1989. 43(9):134-146. Copyright © by Institute of Food Technologists.

whether the chemical is highly toxic, moderately toxic, or slightly toxic. "Danger" means the pesticide is highly toxic and has an LD_{50} value of 50 or less. "Warning" means the chemical is moderately toxic and has an LD_{50} value of 50 to 500. "Caution" means the pesticide is slightly toxic and has an LD_{50} value greater than 500.

An LD_{50} value simply indicates what dose of the chemical will kill 50 percent of the test subjects. It does not mean that humans will not suffer chemical burns, organ malfunctions, or other internal injuries.

Natural Pesticides

Natural pesticides offer one alternative to the use of commercial pesticides. Organic farming can be defined as "growing produce without chemical fertilizers and pesticides on land that has been chemically free for a number of years."

Plants emit their own natural pesticides to protect against fungi, insects, and other predators. These natural pesticides, many of which are carcinogens, are present at levels 10,000 times higher than synthetic chemicals in processed foods.

A consensus is slowly evolving that there are dangers associated with the beneficial uses of chemical pesticides. An integrated approach to pest control is needed. Considerable research is needed to isolate and identify natural control agents that might replace some chemical pesticides. Some already have been identified.

Pyrethrin, which is a naturally occurring, fast-acting component of modern insecticides, is produced from the flowers of several species of chrysanthemum grown in Africa. Derivatives from the Neem tree, which is native to India, have been found to repel 123 species of insects, including pests which destroy grains during storage. Some plants commonly grown in developing countries such as sorghum and sunflowers, produce substances that act as efficient weed killers. Oil from citrus fruit peels, not harmful to humans, kills a wide range of insects.

In Sierra Leone, farmers often mix Black Sesame (*Hyptis spicigera*) and Fly's Talo (*Cassia nigrican*) with their stored cowpea crops. Chemicals produced by these two plants inhibit reproduction in Burchid beetles, the major pest of cowpeas.

Integrated Pest Management (IPM)

Integrated Pest Management (IPM) is a strategy that manages pests while considering the many factors associated with insect, plant, and animal growth. IPM does not advocate the complete elimination of pesticides; it encourages using them judiciously in combination with nonchemical control techniques such as removing plant and animal matter, using pest resistant or tolerant varieties, and incorporating biological controls that rely on natural enemies and insect attractants and repellents.

Wasps and alfalfa weevil. The use of biological control agents to control alfalfa weevil may be a reality in the state of Missouri within the next few years. Parasites contributing to alfalfa weevil control include three kinds of tiny parasitic wasps: *Bathyplectes curculionis*, *Bathyplectes anurus*, and *Microtonus aethiopoides*. Both *Bathyplectes sp.* attack larvae in early spring with *Microtonus sp.* parasitizing overwintering adult weevils and causing sterility. For each adult female weevil parasitized, 500 fewer larvae will be produced the following spring. A fungal pathogen, *Erynia sp,* also contributes to alfalfa weevil larval control in most years.

As these parasites increase in numbers, the need for chemical alfalfa weevil control will be reduced. In the northeast U.S., where these introduced parasites have been present for many years, insecticide use has been reduced by 70 percent.

Parasitic wasps will never eliminate the weevil but should reduce weevil numbers below economic threshold levels in most alfalfa levels. There will be some fields that will require spraying with insecticides, but the ultimate aim of an integrated approach to alfalfa weevil control depends on the scientific and frugal use of pesticides along with nonchemical control methods.

Extent of Pesticide Residues

Many factors influence the nature and extent of pesticide residues on crops. Sunlight, water, soil bacteria, and other physical factors are responsible for breaking down some fraction of the pesticide. These breakdown products may be biologically inactive compounds or they may be toxic chemicals. Once pesticides enter the soil, they may be further degraded or they may reach a water source. Some pesticides remain in the crop foliage and are reintroduced to the soil through postharvest farming techniques. Some pesticides persist in the environment for many years. Pesticides may be evenly distributed in the plants or they may be fractionated into various parts of the plant. When plants metabolize the pesticides, breakdown products with similar or different biological properties are formed.

HERBICIDES AND AGRICULTURAL PRODUCTION

Problems associated with the widespread use of herbicides in agricultural crops are leading to investigations of naturally occurring herbicides. For example, in the maize fields of Mexico, excessive herbicide use has resulted in the elimination of a number of indigenous plants that had been regular, vitamin-rich additions to the diet of people there.

Natural Herbicides and Allelopathy

Innovative agricultural practices in the U.S. involve using crop residues and mulches with allelochemical properties in new conservation tillage practices. Allelopathy can be defined as "chemical warfare among plants." When properly managed, the science of allelopathy may reduce or eliminate the need for some chemical herbicides and, thus, some of the hazards associated with herbicide resistance.

For example, black walnut trees produce a potent toxin, juglone, which washes into the ground with rainfall and prevents the growth of some broadleaf plants. Juglone is also toxic to insects. In the nineteenth century, farmers rubbed "juice" of the black walnut on their livestock to repel flies. These natural chemicals play a role in a plant's defense against disease, insects, and other plants. This growth-inhibiting phenomenon is known as allelopathy.

Certain plants can potentially harm each other. For example, rye deters the growth of some vegetables, and wheat straw can harm sugar beets. Rye has also been used to control weeds in no-till corn-soybean field rotations. A rye cover crop seeded the previous fall may offer a solution for soybean growers wishing to reduce their herbicide applications. Living or dead, the rye mulches release natural plant compounds into the soil to protect against weeds. While rye deters the growth of many annual weeds, including lambsquarters, it does not harm large-seeded crops such as corn and soybeans or perennials such as bindweed and Canada thistle.

Plant scientists speculate that they could breed plants for their ability to produce allelopathic compounds in the same way insect-resistant traits have been developed. It may be possible to isolate allelopathic toxins from allelopathic plants and use them as "natural herbicides." Perhaps they could be sprayed on plants or the soil's surface to remove weeds with little risk of contaminating the soil or groundwater and without leaving harmful residues for humans, livestock, and wildlife.

NATURAL FERTILIZERS

The fact that our world food supply would not exist without the use of fertilizers has been well documented. However, there is a source of fertilizer, namely human excrement, which has not received in-depth investigation.

Human excrement is a surprisingly rich source of fertilizer, but it is exploited by very few societies. The same nutrients that flow from farm to city in the form of food, i.e., nitrogen, phosphorous, and potassium that farmers purchase in chemical fertilizers, retain a large part of their value after the human digestion process. Today, in developed countries, they are treated like garbage. Specifically, they are incinerated, discarded in landfills, or dumped at sea. These procedures have been developed because of the very real public health dangers. However, the systematic recycling of human wastes for their nutrient value, if treated properly to reduce all risks from disease organisms, could lead to indirect improvements in the health of people and the environment.

In the U.K., a new process has been found which converts sewage sludge into high-quality, organic compost that can substitute for nitrate fertilizers. The process is particularly suited to developing countries. A crumbly odorless material is produced that is extremely cheap. In addition to fertilizing, it also keeps moisture in the soil, enabling different kinds of crops to grow.

This process is labor-intensive and involves several steps. The sludge is first sprayed on wheat straw. Then chicken manure is added to initiate the fermentation process. After one week, the mixture is arranged into rows and turned to increase the rate of fermentation. The sludge and straw generate heat of more than 150°F, eliminating the agents of disease. In another two weeks, the sludge is ready for the field.

Again, societal issues come into play with this option. However, as the problems of sea pollution from untreated sewage are becoming more serious and frightful to populations, (reflected in the fact that the AIDS virus can survive in sea water for up to 24 hours near public beaches), this natural fertilizer option may have additional incentives which would also make it more cost-effective.

CHEMICAL RESIDUES AND FOOD PRODUCTS

Pesticides enable seasonal fruits and vegetables to be consumed throughout the year. They are listed in Exhibit 13.1 as an environmental contaminant. As such, their residues on food products are regulated. Pesticidal substances and other toxicants occur naturally in some fruits, vegetables, and cereal grains at concentrations several thousand times higher than the dietary intake of synthetic substances. The National Academy of Sciences (NAS) has recommended adopting a "negligible risk" standard which could be applied to both commodities and processed foods.

In 1989, the U.S. National Food Processors Association (NFPA) reviewed pesticide residue data on 20,300 samples from commodities packed between 1980 and 1988. They found that 93 percent of the samples had no detectable residues. Furthermore, none of the samples in which some residue was found approached the tolerance established by the EPA. The scientists in this agency attributed these findings to a pesticide protective screen program which delineates proper pesticide control and monitoring practices for the growers who produce crops for the food industry.

Effect of Food Processes

In addition, washing, peeling, and other commercial food preparation steps such as those used during sugar refining and the refining of vegetable oils significantly reduce pesticide residues in packaged food products.

The steps taken to process foods, i.e., washing, scrubbing, blending, blanching, and heating, can significantly reduce most pesticide residue levels in processed food products. Scientists have determined that pesticide residues can be reduced by 99 percent through washing and other processing steps depending on the kind of pesticide and crop and the length of time the chemical spent in contact with the crop.

ENVIRONMENTAL CONTAMINANTS
IN HUMANS AND MAMMALS

When the adipose or fatty tissue of human cadavers in Canada was recently examined, the compounds listed in Exhibit 13.3 were identified. Findings for benzene-related compounds were particularly disturbing.

Benzene is a clear solvent derived from petroleum. Three hundred years ago, the only traces of benzene on the planet were found

Exhibit 13.3. Chemical Compounds Identified in the Adipose Tissue of Canadians.

	Selected Notes
Chromium	
Chlorinated Benzenes	
PCBs	
DDT	
Dioxins	
Furans	
Chlorinated Ethans	High-volume solvents produced for the dry cleaning industry.
Hexachlorobenzene	Pesticide used to treat seeds, no longer in use in Canada.
Oxycholorane	
Trans-nonachlor and Cis-nonachlor	Breakdown of insecticide restricted in Canada in 1985.
Heptachlor Epoxide	Product of insecticide not used in Canada since 1977.
Mirex	Never used in Canada.
Dieldrin	Strictly regulated in Canada since the 1970s.

Source: Our Fragile Earth, A Southam Environment Project, The Kamloops Daily News, Kamloops, B.C., Canada; October 7, 1989.

in the garden, specifically minute amounts in Swiss chard and spinach. Unfortunately, today benzene is found in drinking water, fish, fruits, vegetables, dairy products, eggs, and the air. In early 1990, the presence of benzene in Perrier™ caused a stir around the world and led to a massive global recall of the mineral water product by the French manufacturer.

In humans, benzene causes cancer, mostly leukemia. It also damages the central nervous system which transmits messages to and from the brain. In high enough concentrations, benzene can actually destroy human tissues. Of the benzene found in humans, about 48 mg per year for urbanites and 12 mg for rural dwellers, small amounts are stored in fat as shown in Exhibit 13.3. About 20 to 50 percent of benzene that reaches the human body is absorbed through the blood supply.

Every day in Canada alone, more than 90 tons of benzene are excreted into the air. Much of it comes from the exhaust pipes of cars, trucks, and motorcycles. As a component of gasoline, benzene helps increase the octane rating. Benzene is also an intermediary in the production of rubber, polyester, nylon fibers, and resins. Once emitted into the atmosphere, much of it is broken down into other compounds. However, some of it evaporates, eventually getting into water as well as the food chain. Benzene does not affect the ozone layer.

Synthetic PCBs have also found their way into the food chain and have been absorbed by the human body as shown in Exhibit 13.3.

Recent Research Findings

The scientific evidence about the effect of chemical exposures on humans is very incomplete. Obtaining valid research results is compounded by the fact that most chemicals have only been around since the Second World War. As a species, humans lived for thousands of years dealing only with natural toxins like poison mushrooms. In the past 50 or 60 years, a tick of the evolutionary clock, 60,000 new chemicals have been created. The entire line of pesticides was developed in the past 40 years.

The human brain contains a high concentration of fat. The central nervous system, which transmits signals from the brain, also has a high content of lipids. Thus, studies are in progress to see if these fat deposits contain harmful, fat-soluble chemicals.

A recent study in the state of Michigan compared the babies of women who consumed considerable quantities of fish from the Great Lakes with a control group that did not consume these fish. The scientists found a significant difference in the mental development of the children of females who consumed fish. One of their conclusions was that the chemicals that accumulated in the fish may have been responsible. Numerous scientific studies such as this one are now in progress.

In 1985, scientists studied children born to women who had been exposed to polychlorinated biphenyls (PCBs) that had been responsible for contaminating cooking oil in Taiwan in 1979. The children showed delayed development and abnormal behavior. Depression, agitation, and an inability to function have been linked to low-level chemical exposure.

The scientific literature also demonstrates links among some food additives, drugs, and pollutants in the air with unexpected behavioral disturbances including paranoia, hyperactivity, anxiety, and hallucinations.

Environmental Contaminants in Mammals

The Arctic is widely considered to be a sink for industrial pollutants carried north from Europe, the U.S.S.R., and North America by rivers, ocean currents, and northerly winds. Contamination levels in polar bears, whales, and plankton are currently at unprecedented levels. These toxins are accumulating in aboriginal and northern peoples who subsequently consume contaminated fish, sea mammals, and wildlife.

In 1989, an autopsy of a killer whale found at Long Beach, British Columbia revealed an extremely high mercury level. The analysis of the whale's liver indicated a mercury level of 1,272 ppm. The animal was part of a pod of about 400 whales that migrates between Campbell River on Vancouver Island and Puget Sound in Washington State. Although the killer whale's life expectancy is about the same as that of humans, this whale died at about age 15. The cause of death was an intestinal infection, suspected to be related to the high mercury levels. Scientists suspect there is a link between pollutants and the lowering of the effectiveness of immune systems in animals and humans.

High levels of mercury and other heavy metals have also been found in the St. Lawrence River between the U.S. and Canada. In the massive river system, beluga whales have died of such diseases as bronchial pneumonia, hepatitis, ulcers, and cancer.

Chemical Fingerprints

Projections have been made that individuals will eventually have "chemical fingerprints" whereby analyzing their blood can identify what geographic area they reside in. This will be particularly true for those populations that do not have an extensive resource of imported foods.

INTERNATIONAL FOOD REGULATIONS

Historically, science and the law are not synchronized. Scientists thrive on uncertainty; lawyers need conclusive evidence to achieve their goal. This situation continues to challenge the establishment of international food regulations.

In the early 1900s, infectious diseases in developed countries were still the major causes of mortality and morbidity. Scientific advances and the improvement of socioeconomic factors have reduced the incidence of infectious diseases today in developed countries. Currently, their major health concerns have shifted to chronic degenerative diseases of very complex etiologies such as cardiovascular diseases and cancer. The intentional use of food additives and the identification of environmental contaminants have lead to a concern for their chronic health effects.

The role of chemicals, both of natural and synthetic origin, is the major issue confronting regulators of the food industries in developed countries. Issues of concern involve the safety of added chemicals as well as chemical contamination. Whenever the regulatory requirements in different countries are compared, obvious national characteristics and economic needs are involved.

Since 1960, numerous international expert committees have been striving to establish rules applicable to all countries. These committees have included: the Joint FAO/WHO Committee; the European Committee for Research on the Protection of Populations Against the Risks of Long-Term Intoxication (Eurotex Committee); the International Union Against Cancer; and various committees of the European Council including the Scientific Committee for Human Nutrition of the European Communities.

A partial list of the international organizations that promote the use of, as well as the safety of, food products is given in Exhibit 13.4. All of these organizations contribute to the daily trade of food products among nations; many national organizations, such as the Institute of Food Technologists (IFT) in the U.S., also have an international component. International members, frequently alumni from domestic universities, greatly assist the international food policy actions of these national organizations.

In countries such as the U.S., Canada, Australia, many European nations, and certain others, adequate food regulations for additives have existed for many years. Because of the radical changes in food technologies, the need for the constant updating of rules, regulations, and scientific testing facilities has become apparent.

Unfortunately, many countries have yet to formulate national food policies which would appropriately respond to their health situation and their economy. In addition, when formal food policies have been established, they frequently do not respond to the true nature and/or extent of current or emerging food safety problems.

International organizations with mandates for the promotion of agriculture, food production, nutrition, and health have been asked to look into the problems of chemicals in the food supply. The Joint FAO/WHO Expert Committee on Food Additives (JECFA) (Exhibit 13.4) has provided recommendations based on scientific evidence and has established a rational model of sound national food legislation.

Many countries have instituted a national residues program to prevent, detect, and control the use and levels of agricultural chemicals that enter the food supply. The problem related to the residual appearance of pesticides in foods has an international component; a dynamic international management system has long been advocated.

Exhibit 13.4. Selected International Food-Related Organizations.

Joint FAO/WHO Expert Committee on Food Additives
Joint FAO/WHO Expert Committee on Irradiated Foods
Joint FAO/WHO Food Standards Program
Joint FAO/WHO Meeting on Pesticide Residues
Joint FAO/WHO European Committee for Research on the Protection of
    Populations Against the Risk of Long-Term Intoxication (Eurotex
    Committee)
    European Council
    International Union Against Cancer
    Scientific Committee for Human Nutrition of the European Communities
    International Project in the Field of Food Irradiation
    International Committee on Food Microbiology and Hygiene
    International Union of Microbiological Societies
    Joint FAO/WHO Meeting on Pesticide Residues
    FAO Panel of Experts on Pesticide Residues in Food and the Environment
    WHO Expert Group on Pesticide Residues
    Food Standards Program (Codex Alimentarius)
        Codex Committee on Food Additives
        Codex Committee on Pesticide Residues
International Agency on the Evaluation of the Carcinogenic Risk of Chemicals
    to Humans
International Cheese and Deli Association
International Council of Scientific Unions
International Dairy Federation
International Federation of Bee-Keepers Association
International Food Additives Council
International Food Service Executives Association
International Foodservice Distributors Association
International Foodservice Manufacturers Association
International Frozen Food Association
International Jelly and Preserve Association
International Life Sciences Institute -- Nutritional Foundation
International Maple Syrup Institute
International Olive Oil Federation
International Organization of the Flavor Industry
International Program on Chemical Safety
International Research and Development Corporation
International Research Services, Inc.
International Society of Regulatory Toxicology and Pharmacology
International Standards Organization
International Union of Pure and Applied Chemistry

Source: Middlekauff, Roger D. and P. Shubik, eds. 1989. International Food
        Regulation Handbook. New York and Basel: Marcel Dekker, Inc.

Joint WHO/FAO Food Standards Program (Codex Alimentarius)

Established in 1963, the Codex Alimentarius includes standards for food including food hygiene and food additives in an attempt to have international action prevent barriers to food trade. This organization was established in recognition of the need to protect the health of consumers, ensure fair practice in food trade, and to facilitate international trade in foods.

The Need for Regulations

Any substance can be toxic under certain exposure conditions. Risk may be defined as: "the probability that a substance will cause harm under anticipated conditions of human exposure." Unfortunately, scientists can reach different conclusions by making different assumptions when they consider the intrinsic biochemical properties and the level and duration of exposure to the chemical. This fact adds to the complexity of establishing regulations.

Much of the concern about pesticide residues focuses on chronic rather than acute toxicity since the levels of residues are extremely low. The basis for concern focuses upon long-term exposures with the inherent potential for chronic toxicities such as cancer. In some cases, pesticides reduce health risks for humans. For example, fungicides help prevent the formation of aflatoxin, a potent carcinogen, on some crops.

Children face a greater health risk from pesticides than adults because they have a greater exposure, consuming more foods per body weight than adults. They eat more fruits and, once exposed, their bodies have more time to manifest cancers. Their enzyme systems are not fully developed to give them the capabilities for detoxifying some chemicals in their bodies. The magnitude of the increased risk to children is being debated in scientific forums.

U.S. Food Regulations

In the U.S., tolerances are set by the Environmental Protection Agency (EPA) for the Acceptable Daily Intake (ADI) for each chemical, at least 100 times lower than the level at which no toxic effect has been observed in humans (Exhibit 13.5). The ADI represents how much pesticide residue can be ingested by an average person every day for a 70-year lifetime without adverse effects. The human body is capable of metabolizing and excreting small amounts of both naturally-occurring and synthetic substances which would otherwise be toxic if ingested in large amounts.

The EPA is responsible for setting tolerance levels that are fully protective of public health and the environment, and that take into account the special circumstances of vulnerable groups such as young children and pregnant women, as appropriate.

In the U.S., proposals have been made to include pesticides on food products that have a tolerance which poses a negligible risk standard. This new tolerance would apply to all pesticides posing a carcinogenic risk on both raw and processed foods. Before establishing this tolerance, EPA would consider the extent to which three factors justify exceeding the negligible risk standard:

1. impacts of the tolerance on public health;
2. economic impacts on consumers and food producers;
3. whether efforts are being made to find safer alternatives to the pesticide being investigated.

EPA develops tolerances for pesticides which are limits on the pesticide residue level permitted for a specific crop. They represent the highest measurable residue levels found when the pesticide is applied at its maximum allowable level and for the maximum number of applications. A pesticide cannot be registered for a food use without the establishment of a tolerance.

The EPA has approved 300 pesticides for food uses; 200 of these are in common use in the U.S. Surveillance sampling, the spot checking of both domestic and imported foods, uses a method that can detect more than 100 different pesticides in one sample.

Information given in Exhibit 13.6 includes information that companies submitting an application for registration of a pesticide must supply to the EPA. Note that the word "potential" is used for these criteria. The data requirements given in Exhibit 13.6 are modified as additional knowledge about potential health and environmental effects becomes available.

Exhibit 13.5. Risk Assessment Definitions of Chemical Compounds.

COMPOUNDS THAT DO NOT CAUSE CANCER:

NOEL (no observable effect level)

Determined from a series of toxicity studies, this is the highest dose level of pesticide, consumed in the daily diet per unit of body weight, at which no adverse effect is observed.

ADI (acceptable daily intake)

Calculated from the NOEL, the NOEL divided by a safety factor of 100 or greater, gives the ADI, expressed in milligrams of pesticide per kilogram of body weight per day. The safety factor is based on the assumption that humans are 10 times as sensitive as the most sensitive animal tested, and some humans are 10 times as sensitive as the least susceptible human.

TMRC (theoretical maximum residue contribution)

Based on the assumption that each pesticide residue is present at the full tolerance level on all foods, for which it is approved, the sum of the TMRCs for all food forms, represents the cumulative TMRC for each pesticide. When the TMRC for a proposed use, combined with the TMRC for all approved uses, is less than the ADI, the proposed new tolerance is generally approved, provided that it meets the other requirements stated in Exhibit 13.6. When the TMRC exceeds the ADI, further data and investigations are required.

CANCER-CAUSING COMPOUNDS:

Quantitative Risk Assessments

Mathematical models are used to provide upper bound estimates of human cancer risks. Estimates are based on animal bioassay data, assuming a lifetime exposure to the chemical. Judgments are made about whether a given tolerance for a specific pesticide use poses an unreasonable risk to humans. When the estimated upper bound risk is less than 1 in 1 million, tolerances are usually approved.

Source: Thonney, P.F. and C.A. Bisogni. Residues of agricultural chemicals on fruits and vegetables: pesticide use and regulatory issues. Nutrition Today Nov/Dec. 6-12. ©by Williams & Wilkins, 1989.

Exhibit 13.6. Documentation Needed for Pesticides When Applying for U.S. Registration.

Usefulness of chemicals.

Chemical and toxicological properties, including potential human health risks.

Methods of analysis for residues.

Likely distribution of the chemical in the environment after intended use.

Potential effects on wildlife, plants, and other elements in the environment, after intended use.

Source: Thonney, P.F. and C.A. Bisogni. Residues of agricultural chemicals on fruits and vegetables: pesticide use and regulatory issues. Nutrition Today Nov/Dec. 6-12. ©by Williams & Wilkins, 1989.

Establishing Tolerances

A tolerance may be defined as "the maximum level of residue allowed in or on a food at the time the crop is harvested." Before tolerances are established, the chemicals are field tested under the most extreme conditions of their usage. The tolerances are based on the worst case potential residue level for their intended use. A pesticide can have several different tolerances. For example, a pesticide could have a raw agricultural tolerance on peas, a food additive tolerance on frozen peas, and a feed additive tolerance on pea wastes used as animal feeds. Products which exceed the tolerances are considered to be adulterated and are subject to seizure.

When hydroponic vegetables, where growing occurs in water instead of soil, were found to have illegal pesticide residues, they were removed from the U.S. market.

Detection levels. Many pesticides can be detected at the level of 1 ppb. One part per billion is equivalent to four drops of water in an olympic-size swimming pool. Sophisticated technologies such as gas liquid chromatography enable scientists to measure minute residue levels. A major challenge is not to determine whether or not 1 ppb of a residue exists in food or water, but to determine if there is any biological significance to this level which could adversely affect human health. From the scientific data, scientists and statisticians describe the potential health risks and quantify the probability that consumers of the food in question would be subjected to risks described in Exhibit 13.5.

Testing reliability. The reliability of animal test data has been questioned. Animal test data must be shown to be consistent, reproducible, and adaptable for extrapolation to the human condition. If animals are to be employed as surrogates, they must be shown to be reliable in this role. Because the limit of detection of chemicals continues to decrease to at lower levels, actually detecting compounds which could not previously be identified, decisions must be continually updated related to the significance of these findings.

Role of Carcinogens

Possible chemical carcinogens are one of the greatest concerns of adding chemicals to the food supply. Certain chemicals cause cancer. Fortunately, no epidemic has yet been associated with the food supply. However, in certain developing countries, a possible connection between liver cancer and aflatoxin is being investigated.

When cancer risks are projected, the potential increase for tumor formation is based on maximum assumptions, including:

1. all crops being treated with all pesticides for which the crop has a tolerance level established;
2. the highest level residue tolerances are found on these crops;
3. human exposure to these levels occurred daily for 70 years or 25,567 days.

Because this scenario is unlikely, scientists feel justified that inherent safety levels are included in their recommendations.

Bruce Ames contends that obsessive concern with cancer-causing chemicals in foods, pesticides, and toxic wastes has produced regulatory restrictions, problems, and conflicts at EPA. Ames has claimed that government restrictions on man-made chemicals are too stringent in proportion to their risk to humans. He notes that while the U.S. public panicked during the spring of 1989 because of trace amounts of the synthetic growth regulator Alar found on apples, many fruits contain natural carcinogens in concentrations 1,000 times greater. Ames has made the following statement: "Eating vegetables and lowering fat intake will do more to reduce cancer than eliminating pollutants."

In the U.S., the Delaney Amendment of the Food Additive Law prohibits any chemicals which have been shown to cause cancer in experimental animals from entering the food supply at any level. Exceptions have occurred only when estimated risks have been considered to be insignificant. This extreme philosophy has not been enacted when other international regulations have been established. However, the Delaney Amendment has played a major role in the thinking of scientists and policymakers responsible for regulations throughout the world. Today, the Delaney Amendment represents a prohibition premised on the scientific knowledge of an era which lacked full understanding of the process and causes of concern. Scientists can now identify those chemicals which constitute significant risks of cancer.

Although not yet approved in the U.S., recommendations have been made to add a negligible risk classification to Exhibit 13.5 for carcinogenic compounds. This category would limit approval to a pesticide for use on a particular crop to compounds with a combined estimated cancer risk from residues on both raw and processed foods, not in excess of 1 in 1 million people.

Pesticide Residues on Imported Foods

Foods grown in other countries and imported to the U.S. are monitored with the same procedures as those domestic foods. Thus, tolerances include all imported commodities, both raw and agricultural crops and processed food items.

An increase in food imports over the last several years in the U.S. has prompted increased attention to pesticide residues in such foods, especially fresh produce. Note that in Canada, residues of the chemical compound, Mirex, have been found in humans even though this chemical has never been used in that country (Exhibit 13.3).

The Battelle World Agrochemical Data Bank is a computerized information system on worldwide pesticide use. This is an extremely valuable resource for the screening of imported foods. If the FDA finds problems with imported foods and suspects that they may continue, they prohibit its distribution in interstate commerce. Subsequent shipments from that country or point-of-origin may require a certificate from a qualified laboratory stating that the testing indicates no illegal residues of the pesticide.

Although banned from use in Canada, DDT sometimes enters the food chain in small amounts on foods such as Mexican tomatoes and celery produced in poorer countries where restrictions to DDT either do not apply or are not adhered to.

Toxicological Risks

The toxicological risks and likelihood of dietary exposure to individual pesticide residues varies widely. Current information on toxicological hazards, usage volume and patterns, monitoring results, and the chemical and physical characteristics of pesticides indicates little need to analyze about 40 percent of the pesticides currently subject to tolerances. When residues are found in foods, the cause is attributed to misuse, unusual weather conditions, and/or inadequate agricultural practices. Calculated dietary intakes of pesticide residues are generally less than 1 percent of the Acceptable Daily Intake (ADI) established by the WHO and the FAO.

FOOD ADDITIVES

Food additives such as the ones included in Exhibit 13.1 can be classified as either intentional or unintentional. The latter category can happen during agricultural production or food processing and food packaging operations. For example, iodine, a component of cleaning compounds in dairy plants, can be unintentionally added to milk during processing. Many countries have unique regulations about the intentional use of food additives. A few examples will be presented.

Belgium

Belgium was one of the first European countries to introduce a system of allowed food additives. Currently, regulations contained in the "positive list" are also applied to other fields such as packaging materials that come into contact with foods. In certain foods, e.g., milk, honey, and mineral water, no additives are allowed.

Israel

In addition to labelling additives with their group or specific names, Israel has a requirement for more complete designations of all additives that have any hyperallergenic properties. Sulfites are one example.

In Israel, any product labelled with the word "kosher" should also have such phrases added as: meat, dairy, for meat or dairy food, for Passover, donations and tithes set aside, free from suspicion of "orla" or fourth-year fruit, not from a Shmitta year, and so on.

France

The intrigue of French cuisine, known throughout the world, is made possible by numerous decrees, decisions, and circulars regulating the use of different additives in foodstuffs as well as materials and objects in contact with food and drink products intended for human and animal consumption. France requires that tests be completed on at least two animal species, one of which should not belong to the rodent species. Testing on both a rat and a dog would be acceptable, followed by the examination of all organs where the effect of the chemical is unknown. However, France takes the position that the tests for allergenic properties and possible effects on the immune functions have not been perfected. Therefore, these factors are not included in their regulations.

Egypt

In Egypt, imported and exported food products must comply with Codex regulations regarding the maximum residue limits of pesticides and other toxic chemicals used during production, manufacturing, and transportation.

Australia

The Australian food industry has established maximum residue limits (MRLs) which must not be exceeded in human foods, and agricultural and veterinary chemicals, including additives to animal feeds. Where possible, efforts are made to harmonize recommendations with those of the Codex Alimentarius.

European Community

Categories of food additives proposed for legislation in the EC are given in Exhibit 13.7. Those labelled with an asterisk had already been adopted by 1989; committees continue to work on others.

Within the EC, the Scientific Committee for Food is establishing general criteria for the use of food additives. Before an additive may be used in food, it has to have the appropriate toxicological testing and evaluation. Attempts are being made to take into account any cumulative, synergistic, or potentiating effects of their use. The need for the additive must be justified. Scientists are required to give technological, economic, and other advantages that can be demonstrated for the benefit of the consumer. The use of food additives in the EC will likely follow those guidelines endorsed by the FAO/WHO Codex Alimentarius given in Exhibit 13.8. The requirements appearing in the EC directives on additives must be applied to the Member States, two of which were listed above.

Exhibit 13.7. Categories of Food Additives Proposed for EC Legislation.

Color*	Sweetener
Preservative*	Raising agent
Antioxidant*	Antifoaming agent
Emulsifier*	Glazing agent
Thickener*	Flour-treatment agent
Gelling agent*	Firming agent
Stabilizer*	Humectant
Flavor enhancer	Sequestrant
Acid	Yeast nutrient
Acidity regulator	Foam stabilizer
Anticaking agent	Enzyme
Modified starch	

Source: Middlekauff, Roger D. and P. Shubik, eds. 1989. International Food Regulation Handbook. New York and Basel: Marcel Dekker, Inc.

BIOTECHNOLOGY AND CHEMICAL REDUCTION

Newer techniques in biotechnology will result in more changes in the food supply than could have been envisaged 10 years ago. To cope with the potential hazards, whether real or imagined, scientists with training in fields not previously associated with food safety will have to be involved in food regulations. In 1986, Denmark passed The Environmental and Gene Technology Act. Under these regulations, gene technology production and products must be approved in advance so that organisms produced by these means are not released until all possible risks have been evaluated. These regulations apply both to food products and food ingredients. The intent of these regulations is to ensure that gene technology is introduced without risk to the environment, nature, health, and food.

Exhibit 13.8. Guidelines for the Use of Food Additives.

The use of food additives is justified when they serve at least one of these purposes:

Preserve the nutritional quality of the food.

Produce necessary ingredients or constituents of foods processed for groups of consumers with special dietary needs.

Enhance the keeping quality or stability of a food or improve its sensory properties, provided that it does not change the nature, substance, or quality of the food.

Provide aids in manufacture, processing, preparation, treatment, packing, transport, or storage of food, provided it is not used to disguise faulty raw materials or undesirable practices of techniques.

Source: Haigh, R. and P. Deboyser. 1989. Food additives and the European Economic Community. In International Food Regulation Handbook. 507-526. R.D. Middlekauff and P. Shubik, eds. New York and Basel: Marcel Dekker, Inc.

Biotechnology entrepreneurs envision a future when genetically altered bacteria will be able to digest oil spills and toxic wastes, kill crop pests, and immunize wild animals against rabies. In the U.S., 60 million tons of hazardous chemical wastes are produced each year. These predictions about the use of bacteria could have positive economical and health consequences.

CONSUMER CONCERN

Informed consumers are concerned with such matters as pesticide and herbicide residues on produce, antibiotics in meats, and overall food quality. However, these same consumers, as homeowners, use more pesticide and chemical fertilizer per acre of lawn than farmers do on the same amount of land.

Some recommendations have been made to better inform consumers about the use of chemicals on foods. Several of these suggestions are almost scare tactics designed to reduce drastically the use of agricultural chemicals. One suggestion recommends the prominent listing of the chemicals used, along with the prices, on supermarket shelves.

Other scientists state that the problems are just too complicated to solve by sticking labels on things at the supermarket with the assumption that consumers will care or know enough to make different selections. Some consumer advocates favor a system of pollution taxes and permits to price environmentally offensive products off the market.

In the late 1980s, the Prime Minister of Canada, Brian Mulroney, promised to "empower" consumers by labelling products that were least destructive to the environment. This gives Canadian consumers an option to choose goods carrying the government's environmental seal of approval for such products as recycled plastic materials and papers used by the food industry.

SUMMARY

A clear understanding needs to be developed regarding the importance of the role of science in food regulations. Without scientific information that is valid and reliable, the regulation of the global food supply will continue to be somewhat arbitrary. Furthermore, if scientific information does not lead to effective food regulations, consumers will be continually confused and misled by governmental actions regarding those regulations.

REFERENCES

"All natural" herbicide isn't just a pipe dream. *The College of Agricultural and Life Sciences Quarterly* 8(4):1-4, 1990.

Brown, Judith E. 1990. *The science of human nutrition*. New York: Harcourt Brace Jovanovich, Inc.

Eisenberg, A. and E. Mayshar. 1989. Statutory and regulatory requirements for food in Israel. In *International food regulation handbook*, eds. R. D. Middlekauff and P. Shubik, 369-396. New York and Basel: Marcel Dekker, Inc.

El-Sebae, Abdel Khalek H. 1989. Statutory and regulatory requirements for food and beverages in Egypt. In *International food regulation handbook*, eds. R. D. Middlekauff and P. Shubik, 397-410. New York and Basel: Marcel Dekker, Inc.

Farley, Dixie. 1989. Setting safe limits on pesticide residues. *Dairy, Food and Environmental Sanitation* 9:135-137.

Haigh, R. and P. Deboyser. 1989. Food additives and the European Economic Community. In *International food regulation handbook*, eds. R. D. Middlekauff and P. Shubik, 507-526. New York and Basel: Marcel Dekker, Inc.

Jones, Edwin L. 1989. Pesticide residues. In *International food regulation handbook,* eds. R. D. Middlekauff and P. Shubik, 253-282. New York and Basel: Marcel Dekker, Inc.

LaFontaine, A. 1989. Regulations governing additives in Belgium. In *International food regulation handbook*, eds. R. D. Middlekauff and P. Shubik, 329-331. New York and Basel: Marcel Dekker, Inc.

Maga, Joseph A. 1983. Organically grown foods. In *Sustainable food systems*, ed. D. Knorr, 305-351. Westport, Conn.: AVI Publishing Company, Inc.

Middlekauff, R. D. and P. Shubik. 1989. Introduction. In *International food regulation handbook*, eds. R. D. Middlekauff and P. Shubik, 1-5. New York and Basel: Marcel Dekker, Inc.

Nguyen Phy Lich, H., H. Dutertre-Catella, and R. Truhaut. 1989. Principles applied in France for the regulation of the use of food additives. In *International food regulation handbook*, eds. R. D. Middlekauff and P. Shubik, 333-360. New York and Basel: Marcel Dekker, Inc.

Norris, B. and A. L. Black. 1989. Food administration in Australia. In *International food regulation handbook*, eds. R. D. Middlekauff and P. Shubik, 455-479. New York and Basel: Marcel Dekker, Inc.

Pelto, G. H. and P. J. Pelto. 1983. Diet and delocalization: dietary changes since 1750. In *Hunger and history*, eds. R. I. Rotberg and T. K. Rabb, 309-330. Cambridge: Cambridge University Press.

Peterson, B. and C. Chaisson. 1988. Pesticide and residues in food. *Food Technology* 42(7):59-64.

Pimental, D. and M. Pimental. 1979. *Food, energy, and society*. New York: John Wiley & Sons.

Pothisiri, P. and N. Komolsewin. 1989. Food laws, regulations, and standards in Thailand. In *International food regulation handbook*, eds. R. D. Middlekauff and P. Shubik, 411-453. New York and Basel: Marcel Dekker, Inc.

Poulsen, Emil. 1989. Food regulation in Denmark. In *International food regulation handbook*, eds. R. D. Middlekauff and P. Shubik, 361-368. New York and Basel: Marcel Dekker, Inc.

Schneeberger, Ken, ed. 1989. Farms and Centers Reporter, University of Missouri-Columbia Agricultural Experiment Station. No. 24.

Thonney, P. F. and C. A. Bisogni. 1989. Residues of agricultural chemicals on fruits and vegetables: pesticide use and regulatory issues. *Nutrition Today* Nov/Dec. 6-12.

Too much fuss about pesticides? *Consumer Reports*, October 1989. 655-658.

Wittwer, Sylvan H. 1983. The new agriculture: a view of the twenty-first century. In *Agriculture in the twenty-first century*, ed. J. W. Rosenblum, 337-67. New York: John Wiley & Sons.

Yermanos, D. M., M. Neushul, and R. D. MacElroy. 1983. Crops from the desert, sea, and space. In *Agriculture in the twenty-first century*, ed. J. W. Rosenblum, 144-65. New York: John Wiley & Sons.

Chapter Fourteen

Global Warming and Agriculture

INTRODUCTION

As this chapter is being written, scientists are still unsure about many of the issues surrounding global warming. Recently, the statement has been made that we need two more decades of data about climatic changes before we will know whether recent weather changes are, in fact, caused by global warming. However, in the meantime, you need to become aware of the possible effects of global warming. Since many of the recommendations for reducing this effect have other positive influences on the environment, i.e., reducing the level of pollution, implementing them could have a positive impact on agriculture whether or not we actually experience global warming to the extent that is being predicted. By studying information in this chapter, you will become aware of several issues:

- The concept of global warming has grave potential impacts for global agriculture as entire agricultural production areas could be altered and entire countries could disappear, further aggravating the worldwide refugee situation.
- Increasing atmospheric pollutants, especially carbon dioxide, have both positive and negative effects on the production of crops, and offer numerous areas where further research investigations are required.

Given the lack of precise knowledge about global warming, you will be exposed to predictions throughout this chapter. Some of these predictions will be conflicting ones. With your knowledge of crop production, you will be able to understand why current atmospheric pollutants, coupled with any future global warming effects, will have a drastic impact upon agriculture and our ability to cope with the global world food situation.

GLOBAL WARMING

The planet is getting warmer but no one can say how hot it will get or what, precisely, global warming will mean. There are vast differences in the temperature projections made by various computer models developed by scientists. These differences are especially important when studied in an historical context. The average temperature of the earth during the last ice age was 5 degrees cooler than it is today. Scenarios for the future vary by as much as 4 degrees. Assertions made about global warming, i.e., that average temperatures have risen 1 degree since 1899, and will rise by 3 and 6 degrees by the years 2030 and 2065, respectively, are being widely challenged.

Global warming does seem to be happening; the rate of warming is increasing as the decades pass. Although the numbers are far from firm, most scientists believe that global temperatures rose about one-quarter of a degree between 1780 and 1880, 1 degree between 1880 and 1950, and more than one-half of a degree since then. These findings agree with recent predictions made by scientists, given the amount of greenhouse gases poured into the atmosphere during these time periods.

The precise direction and acceleration of this trend are unclear. At the current rate of warming, by the turn of the century the seas could theoretically rise by about 1 foot above their mean level in 1980. However, an increase of several inches is more likely. By 2050, the earth will be anywhere from 1.5 degrees to 8 degrees warmer. This forecast is very broad and imprecise because many of the factors that shape such estimates are still impossible to forecast. If the higher temperature occurs by 2050, the oceans will wash over much of the U.S. coastline. In the southern state of Louisiana, land is currently being lost to the Gulf of Mexico at a rate of one acre every sixteen minutes.

The theory behind the greenhouse effect is well established. Carbon dioxide, nitrogen oxide, methane, the chlorofluorocarbons used in aerosol cans, and a few other gases absorb heat from the sun and hold this heat in the atmosphere. At the same time that this is occurring, trees are being destroyed throughout the world. Trees naturally absorb carbon dioxide. With fewer trees, the planet's ability to cope with this pollution is reduced. The combination of more gas with less opportunity to get rid of it causes the earth to become warmer. When the planet becomes warm enough, local climates will change dramatically throughout the world.

The concept of global warming poses the biggest universal threat to the planet. The accumulation of gases in the atmosphere threatens to warm the planet with catastrophic consequences. The 4.5 to 5.5 billion tons of carbon released into the atmosphere each year by cars, factories, and power plants come mainly from developed countries. Increasingly, socialist countries such as China are being investigated for their contributions.

Some scientists assert that the computer models used to predict the greenhouse effect are so weak that they cannot even account for the modest warming that has occurred over the past 100 years. Scientists understand the physics of the greenhouse effect in that they know it can occur. However, they disagree about the timing, as well as the magnitude, of changes. A complicating research issue is that they cannot determine its precise geographic distribution.

Recommendations being made to react to global warming include building dikes and sea walls to keep the oceans from reaching low-lying urban and agricultural areas, establishing more refugee camps in anticipation of mass movements of people, developing drought-resistant crops, and establishing economical irrigation systems that use more sea water without contributing to the salinity problem in soils. Proponents of these actions state that we cannot afford to wait until the effects of global warming are upon us.

These and other precautions are being recommended by scientists, social scientists, and environmentalists who have grim visions of the future. Their images are dark, forlorn, and surprisingly familiar. To illustrate their fears, they stress the television images that we are becoming familiar with, i.e., the faces of the starving in the Sudan, the homeless in Bangladesh after extensive flooding, and the dead bodies from the 1988 killer heat wave in China and Greece.

When the severe drought of 1988 left crops parched and dying throughout much of the U.S., projections about global warming were frequently made by the media. The six warmest years in recorded history occurred in the 1980s; 1988 being the warmest year. During that period, it seemed that all the pollution that cars and industry had spewed into the atmosphere for the last century had warmed the earth beyond its ability to adapt. These near-desert conditions could be the North America of the future, but not by the year 2000.

Although the pollution responsible for planetary warming is undeniably a global problem, the U.S. bears a disproportionately large part of the responsibility. American cars and industry emit nearly one-fourth of the carbon dioxide produced in the world each year, and significant fractions of the other greenhouse gases. Some scientists feel that changing this situation could delay catastrophic changes in the world's climate for many years.

Climate Changes

With projected warmings of the climate, areas of the world that are likely to experience higher temperatures and lower rainfall include some of the earth's key food-producing regions, such as the middle of North America. Rising temperatures could transform Canada's north and lead to massive droughts on the Prairies. If the frequency of dry hot summers increases in Canada and the U.S., even the event of a mild drought would cause world food prices to soar. A severe drought could cause a global food emergency.

Furthermore, hurricanes might destroy heavily populated areas more frequently. Scientists are still very uncertain about how quickly the warming will progress and what its impact on production will be.

Obviously, climatic changes will affect both urban and rural areas. Washington, D.C. normally has 14 days of temperatures over 100°F, annually. According to some projections, it is possible that this area will have 96 days of temperatures over 100°F by the year 2010. With this latter projection, the use of air conditioners could increase, thereby increasing some of the atmospheric pollutants which affect agricultural crops.

Crop land might wither and become infertile in the U.S., considered to be the breadbasket of the world. Projections have been made that the entire climate will move north 500 miles. The central U.S. will become hotter and drier, bringing semitropical weather to the central plain states of Kansas and Nebraska and destroying much of American agriculture as it is known today.

Changing Sea Levels

More than one-third of the world's population lives within 1 meter of sea level. If rising temperatures cause the two polar ice caps to begin melting, the oceans will be raised enough to inundate much of the coastal U.S. However, the ten countries which are most vulnerable to a rise in sea levels are given in Exhibit 14.1. Most of them have large populations and per capita incomes that hardly justify taking any expensive advance measures, such as sea walls, to prevent their destruction.

As ice caps melt and the seas expand, scientists expect the ocean will rise at least a meter over the next century. If the two polar ice caps melt and sea levels rise, as some scientists are predicting, salt water could cover land where one-third of the world's population now lives including places like Bangladesh (Exhibit 14.1). Furthermore, rising sea levels could change boundaries between nations and alter the shape and importance of international waterways used for food transportation.

Rising sea levels could drown out low-lying lands including up to 15 percent of Egypt's arable land, and western Canadian suburbs and agricultural areas such as Richmond, B.C., near the mouth of the Fraser River, over the next century. The Maldives, in the Indian Ocean, would disappear. Rising sea levels would displace millions of people in the delta regions of the Nile and Ganges rivers, in Egypt and India, respectively. These and other projections are based on the fact that water levels could rise by 30 feet.

Even without the onset of global warming, flooding of agricultural lands around the world is becoming an increasing concern. For example, the area subject to annual flooding in India expanded from 47 million acres in 1960 to 124 million acres in 1984, an area larger than the U.S. western state of California.

Exhibit 14.1. Ten Countries Most Vulnerable to Sea Level Rise.

Countries	Population	Per Capita Income
	(million)	(dollars)
Bangladesh	114.7	160
Egypt	54.8	710
The Gambia	0.8	220
Indonesia	184.6	450
Maldives	0.2	300
Mozambique	15.2	150
Pakistan	110.4	350
Senegal	5.2	510
Surinam	0.4	2,360
Thailand	55.6	840

Source: Reprinted from STATE OF THE WORLD 1990, A Worldwatch
Institute Report on Progress Toward a Sustainable
Society, Project Director: Lester R. Brown. By
permission of W. W. Norton & Company, Inc.
Copyright (c) 1990 by Worldwatch Institute.

ATMOSPHERIC POLLUTANTS

Agricultural practices contribute a number of gases that can affect the atmosphere, including nitrogen, ammonia, and methane. The emission of nitrogen compounds may affect climate and stratospheric ozone contents on a global scale, and lakes and forests on both a local and regional scale.

Chemicals are transported from sources primarily through atmospheric processes and are deposited on agricultural ecosystems. Chemicals can be released into surface or ground waters and arrive in agroecosystems through irrigation waters. These chemicals may enter the plant system directly from the atmosphere through the leaves or through the soil by way of the root systems.

Crops in different regions of the world may respond to pollutants in different manners. Sulfur gasses may either be a beneficial nutrient or a toxic disaster. The effects of acid rain can only be observed over decades. A complicating factor is that air pollutants interact with man-made and environmental stresses such as drought and biological stresses.

Nitrous oxide is produced in agroecosystems as a result of microbial denitrification of nitrate under relatively anaerobic conditions. The increased use of fertilizers has led to greater nitrous oxide losses into the atmosphere. The process of denitrification is being increased by the increased use of ammonia fertilizers and the increased production of legume crops as well as atmospheric depositions.

Ammonia volatilization losses are emitted from fresh manures. Significant volatilization also occurs when aqueous ammonia fertilizer is applied to neutral or alkaline soils. Both the clearing of forested lands and the burning of vegetation results in large losses of nitrogen, especially in tropical forests where many of the nutrients are found in the above-ground biomass.

Research is needed to seek means of alleviating the sensitivity of agricultural crops to atmospheric pollutants such as sulfur and nitrogen compounds, ozone, carbon monoxide, methane, and acid deposition. An important issue is to determine the combined and synergistic effects of multiple pollutants. Some progress is being made in identifying chemicals that reduce the damage in plants. The application of these chemicals in fertilizers requires further investigation.

Carbon Dioxide

Deforestation and burning of fossil fuels around the world have spewed at least 19 billion tons of carbon dioxide into the atmosphere. The carbon dioxide concentration in the air has risen 25 percent since 1850. It is expected to more than double by the middle of the next century if the global use of oil, gas, and coal is not drastically curtailed. Every litre of gasoline used in automobiles sends 0.7 kilograms of carbon or 2.2 kilograms of carbon dioxide down the tailpipe and into the atmosphere. Information in Exhibit 14.2 gives global carbon emissions and goals for their reductions in the next 20 years.

There are other natural causes for the release of carbon dioxide into the atmosphere. American drivers burn about 100 billion gallons of gasoline each year. Even if our total industrial carbon dioxide production or pollution could be stopped tomorrow, the level of carbon dioxide in the atmosphere would continue to rise. One reason is that forest fires would continue to liberate the vast stores of carbon tied up in trees.

Until China has effective policies about the environment, including reducing their reliance on high sulphur coal reserves, efforts being made to reduce atmospheric levels of carbon dioxide by other nations in the world will be largely wasted. Some experts say that even if North America, Europe, and the U.S.S.R. were able to

Exhibit 14.2 Global Carbon Emissions, 1988, and Goals for 2000 and 2010.

Area	1988 Carbon (million tons)	1988 Per Capita (tons)	2000 Carbon (million tons)	2000 Per Capita (tons)	2010 Carbon (million tons)	2010 Per Capita (tons)
North America	1,379	5.07	897	3.03	662	2.13
Soviet Union and Eastern Europe	1,428	3.55	964	2.23	872	1.91
Oceania	336	2.27	284	1.79	270	1.65
Latin America	910	2.09	803	1.46	764	1.18
Western Europe	774	2.03	699	1.79	664	1.67
Middle East	187	1.14	187	0.83	217	0.74
Africa	534	0.86	646	0.73	749	0.64
Centrally Planned Asia	774	0.66	932	0.69	1,082	0.73
Far East Asia	833	0.55	998	0.52	1,158	0.52
World	7,319	1.42	6,435	1.03	6,438	0.93

dramatically reduce coal emissions, a major contributor to global warming, the predicted growth in China's use of coal would counter their efforts on a global scale. Modernizing factories in Eastern Europe, thereby reducing pollution levels, is a high priority item as they adopt free market systems.

Scientists are not sure what happens to about one-half of the carbon dioxide that humans produce every year by burning fossil fuels. Carbon is a primary cause of the greenhouse effect. Scientists know that 50 percent of this carbon dioxide goes into the atmosphere. They believe the other 50 percent ends up in the oceans but they are unsure of its actions there.

Carbon Dioxide and Crop Production

The rising levels of carbon dioxide may have both negative and positive effects on food production. Increased levels of carbon dioxide can have favorable effects on the yield of crops. Virtually all crops respond favorably to levels of carbon dioxide higher than the normal current atmospheric level of 340 ppm.

Scientists have extensively reviewed the direct effects of elevated levels of atmospheric carbon dioxide on plants. Their findings indicate a potential for improved photosynthesis and product yield; greater biological nitrogen fixation and mycorrhizal activity; enhanced water efficiency usage; greater resilience to stresses of water, light, and temperature; and increased protection against air pollutants.

Carbon dioxide concentration could double over the next 100 years, based on current projected fossil fuel uses. A doubling of carbon dioxide could increase plant biomass and seed yield of some C3 crops by more than 30 percent.

Although the direct effect of rising carbon dioxide levels will be to increase photosynthesis and crop productivity, there is some uncertainty among scientists about the other environmental consequences of continued increases in atmospheric carbon dioxide. There is general agreement that this trend will lead to an increase in air and sea-surface temperatures and a change in rainfall patterns.

Positive carbon dioxide effects include:

1. larger plants and plant parts;
2. increased leaf turgor;
3. decreased stomatal conductance;
4. decreased transpirational flux density;
5. increased storage of carbohydrates in the leaf.

Plant scientists have shown that increased growth and yield occurs even when nutrients are supplied at levels below normal.

Increasing the carbon dioxide concentration around the globe induces partial stomatal closure and may alleviate the negative impact of other environmental constraints, i.e., ozone or high vapor pressure deficits. Lower stomatal conductances may help alleviate the effects of climatological drought. Even though these rather positive effects have been observed, several additional questions need further investigation.

Several of these unknown situations are asked in Exhibit 14.3.

Exhibit 14.3. Areas that Require Further Investigation as the Levels of Atmospheric Carbon Dioxide Increase.

1. Can plant breeding increase the harvest indexes beyond those presently expected using increased levels of carbon dioxide?

2. Will preferential stimulation of C3 plants encourage better competition, production and survival of legumes in grass-legume mixtures, ie. pastures and range lands?

3. Will forage quality be affected by increased levels of carbon dioxide?

4. Will insect and/or disease infestation be enhanced or reduced?

5. Will soil organic matter and litter be increased and thus improve soil properties?

Source: Davidson, J.M., A.D. Hanson and D.R. Nielsen. 1985. Environmental constraints. In Crop productivity - research imperatives revisited. Gibbs, M. and C. Carlson, eds. 196-215. An international conference held at Boyne Highlands Inn, October 13-18, 1985 and Airlee House, December 11-13, 1985.

Once these questions have been answered, the reasons why the effects occur will have to be established. Scientists are working on many projects in these areas; new information is being introduced at a rapid rate.

Possible interactions of increasing carbon dioxide levels with other components of the agricultural production system and other environmental constraints need to be studied. For example, what happens if two chemicals, in addition to carbon dioxide, are all found in the atmosphere in increasing levels, and all three of them are able to enter the plants at increasing rates? What is the combined effect of their actions? What happens when one or more of the chemicals is reduced or prevented from entering the plant? Which of the chemicals has the most disastrous effect upon the questions asked in Exhibit 14.3?

Research efforts will address these and numerous other issues. In summary, the long-term consequences of an increasing carbon dioxide concentration on agroecosystems on a global basis needs to be assessed.

Production of Trees

A small, symbolically important step towards reducing the effect of the carbon dioxide in the atmosphere would be to halt deforestation of ancient forests in the Pacific Northwest of the U.S. and Canada, including Alaska. The U.S. spends $40 million each year for building logging roads and subsidizing the logging industry. These actions financially support the destruction of virgin forests on public lands. If the U.S. protected these old growth woodlands, the nation could have more credibility when asking tropical nations to stop the cutting of their rain forests.

Planting an extra 120 million hectares of trees, representing about 46.6 million acres or 463,000 square miles, would clear the atmosphere of about 15 percent of the carbon dioxide produced in the world each year. Planting trees on commercial and residential properties could save the U.S. enough energy, used for either heating or cooling these properties, to reduce atmospheric carbon pollution by 18 million tons a year.

The carbon dioxide would be released again when the trees died and decayed or were burned, but the delay would provide some time in which to develop other methods of coping with this problem. Some farming methods which employ trees and crops are being investigated.

Methane

Methane is the second largest volume of gas associated with global warming. Scientists are not sure where all of it is coming from. Jokes are being made about the "flatulent cow hypothesis" and modern agricultural methods are being blamed. Increases in the emissions of nitrous oxide and methane may lead to a global warming as drastic as that predicted from increased carbon dioxide concentrations in the atmosphere.

The production of paddy rice contributes methane to the atmosphere. Methane is one of the end-products of the decomposition processes prevailing in paddy rice fields. In Australia, the large termite mounds located above the ground directly contribute methane gas to the atmosphere.

The emission of gaseous compounds from agricultural practices is of concern on a local and global scale. There is a need to continually monitor the quality of the atmosphere and to develop quantitative estimates of gaseous emissions.

Ozone

Ozone is both an essential component of the earth's stratosphere and a natural component of the earth's troposphere. Through photochemical reactions involving nitrous oxide and hydrocarbons, ozone is produced as a direct result of human activities. Because ozone can be distributed for long distances in the atmosphere and because there are frequently long periods of air stagnation, ozone concentrations during the growing season are sufficiently high to cause crop losses throughout the U.S. Estimates of yield reductions have been reported from almost negligible to as high as 25 percent depending upon the crop being investigated, the location of the fields, and the season.

Scientists first discovered that the ozone layer was decreasing in 1985 when satellite pictures revealed a "hole" in the ozone layer over the South Pole. The hole grows and shrinks with the seasons and the weather. The ozone hole over Antarctica has been reported as "alarmingly" large, and scientists have reported evidence that a second hole could be developing over the Arctic. It is still believed that turbulent winds will prevent the formation of a similar large bald spot over the North Pole. However, ozone levels in the high northern latitudes have been reduced by about 5 percent since 1972.

The Antarctic hole has scientists worried because it may be a warning of things to come. If the entire ozone layer were depleted, the excess energy from the sun would add 4 degrees to the global warming caused by the greenhouse effect.

In the meantime, the protective layer that shields the earth from ultraviolet radiation is thinning. Even if all of the chemicals that damage the ozone layer were immediately banned from use around the world, the destruction would continue for at least another century. There are tons of chlorofluorocarbons and other compounds already in the atmosphere. They will continue to react for at least decades and maybe centuries. The ozone hole above the Antarctic cannot get much deeper, so some scientists fear it will spread outward, encompassing larger areas of Argentina, Brazil, New Zealand, and Uruguay.

Ozone is one of the most damaging anthropogenic chemicals to agroecosystems in the U.S. and Canada. Because it is an important problem in all industrialized countries, projections have been made that it will become a global problem as less developed countries become more industrialized.

Ozone and Crop Production

Ozone affects crops and crop systems in several ways. First, the stomatal functions may be directly affected. Second, plant cell membranes and a number of other cellular processes are affected. Third, the level of photosynthesis is reduced and partitioning favors vegetative growth of the top over the root or reproductive growth.

The actual plant response to ozone is affected by both abiotic and biotic stresses. One protective measure exhibited by some plants is stomatal closure. In addition, some pesticides can protect plants from ozone damage. One complicating factor known by researchers who are attempting to minimize ozone plant damage is that species and cultivars have different levels of known sensitivities to ozone levels.

Ozone pollution, largely from auto emissions, reduces crop yields from 5 to 10 percent, in effect making farmers subsidizers of the people or commuters who are driving the automobiles. Yields of some soybeans are reduced by the increased ultraviolet radiation associated with stratospheric ozone depletion. Ground level ozone from fossil fuel burning is reducing the U.S. corn, wheat, soybean, and peanut harvests by at least 5 percent. Reducing the levels of ground-level ozone by even one-half would reduce these crop losses by about $5 billion.

Ultraviolet Radiation

Life can survive on earth because it is shielded from the sun's ultraviolet light. The shield is the ozone layer located 10 to 30 miles above the planet's surface. Ozone is an unstable molecule consisting of three oxygen atoms, and it absorbs ultraviolet light. The small amount of ultraviolet light that penetrates the ozone layer is enough to cause sunburn, cataracts, and skin cancer. If the layer were to disappear, major ecological disruptions would follow. Initially, land animals, including humans, would experience a plague of skin cancers induced by ultraviolet light. Life itself would survive, but probably not without a period of mass species extinctions similar to the one that apparently destroyed the dinosaurs.

Plants and animals are also sensitive to ultraviolet radiation. Aquatic ecosystems may be severely threatened by the enlarging ozone holes above the two polar regions. Single-celled organisms or phytoplankton turn the sun's energy into food. They cannot avoid the sun, and thus they cannot escape incoming ultraviolet radiation. As they are the backbone of the food chain, their destruction could have drastic effects on fish and other species. Obviously, this would have a severe effect upon the human food supply.

Chlorofluorocarbons (CFCs)

One of the causes of the depletion of the ozone layer is the use of chlorofluorocarbons (CFCs), a group of chemicals used in aerosol sprays, air conditioners, foamed plastics, and the manufacture of microchips. Food industries around the world are contributing to the use of CFCs. Every time an air conditioner leaks or the plastic box from a fast-food hamburger is broken, CFCs are released into the air. Eventually, winds carry CFCs up into the ozone layer. Once in this atmospheric zone, CFCs are no longer protected from ultraviolet light. They subsequently break down, releasing chlorine and other chemicals. By a complicated process, one molecule of chlorine released into the ozone layer can destroy as many as 100,000 molecules of ozone.

Because CFCs are also twenty thousand times more efficient than carbon dioxide at trapping heat, even tiny amounts can greatly increase the greenhouse effect. According to one estimate, about 12 percent of global warming can be traced to CFCs.

The U.S. made the first move against CFCs in 1978, when it banned their use in aerosol cans. In 1987, representatives of 46 nations met in Montreal and agreed to reduce the production of CFCs by 50 percent by 1999. Reportedly, the U.K., Netherlands, and West Germany would like to make an 85 percent reduction, and the Nordic countries have asked to ban CFCs altogether.

One obstacle to that goal is the lack of substitutes for CFCs. A few candidate chemicals are available, but most of them are far more expensive than the compounds they would replace. The chemical conglomerate DuPont expects to spend at least $1 billion in the 1990s to develop an alternative to CFCs. The worldwide market for CFCs is large and growing. Further progress on this issue will require a major international effort.

CHANGING AGRICULTURAL PRACTICES: EFFECTS ON GLOBAL WARMING

Global warming is affected by some shifts made in agricultural practices. For example, in Brazil, a shift has been made to growing sugarcane for fuel instead of other food crops. Specifically, on the gently sloping hills and flat valleys of Sao Paulo in Brazil, agricultural production is now limited to sugarcane. Formerly, these fields were used to grow coffee, soybeans, citrus trees, as well as grains. These sugar plantations produce 70 percent of Brazil's ethanol. To protect workers from the sugarcane's sharp leaves, the fields are burned before harvest. Each year, the scorched area exceeds the acreage burned in the Amazon, and may contribute to the greenhouse effect. In Australia, this problem has been solved by using automated sugarcane harvesting equipment which eliminates the need for burning, thereby saving the nutrients and the biomass for the next year's crops.

SUMMARY

Higher sea levels, more droughts, and more hurricanes are expected as the temperature of the planet rises. Primarily the result of fossil fuel consumption in the developed world, global warming could be disastrous for many of the developing countries.

Scientists are still studying the greenhouse threat and are debating the seriousness of the problem. Obviously, initiating strong actions or steps to prevent the severity of the greenhouse effect will cause severe economic dislocations throughout the world. The UN is sponsoring a major study that could provide the basis for a coordinated international approach to global warming. Waiting for the absolute certainty about global warming is projected to produce many years of policy paralysis throughout the world.

Today, poor land use and encroaching deserts are the major reasons people are forced to abandon their homes, but that is expected to change as global warming occurs. Deforestation in Haiti and drought in Africa have prompted large cross-border refugee movements. Mass migrations will likely result if rapid population growth outstrips world food and energy resources.

Food scarcity could emerge as the most profound and immediate consequence of global warming, responding to the environmental degradation effects which could include tremendous levels of deforestation, soil erosion, air pollution, and acid rain in addition to the projected climatic effects.

Part of the sociological problem of dealing with issues such as global warming and ozone depletion is that life in areas that could be affected usually seems far removed from disasters. Exceptions do occur during prolonged droughts or severe weather such as hurricanes. Fortunately, so far, life has been able to return to normal. Eventually farmers get the rains they need and we are able to clean up damage caused by hurricanes. What scientists are warning is that if their projections prove to be correct, as a society we will not have the capacity to continually recover from these occurrences.

REFERENCES

Brown, Lester R. 1989. Feeding six billion. *World-Watch* 2(5):32-40.

Brown, Lester R. 1989. Reexamining the world food prospect. In *State of the world 1989*, ed. L. R. Brown, 41-58. New York: W. W. Norton & Company.

Cetron, Marvin and Owen Davies. 1989. *American renaissance – our life at the turn of the 21st century*. New York: St. Martin's Press.

Davidson, J. M., A. D. Hanson, and D. R. Nielsen. 1985. Environmental constraints. In *Crop productivity – research imperatives revisited*, eds. M. Gibbs and C. Carlson, 196-215. An international conference held at Boyne Highlands Inn, October 13-18, 1985 and Airlie House, December 11-13, 1985.

Flavin, Christopher. 1990. Slowing global warming. In *State of the world 1990*, ed. L. Starke, 17-38. New York: W. W. Norton & Company, Inc.

Jacobson, Jodi L. 1990. Holding back the sea. In *State of the world 1990*, ed. L. Starke, 79-97. New York and London: W. W. Norton & Company, Inc.

Wittwer, Sylvan H. 1983. The new agriculture: a view of the twenty-first century. In *Agriculture in the twenty-first century*, ed. J. W. Rosenblum, 337-67. New York: John Wiley & Sons.

Yermanos, D. M., M. Neushul, and R. D. MacElroy. 1983. Crops from the desert, sea, and space. In *Agriculture in the twenty-first century*, ed. J. W. Rosenblum, 144-65. New York: John Wiley & Sons.

Chapter Fifteen

World Food:
Research, Policies, and Actions

INTRODUCTION

Throughout the previous fourteen chapters, you have become aware of the severe problems and issues facing global agriculture today. You are now familiar with the complexity of the issues involved. Without a sense of hope, you could become depressed and somewhat fatalistic about the world's future food and agricultural situation. Fortunately, for the first time in human history, we are now equipped with two powerful tools which, if used effectively, offer us hope that the world food problem can be solved. These two tools are multidisciplinary agricultural research and development programs, and outstanding capabilities related to information technologies. We are capable of developing the abilities to cope; informed political actions must follow.

Information in this chapter should give you the sense of hope that is required if our global society is to succeed. By studying this information, you will be in an informed position to discuss:

- the role of physical and social scientists in multidisciplinary research programs, with inherent objectives of improving the nutritional status of a targeted population;
- the components of an effective food policy;
- examples of current and future research projects throughout the world that, coupled with the latest informational and educational technologies, will help to alleviate malnutrition and hunger.

Although the need for multidisciplinary research projects has been alluded to throughout previous chapters, this chapter will include one example of an effective one involving a single commodity, peanuts, and part of the research project conducted in the Sudan. Once you have studied this example, you should be in a good position to learn about and discuss other research projects as they come to your attention during the next decade.

Components of effective food policies will be outlined for you, also enabling you to analyze future policies as they evolve around the globe. Policies of the EC are stressed for you in this chapter because these developments will affect world agriculture and trade during the 1990s. Ten years from now, it could be developments in the U.S.S.R. that will have the biggest impact upon world food trade and policies.

All issues could not be summarized for you; key points and issues for you to think about are included. Hopefully, this information has helped you decide what your personal role will be in dealing with the world food situation. A summary of international employment opportunities is given in Appendix B.

INFORMATION EXPLOSION: THE ROLE OF SCIENTISTS

By the time children who are enrolled in kindergartens today graduate from high school, the amount of knowledge in the world will have doubled four times! The Class of 2000 will be exposed to more information in one year than their grandparents encountered throughout their lives. These graduates will have to assimilate this information and the inventions and developments resulting from it. By 2010, there will hardly be a single job in developed countries that does not require some skill in using computers and telecommunications systems. The food and agriculture section will be no exception.

No nation can prosper in the age of information and technology without being interdependent with a variety of other nations around the world. Today, the world is experiencing the age of information and telecommunications, galloping technological developments, and an increasing interdependence among nations. This is having a tremendous impact upon people living in both urban and rural areas.

For example, in China, recent government propaganda cannot completely eliminate the images of relative progress elsewhere that the people have seen for years. This has been conveyed to them by: television sets reaching over 800 million Chinese; millions of tourists; thousands of businessmen, scientists, and scholars; images and text transmitted by FAX; and by the elite population of China returning from developed countries.

To implement effective food policies, administrators must have access to valid and pertinent data. This information has to be presented in an appropriate form. Policymakers have to be able to analyze data to understand any given situation in their countries. The effects of their policies should be known before they are implemented. This fact offers challenges to both nutritionists and food scientists who are often responsible for interpreting data for submission to the policymakers. No nation can compete in the world food and agriculture market without competent scientists and engineers.

The ability to address and manage the numerous complex issues of today's agricultural production systems requires an increased understanding of the numerous interactions among plants and their growing environments and required inputs. Using recent advances in computer and sensor technology, tools are being developed for specific research purposes. They are being designed and developed through the cooperative efforts of engineers and scientists from many disciplines.

For example, the techniques of remote sensing use planes and satellites to scan the earth from altitudes of 5 to 200 miles. Soil maps and environmental maps are overlaid with a specific crop production system, giving a precise diagnosis or prognosis. The use of computers has made it possible to map the worldwide distribution of disease-transmitting insects and reservoirs of vector borne disease in nature. We are on the threshold of being in a position to predict outbreaks of insect-borne diseases and to institute control measures before the outbreaks occur.

EFFECTIVE FOOD POLICIES

A broadly based, integrated policy approach to food supply, distribution, and consumption is essential if everyone is to be assured of access to food. Previous experiences attest to the fact that such policies are not easy to implement. Three minimal components of an effective food policy are listed in Exhibit 15.1.

The food sector is complex and interacts dynamically with all other sectors of the economy. Problems arise when policies are not multidisciplinary. In many countries, agriculturists focus on production; those active in the commercial food sector, on market improvement; and physicians and nutritionists, on the clinical aspects of malnutrition. Thus, when governmental ministries are established in these nations, they are centered around these disciplines i.e., ministry of agriculture (production), ministry of health (malnutrition), and marketing board (agricultural marketing). Few governments have a ministry whose responsibility is to address all aspects of food policy.

International agencies face the same limitation. For example, FAO focuses on food production issues, and WHO on health and nutrition issues. Within the World Bank, several departments deal

Exhibit 15.1. Components of an Effective Food Policy.

---

1. Be concerned with both short and long term needs of the population.

2. Include programs to alleviate current malnutrition, such as fortifying food, providing school lunches, establishing ration shops, and distributing vitamin A capsules.

3. Include programs to increase supply and access to food and nutrition in the long term, such as research to increase crop yields, improved transportation, incentives for farmers, expanded employment and income-generating opportunities, and appropriate use of futures markets.

Source: Gittinger, J.P., J. Leslie and C. Hoisington. 1987. Food Policy Integrating Supply, Distribution, and Consumption. Baltimore: The John Hopkins University Press. "A World Bank Publication."

with food production and nutrition interventions. In spite of its commitment to a broader food policy, the World Food Council supports discipline-oriented programs.

As a direct result of these organizational structures and lack of effective organizational decision making, some aspects of food policy are ignored and policies may be developed with inherent inconsistencies. For example, agriculturists may assume nutritionists deal with food consumption issues, and nutritionists may assume someone else is responsible for monitoring economically vulnerable groups that are not yet suffering from overt malnutrition.

In many nations, food distribution and market improvement issues do not receive sufficient attention because they are not the core responsibility of any ministry. To deal with a nation's food problems, close and coordinated consultations among many diverse government ministries are needed. Effective communication among departments may be as important as achieving their respective missions. For example, the ministry of agriculture may be concentrating efforts on high status foods or export crops while the ministry of health would prefer that the focus be placed on increasing the production of indigenous foods consumed by the poor. Without effectively coordinated policies, the poor populations are adversely affected.

Attaining this kind of cooperation requires solid and unwavering political support from the highest level of the government. This kind of support may represent the ultimate test of a country's commitment to confront its food problems. The kinds of decision making involved may be counter to those made by the long-standing economic and bureaucratic institutions within the country.

What is the role of government and how will effective food policies be established to assist in the future? Simply stated, the role of government is to help assure a balanced, motivating regulatory environment; to negotiate reasonable and consistent health, sanitary, and safety codes across national boundaries; to provide basic research to improve the technological competitiveness of the food industry; and to assist with the development of long-term export food strategies and policies. At present, nations in Eastern Europe have the opportunity to establish new governments with all of these qualities for improving their quality of life, and thus ensuring their food security and nutritional status.

Food Policy Changes:
U.S. and the EC

The problems the world faces now and in the future are clearly ones that make close cooperation between the U.S. and Europe essential. Massive debt, growing poverty, famine, overpopulation, land erosion, and other environmental deterioration are all global problems demanding global solutions. Many are extremely threatening and some are growing more dangerous in an exponential manner.

The EC will create an entity of 322 million people with a combined GNP of $4.2 trillion. There is a great need for cooperation between the EC and the developing countries. Wars, political tension, poverty, famine, and environmental disasters are current and future problems which must be dealt with jointly.

Until 1989, Europe allowed the U.S. to shoulder most of the responsibility. The U.S. has been highly active in helping many developing countries and has also felt free to intervene in their affairs, sometimes with less-than-perfect results. Given the desirability for Europe to accept greater responsibility toward the developing world, unification will give it the means to make a greater difference in world affairs.

More than $50 billion in annual farm subsidies and incentives in North America and Europe encourage farmers to produce more than the domestic demand. The export of their subsidized surpluses depresses international prices and undercuts foreign exchange earnings in some of the unstable agriculturally based economies of developing countries.

There is a growing movement in the U.S. Congress to reduce federal spending for farm subsidies. In spite of strong opposition from farmers, this movement is eventually projected to succeed. Large farm corporations will be able to absorb these losses. Midsized farms, already hard-pressed, may not survive the loss.

By 2000, most farm subsidies will be drastically reduced in the U.S. In part, this will be a response to the consolidation of the EC in 1992. Although individual European governments will resist, they are projected to eventually eliminate subsidies to their own farmers, a key part of their agreement to remove all trade barriers among the Common Market nations. Once those subsidies are gone, the U.S. will dismantle its own agricultural welfare system in order to gain access to the vast European market.

How well farmers survive this loss of income will depend largely on the size of their operations. The large corporations with substantial capital reserves will thrive, in part because the opening of European markets will bring greater competition for their products. Most small farms will survive because their agricultural profits are supplemented by outside incomes. Pessimistic projections are given for some mid-sized American farms, however.

Projections have been made that some of the current barriers to trade will be reduced. This will impact upon the U.S. food processing industry. As trade barriers are eliminated, local and international market competition will increase. To survive, the U.S. food industry will have to produce superior products and packaging. Desired tastes and food textures of consumers around the globe will have to be researched for the food products that are made available to them. The product prices will have to be very competitive with those from other areas, i.e., Japan and the EC. In summary, to survive on the international market, the U.S. food industry will have to offer world-class service.

FOOD SECURITY

A nation's food security is achieved when it can assure both physical and economic access to food for all of its citizens on both a short- and long-term basis. Food security may be best served by a combination of agricultural production and imports.

An analogy can be made between the nutritional status of an individual and the food sector of a society. Specifically, a person with marginally inadequate food intake cannot build up reserves of energy and other nutrients to resist a crisis. Such an individual is vulnerable to infectious disease or variations in seasonable food availability, both of which can precipitate severe malnutrition. A society in which a substantial proportion of the population receives only a marginal food intake is vulnerable to the food shortages and high prices resulting from a poor crop or an economic crisis. The result can be famine.

THE ROLE OF DEVELOPMENT

The notion of development has been consistently present in the connotations of the terms, "North" and "South." The word "development" is now permanently associated with the non-industrialized, often recently independent countries. Policymakers in the postwar period after World War II grappled with development issues framed by the experience of the colonial era and the anxieties of an increasingly polarized world.

In 1979, the Brandt Commission signaled alarm that Northern interests were imperiled by the inability of the South to better meet its needs. The 1980s saw the great debt crisis of developing countries with the coincidental circumstances of extreme drought and famine in Africa and unprecedented economic vitality and export performance in the newly industrialized countries of Asia. The Brundtland Commission warned that, in the absence of sustainable development practices, the planet would lose its life support abilities.

At the present time, the governments of the North have not yet been able to resolve and offer effective responses to these bewildering circumstances. There are a number of reasons. First, the North seems unable to show the political stamina needed for the lengthy periods of transformation in the South. Their problems are challenging and require a continuing commitment. Second, arrogance and ignorance combine to prescribe inept remedies. Technologies that are inappropriate and ineffective continue to be transferred from North to South. When they fail, the South is frequently blamed. Third, abuses of human rights, corruption, and privilege in some developing countries enable excuses for the strong reluctance to respond adequately. Fourth, a latent fear of competition from producers paying low wages deters their full cooperation. Evolving Southern economies are often denied access to Northern markets or are forced to absorb subsidized agricultural produce from the North at the expense of their own farm sector.

Other limitations to agricultural development are the paucity of roads, fertilizers, improved seeds and agro-chemical products, bank services, tools and equipment, maintenance services, storage installations, and marketing services found in developing countries. If these facilities were available, they could enable landless farmers, or those with insufficient land, to find local jobs. They would then not be obliged to move to the overcrowded towns but could remain in the countryside bringing rural areas back to life.

The World Bank has emphasized helping governments realize the objective of providing sufficient food of adequate nutritional quality for everyone. One philosophy is that economic growth will ultimately provide most households with the purchasing power needed to secure an adequate diet. However, even when national income is relatively high, special health and nutrition measures are needed for vulnerable groups.

The next revolution in agriculture should be a move to set up, or reinstate, industries in rural areas that should never have been transferred because their resources, particularly labor, come from those areas. Their markets are also contained there.

WORLD AGRICULTURAL RESEARCH

Research is the key to attaining and retaining a competitive edge in a global society. Research is needed for many of the multidisciplinary problems associated with food production, processing, distribution, marketing, and consumption. In most countries, research activities have centered around food production. For example, in the U.S. only 15 percent of public funds spent on agricultural research and development is devoted to postharvest programs. In 1984, the U.S. food industry only spent 0.4 percent of sales on research and development.

The eighteen areas listed in Exhibit 15.2 represent many experts' opinions of the future agricultural situation in the U.S. Since they were presented in 1983, many of these developments have occurred or are being intensified. The implementation of others will require considerable scientific research including, but not limited to, biotechnology.

Biotechnology, the communication revolution, and automation

Exhibit 15.2.　Recent and Projected Developments in U.S. Agriculture.

---

1. Appropriate mechanization.
2. Improved crop varieties.
3. Increased productivity of land and labor.
4. Genetically engineered vaccines for disease control in livestock.
5. Highly potent pesticides.
6. Monoclonal antibodies.
7. Growth hormones.
8. Interferons for improved performance and health.
9. Explants from super-plant selections, clonally propagated by new techniques for culturing tissue.
10. More fertilizers and pesticides of natural and synthetic origin will be used more efficiently and scientifically.
11. More cultivated land will be irrigated with greater efficiency of water use and with increased supplemental applications in subhumid crop production areas.
12. Conservation tillage and drip irrigation.
13. Improved water management, including irrigation and drainage.
14. Production practices, management procedures, and genetic improvements for both crops and animals making them more climate adaptable.
15. Expanded use of plastics as soil mulches and for covers in protected cultivation.
16. Computerization of essential farm operations.
17. Computers at the farm level being used for: management decisions, improved communications, and instrumentation control.
18. The resource base will change with time and technology.

Source:　Wittwer, Sylvan H.　1983.　The new agriculture: a view of the twenty-first century.　In <u>Agriculture in the twenty-first century</u>. ed. J.W. Rosenblum 337-67. New York: John Wiley and Sons.

are new dimensions of crop productivity in the 1990s. Biotechnological possibilities include creating plants which will synthesize their own pesticides, and creating genetically engineered microorganisms for soil treatments. The latter could control pests in the soil or could be sprayed on plants to achieve greater resistance to environmental stresses.

Knowledge is needed in interorgan communication where knowledge in crops lags far behind that for similar processes in animals. Knowledge to bridge these gaps is crucial for controlling growth and development; root, tuber, seed and fruit production; water requirements; stress resistance; crop maturity; and senescence.

The future success of U.S. agriculture will become increasingly dependent on the interaction between U.S. scientists and institutions and those in other nations. Nations receiving technical aid from the U.S. are often the primary source of food products imported from the U.S. These countries are rich in germ plasm resources essential for future biotechnological efforts for agricultural development.

The U.S. may be falling behind in the very area it has long dominated, i.e., basic scientific research. Today, basic research accounts for only one-eighth of total U.S. research and development funding, totalling $125 billion. For the first time since World War II, the U.S. is spending less than one-half of the world's research outlays. Japan now spends 25 percent of all research money, twice what it spent just 10 years ago. Although these data are given for the totality of U.S. industries, similar trends have been reported for the food and agricultural industries.

International Agricultural Research Centers (IARCs)

In 1985, funds for international agriculture research totalled $200 million at all of the International Agricultural Research Centers (IARCs). National agricultural research centers have taken on a new prominence in China with an Academy of Agricultural Science in every province. India has 36 agricultural research institutes and 22 agricultural universities. In the U.S.S.R., Academies of Agricultural Sciences in the various republics include both research and advanced training responsibilities. In recent years, countries such as Indonesia, Brazil, Mexico, Japan, and Thailand have greatly improved their national agricultural research capabilities. In a host of nations, including the U.S., there have been major shifts in research funding from publicly- to privately-supported programs.

Numerous recommendations have been made to broaden the missions of the IARCs to include both crop production and utilization. Intense scientific exchanges, rather than technology transfers, should help to characterize major scientific interactions among developed and developing nations.

Role of Automation

Researchers at numerous universities and companies are developing farm robots to do everything from harvesting tomatoes to milking cows. Agriculture needs the cost savings that automation enables. While the direct labor content of manufactured products can be as little as 5 percent of the selling price, labor represents a much greater portion of the price of farm produce. For example, 30 percent of what you pay for an apple can be attributed to the cost of picking it.

Researchers have termed farm automation "agrimation." They envision a day when, even during the night, "agribots" will move among an orchard's trees picking fruit at just the optimal stage of ripeness. In Florida, human workers hired at harvest time gather about one thousand oranges an hour for 6 to 8 hours per day. Robots could work the citrus groves 24 hours per day. Currently, experimental machines with only one picking arm are about as productive as one two-armed person. Robots ultimately could have more than two arms.

Multidisciplinary Research

The following example illustrates how a multidisciplinary research study can be effective and meet their established goals. Activities will be briefly highlighted along with some of the results.

Peanut Research Program: An Example

A peanut Collaborative Research Support Program was initiated in 1980. The technical advisory committee was assembled to represent global peanut research interests. Members came from:

1. USDA and land grant university plant, food, and social science departments;
2. The International Crop Research Institute for the Semi-Arid Tropics (ICRISAT);
3. The African Groundnut Council;
4. The Institute of Research for Oils and Oilseeds (IRHO);
5. Latin American and Caribbean research organizations;

6. The World Bank;
7. The U.S. Peanut Council.

Fact-finding trips were made to international peanut meetings and research sites in peanut-producing countries. Scientists from 20 countries were interviewed. Some of the production constraints for the efficient production of peanuts were identified as: high labor demands for planting and weeding, high costs for seeds, inhibited planting until sufficient rains occur, and drought-related risks. Researchers concluded that more focused farming systems and market price-policy analysis appeared to be needed in order to understand peanut production and their domestic market potential.

Why peanuts? They are an important foreign-exchange earner and are a source of vegetable oil. More information was needed about their consumption patterns in order to assess their market potential. The initial team concluded that all socioeconomic groups ate peanuts, but in very small quantities.

After these preliminary findings, research projects were initiated in several areas:

1. advanced line, variety testing, and cultural practices;
2. breeding and cultural practices;
3. mycotoxin management;
4. weeds, insects, diseases, and nematode control;
5. food technology;
6. physiology and soil microbiology;
7. socioeconomics.

Sudan was one of the countries chosen for intensive multidisciplinary study. The objective of the peanut project in this country was to determine the role of peanuts in the diet and food budgets of Sudanese households and to explore the potential for improved or new peanut products and increased consumption.

Two research instruments were required to meet the research objectives:

1. to estimate demand for various peanut products, both in producing areas and in urban markets stratified by income levels;
2. to evaluate the role of peanuts in food security at the farm level vis-à-vis postharvest peanut storage, handling, utilization, marketing practices, and aflatoxin contamination levels.

Multidisciplinary data collection. The following data were collected about peanuts and foreign exchange in Sudan:

1. From 1974-1978, peanuts represented 16 percent of the foreign-exchange earnings.
2. In 1976, the peanut export volume peaked at 280,000 tons.
3. In 1977, Sudanese peanut production peaked at 1.027 million metric tons.
4. From 1979-1983, peanut exports dropped to less than 7 percent of the foreign-exchange earnings.
5. From 1980-1981, peanut exports amounted to 80,000 tons. This corresponded with a drought in the U.S. which reduced peanut production by one-third and U.S. imports increased more than tenfold to 3.6 million pounds. In this year, Sudan's share of U.S. imports rose from 2.4 to 8 percent and then returned to 2.6 percent the following year.
6. In 1980-1982, Sudan's farm prices were 50 percent below world price and one-sixth of the quota price of 27.5 cents per pound received by U.S. farmers.
7. During 1982 and 1983, the increased domestic demand, poor growing conditions, and aflatoxin contamination problems resulted in declining exports.
8. During 1984 and 1985, Sudan had no exports of peanuts.

The domestic demand for peanut oil for cooking was increased by population growth and the diversion of all of the cottonseed oil to the domestic soap industry. Peanut cake production increased as a by-product of the oil industry, but its export market faltered when aflatoxin detections proved excessive for European livestock feed markets. Peanut exports were curtailed by aflatoxin restrictions in the EC. Furthermore, drought in western Sudan reduced peanut production in favor of more drought-resistant food and export crops such as sesame, sorghum, millet, rosette, and gum arabic.

Labor shifted from rain-fed agriculture to more drought-tolerant crops in western Sudan, to irrigated schemes in central Sudan and to labor markets in Saudi Arabia and other Middle Eastern countries. The area planted in peanuts had decreased from 2.47 million acres in 1977 to less than .95 million acres in 1984.

After obtaining these facts, the researchers concluded that peanut production and prices in Sudan would depend increasingly upon growth in domestic demand and decreasingly upon their exports. They concluded that a comparative advantage for peanut production for the world market probably existed given that rainfall returned to normal in the rain-fed peanut-producing areas, trade and foreign exchange policies continue to encourage exports, and the area's labor supply stabilized. Given good conditions, Sudan could probably expand trade to China, Japan, Saudi Arabia, Egypt, and other peanut and peanut-oil markets.

In the domestic market, Sudan depended heavily upon the peanut as a source of dietary oils and calories. For 1979-1981, FAO indicated per capita availability of 2,291 calories per day in Sudan. There is a considerable caloric inequality in Sudan, one of Africa's largest and most climatically diverse countries. Egypt, Uganda, and Central African Republic had a per capita availability of 3,174, 1,691, and 2,079 calories per day, respectively. Central Sudan's supplies may have been within 500 calories of Egypt, but in the western and southern regions, availability was closer to the 2,000 calories of its neighbors.

In 1979-1981, 43 percent of Sudan's fat supply and 12 percent of its food energy came from peanuts and peanut products. Of Sudan's 2,291 calories consumed per capita each day, 220 came from peanut oil, and 55 from peanuts. In 1983 and 1984, their per capita calorie supplies were dramatically dropped in response to the low peanut yields.

When groundnut cakes were made, they were found to be prolific mediums for *Aspergillis flavus* and mycotoxin by-products, including B1 aflatoxin. Therefore, recommendations were made that, when these peanut products were designed for the export trade, the production of this toxin had to be carefully controlled. Obviously, this control was equally important for the health of the domestic population.

Multidisciplinary field surveys. Two major multidisciplinary field surveys were conducted to document purchases of raw, roasted, paste, and peanut butter in urban areas, i.e., Khartoum, according to three income classifications: low, medium, and high. In addition, surveys were performed to document the importance of peanuts as a cash crop, documenting variation in peanut cultural practices, both pre- and postharvest, that could be associated with aflatoxin contamination of farm-stored peanuts. Peanut samples for laboratory analysis were also collected from the farmers that were interviewed for the two surveys.

As was expected, high-income households purchased different peanut products than low-income households. Products with more value-added processing were generally preferred by higher-income households. Further, roasted peanuts were more likely to be purchased from street vendors and consumed as snacks, with peanut paste, butter, and oil more likely to be consumed for the home. Boiled peanuts were more frequently purchased in rural peanut-producing areas. Since peanut butter and oil were more likely to be used to complement a variety of foods, i.e., in soups, salads, cakes, candies, and on breads, higher-income households with more diverse diets were more likely to consume these products.

Survey results revealed that in Khartoum, 15 pounds of shelled or processed peanuts (excluding oil) were purchased per person per year. Elasticities of demand for peanut products were calculated according to income level and household size. These survey findings were compared with similar ones in three other countries: Jamaica, St. Vincent, and Trinidad.

These research findings should be of value to social, food, and agronomic scientists in making future research decisions about peanut production, storage, processing, and marketing. Agronomic experiments, suggested by the farm surveys of cultural practices that were conducive to aflatoxin growth, were beyond the scope of the food science projects. Together, these two type of scientists could conduct experiments to minimize this mycotoxin, which proved to be a huge barrier to the success of the international trade peanut market.

Commodity research coordinators in each country met to negotiate technical issues and research budgets for both domestic and international projects. In this manner, the participants of these multidisciplinary research efforts sought to optimize the role of peanuts in both the economy of Sudan and in the diet of its population. Their goal was to optimize the benefits achieved from one commodity, peanuts, in terms of its benefits to the country's poor population, its need for public research dollars to maximize its production, its contribution to the foreign-exchange rate, and its type of product mix which would meet more of the nutritional needs of the population.

In addition to these findings with the peanut industry, several inherently valuable events occurred during this project:

1. Students were trained in research techniques.
2. The laboratories of some scientists were equipped to perform the analyses required.
3. Research collaborations forced an exchange of ideas among many diverse scientists.
4. Methods and measurement procedures were developed, refined, and reported in accordance with international standards.
5. Improved technologies for peanut production, processing, and storage were designed and tested for use on small farms, in low-income homes, and in small cottage industries.
6. Research findings were debated and published for wider application around the world.

The end result of this multidisciplinary project, only briefly highlighted here, was that significant benefits were received from the research and development investment. If Sudan becomes the "Number One" country in northern Africa for the export of peanut products to the EC, the impetus for this achievement started with this project and the combined ideas of all the administrators and scientists involved. Further, the knowledge that was gained by the six areas listed above can be applied to other research problems with other crops. Hopefully, the research cycle of acquiring knowledge and applying results will continue.

WORLD POLICIES AND ACTIONS

A golden age of agricultural science is now at hand. Major achievements have been made in such diverse and complementary fields as: microbiology, genetics, biochemistry, physics, plant physiology, environmental stresses, intensive crop management, food science and nutrition, food engineering, and veterinary medicine, to name a few.

An optimistic vision of the future of the globe includes a world where hunger and poverty are decreased and all nations work together to clean up the oceans and the atmosphere. For this miracle to occur, it appears that a portion of the $1 trillion per year now spent on global military expenditures will have to be redirected to protect and repair the environment and support sustainable agricultural systems.

Achieving this idealistic world will require unprecedented vision and cooperation, redistribution of wealth, and effective decision making for extremely complex issues. To date, world leaders have not lived through such a situation; comprehension of its seriousness is just now beginning to be reflected in institutions and politics around the world. For example, the International Geosphere-Biosphere Program is being proposed to bring together experts in oceans, atmosphere, climate, the Arctic, the Antarctic, chemicals, population, plants, animals, bacteria, geology, geography, and dozens of other disciplines.

National committees, scientific societies, government agencies, and an informal global college of scientists are assembling the program. Each country is responsible for its own national initiative and for funding its own programs. Research activities, largely multidisciplinary, will occupy the 1990s and beyond.

An optimistic argument for the world food problem is presented in Exhibit 15.3. Although written in 1983, similar arguments are still being made today. The optimistic viewpoint points out that we should appreciate the tremendous potential opportunities that science and technology promise to deliver to society.

Today, plans are evolving to counter many environmental threats including programs to save tropical forests, roll back the deserts, bring clean water to developing countries, and stabilize popula-

Exhibit 15.3. An Optimistic Viewpoint of World Food Security.

One key aspect of every modern economy is its ability to deal quickly with newly arising problems. There will be temporary increases in food scarcity in the future, due to increases in population, political errors, war, and natural causes. Together with modern transportation systems, the organized system of agricultural research, information contained in libraries dealing with unused technologies, and economic flexibility, we can prevail against these scarcities, in a relatively rapid manner. Usually we will find ourselves to be better off than we were before the scarcity arose, because of the continually positive effects of the solutions to the vanquished problems. Such is the hope, based on the experience of the past.

Adapted from: Simon, Julian L. 1983. The effects of population on nutrition and economic well-being. In Hunger and History 215-239. Ed. Rotberg, R.I. and T.K. Rabb. Cambridge: Cambridge University Press.

tions. Unfortunately, many of these programs are crippled by lack of funds.

Projections have been made that by 2000, developed countries will have effectively joined together to create cooperative development programs for the developing world. These projections are made with the understanding that no country stands to gain anything from a world that is increasingly ravaged by war, famine, and disease. If just 10 percent of the money that the U.S. and U.S.S.R. spend on weapons was given as aid to the underdeveloped countries of the world, measurable improvements would be possible.

Developing countries may never be as prosperous as the West; we may not be able to reduce the gap between the income levels of developed and developing countries. However, a joint effort among the world's richest nations should be able to contain the gap between rich and poor nations, at least.

So far, there have been relatively few international efforts to control environmental problems, of which agricultural problems are inherent. Some efforts are being made; others should be in place by the year 2000. The Montreal Protocol to reduce CFC production was one tentative step. Another was a private environmental group's deal with Bolivia in which the organization paid off $650,000 of the nation's debt and Bolivia agreed to create a

4-million-acre tropical forest preserve. The World Wildlife Fund bought up $1 million worth of Ecuadoran debt, paying only $354,000 for it. The Fund now receives the loan payments and passes the money on to an organization in Ecuador to support national parks and wildlife preserves. Other efforts which include significant impacts for food and agriculture will be initiated throughout the 1990s.

In almost every cloud, no matter how dark it appears, there is always a silver lining. Will we ensure that this African proverb will continue to hold true?

REFERENCES

Cetron, Marvin and Owen Davies. 1989. *American renaissance – our life at the turn of the 21st century*. New York: St. Martin's Press.

Falcon, W. P., C. T. Kurien, F. Monckeberg, A. P. Okeyo, S. O. Olayide, F. Rabar, and W. Tims. 1987. The world food and hunger problem: changing perspectives and possibilities, 1974-84. In *Food policy integrating supply, distribution, and consumption*, eds. J. P. Gittinger, J. Leslie, and C. Hoisington, 15-38. Baltimore: The Johns Hopkins University Press.

Gever, J., R. Kaufman, D. Skole, and C. Vorosmarty. 1986. *Beyond oil*. Cambridge: Ballinger Publishing Company.

Gittinger, J. P., J. Leslie, and C. Hoisington. 1987. *Food policy integrating supply, distribution, and consumption*. Baltimore: The Johns Hopkins University Press.

Lee, John E. 1988. Trends in world agriculture and trade in high-value food products. *Food Technology* 42(9):119-27.

McGovern, R. Gordon. 1988. Worldwide consumer trends and the competitive position of the U.S. food industry. *Food Technology* 42(9):128-9.

Puchala, Donald J. 1989. The road to Rome: the production and distribution of food. In *Global issues in the United Nations' framework*, eds. P. Taylor and A. J. R. Groom, 177-204. New York: St. Martin's Press.

Simon, Julian L. 1983. The effects of population on nutrition and economic well-being. In *Hunger and history*, eds. R. I. Rotberg and T. K. Rabb, 215-239. Cambridge: Cambridge University Press.

Taylor, Paul. 1989. Population: coming to terms with people. In *global issues in the United Nations' framework*, eds. P. Taylor and A. J. R. Groom, 148-176. New York: St. Martin's Press.

Wanniski, Jude. 1978. *The way the world works*. New York: Basic Books, Inc.

Wheelock, G. C., H. S. Jones, B. Singh, and V. Caples. 1989. Social science and food science research in the peanut CRSP. In *The social sciences in international agricultural research*, ed. C. M. McCorkle, 175-192. Boulder and London: Lynne Reinner Publishers.

Wittwer, Sylvan H. 1985. Crop productivity—research imperatives: a decade of change. In *Crop productivity—research imperatives revisited*, eds. M. Gibbs and C. Carlson, 1-6. An international conference held at Boyne Highlands Inn, October 13-18, 1985 and Airlie House, December 11-13, 1985.

Yermanos, D. M., M. Neushul, and R. D. MacElroy. 1983. Crops from the desert, sea, and space. In *Agriculture in the twenty-first century*, ed. J. W. Rosenblum, 144-65. New York: John Wiley & Sons.

Appendix A:
FAO Country Classifications

Data in all exhibits based on the FAO Production Yearbook (1988) have classified countries and regions according to the following scheme:

CLASS I: DEVELOPED MARKET ECONOMIES

Region A—*North America:* Canada, United States.

Region B—*Western Europe:* Andorra, Austria, Belgium-Luxembourg, Denmark, Faeroe Islands, Finland, France, Federal Republic of Germany (incl. West Berlin), Gibraltar, Greece, Holy See, Iceland, Ireland, Italy, Liechtenstein, Malta, Monaco, Netherlands, Norway, Portugal (incl. Azores and Madeira), San Marino, Spain (incl. Spanish North Africa), Sweden, Switzerland, United Kingdom (incl. Channel Islands and Isle of Man), Yugoslavia.

Region C—*Oceania:* Australia, New Zealand.

Region D—*Other developed market economies:* Israel, Japan (incl. Bonin and Ryukyu Is.), South Africa.

CLASS II: DEVELOPING MARKET ECONOMIES

Region A—*Africa:* Algeria, Angola, Benin, Botswana, British Indian Ocean Territory, Burkina Faso, Burundi, Cameroon, Cape Verde, Central African Republic, Chad, Comoros, Congo, Cote d'Ivoire, Djibouti, Equatorial Guinea, Ethiopia, Gabon, Gambia, Ghana, Guinea, Guinea-Bissau, Kenya, Lesotho, Liberia, Madagascar, Malawi, Mali, Mauritania, Mauritius, Morocco, Mozambique, Namibia, Niger, Nigeria, Reunion, Rwanda, Saint Helena, Sao Tome and Principe,

Senegal, Seychelles, Sierra Leone, Somalia, Swaziland, Tanzania, Togo, Tunisia, Uganda, Western Sahara, Zaire, Zambia, Zimbabwe.

Region B—*Latin America:* Anguilla, Antigua and Barbuda, Argentina, Aruba, Bahamas, Barbados, Belize, Bolivia, Brazil, British Virgin Islands, Cayman Islands, Chile, Colombia, Costa Rica, Cuba, Dominica, Dominican Republic, Ecuador (incl. Galapagos Islands), El Salvador, Falkland Islands (Malvinas), French Guiana, Grenada, Guadeloupe, Guatemala, Guyana, Haiti, Honduras, Jamaica, Martinique, Mexico, Montserrat, Netherlands Antilles, Nicaragua, Panama, Paraguay, Peru, Puerto Rico, Saint Kitts and Nevis, Saint Lucia, Saint Vincent and the Grenadines, Suriname, Trinidad and Tobago, Turks and Caicos Islands, Uruguay, U.S. Virgin Islands, Venezuela.

Region C—*Near East: Africa:* Egypt, Libyan Arab Jamahiriya, Sudan. *Asia:* Afghanistan, Bahrain, Cyprus, Gaza Strip (Palestine), Islamic Republic of Iran, Iraq, Jordan, Kuwait, Lebanon, Oman, Qatar, Kingdom of Saudi Arabia, Syrian Arab Republic, Turkey, United Arab Emirates, Yemen Arab Republic, Democratic Yemen.

Region D—*Far East:* Bangladesh, Bhutan, Brunei Darussalam, Burma, East Timor, Hong Kong, India, Indonesia, Republic of Korea, Laos, Macau, Malaysia, Maldives, Nepal, Pakistan, Philippines, Singapore, Sri Lanka, Thailand.

Region E—*Other developing market economies: America:* Bermuda, Greenland, Saint Pierre and Miquelon. *Oceania:* American Samoa, Canton and Enderbury Islands, Christmas Island (Australia), Cocos (Keeling) Islands, Cook Islands, Fiji, French Polynesia, Guam, Johnston Island, Kiribati, Midway Islands, Nauru, New Caledonia, Niue, Norfolk Island, Pacific Islands (incl. Marshall Islands, Federated States of Micronesia, Northern Mariana Islands and Palau), Papua New Guinea, Pitcairn, Samoa, Solomon Islands, Tokelau, Tonga, Tuvalu, Vanuatu, Wake Island, Wallis and Futuna Islands.

ALL DEVELOPED COUNTRIES

Includes developed market economies and Region B of centrally planned economies.

ALL DEVELOPING COUNTRIES

Includes developing market economies and Region A of centrally planned economies.

Source: *FAO Production Yearbook*. Vol. 42. 1988. Food and Agriculture Organization of the United Nations: Rome.

Appendix B:
Career Opportunities
in International Agriculture

Agriculturalists face challenges in food production, processing, distribution, and marketing, as well as in agro-industrial products throughout the world. The opportunities presented by the challenges are wide and varied. Specialized skills and knowledge of agriculturalists are in increasing demand by governments; commodity export associations; commercial firms; educational, research, and technical institutions; and international agencies.

Although a few organizations accept practical work experience in lieu of academic credentials, the majority require at least a BS degree in such fields as: agricultural economics, agricultural business management, animal science, soil science, plant science, horticulture, plant pathology, food science, nutrition, forestry, veterinary medicine, or food and agricultural engineering. Many agencies and international organizations employ professionals with MS and PhD degrees.

When being considered for entry into the international employment market, other personal qualities are also assessed, including, but not limited to: language facility, a flexible and adaptable personality, previous exposure to a foreign setting, and the ability to function and communicate effectively in foreign environments. Information about employment opportunities abroad can be obtained in the source reference cited for this appendix, and from the following contacts:

1988 Agricultural Consultants Directory, Agribusiness Worldwide, P.O. Box 29155, Shawnee Mission, KS 66201.
Current Technical Service Contracts and Grants, as of September, 1986, Office of Procurement, Procurement Support Division,

U.S. International Development Cooperation Agency, Agency for International Development, Washington, DC 20523.

The Directory of the Association of State Departments of Agriculture, NASDA, 1616 H Street N.W., Washington, DC 20523.

The Directory of U.S. Nonprofit Organizations in Development Assistance Abroad, Technical Assistance Information Clearing House, American Council of Voluntary Agencies for Foreign Service, Inc., 200 Park Avenue South, New York, NY 10003.

Encyclopedia of Associations, International Organizations, 1986 Edition, Volume 4, Gale Research Company, Book Tower, Detroit, MI 48226.

Home Offices of U.S. Market Development Cooperators and Targeted Export Assistance Participants, Operating under continuing FAS project agreements, January 1988, U.S. Agricultural Export Development Council, 600 Maryland Avenue S.W., Suite 510, Washington, DC 20024.

InterAction Member Profiles, InterAction, American Council for Voluntary International Action, 1815 H Street N.W., 11th Floor, Washington, DC 20006.

International Research Centers Directory 1986-1987, Gale Research Company, Book Tower, Detroit, MI 48226.

Rural Economic Alternatives, Technical Assistance Bulletin, No. 5, Center for Agriculture and Rural Development, The Council of State Governments, Iron Works Pike, P.O. Box 11910, Lexington, KY 40578.

Source: Warnken, P. F., E. J. Scherff, and T. C. Love. 1990. *International Agriculture: A World of Opportunities*. Bulletin M-107/January 1990/3M. Available from: Extension Publications, 115 South 5th Street, University of Missouri-Columbia, Columbia, MO 65211. Charge: $7.00 per copy plus postage and $1.00 handling.

Index